1995

DIVERSITY AND UNITY IN EARLY NORTH AMERICA

"For many years, critics have been calling for a 'new synthesis' of American history. Philip Morgan's judicious selection of pathbreaking recent work in early American history demonstrates that the new narrative is already here.... In this powerful and readable collection, we find a complex and ironic history in which men and women, black and white, Native American and immigrant from the entire Atlantic world struggled to shape private lives and public authority."

Linda K. Kerber, University of Iowa

"It will be enlightening and stimulating for students and teachers of Early America."

Rachel N. Klein, University of California

Philip Morgan's selection of cutting-edge essays by leading historians represents the extraordinary vitality of recent historical literature on early America. The book opens up previously unexplored areas such as cultural diversity, ethnicity, and gender, and reveals the importance of new methods such as anthropology, and historical demography to the study of early America.

Philip D. Morgan is Associate Professor of History at Florida State University.

Rewriting Histories will focus on historical themes where standard conclusions are facing a major challenge. Each book will present 8-10 papers (edited and annotated where necessary) at the forefront of current research and interpretation, offering students an accessible way to engage with contemporary debates.

Series editor **Jack R. Censer** is Professor of History at George Mason University.

REWRITING HISTORIES
Series editor: Jack R. Censer

DIVERSITY AND UNITY IN EARLY NORTH AMERICA

Edited by Philip D. Morgan

London and New York

First published 1993
by Routledge

11 New Fetter Lane, London EC4P 4EE
Simultaneously published in the USA and Canada
by Routledge, Inc.
29 West 35th Street, New York, NY 10001

Typeset in 10 on 12 point Palatino by
ROM-Data Corporation Ltd, Falmouth, Cornwall
Printed in Great Britain by
T J Press (Padstow) Ltd, Cornwall

British Library Cataloguing in Publication Data
A catalogue record for this book is available from the British Library

Library of Congress Cataloging in Publication Data
Diversity and unity in early North America / edited by
Philip D. Morgan.
p. cm. - (Rewriting historeis [i.e. histories])
Includes bibliographical references and index.
1. United States–Civilization–To 1783.
2. Great Britain–Colonies–America.   I. Morgan, Philip D.
II Series: Re-writing histories.
E162.D58   1993
973–dc20   93–16763

ISBN 0–415–08798–8   0–415–08799–6 (pbk)

CONTENTS

EDITOR'S PREFACE

Rewriting history, or revisionism, has always followed closely in the tow of history writing. In their efforts to re-evaluate the past, professional as well as amateur scholars have followed many approaches, most commonly as empiricists, uncovering new information to challenge earlier accounts. Historians have also revised previous versions by adopting new perspectives, usually fortified by new research, which overturn received views.

Even though rewriting is constantly taking place, historians' attitudes toward using new interpretations have been anything but settled. For most, the validity of revisionism lies in providing a stronger, more convincing account that better captures the objective truth of the matter. Although such historians might agree that we never finally arrive at the "truth," they believe it exists and over time may be better and better approximated. At the other extreme stand scholars who believe that each generation or even each cultural group or subgroup necessarily regards the past differently, each creating for itself a more usable history. Although these latter scholars do not reject the possibility of demonstrating empirically that some contentions are better than others, they focus upon generating new views based upon different life experiences. Different truths exist for different groups. Surely such an understanding, by emphasizing subjectivity, further encourages rewriting history. Between these two groups are those historians who wish to borrow from both sides. This third group, while accepting that every congeries of individuals sees matters differently, still wishes somewhat contradictorily to fashion a broader history that incorporates both of these particular visions. Revisionists who stress empiricism fall into the first of the three camps, while others spread out across the board.

Today the rewriting of history seems to have accelerated to a blinding speed as a consequence of the evolution of revisionism. A variety of approaches has emerged. A major factor in this process has been the enormous increase in the number of researchers. This explosion has reinforced and enabled the retesting of many assertions. Significant ideological shifts have also played a major part in the growth of revisionism. First, the crisis of Marxism, culminating in the events in Eastern Europe in 1989, has given rise to doubts about explicitly Marxist accounts. Such doubts have spilled over into the entire field of social history which has been a dominant subfield of the discipline for several decades. Focusing on society and its class divisions implied that these are the most important elements in historical analysis. Because Marxism was built on the same claim, the whole basis of social history has been questioned, despite the very many studies that directly had little to do with Marxism. Disillusionment with social history simultaneously opened the door to cultural and linguistic approaches largely developed in anthropology and literature. Multiculturalism and feminism further generated revisionism. By claiming that scholars had, wittingly or not, operated from a white European/American male point of view, newer researchers argued other approaches had been neglected or misunderstood. Not surprisingly, these last historians are the most likely to envision each subgroup rewriting its own usable history, while other scholars incline toward revisionism as part of the search for some stable truth.

Rewriting Histories will make these new approaches available to the student population. Often new scholarly debates take place in the scattered issues of journals which are sometimes difficult to find. Furthermore, in these first interactions, historians tend to address one another, leaving out the evidence that would make their arguments more accessible to the uninitiated. This series of books will collect in one place a strong group of the major articles in selected fields, adding notes and introductions conducive to improved understanding. Editors will select articles containing substantial historical data, so that students – at least those who approach the subject as an objective phenomenon – can advance not only their comprehension of debated points but also their grasp of substantive aspects of the subject.

Phil Morgan's understanding of the newest historiography of colonial America owes much to the broader developments influencing history. Cultural diversity, anthropological techniques, and feminist perspectives have in particular penetrated the writing of early American history. In this work Morgan shows that historians have also taken up one more challenge as yet generally untested. Unlike most of their colleagues in other fields, colonial historians have begun the laborious, daunting but absolutely essential task of integrating the new findings into a rich whole.

Jack R. Censer

TABLES AND MAP

Tables

Map

Table 1 Population of British North America, 1610–1780 (in thousands)

Year	New England	Mid-Atlantic	Chesapeake	Lower South	Total
1620	–	–	1	–	1
1660	33	5	25	1	64
1700	92	53	98	16	259
1740	290	220	296	108	914
1780	698	723	786	506	2713

Note: Indians, except those who lived in colonial settlements, are not in-
cluded in these population figures.
Source: John J. McCusker and Russell R. Menard, *The Economy of British
America, 1607–1789* (Chapel Hill, N.C., 1985): 103, 136, 172, 203.

Table 2 Percentage of blacks in the population of British North America,
1660–1780

Year	New England	Mid-Atlantic	Chesapeake	Lower South
1660	2	11	4	2
1700	2	7	13	18
1740	3	7	28	46
1780	2	6	39	41

Source: McCusker and Menard, *The Economy of British America, 1607–
1789*: 222.

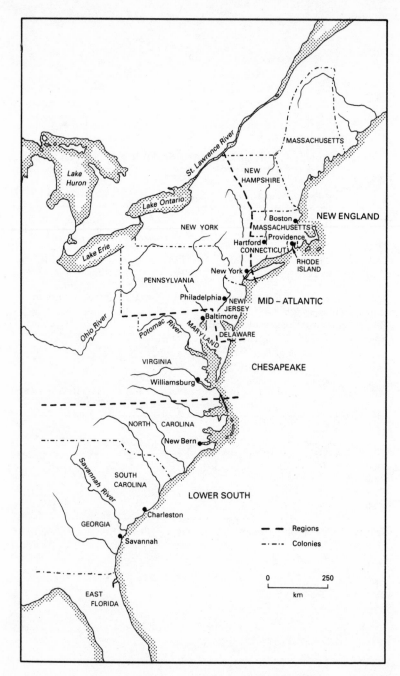

Regions and colonies of early North America, ca. 1775

GENERAL
INTRODUCTION

Over the last few decades, the study of early America has been transformed. As with other periods of American history – and indeed with modern historiography, in general – the revolution has given rise to profoundly mixed results. On the one hand, recent history has enfranchised groups that were previously neglected or excluded; the historically silent, whether women, minorities, or workers, have been given their voice. The downtrodden and illiterate have been rescued from what E. P. Thompson described as the "enormous condescension of history." Scholarly horizons have expanded in other ways to encompass feelings, emotions, attitudes, even smells and sounds. This proliferation of knowledge has deepened and enlarged our appreciation of the diversity of human experience. History is now more comprehensive, complex, and multidimensional. On the other hand, the explosion of historical information has led to few new syntheses, few coherent or integrated visions of the past, few organizing frameworks. Rather, reflections upon the overall effects of the so-called "new history" are more likely to focus upon the splintering, fragmentation, disarray, shapelessness, inaccessibility, incoherence, chaos, anarchy, and meaninglessness of it all. An oft-heard lament is the disappearance of a unitary, monolithic story, a master narrative. Peter Novick concludes that "A striking feature of the American historical profession in the last twenty years has been its inability to move toward any overarching interpretation which could organize American, or for that matter, non-American, history."[1]

Although Novick's assessment may be broadly accurate, it will be the burden of this collection of essays to suggest that the study of colonial America has not become so specialized or fragmented as to reach the point of disintegration. To be sure, few historians of

1

colonial America now write purely in heroic or epic terms of the Rise of Democracy or Liberty – as, say, George Bancroft and Francis Parkman in the nineteenth, and Thomas J. Wertenbaker and Daniel J. Boorstin in the twentieth, century largely did.[2] There once was a time when history was written by those who had a sense of the entire tradition, who wrote of the whole, not its parts, who aimed to unite rather than divide. But these single stories, these master narratives, were based on the forcible exclusion of a variety of other stories – of followers as well as leaders, of the margins as well as the center, of folk as well as high culture. Such syntheses were not really syntheses at all. Rather than thinking that attention to minorities or to the margins or to the common folk subtracts from the central story, new versions of the past see the possibilities in terms of enrichment, of a greater sensitivity to the diversity of human experience. The aim is to point directions toward recapturing a whole world, telling a plurality of stories, and, in this way, redefining the meaning of colonial America. These goals may not amount to a new architectonic vision, but they are a long way from cacaphonous confusion. In William McNeill's words, the result will be "an ecumenical history, with plenty of room for human diversity in all its complexity."[3]

This collection of essays first approaches colonial America from three illuminating angles of vision, which together enrich our understanding. These are not the only frameworks, the only organizing ideas, for comprehending early America, but they are unquestionably among the most significant and promising. The concluding section indicates how these new approaches can yield a structural coherence to the subject.

First, scholars of early America have refined and redefined the spatial dimensions of their subject. A twofold perspective on the colonial American experience is now emerging. On the one hand, it has become increasingly clear that sharp regional differences separated colonial Americans one from one another. On the other hand, a resurgence of interest in the Atlantic dimensions of American colonization has emphasized that colonial Americans lived in an Atlantic world. David Hackett Fischer has combined both approaches by arguing that British North America is best understood as four regional cultures, each of which had separate origins in four British regions.[4] The validity of Fischer's interpretations aside, a Janus-faced approach, sensitive to both the regional and transatlantic dimensions of the early American experience, will help us understand what united Americans as much as what separated them.

Although historians increasingly view colonial America from the perspective of distinct regions, few employ exactly the same regional categorizations – as will become clear from comparisons of the essays in this volume – but New England, the Mid-Atlantic (or Middle Colonies), the Chesapeake, the lower South, the Backcountry, and the West Indies have emerged as the major regional constituents of British America. In a contemporary world where regions – whether Quebec in Canada, Catalonia in Spain, Lithuania in the old Soviet Union, or Croatia in former Yugoslavia – have been asserting themselves, sensitivity to provincial identity has been enhanced. Indeed, increasing attention to the regional diversity of early America has led some to argue that the notion of a single colonial America should be laid to rest once and for all.

Representatives of this opinion can be found in many quarters. Bernard Bailyn notes that "the settlement and development patterns for the whole of British North America reveals not uniformity, but highly differentiated processes." There was no single "American" family or community structure, he continues; rather, colonial America was "a variegated, dynamic world. No simple pattern seems to fit any part of it." John M. Murrin concurs: "The seventeenth century created, within English America alone, not one new civilization on this side of the Atlantic, but many distinct colonies that differed as dramatically from one another as any of them from England." These seventeenth-century settlements "produced not one, but many Americas, and the passage of time threatened to drive them farther apart, not closer together." Most emphatic is Ian K. Steele who detects "the evaporation of a single 'colonial America' as a serious historical subject." Instead, "historians are finally abandoning efforts to assert it as a context within which anyone ever really lived. It was an impossible intellectual burden to contrive a single, complete, and autonomous 'colonial America.' "[5]

If many historians are prepared to jettison the idea of a single colonial America, others insist that the continent be viewed as part of a larger Atlantic world. Conceiving of the Atlantic as a waterway rather than a moat, a bridge rather than a barrier, they are impressed by the links and continuous exchanges between colonies and mother countries. These connections emerge in Bailyn's conception of homeland and marchland (the latter a border territory or frontier), in Greene's and Murrin's emphasis on Anglicization (the process by which the colonies became more English), in Butler's transatlantic perspectives on American religion, and in Breen's discussion of an Anglo-American consumer revolution. They could be equally well demonstrated in other ways, from increasing commercial ties of Britain and its colonies to improved communications drawing Barbados and Boston closer to London than parts of rural Ireland or Scotland. In short, centripetal as well as centrifugal forces were at work in early America.[6]

The most important centripetal force, many historians argue, was the empire. As Ian Steele has put it, "Most historians who take an Atlantic approach to early America argue that the English Atlantic empire was the most meaningful large-scale community within which colonial Americans lived."[7] By the late seventeenth century, the empire was a far more intrusive force in people's lives; and its impact waxed rather than waned over the course of the eighteenth century. Commerce increased markedly not only between the major American regions and the mother country but also among the American regions themselves; legal procedures in the colonies became more standardized and imitative of metropolitan practices over time; frequent wars against common enemies bound the empire together; a shared political ideology increasingly characterized the provinces and the metropolis. In these and many other ways, the empire became more thoroughly integrated over time. From this perspective, the American Revolution was not an inevitable drift away from the mother country, but rather a more complicated process by which growing assimilation and integration provoked resentment and separatism. Because the colonists became more closely tied to Britain over time, so they were able to resist Britain with all the weapons in the British arsenal – everything from petitions to boycotts, constitutional arguments to crowd action.

Just as regional and imperial identities helped define early America, recognition of the continent's multiracial and multiethnic character is indispensable to any understanding of the American experience. America has always been a heterogeneous country. The mingling, jostling, and outright clashing of diverse racial and ethnic groups and cultures has shaped, and continues to shape, the society. Even when Europeans, Indians, and Afro-Americans were at loggerheads, their fates were, in T. H. Breen's words, "intricately

4

intertwined"; America's colonization involved a "kaleidoscope of human encounters" among an astonishing array of ethnic and racial groups.[8] How they interacted, what they preserved of their original cultures, and how much they borrowed from one another tells us much about early America – and modern America too. The American experience must reflect this polyphony – not cacophony – of voices.

Early America was preeminently a place of multiple cultural frontiers. Frontiers varied because relationships between and among ethnic groups were in constant motion. The extent of assimilation and autonomy among cultures varied from place to place and from period to period. These geographical and chronological variations are key themes in the essays of Merrell and Berlin. People drew and redrew their own cultural maps in response to changing, always complex conditions, ranging from the demographic to the environmental, from the economic to the political. Although blacks and Indians were cruelly exploited and subject to enormous constraints over which they had no control, they were never just passive victims. Rather, both Indians and Afro-Americans made choices about their lives and reconstructed new societies and cultures, stitching together shreds of their old ways with fragments borrowed from the new. Cultural exchanges between peoples formed a continuous process, involving loans and rejections, conflict and cooperation, accommodation and resistance, reinterpretation and syncretism.

Frontiers varied because cultural adaptations between peoples proceeded at different rates in different arenas of contact. In some spheres, tensions often flared into violence; in others, peaceful cooperation was the norm. In some areas, cultural fusion was commonplace; in others, the retention of old ways remained strong. The range of human interaction was immense. And while general patterns can be discerned, individuals always shaped their own lives in reaction to specific, particular conditions.[9]

Increasingly, historians of colonial America make ethnic and racial groups part of the stories they tell. They are joining ethnic and racial voices to a chorus that previously turned a deaf ear to them. Part of the goal is simply to win a place within history for the losers. Attempts at redressing the balance need not be a zero-sum game, where the addition of new groups means the subtraction of traditional ones. Rather, the recognition that ethnic and racial diversity helped to define America should be seen as enriching.

Unfortunately, diversity, by its centrifugal nature, can prove threatening, because it seems to attenuate, even dissolve the identity it helps to define. But the American vision lives in recognition of difference. Only acceptance of this variety permits a multifaceted and rounded view of the early American past.

Another major theme of recent historical work that promises a comprehensive and complex approach to the past is the attempt to connect private and public worlds, interior experience and external events. As never before, contemporary historians attend to the intimate details of everyday life, the actualities of domestic life, the ideas and beliefs of ordinary people. They have broadened the boundaries of subjective experience to encompass nonverbal expression, gestures, fears, and aspirations. They have explored artifacts of all kinds – from furniture to folk songs, from poems to pottery, from games to gravestones – in order to comprehend people's construction of their world. They have become more sensitive to visual signs, viewing architecture, dress, ceremonies, and art as vehicles for the transmission of cultural messages. And they have begun to connect these personal maps of reality, the private worlds of ordinary people, to public events, both political and nonpolitical.[10]

Many essays in this volume are influenced by these trends. Studies of family structure, a number of the essays indicate, are essential to an understanding of colonial society. Religious sensibilities too have much to tell us about external events. Although few agree on the precise relationship of evangelicalism to the Revolution – as the essays by Greene, Butler, and Murrin reveal – there can be no doubt of a connection. Others probe the mundane details of domestic life: how families divided labor is linked to community organization and development, what consumers bought is tied to the coming of the American Revolution. Bailyn uses architecture to limn the emergence of the gentry in the late seventeenth-century Chesapeake; Isaac uses it to delineate gentry hegemony by the mid-eighteenth century.

Despite the apparent ascendancy of social history, these essays on society take the public realm seriously. Wars – whether the Indian wars emphasized by Bailyn, Merrell and Murrin, or the Anglo-French wars discussed by Murrin – are seen as important agents of change, both in private and public life. Greene's ultimate quarry is the set of public values that governed an emerging

6

American culture. He identifies personal independence as the most powerful imperative in early America. Others discuss individualism more indirectly: Isaac, for example, discerns a growing individual separateness in the restructuring of gentry houses and new domestic lifestyles. Of all the essayists, Tim Breen confronts issues of private and public most directly, as he explores the relationship between the growth of national consciousness among the colonists and their rejection of British goods.

Taken together, these essays demonstrate the creative ferment in the scholarship of early American history. Over the past generation or so, the examination of new issues, problems, and groups that traditional historiography largely ignored has broadened and deepened our appreciation of the diversity of human experience. The new history attempts to preserve the complexity of the past, not homogenize it; paint in bold hues not in drab colors; reconnoitre the jagged peaks and plunging valleys, not flatten the landscape. Ordinary folk are seen as actors, able to make choices, create alternatives, affect the situations they found themselves in. Agency, so long a preserve of elites and great men, once considered the main historical actors, has now been restored to ordinary people. In all of these ways, the new versions of the past are more satisfying in that they are more comprehensive, more multidimensional, more tentative, and more sensitive to the diversities of human cultures.

The concluding essay by John Murrin demonstrates how all these rich possibilities can be synthesized. His is a balanced account, devoting as much attention to the Indians and Africans as to the Europeans in America. He is sensitive to the striking diversity of early America and indeed shows how "the colonists sorted themselves into a broad spectrum of settlements." Yet he also argues that the expanding impact of empire tended to draw the regions of America closer together. He links private and public worlds: life expectancy helps explain a region's culture; family size and structure are connected to community development; newspaper reading is coupled to imperial integration; the political allegiances of religiously awakened settlers are explored. It is not just the combination of approaches that makes Murrin's essay so rewarding, but its recognition of paradox and irony: the enormous human costs that accompanied the achievements of early Americans; the sheer luck of the relatively few religious idealists who won the demographic lottery of early America by settling in northern climes; the many ironic legacies bequeathed by the Great War for Empire. Murrin's essay exemplifies the greater range, richer insight, and deeper sympathy which are the keynotes of the best, modern historiography.

NOTES

1 E. P. Thompson, *The Making of the English Working Class* (London, 1963): 13; Peter Novick, *That Noble Dream: The "Objectivity Question" and the American Historical Profession* (New York, 1988): 457–8.
2 George Bancroft, *History of the United States from the Discovery of the American Continent*, 10 vols (Boston, 1834–75); Francis Parkman, *France and England in North America*, 2 vols (New York, 1983 [orig. publ. 1865–92]); Thomas J. Wertenbaker, *The Founding of American Civilization*, 3 vols (New York, 1938–47); Daniel J. Boorstin, *The Americans: The Colonial Experience* (New York, 1958).
3 William McNeill, "Mythistory, or Truth, Myth, History, and Historians," *American Historical Review*, 91 (1986): 7.
4 Fischer, *Albion's Seed: Four British Folkways in America* (New York, 1989). See also "Forum" in *William and Mary Quarterly*, 3rd Ser., XLVIII (1991): 224–308.
5 Bailyn, *The Peopling of British North America: An Introduction* (New York, 1986): 49, 58, 59; Murrin, "A Roof without Walls: The Dilemma of American National Identity," in Richard Beeman, Stephen Botein, and Edward C. Carter II, eds., *Beyond Confederation: Origins of the Constitution and American National Identity* (Chapel Hill, N. C., 1987): 334, 336; Ian K. Steele, "Empire of Migrants and Consumers: Some Current Atlantic Approaches to the History of Colonial Virginia," *Virginia Magazine of History and Biography*, 99 (1991): 489.
6 Ian K. Steele, *The English Atlantic, 1675–1740: An Exploration of Communication and Community* (New York, 1986).
7 Steele, "Empire of Migrants and Consumers": 490.
8 T. H. Breen, "Creative Adaptations: Peoples and Cultures," in Jack P. Greene and J. R. Pole, eds., *Colonial British America: Essays in the New History of the Early Modern Era* (Baltimore, 1984): 195, 197–8.
9 See, for example, Bernard Bailyn and Philip D. Morgan, eds., *Strangers within the Realm: Cultural Margins of the First British Empire* (Chapel Hill, N. C., 1991).
10 Bernard Bailyn, "The Challenge of Modern Historiography," *AHR*, 87 (1982): 19–22.

Part I

WHOLES AND PARTS: REGIONS AND AMERICAN SOCIETY

To comprehend the early North American experience requires an understanding of the acute regional differences that fragmented Americans and of the distinctive ties that bound those same Americans together. Bernard Bailyn's essay highlights regional variety, although also identifying some emerging features shared by all colonial Americans. Jack Greene's essay is sensitive to regional variety but devotes more attention to the development of a single American society and culture. The reader ought to assess the reasons for the difference in emphasis between the two essays. Is it best explained, for example, by recognizing that Bailyn is considering the seventeenth century and Greene the eighteenth century?

1

A DOMESDAY BOOK FOR THE PERIPHERY

Bernard Bailyn

After conquering England in the eleventh century, William I ordered investigators or legati *to survey his new realm. The information they collected became known as the Domesday Book. Six centuries later, another foreigner, William of Orange, succeeded to the English throne. In an illuminating flight of fancy, Bailyn wonders what a group of* legati *would have discovered in 1700 had they constructed a domesday book for William III. In an imaginative* tour de force, *Bailyn emphasizes two findings. First, the investigators would have noted great differences between the four major zones of settlement in mainland North America. The contrast between the plodding, pious, puritanical New Englanders and the crude, cruel, "Conquistador-like" Carolinians could not have been more stark. Second, they would have glimpsed common elements, all stemming from North America's status as a marchland, a border country, where violence mingled with civility.*

Bailyn's profound insights and pungent prose invite reflection. Did, for example, the differences between regions outweigh the similarities in 1700? Do the sharp distinctions ascribed to the various regions sit awkwardly with a view of North America as one single marchland? In addition, should England be the only or primary standard of measurement for judging colonial developments? For Bailyn (and for many colonists, it should be added), England was the appropriate yardstick; consequently, he is most impressed by the backwardness of the colonies, their "diminishment of metropolitan accomplishment." But if other colonies were the gauges of British American achievements, would a more positive view be possible? Although recognizing growing refinement in turn-of-the-century America, Bailyn emphasizes the violence, crudity, and primitiveness of so much of early American life. Is this emphasis overdrawn? Compare Bailyn's emphasis on the ferocity that marked Indian–white relations with Merrell's argument that mundane, peaceful, and even

11

cooperative contacts were commonplace. Moreover, is the early American language of civilization and savagery appropriate for twentieth-century historians?

* * *

Suppose William III had set out to survey his empire in North America as of, say, 1700. And suppose, further, that he had wanted not only a record of land tenures but also a social description of North America as it then existed, and to accomplish this had sent out teams of *legati* to report on this great territory in four large circuits.

In each of the areas these *legati* would have found developments under way that fundamentally shaped the emerging local characteristics of early American culture. But in addition, and more important, they would have found a strange common element running through all of these regions, a peculiar quality that persisted in the generations that followed. This common characteristic could not have been found in an earlier age; and at any later stage it would seem immutable, too deeply set, too elaborately interwoven into the general fabric of society, to be clearly identified. The crucial phase of origins lay in these transition years at the turn of the century – a soft, plastic moment of history when what would become familiar and obvious to later generations was just emerging, unsurely, from a strange and unfamiliar past.

Change was everywhere, together with confusion and controversy. The *legati* in the first circuit, New England, would have reported an agonizing transformation, impelled by the inmost tendencies of a highly self-conscious and cultivated religious culture and by the buffeting of external events. They would have found a Puritan world whose inner spirit, once powerfully creative and fearless, had survived into a third generation in a faded and defensive form. The fierce religious intensity, the sense of daring and risky enterprise in the service of a demanding God – an enterprise of great relevance to the whole informed Protestant world – all of that had passed. The first generation's accomplishments had been products of passionate striving in an atmosphere of fear and desperation; but to their children the founders' world was an inheritance they were born into – respected but familiar and routine. And to *their* children,

12

adults at the end of the century, what had once been rebellious, liberating, and challenging had become a problematic anachronism.

So John Winthrop, Jr.,[a] a second-generation Puritan, physician, amateur scientist, and imaginative entrepreneur, lived out his life in backwoods Connecticut struggling to maintain contact with the larger world from which his parents had dared to escape. He wrote letter after letter to the Royal Society in London, of which he was the first American member, in an effort to keep in touch. He sent over scientific specimens, anything he could get hold of – rattle-snake skins, birds' nests, plants, crabs, strange pigs. He studied the Society's *Transactions* so as not to fall too far behind. And to those concerned with the propagation of the Gospel he dispatched John Eliot's Algonquian translation of the Bible and two essays written in Latin by Indian students at Harvard. But these were failing efforts. In the end loneliness and isolation overcame him. He died, venerated in the villages along the Connecticut River – themselves changing like autumn leaves from vital, experimental religious communities to sere, old-fashioned backwoods towns – but forgotten in the greater world at home. His sons, however, provincial land speculators and petty politicians, had no such memories as their father had had, and no such aspirations; they suffered, therefore, no such disappointments. They were altogether native to the land, and their cultural horizons had narrowed to its practical demands.

The third generation, adults at the end of the century, were dull, rather rustic provincials, whose concerns had little to do with the spiritual yearnings and ascetic self-discipline of their grand-parents. Their interests centered on much more mundane matters – on the struggle to profit from their farms, on the conduct of trade; above all, on the consequences of extraordinary population growth.[1]

The New England population – self-enclosed, lacking in signifi-cant accretions from abroad – was growing, in the seventeenth century, at a rate of 2.6 or 2.7 percent in a year, hence doubling every twenty-seven years. This phenomenal growth was no consequence of a peculiarly high birth rate – New England and old England scarcely differed in this – but of a low death rate, the result not of the absence of epidemics but of their low intensity, which allowed swift demographic recoveries. This regional population growth and low mortality rate – which declined in the eighteenth century – had the effect of propelling the boundaries of Anglo-American settlements out from the original coastal and riverbank enclaves. By the early eighteenth century, a settlement map would show a pattern surprisingly like the Soviet crossed hammer and sickle, the sickle being a fifty-mile-wide band of British settlements south along the coast from New Hampshire around the Cape to the New York boundary, the hammer being the northern penetration of settlement up the Connecticut River – a solid arm two or three townships wide, reaching inland straight up from Long Island Sound north to the level of Brattleboro, Vermont. Between 1660 and 1710, 209 new townships had been settled in New England, an average of over four per year.[2]

Behind this remarkable spread of settlement lay the central mechanism at work in this northernmost circuit of the turn-of-the-century Domesday survey. In any newly established New England town, founding families were able to subdivide their land to the satisfaction of at most only two successive generations. The fourth, sometimes even the third, generation felt a relative land shortage, or rather a land hunger created by their expectations, which led some to venture out into new settlements, often on land earlier invested in, speculatively, by far-sighted kin. There is no absolute lower boundary of acreage per child that marks the point at which a family broke out of its original location. Some sent representatives out soon after their establishment; some managed to maintain four generations in the original community by the comprehensive utilization of the family's initial properties. But the common experience was for families to reach out to newly opening territory in the third or fourth generation, when some kind of threshold of optimal town population and maximal morselization of land was reached – optimal and maximal in terms of certain widely shared expectations.[3]

None of this concern with population growth and land distribution – any more than with local trade and overseas commerce – was felt to be incompatible with the restrained and serious way of life instinctive to these third-generation provincial Puritans. But, combined with the cooling of religious passion, it shifted the tone and quality of New England culture in fundamental ways. New England was culturally and ethnically a homogeneous world, derived from a single period of English emigration, 1630–40, spreading out quickly, westward and northward, into uncultivated lands and forming a network of communities set in forest clearings and natural meadowland and linked by hundreds of footpaths, by rough, stump-filled horse-and-wagon trails, and by river routes. In these isolated but associated communities lived a population of austere and prolific country folk, pious without passion, ambitious for worldly things, yet still attuned, in some degree, to the appeal of their ancestors' spiritual quests, still aware of, and to some extent unified by, a distinctive cultural heritage.

No such homogeneity would have been found in the area of the second circuit. It was a remarkably different world. In the settlements scattered from the Hudson River south to the Delaware, the legates would have found ethnic diversity of the most extreme kind, and not a single expanding network of communities impelled outward by the dynamics of a distinctive demographic process, but half a dozen different demographic processes moving in different phases at different speeds.

Small migrant flows over many years had produced New York's population of 1700. Originally people had come from the Netherlands; then, in small numbers, from New England, from England, from France, from the German principalities, from Brazil, indirectly from Africa, and from Virginia and Maryland. Still only slowly growing, the colony of only 18,000 souls was a mosaic of groups, ill-integrated and often hostile to each other. In the Hudson Valley there were Dutch, French, Walloons, Palatines, and English. Manhattan, with a population of only 5,000, was dominated numerically by the Dutch but politically, socially, and economically by the English and French; it had a small community of Jews and a sizable group – perhaps as much as 15 percent of the population – of Africans, almost all of them slaves. And the religious scene was even more complex than the ethnic, and had been from the colony's earliest years. "Here," Governor Dongan reported in 1687, "bee not many of the Church of England, [and] few Roman Catholicks, [but] abundance of Quakers – preachers, men and women, especially – singing Quakers, ranting Quakers, Sabbatarians, Antisabbatarians, some Anabaptists, some Independents, some Jews; in short, of all sorts of opinions there are some, and the most part of none at all."[4]

Elsewhere in this middle circuit the ethnic complexity was similar. The Jerseys had been settled by widely differing groups entering from different directions. Originally Dutch from Manhattan and New Englanders had settled in the northeast of the colony; then English Quakers began the occupancy of West Jersey,

15

approaching from the Delaware River in the southwest. Some Swedes, long established on the Delaware, moved east to the Atlantic coastal plain; and hundreds of Scots – clients of the Scottish East Jersey proprietors – settled a hopeful new capital at Perth Amboy, an excellent harbor opposite the tip of Staten Island, and then fanned out in an inland arc, joining in with New Englanders and Dutch to populate, in the 1680s, a series of poly-ethnic settlements in the Raritan Valley. Only a few original settlements of New Englanders and Dutch in the northeast remained ethnically homogeneous.

Pennsylvania's diversity was similar. By 1700 the settlements there, expanding back westward from the Delaware River, filled out the whole south-eastern corner of the colony, and throughout that large area, as in New Jersey and New York, settlement had advanced without central organization or control, creating a mosaic whose pattern was formed simply by ease of routes of access, accidents of land claims, and the contours of the terrain.

This whole middle circuit of British North America, founded by diverse peoples from all over the American colonies, and from Britain, western Europe, and West Africa, was the scene of continuous contention: Dutch vs. Anglo-French; Scots vs. English; Quakers vs. Quakers. The worst struggle was in New York City. There the animosities between numerically dominant Dutch and the politically and economically dominant Anglo-French had led to a violent upheaval – Leisler's Rebellion[b] – that tore the colony apart in 1689 and was only temporarily resolved two years later by the judicial murder of the ringleaders. In 1700 that fierce politico-ethnic struggle, whose origins lay deep in the peopling process, was still the dominant fact in the colony's public life, though it was beginning to fade and to reshape into a new configuration.

Pennsylvania too had had turmoils rooted in political and ethnic diversity. William Penn,[c] harassed at every turn and frustrated in his hopes for a tranquil, well-structured society in Pennsylvania, cursed and cursed again what he called these "scurvy quarrels that break out to the disgrace of the Province." And so too did a succession of governors in the other colonies of this region, who struggled to maintain public authority and a modicum of community spirit and social order in widely scattered settlements of different peoples, living, often, in primitive conditions.

It was a strange, disorderly world, the commissioners for the second circuit would have had to report – lacking anything like a uniform land system; lacking social cohesion; and chaotic in public affairs to the point of political violence. Yet, amid all this diversity and turmoil a more coherent world was emerging, with something of the normal hierarchy of statuses and wealth, if not of rank, which in traditional societies reinforced private as well as public order. In New York a small provincial aristocracy of sorts was taking stable form. It was largely Anglo-French in origins, though it included significant Dutch elements too. Based on political and economic privilege, it was just then, at the turn of the century, being secured by a series of spectacular land grants along the Hudson and on Long Island, grants that had been and still were being hotly contested, but would soon be solidly confirmed. The Dutch dominated only the upriver center at Albany, with its monopoly of the Indian trade, but the leaders there were doubly provincial: gentry on the outer frontier of a frontier world. And in Pennsylvania too a leadership group was emerging from the confusion of the settling years – Quaker merchants for the most part, together with a few Anglicans who arrived with some capital and connections throughout the Atlantic trading world and who knew how to turn political advantage to economic profit.[5]

But if these were provincial aristocracies, they were still supple, still without the full external attributes of superiority, their distinction still well within the range of competition by ambitious but disadvantaged natives and by well-connected or prosperous newcomers.

Something of the same development was overtaking the world of the third circuit, the Chesapeake colonies – but at a different pace, and emerging out of entirely different demographic circumstances. There a transformation was underway that would affect the entire course of American history, and the history of the Western world indirectly.

The population history of the tobacco country of Virginia and Maryland, the commissioners would have discovered, had two, but only two, characteristics in common with that of New England: its white population was largely derived from English sources, and its numbers, at the time of the survey, were approximately the same as those of the Puritan colonies. But the number of immigrants that had arrived, the timing of their arrival, and their social, physical, and legal condition had been entirely different. New England's original immigration had taken place in a single short span of years early in the century; these Puritan immigrants and their followers had settled in a temperate and healthy environment; and they had been overwhelmingly free people, not bound servants, and organized for the most part in family groups, with only a relatively small preponderance of males over females. The English immigration to the Chesapeake had not been confined to a short period, but had been continuous, from 1607 on, with various peaks of intensity – in all, an immigrant population eight times as large as the Puritan migration. This century-long flow had consisted overwhelmingly of unmarried male indentured servants[d] (males outnumbered females by well over six to one), bound in indentures to four or more years of servitude, depending largely on age, and traveling not in family groups but as individuals. They had arrived and had been put to work in an unfamiliar, unhealthy environment in which malaria, which opened its victims to the ravages of a dozen other diseases, was endemic, and they had died like flies.

A deadly cycle had been at work. Survival in this environment had depended on building up immunities to the worst diseases, and these immunities were strongest in those born in the land. But there was no quick development of a native-born population. The immigrant women, too few under the best of conditions to reproduce the local populations, were kept by servitude from early marriages, and they succumbed like the men to the diseases that swept the land. The children they bore, hence the native population, were too few to replace the losses, even if all their children had lived. In fact, approximately half of the children born in these disease-ridden colonies in the seventeenth century died before the age of twenty, and those who survived to that age – the most-seasoned and best-acclimatized people of the region – had a further life expectancy of little over twenty years; New Englanders aged twenty had almost twice that life expectancy. And these were the natives; most immigrants to the Chesapeake who survived to the age of twenty died before reaching forty.

The deadly cycle of high death rates requiring more and more immigration to stock the work force, hence a constant renewal of the same disease vulnerability – this cycle could only be broken either by the slow growth of a native-born population, which would eventually have the advantages of a balanced sex ratio and inborn resistance to local diseases, or by the shift to a different source of manpower. Both were taking place in the years when our legates were touring the land. Slowly the proportion of native-born

Virginians and Marylanders had grown. It was just at the time we are discussing – at the end of the seventeenth century – that the number of native-born whites finally became greater than that of white immigrants; it was then, and then only, that the white population was beginning to reproduce itself without immigration. At the same time the work force was in the midst of a dramatic shift to slave labor. As late as 1680 less than 8 percent of the Chesapeake population had been black slaves; by 1690 the figure was 15 percent; by 1710 it was 25 percent. And the percentage was continuing to rise, not because planters preferred blacks to whites, and not because they feared open revolt by a rural proletariat of freed white servants, but because the available sources of British indentured servants were disappearing. In the late seventeenth century the supply of indentured servants dropped by 3 percent a year while the demand for labor grew at about the same rate. To fill the growing gap in field labor the planters turned increasingly to slaves, whose availability soared after 1697, when the monopoly of the Royal African Company[e] was broken and the African slave trade was thrown open to all comers.

As a result of this shift there was under way in 1700 – our legates would have observed – a massive transformation. A slave labor force that could be recruited at will by those with capital to invest was creating a growing disparity in the size of the producing units, and at the same time generating a self-intensifying tendency toward oligarchy. More and more of the productive land was devolving into the hands of a few large-scale operators, while more and more of the white population owned less and less of the best agricultural lands, were in a weak competitive situation, and were drifting into tenancy and moving off to more easily accessible frontier lands. At the same time a small number of ambitious landowning planters – a William Byrd I, a William Fitzhugh, a Wormeley, a Lee, a Carter, a Beverley – were able to parlay small gains into the critical capital of slaves, maneuver politically to get the lands they wanted, and begin the process of gentrification.[6]

Their achievements by 1700 were still modest by metropolitan standards. Byrd, a goldsmith's son who made his fortune by aggressive exploitation of the backcountry Indian trade, was able to send *his* son to England for his entire education and to support him in style as he learned commerce, law, and the ways of the polite world. But the senior Byrd's Westover plantation house was not the elegant riverside mansion it would later become; it was a four-square wooden farmhouse built for utility and with no pretense to elegance. The greatest house of the late seventeenth century was probably Greenspring, which had been Governor Berkeley's[f] home and political headquarters during his long tenure in office. The legates would have found that house in a significant state of transition. At the time of their visit the original manor house – "a typical small English brick country house" of the 1640s, which measured in all only sixty feet by sixty – was being renovated and rebuilt into a two-and-a-half-story mansion house a hundred feet long, boasting two tiers of dormers in its high-pitched roof, a five-arched arcade shading the lower front, and a second-floor porch with ornamental brickwork. Even so, a century later, just before the house was demolished, the noted architect Benjamin Latrobe inspected it and described it as "a brick building of great solidity but no attempt at grandeur"; its ornamented brickwork, he wrote, was "clumsy," and "about the style of James the first."[7]

There were, in 1700, other houses of some amplitude if no great technical elegance – Ralph Wormeley's Rosegill, the ten-room "great house" of a sprawling, multibuilding farm establishment built on a bluff overlooking the Rappahannock River; William Fitzhugh's Bedford, a thirteen-room wooden structure on the Potomac, four rooms of which were hung with tapestries and which was surrounded by the usual cluster of outbuildings, by an orchard of 2,500 apple trees, and by a large fenced-in garden. In Maryland too a nascent aristocracy was beginning to express its social ambitions and self-regard in the enhancement of the physical setting of its existence. But these late seventeenth-century establishments, much remarked on at the time, were the merest winks of light in a universe of frontier desolation. Virginia, a group of residents reported in 1697, "looks all like a wild desart; the high-lands overgrown with trees, and the low-lands sunk with water, marsh, and swamp … perhaps not the hundredth part of the country is yet clear'd from the woods, and not one foot of the marsh and swamp drained." Where the still heavily forested land was cleared, there were tree stumps and tangles of shrubs in and around small patches of cultivation.

The typical house of an ordinary farmer was a dark, drafty, dirt-floored, insect-ridden, one- or two-bedroom box made of green wood and scarcely worth maintaining in good condition, since it would be abandoned as soon as the few acres of farmland it adjoined were exhausted by ruthless tobacco cultivation. These ill-kept, ramshackle, crowded little farmhouses, so flimsy they were "virtually uninhabitable after a decade unless they were substantially reconstructed," were "dribbled over the landscape without apparent design." Most were a mile or so from the next habitation (some were completely isolated), and there were ruins and debris all along the banks of Chesapeake Bay and the lower reaches of the rivers that empty into it, wherever there was, or had been, habitation.[8]

Precisely what our legates would have seen in their water-borne inspection tour of 1700 has been vividly, and accurately, described by a modern scholar. Riding along the Maryland rivers at that time, Gloria Main has written, one would have seen

> vast unbroken stands of gigantic trees along the spines of higher ground, interspersed by abandoned fields and over-grown thickets with occasional sagging houses and dilapidated barns. The long intervals of green shoreline are only occasionally interrupted by villagelike clusters of small buildings that mark the home plantations of the larger planters, but nowhere would we see great mansions rising from grassy knolls or long sweeps of lawn leading down to the waterside. The landings to which we tie up our boat lead us instead to small wooden houses, unpainted and unadorned. No formal space stands before or behind the principal structure, if one can so be defined, nor is there an orderly disposition of the farm buildings. Only the beaten pathways between link them together as a working whole.
>
> If the untidy, unplanned, and unsymmetrical layout of the typical plantation is dismaying, the interiors of the homes prove even bleaker. There we find few comforts and no conveniences. Most colonial furniture consists of homemade pieces from local soft woods, roughly dressed and nailed together. Dirt or plank floors bear no coverings, nor do curtains hang at the glassless windows.

The commissioners would have found few concentrations of people, red, white, or black, anywhere. There were no towns, nor any general interest in creating them because the House of Burgesses,[8] the report of 1697 stated, consisted largely of country people born in the land, people who had never seen a town and had no idea of their "conveniency."[9] Even small groups of people would have been found only in a few of the inland villages, which consisted of a courthouse, a church, and a market of some kind. And the outer frontier was still close to the coast – in the near piedmont region, just beyond the reach of river navigation, between eighty and a hundred miles distant from the sea. It was in that piedmont frontier, in the years of this Domesday survey, that new lands were being claimed and opened up, and it seemed a wilderness world. When in 1714 Governor Spotswood[h] settled Virginia's first German colony, a group of forty ironworkers from Nassau-Siegen on the Rhine, in an encampment of palisaded log cabins just inside the fringe of the piedmont forests, he knew he was condemning them to a wilderness existence. In fact this crude settlement, which he called Germanna, was only thirty miles from the fall line and equally close to well-settled territory to the north, along the Potomac River.[10]

Touring deeper inland along the Virginia rivers, our legates would have passed through a succession, not of massive plantation estates and genteel establishments manned by platoons of slaves, but of moderate-sized and small farms, most of them worked by their owners with one or two servants or slaves. Virginia's rent roll of 1704, covering the area from the Rappahannock River south, reveals approximately 5,500 separate units of landownership. While there were a few tracts of several thousand acres (most of them only lightly cultivated frontier reserves), the great majority of these Virginia farms were holdings of from fifty to five hundred acres, and the mixed work force of servants and slaves (the slaves outnumbering the servants by 20 percent) was distributed thinly through these plantations. The average Virginia farm had only one or two servants or slaves; "a bare handful of well-to-do men each [had] from five to ten, or in rare cases 20 or 30, servants or slaves." And as they progressed still deeper inland, the main habitations the legates would have found would have been Indian cabins, "built," a contemporary wrote, "with posts put into the ground, the one by the other as close as they could stand ... and a sort of roof upon it, covered with the bark of trees. They say it keeps out the rain very well. The Indian women were all naked, only a girdle they had tied around the waist and about a yard of blanketing put between their legs.... . Their beds were mats made of bulrushes.... . All the household goods was a pot."[11]

The only busy scenes anywhere would have been the dock areas at the mouth of the James River and a few other spots along the Chesapeake Bay basin where the tobacco fleet, loaded with huge barrels of the weed that had been rolled to the river banks and carried downstream on rafts or skiffs, rode at anchor awaiting departure. There incoming vessels, arriving with loads of goods, servants, and slaves, carried news of an incomparably greater world far over the horizon.

But however crude and thinly populated the Chesapeake world was, it was active, more or less stable, and beginning to produce a culturally ambitious gentry leadership. In comparison with the settlements in the Carolinas – the fourth and last area of the legates' inspection – it was civilization itself.

There were two centers of British habitation south of Virginia which together would have formed the commissioners' fourth and final circuit. The older, which would become North Carolina, was only twenty to thirty miles south of Virginia. In 1700 this cluster of settlements around Albemarle Sound was a scraggly sprawl of farms and tiny villages set in the midst of pine forests and planted in the sandy soil of a coastal region cut off from the ocean by a ring of sand reefs. To this sheltered, almost inaccessible, region had come as early as the 1650s a ragtag collection of farmers, trappers, petty merchants, Indian traders, and rather desperate fortune hunters. Most had come from, or via, Virginia, which at that time regarded this pine-forest wilderness as its southern frontier; later they were joined by groups of Marylanders, New Englanders, and Barbadians. By 1700 new and alien groups were beginning to arrive. In 1704–5 a colony of Huguenots, escaping from crowded conditions in Virginia, joined the settlements. And in 1710 a colony of Swiss and Germans formed a separate settlement somewhat to the south, on the Neuse River. Some of these new settlers were religious radicals – Baptists, Anabaptists, and Mennonites – seeking refuge from a strict Protestant regime in Bern, Switzerland. But to this original group had been added several hundred of the 10,000 refugees from the southwest Rhineland who had arrived in England in 1710 and had then scattered into remote corners of the British world – some to Ireland, some to the Schoharie Valley of New York, some to the backcountry of Pennsylvania, some to the pine woods of North Carolina.

So the northern Carolina settlement of a few thousand souls was being peopled – quite randomly – from several quite different sources. The inhabitants, living in rough, scruffy clearings at the edges of pine forests and in dwellings even cruder than those of the

Chesapeake farmers, were engaged in tobacco-growing, mixed farming, and cattle-raising. They were few in number; they formed no towns of any size; and they nourished no gentry leadership. Their still primitive settlements were highly unstable, and the commissioners, as they left, must have wondered if they would survive at all. For the establishment of New Bern, North Carolina, had touched off an Indian war, which broke out in September 1711 and raged for two years. It would end, after orgies of atrocities on both sides, with the neighboring Tuscarora tribes decimated and driven off the land. That it was "won" at all – that is, that the northern Carolina settlements survived at all – was due in part to the help provided by the southern Carolina settlements. Several expeditions of southern Carolinians together with warlike Indian allies marched across the 300 miles of unmapped forests that separated the two regions, through veritable jungles and scarcely passable swamp land, to help repel the Tuscaroras' attacks in the north.[12]

These southern Carolinians had come from a tiny but surprisingly prosperous community centered on the port of Charles Town, at the juncture of the Ashley and Cooper rivers. In 1703, in this southernmost British settlement there were just over 7,000 inhabitants (somewhat more than lived in the northern area). It was a population strangely proportioned: almost half were black slaves, Indians, or white indentured servants. The free whites – a mere 3,600 – were the product of a straggling immigration, chiefly from Barbados. Desperately attempting to wring profits from the wild land, they were experimenting with raising silkworms, cotton, flax, and rice while developing forest industries and raising cattle. Their way of life, at the turn of the century, was primitive. Working in the semitropical climate side by side with their black and Indian slaves, they shared at times "a common undertaking as members of an interracial family unit," but it was a unit that was explosive with half-controlled tensions, fears, and hostilities. Miscegenation was common-place; mulatto and "mustee" (mixed Negro and Indian) children were everywhere; and manumission was frequent – of mulatto children and of black and Indian women (not men). These were no tender, affectionate relationships. This was a brutal, half-primitive world of bushwhacking frontiersmen, who "can't be persuaded," the Anglican missionary Francis Le Jau, reported in 1709, "that Negroes and Indians are otherwise than beasts, and use them like such." So Mary Stafford, a young woman who, with her husband, had fled England for South Carolina to escape their debts, wrote in 1711 that there were good possibilities in the colony – for those who could "get a few slaves and can beat them well to make them work hard. [T]here is no living here without."[13]

It was in fact the South Carolinians' toughness, their crudeness, and their fierce Conquistador-like zest for profits that made poss-ible their major source of gain. For the Indian trade was their Potosí, and it was an enterprise of ferocious, often bloody, exploitation. In the early 1700s there were at least 200 white traders working out of Charles Town. They organized caravans of twenty or thirty pack horses which they led or sent not merely 145 miles inland to a central Indian transfer point near present-day Columbia, South Carolina, but deep into southern Georgia to barter – with whatever ruthlessness was effective – with the Creek tribes, and all the way across Georgia, across Alabama, and across Mississippi, on treks that took a year or more, to reach the Chickasaw tribes on the Mississippi River. By 1700 an average of 54,000 deerskins were being exported annually to England from the still primitive settle-ments in southern Carolina – cargoes worth a small fortune. It was this Indian trade – with its half-savage British *coureurs de bois*,[i] many of them accepted members of the Indian tribes in which they lived for most of each year; with its caravans coming and going; with its transfer centers and warehouses, its canoes and flat boats in which skins could be transported in large quantities along river routes – it was all of this strange and exotic traffic that would have struck the commissioners most forcefully as they completed the fourth circuit in Charles Town.[14]

This is what British North America must have looked like in 1700. But there is a larger dimension to the story that the legates should have reported if they were faithful to their instructions.

These widely scattered settlements, for all their differences, shared a single, complex characteristic, a common quality, which was just then emerging and which would continue to characterize American society throughout the pre-industrial era and perhaps afterward as well.

This whole world of the legates' inspection was a borderland, a part of the expanding periphery of Britain's core culture; and its inner quality derived from that fact. Like the Welsh borderland two hundred years earlier, like the Scottish middle marches a century earlier, like Ireland and the Caribbean islands in the colonists' own time, and like Australia later, the mainland North American colonies formed a typically disordered border country in which, as in the Scottish marchland in the fifteenth century, "violence [was] … a way of life."[15] Concentrating, as American historians have done, on the origins of a later American civilization, and hence viewing the colonial world as a *frontier* – that is, as an advance, as a forward- and outward-looking, future-anticipating progress toward what we know eventuated, instead of as a periphery, a ragged outer margin of a central world, a regressive, backward-looking diminishment of metropolitan accomplishment – looking at the colonies in this anachronistic way, one tends to minimize the primitiveness and violence, the bizarre, quite literally outlandish quality of life in this far-distant outback of late seventeenth-century Britain.

Partly this wildness, extravagance, and disorder were simply the products of the inescapable difficulties of maintaining a high European civilization in an undeveloped environment. Partly, too, they were products of the hostility that developed between the Europeans and the native peoples. But in large part, too, they were products of the common European, and indeed British, conception of America as an uncivil place on the distant margins of civilization – a place where the ordinary restraints of civility could be abandoned in pell-mell exploitation, a remote place where recognized enemies and pariahs of society – heretics, criminals, paupers – could safely be deposited, their contamination sealed off by 3,000 miles of ocean, and where putatively inferior specimens of humanity, blacks and Indians, could be reduced to subhuman statuses, worked like animals, and denied the most elemental benefits of law and religion, those fragile integuments which even in England could barely contain the savagery of life. Blackstone's statement in his *Commentaries*[j] that "a slave or negro, the instant he lands in England, becomes a freeman; that is, the law will protect him in the enjoyment of his person and his property," and Mansfield's decision in *Sommersett's Case* (1772),[k] were simply obvious[16]; but obvious too was the obverse understanding that on the outer boundaries of civilization, restraint on brutal exploitation could be abandoned.

There was nothing remarkable in such a view. The peripheries generally were viewed like this. So land-rich Ireland and its brutally subjugated people were seen at the time (and, one might add, after); so too the sugar-rich West Indies; so too, later, Australia and

New Zealand, and ultimately parts of Africa. What was uncommon, and what created the distinctive characteristics of British North American life, was the fact that by the turn of the seventeenth century the settlers in America – the creole,[1] now indigenous population – had attained a state of self-conscious gentility incompatible with the violence and extravagance and disorder of life in a marchland, and they were aware that that was so. It was the juxtaposition of the two – the intermingling of savagery and developing civilization – that is the central characteristic of the world that was emerging in British America. Borderland violence and bizarre distensions of normal European culture patterns had become fused with a growing civility into a distinctive way of life.

Everywhere one turns in this far periphery of the British world one finds examples of this complex mixture. The Indian wars are the most obvious. They bred a brutality so extreme that one almost tries not to comprehend. Kindly, devout, and genteel householders became brutal overnight. The gentle, humane Reverend John Pike of Dover, New Hampshire, calmly recorded in his journal of 1682–1709 a fearful chronicle, not merely of sudden death and kidnapping, but of savagery, on both sides. William Moodey, Pike reported, was captured, then escaped, and was retaken: " 'tis feared he & another Englishman were roasted to death." Two of the white women captured by the Indians in the Haverhill raid of March 1697, he recorded – and Cotton Mather and others celebrated – managed to break free; and then these New England women "slew ten of the Indians, & returned home with their scalps." Pike might have added that among these slaughtered and scalped Indian victims of the two Haverhill women – the mother and nurse of an infant whose brains had been "dashed out ... against a tree" by the Indians – were two native women and six children, and that the colony, following a policy common at the time, paid the Haverhill ladies £50 in bounty money for the scalps they brought back. And he might have noted further that scalping, indulged in by whites as well as by Indians everywhere in this period, was no deft tonsorial operation but a work of butchery in which, more often than not, the cranium was shattered with an axe; the victims were as often living as dead when it was done.[17]

The savagery of the Indian wars was the same everywhere. In the Tuscarora War in North Carolina, terrified white settlers, some newly arrived from Europe, burned Indians alive in retaliation for what had happened to their women: "laid on their house-floors and

27

great stakes run up through their bodies. Others big with child, the infants ripped out and hung upon trees." And so it continued. A half-century later one of the defenders of a besieged fort in South Carolina's Cherokee War (1760-1) wrote the governor, "We have now the pleasure, Sir, to fatten our dogs with their carcasses and to display their scalps neatly ornamented on the top of our bastions." That fierce and bloody war, wrote the eighteenth-century historian David Ramsay, "tainted the principles of many of the inhabitants, so as to endanger the peace and happiness of society." Respectable backcountry people, he said, "acquired such vicious habits that when the war was over they despised labor and became pests of society," creating in the backcountry a constant state of "anarchy, disorder, and confusion."[18]

But the meaning of the Indian wars cannot be measured simply by events like this, nor was their effect confined to those directly involved. The narratives of Indian captivity – best sellers every-where in America with the appearance of *The Soveraignty & Goodness of God ... Being a Narrative of the Captivity and Restauration of Mrs. Mary Rowlandson ...* (1682) – universalized these experiences, cast them into popular literary idioms, and drove them, in ways one will never fully understand, deep into the American psyche. Con-temporary readers of those vivid tales, the more gripping because they told of fearful things that in fact happened to many hundreds of their contemporaries and that might happen to anyone in America,[19] must have incorporated the narrators' experiences into their basic perception of the world. They must somehow have learned to live with the constant apprehension of extreme viol-ence, and they must have wondered, secretly, guiltily, about their own capacity to endure – and to inflict – degradation, humiliation, and pain.[20]

But one need not dwell on the Indian wars, so full of atrocities on both sides, bred of fear and an insensitivity to human suffering. They seem too obvious an example and somehow not a part of the normal pattern of life. But savagery and the breakdown of ordered life lay everywhere in this borderland world, especially on its own margins. The North Carolina backwoodsmen were repeatedly said to be "the lowest scum and rabble ... [who] build themselves sorry hutts and live in a beastly sort of plenty ... devoted to calumny, lying, and the vilest tricking and cheating; a people into whose heads no human means can beat the notion of a publick interest or persuade to live like men." The South Carolina Indian traders were known to be "more prone to savage barbarity than the savages themselves." "Villains," "horse thieves," "banditti" infested the southern border country, it was said again and again. And travelers at the outposts at every stage – Esopus (Kingston), New York, in the mid-seventeenth century; New Bern, North Carolina, in 1710; Pittsburgh and the Ohio country in the 1760s and 1770s – reported hard-drinking trappers and traders mingling with pioneer farmers, scenes of drunken brawls involving whites, blacks, and Indians, at times an almost complete breakdown of normal civility.[21]

Savagery lay not only on the far outer margins, however. In the south, and elsewhere as well, it invaded the very heart of a growing gentility. For in those colonies slavery took on a new and strange existence. In British North America slavery was no exterior and distant phenomenon, sealed off in remote regions as it was for Britain itself, but, in its most brutal form, an everyday fact of life in communities that were otherwise genteel, otherwise decent, and growing more tolerant, reasonable, and benign all the time. In plantation culture, and elsewhere where slavery was an important part of society, an accommodation was somehow made between brutality and progressive refinement. The savagery of chattel slavery was no new thing for people of the seventeenth and eighteenth centuries; brutality in human relations was commonplace, and took many forms. What was new was that chattel slavery, a condition considered appropriate for isolated work gangs at the remote margins of civilization, was here incorporated into a world of growing sophistication.

One can hardly believe William Byrd II's[m] normal way of life, as he so meticulously recorded it in the diary he kept during these years at the turn of the century. The days pass smoothly. Byrd rises "betimes," reads his Bible, a passage in Greek, another in Hebrew, and some poetry, does a few exercises, and attends to the duties of his plantation, Westover, which he was building into the elegant Georgian estate that would become so famous. But in the midst of all this gentility lie his relations with his slaves. His black serving girl Jenny, age sixteen, is beaten repeatedly. Scarcely a month goes by in which she is not thrashed, beaten, soundly whipped (his terms) for all sorts of things, for something and for nothing: for being unmannerly, for concealing the serving boy Eugene's bedwetting, for throwing water on the sofa. She is strapped, beaten with tongs, and on one occasion, when Byrd's neurotic wife flies into a rage, branded with a hot iron. And the eighteen-year-old

29

Eugene is whipped soundly for running away (Byrd could not imagine why he would want to do such a thing), then clamped with the iron boot; thereafter, when his bedwetting becomes chronic and when even the branding iron does no good, "I made him drink a pint of piss."[22]

Yet Byrd was a well-educated and conscientious *paterfamilias*, a would-be *littérateur*, proud of his large, much-used library; he was a man of taste and cultivation who had lived for fifteen years among the literati of London and had studied at the Inns of Court. His treatment of his slaves was by no means exceptionally brutal. For exceptional behavior one need merely turn over the letters of the South Carolina missionary Le Jau, with their tales of slave women being "scalloped" and left to die in the woods or burnt alive on suspicion of arson; of masters who "hamstring, mai[m], & unlimb" their slaves "for small faults," or for falling asleep at work "scourge" them twice a day, then "muffle" them so that they could not eat, and at night bind them into a "hellish machine … [in] the shape of a coffin where [they] could not stirr"; of laws, no longer even remarked on, that required the castration of Negro runaways; and of Indian wars deliberately instigated "for our people to get slaves." Byrd was more typical than these South Carolina masters, and typical too must have been the psychological conflicts that produced the rages of the politically liberal, well-read, and respon- sible Landon Carter. Carter's diary – as I read it – is a tragic and despairing document, and it could have been written nowhere else in the Western world – except, perhaps, in the remote far *Eastern* marchland of European civilization, on the isolated estates of the Russian nobility, whose autonomy was as complete as that of the American plantation owners and who also sought to incorporate a total despotism into the heart of domestic gentility.[23]

Still, slavery, like the Indian wars, may somehow be discounted as being exceptional to most people's way of life (in fact it was not) or as a commonplace of the age. But slavery, like the Indian wars, was only a particular expression of a mingling of primitivism and progressive civilization which in its widest ranges was an under- lying characteristic of all these marchland colonies. It was thus perfectly reasonable for the British government to think of the American colonies as in some sense frontier garrison settlements, and to appoint military officers to rule them, which they did throughout the seventeenth century and for the first third of the eighteenth century. It was equally reasonable for the government to start the practice, which it did in the early seventeenth century, of banishing convicted felons or prisoners of war to the colonies: "so do the Spaniards people the Indies," Governor Dale of Virginia wrote in 1611 in begging the government to send over to the labor-short colony "all offenders out of the common gaols condemned to die." In the course of the eighteenth century Britain would send over to North America, mainly to Maryland and Virginia, an estimated 50,000 convicted felons, approximately the same number of convicts that would be sent to Australia before 1824. Indeed, garrison government and the transport of convicts to America were aspects of the same core-and-periphery relationship. As a form of punishment, transportation was logical enough, for the colonies were assumed to be so remote, so primitive, that merely sending people there would be punitive, and it was also economical, constructive, and socially therapeutic – for Britain, that is: the colonies were seen as different kinds of places.[24]

The colonists, however, were beginning to disagree. As early as 1670 the Virginia Assembly attempted to ban the transportation of "fellons and other desperate villaines sent hither from the several prisons in England." They feared, they said, "the danger which apparently threatens us from the barbarous designes and felonious practices of such wicked villaines." More than that, the Assembly wrote, by importing convicted criminals we "loose our reputation, [whilst] we are beleived to be a place onely fitt to receive such base and lewd persons" – or, as President Stith of the College of William and Mary put it later, in the eighteenth century, Virginia, because of the advent of the convicts, had come to be reputed a "hell upon earth, another Siberia." One well-informed commentator in early eighteenth-century Virginia felt that the only solution, since the government was determined to continue shipping criminals to America, was to set off one whole county in Virginia as a separate penal colony – an American Botany Bay, in effect – and confine all the transported felons to that area. By then, 1724, the incongruity and illogicality of shipping convicted felons to the colonies were disturbing; thirty years later the practice had become shocking. Dismissal of the "terrible herd of exiled malefactors" to the mainland colonies, proud of their gentility, it was then said, was a punishment not to the convicts, for whom it was in fact a blessing, but for the Americans, who had done no wrong. Americans were Britons: "how injurious does it seem to free one part of the dominions from the plagues of mankind, and cast them upon another?"

31

By the 1760s the situation, to many Americans, had become ludicrous, a fit subject for Franklin's choicest wit.[25]

All of these overt violations of ordinary civil order – Indian wars, slavery, garrison government, the transportation of criminals – though they permeated the developing culture, overspecify and overdramatize, make too lurid, an issue that had much subtler and broader manifestations. The less physical aspects of the colonies' peculiarities were equally important. For ultimately the colonies' strange ways were only distensions and combinations of elements that existed in the parent cultures, but that existed there within constraints that limited, shaped, and in a sense civilized their growth. These elements were here released, fulfilled – at times with strange results that could not have been anticipated.

Thus Puritanism, in its various forms, fulfilled itself in New England, reached its limits, unconstrained by a parent church or by any external social or institutional authority. It became complex and engrossing in its unfolding; bred unusual offshoots; and ended by creating a peculiar subculture of its own.[26] So too, late in the century, did the products of a wave of pietistic fervor that broke over the German states. Everywhere in the Rhineland this pietistic awakening created new radical movements, but they were movements whose European shapes were formed and whose European destinies were limited by the establishments in whose interstices alone these movements were able to grow. In the far western American marchlands, where there were no external controls, no central establishment, the results were altogether different.

It was in Pennsylvania that the messianic pietism and the bizarre occultism that swept through the Protestant sects in the German states – perfectionist impulses that tended to exhaust themselves in the dense social environment of Europe – it was in Pennsylvania that they bore the strangest and most plentiful fruit.[27]

It began with the arrival in 1694 of the learned Johannes Kelpius and his mystical sect, until then known as the Chapter of Perfection. Kelpius was a model Rosicrucian mystic, a magus, and also a *magister* of the University of Altdorf, a master both of esoteric lore and of secular scholarship.[n] With his followers, he built just outside Philadelphia, on a ridge overlooking a creek, a log-walled monastery forty feet by forty feet to accommodate the forty brethren. It had a common room for Quaker-like worship, and individual cells where the brethren could search for perfection in trancelike states by contemplating their magic numbers and their esoteric symbols.

In a primitive laboratory they conducted chemical and pharmaceutical experiments aimed at eliminating disease and prolonging life indefinitely. And on the roof they built a telescope, which they manned from dusk till dawn, so that in case, as they put it, the Bridegroom came in the middle of the night, their lamps would be prepared – which is to say, they would be prepared to receive the Deliverer. But the heart of Kelpius's sect – which was renamed here The Woman in the Wilderness, after a passage in Revelation – lay not in the common room, not in the cells, not in the laboratory, and not in the rooftop *Sternwarte*, but in a cave which the Magus found in a nearby hillside and in which he spent most of his life after his arrival in Pennsylvania pondering a truth concealed to ordinary souls but revealed to him by signs, by symbols, by numbers, and by pure contemplation. For he knew with certainty that the wilderness into which the Woman in Revelation (the pure church) had fled was none other than Pennsylvania. It was here, he believed, that mankind would "find the dear Lord Jesus"; it was here that the true Christian, vigilantly trimming his lamp, should await the Bridegroom and prepare for the heavenly feast.[28]

At Kelpius's death the leadership of The Woman in the Wilderness passed to Johann Gottfried Seelig, a theologian and scholar of such immaculate piety and stern austerity that he could not tolerate the worldly demands even of guiding a monastery, and so resigned, "clad himself in pilgrim garb, and retired to one of the small log cabins that were on the tract, where he spent his time in mystical speculations and devout meditations, in which the spiritual bridegroom bore an important part." His successor, Conrad Matthäi, was the last in this succession; he lived until 1748. *Der alte Matthäi*, as he was called, became a familiar figure to everyone in and around Philadelphia, impressive to the end with his snow-white hair and flowing beard, dressed in a coarse homespun gown and sandals, and carrying always a long staff, an alpen-stock, which must have seemed a symbol of office.[29]

But long before the sect's and Matthäi's demise, the brotherhood of The Woman in the Wilderness had been superseded in the Pennsylvania mystics' world by a far more dynamic movement led by the most extraordinary figure of them all.

Johann Conrad Beissel, an ignorant, mystical, tormented baker's boy from the German Palatinate, after flirting with several of the radical sects that struggled for existence in the spiritually burnt-over districts of the Rhineland, had joined the exodus to Pennsylvania;

concocted, in a hermit's cabin near Germantown, his own brand of sabbatarian Dunkerism;° gathered a band of followers at Conestoga; and founded the Ephrata cloister, whose monks and nuns he ruled despotically, neurotically, and cruelly. God-possessed, immersed in the writings of the mystics, entranced by the secret rites of the Rosicrucians, he was a cyclone of energy, and he pursued his dream of a pure religion, unimpeded by state, society, or church. He was bizarre but unconfined, and the fame of his strange sect of emaciated celibates spread throughout the English as well as the German population of Pennsylvania and ultimately throughout the Rhineland and in France, through Voltaire, as well. Beissel preached with his eyes shut tight, passionately, ungrammatically, in incoherent torrents. If by chance his bowed congregation indicated understanding in quiet murmurs of assent, he reversed his chaotic argument to demonstrate the incomprehensibility of God's truth. And he imposed on his half-starved followers – clothed in rough, Capuchin-like habits designed to hide all signs of human shape – a rule of such severe self-mortification that some went mad, while the elite enacted the secret rites of the Rosicrucians, to which neophytes sought admission by bodily ordeals that lasted forty days and forty nights. Yet ... and yet ... the art of book illumination was reinvented in Beissel's Ephrata, and from some spark of hidden genius the *Vorsteher* himself devised a form of polyphonic choral music, complete with his own system of notation, which, when sung falsetto by his followers straining to reach ever higher, more "divine" notes, created an unearthly effect that enthralled everyone who ever heard it – and which caught the imagination, two centuries later, of another German immigrant in America, Thomas Mann, who, brooding on art and the German soul, immortalized Beissel in *Doctor Faustus*.[30]

Beissel's Ephrata was unique – but such unique utopias grew like mushrooms in British North America, flourished, and then wilted and died in that open world. While contemplating a form for a Brotherhood of Zion fit for his prophetic ecstasies, Beissel visited first The Woman in the Wilderness sect; then the Labadists' Bohemia Manor[P] in nearby Maryland; and then the followers of Matthias Baumann, who believed they were as much Christ as Christ and could not sin and whose leader, to prove that he was a special envoy of God to man, proposed to walk across the surface of the Delaware River. And Beissel could have found many more. The sophisticated Moravian leader Count Zinzendorf[q] considered

Beissel to be diabolical, but Zinzendorf's own group, the Unitas Fratrum, contributed to the multiplicity of conventicles in America not only an array of semi-communistic Moravian settlements, but also a missionary movement that spawned dozens of short-lived utopias on the frontier and deep in Indian territory. The sectarian Germans – the so-called "plain Dutch" – who settled much of eastern Pennsylvania shared with Ephrata its alienation from the world and its relentless pursuit of truth; but having compromised to some extent with the world, they flourished. By 1750 there were forty-eight Amish and Mennonite settlements in Pennsylvania, ten Dunkard, and the beginnings of several Schwenkfelder.[31]

Much of the British North American culture was familiarly European, traditional, even conservative. Life on the farms outside Philadelphia, Francis Michel reported with surprise in 1704, was "just like living in Germany." But everywhere there were strange distensions of familiar forms, and an outer boundary of primitivism that entered into the inner lives of a population growing ever more genteel, ever more stable and sophisticated. And so it continued into the later eighteenth century. Sir William Johnson's[r] establishment, Johnson Hall, the spacious, well-furnished mansion he built at the edge of the forest in the early 1760s just north of the Mohawk River in upcountry New York, was called by contemporaries a "superb and elegant edifice." But Johnson Hall was the headquarters building of a biracial manor court where Johnson lived the uninhibited life of a marchland baron, surrounded by his illegitimate children by two successive common-law wives, one a runaway German indentured servant, the other a Mohawk Indian, and by children of other, more casual connections as well. Crowds of Indians were always there. Outbuildings were constructed to accommodate them when they arrived, but many simply camped on the lawn and wandered through the house. Lord Adam Gordon, visiting in 1765, was astonished and deeply impressed by this strange baronial court "cleared," he reported, "in an absolute forest." Johnson's success with the Indians, he felt, and his control of this northern border area, were admirable, but, Gordon added after spending some days with Johnson, "no consideration should tempt me to lead his life.... I know no other man equal to so disagreeable a duty."[32]

Johnson's bizarre establishment was at the far edge of the outer periphery, but every section of the land, no matter how long settled

35

and sophisticated, had direct and continuous contact with the wilderness. Mule skinners plunged deep into strange Indian territories, remained there for months, even years, to return to the coastal towns with packs of animal skins and with strange tales and stranger experiences they could never fully tell. Hundreds of settlers, we do not know how many, who made direct contact with the Indian tribes – even some of those captured and brutalized by the Indians during the wars – found in the Indians' lives an appealing sense of community, of equality, and of unfettered freedom of movement, and they disappeared across the forest pale. All the borderlands bred strange forms of life. William Faulkner's story of the mysterious Thomas Sutpen – erecting in frontier Mississippi, with the labor of twenty "wild" Negroes clothed only in caked mud, a mansion house made of bricks baked on the spot, which he equipped with costly European furnishings – has dramatic counterparts in the pages of history.[s] So William Dunbar, a young Anglo-Scottish intellectual and scientist, constructed, in 1773, with the labor of a battalion of slaves he personally led in chains from Jamaica, a sumptuous wilderness estate at a deserted bend of the Mississippi River near Natchez. Dunbar's life, recorded in a diary that details his scientific studies as well as his struggle with his slaves and with the wilderness, is in some ways stranger and darker than that of any of Faulkner's characters. But the most extraordinary Faulknerian episode took place not on the banks of the Mississippi but in East Florida.[33]

Among the many whose imaginations were fired by the acquisition of East Florida in 1763 was a certain Dr. Andrew Turnbull of London, well connected with the leading politicians, including George Grenville, and with polite society. Like so many others he dreamed of founding an estate in that semitropical land that would produce cotton, silk, indigo, and fruits of all kinds; he also hoped it would provide comfort and affluence for his large and rather burdensome family. Being sophisticated, even scientific in his approach, he recruited settlers for his Florida land grant in places he believed had climates equivalent to Florida's, and so in 1768 arrived at the swampy Mosquito Inlet, seventy-five miles south of St. Augustine, with 1,255 Greeks, Corsicans, Italians, and Minorcans. The Greeks he had recruited in the villages of Mani in the Peloponnesus – villages "built like eagles' nests high on the cliffs of a rocky peninsula."

The saga of Turnbull's settlement, which he called New Smyrna, makes the bizarre early history of Faulkner's Yoknapatawpha County seem tranquil in comparison. The settlers, having deserted their dry, clear, invigorating Aegean and Mediterranean climate for Turnbull's swampy utopia, fell victim to Florida's heat, humidity, and torrential rains. Weakened by semi-starvation and malaria, they died in a rampage of disease. Within twenty-four months half of the settlers were dead, and Turnbull, his dream fading before his eyes, turned savage. Enforcing a criminal code of his own devising, he beat the survivors if they slackened in their work, and appointed sadistic overseers who turned the marshy, floridly overgrown plantation into a concentration camp. Those who attempted to flee were flogged, starved, and chained to heavy iron balls. Yet nothing could create the elysium Dr. Turnbull continued to seek. When the American Revolution loosened the ties of all civil authority in America, the surviving settlers finally managed to escape. Turnbull himself, pursued by creditors and enemies in high places in Florida, worked his way to Charleston, and there he lived out his life, a British subject to the end, a respected and successful physician, a man of property and standing, and one of the founders of the South Carolina Medical Society. His beautiful Greek wife, the last legacy of his earlier, bloody adventure, survived him.[34]

This mingling of primitivism and civilization, however transitory stage by stage, was an essential part of early American culture, and we must struggle to comprehend it.

What did it mean to Jefferson, slave owner and *philosophe*, that he grew up in this far western borderland world of Britain, looking out from Queen Anne rooms of spare elegance onto a wild, uncultivated land? We can only grope to understand.[t]

EDITOR'S NOTES

a John Winthrop, Jr. (1606–76), son of John Winthrop, governor of Massachusetts.
b Jacob Leisler (1640–91) led the rebellion which took his name, and held power for almost two years from 1689 to 1691.
c William Penn (1644–1718), the founder of Pennsylvania.
d Unable or unwilling to pay the costs of migration, an indentured servant entered into a contract with a merchant or ship captain, who paid the costs of transportation. A colonist bought the contract, thereby securing access to the servant's full-time labor for a number of years in return for subsistence and "freedom dues" at the expiration of the contract.
e The Royal African Company, a joint-stock company chartered in 1672, initially held a monopoly on all English trade with Africa.

f   Sir William Berkeley (1606–77), governor of Virginia 1641–52, 1660–76.
g   The Virginia House of Burgesses, created in 1619, was the first repre-
    sentative legislative assembly in British America.
h   Alexander Spotswood, governor of Virginia 1710–23.
i   *coureurs de bois* means literally "woods runners," and refers to those who
    traded illegally with the Indians.
j   William Blackstone's *Commentaries on the Laws of England* (1765–9).
k   In 1772 Lord Chief Justice Mansfield ruled that a master had no right
    forcibly to remove his slave – in the specific case, one James Somerset –
    out of England.
l   Creole means native-born in this context.
m   William Byrd II (1674–1744), a prominent Virginia planter.
n   Rosicrucianism was a strain of German pietism interested in the occult.
    It got its name from Christian Rosenkreuz, who founded the Fraternity
    of the Rose Cross in 1408.
o   Earliest of the organized pietist groups in America was the Church of
    the Brethren, also known as Dunkers, whose most distinctive practice
    was thrice repeated immersion, face forward, in a flowing stream –
    hence the name.
p   Labadists were followers of Jean de Labadie, leader of a quietist move-
    ment within the Dutch Reformed Church.
q   Count Nicholas Ludwig Zinzendorf (1700–60) was a leader of the
    Renewed Church of the United Brethren, otherwise known as the
    Unitas Fratrum or Moravians, the most important pietistic sect in
    America.
r   Sir William Johnson (1715 –74), superintendent of Indian affairs for the
    Northern Department from 1768 onward.
s   William Faulkner, *Absalom, Absalom!* (1936).
t   Thomas Jefferson (1743 –1826), Virginia planter, owner of Monticello,
    and later president of the U.S.A.

NOTES

Reprinted from Bernard Bailyn, *The Peopling of British North America: An Introduction* (New York, 1986). © 1986 Bernard Bailyn. Used with the permission of the author.

1   Richard S. Dunn, *Puritans and Yankees: The Winthrop Dynasty of New England, 1630–1717* (Princeton, 1962), traces this three-generational transition with great care: the treatment of the second and third generations is especially sensitive and revealing. For the attenuation of Puritan culture through the next two generations, see Richard L. Bushman, *From Puritan to Yankee: Character and the Social Order in Connecticut, 1690–1765* (Cambridge, Mass., 1967).
2   Daniel S. Smith, "The Demographic History of Colonial New England," *Journal of Economic History*, 32 (1972): 165–83; Kenneth A. Lockridge, "The Population of Dedham, Massachusetts, 1636–1736," *Economic History Review*, 2nd ser., 19 (1966): 318–44.

3 Philip J. Greven, Jr., *Four Generations: Population, Land, and Family in Colonial Andover, Massachusetts* (Ithaca, N.Y., 1970): esp. chaps. 5–8.

4 Thomas J. Archdeacon, *New York City, 1664–1710: Conquest and Change* (Ithaca, N.Y., 1976): esp. chap. 2 (quotation at 33); Patricia U. Bonomi, *A Factious People: Politics and Society in Colonial New York* (New York, 1971): esp. chap. 2.

5 Peter O. Wacker, *Land and People, A Cultural Geography of Pre-industrial New Jersey: Origins and Settlement Patterns* (New Brunswick, N.J., 1975): chap. 3; Ned C. Landsman, *Scotland and its First American Colony 1683–1763* (Princeton, 1985): chaps. 4–6; Sally Schwartz, " 'A Mixed Multitude': Religion and Ethnicity in Colonial Pennsylvania" (Ph.D. dissertation, Harvard Univ., 1981): esp. chaps. 3–5; James T. Lemon, *The Best Poor Man's Country: A Geographical Study of Early Southeastern Pennsylvania* (Baltimore, 1972): chaps. 1–3; Gary B. Nash, *Quakers and Politics: Pennsylvania, 1681–1726* (Princeton, 1968): 174. On Leisler's Rebellion, besides Archdeacon, *New York City*, chap. 5, see Jerome R. Reich, *Leisler's Rebellion: A Study of Democracy in New York, 1664–1720* (Chicago, 1953). On the emerging aristocracies, see Bonomi, *Factious People*, chaps. 2, 3; Archdeacon, *New York City*, chaps. 3, 4; Frederick B. Tolles, *Meeting House and Counting House: The Quaker Merchants of Colonial Philadelphia* (Chapel Hill, N.C., 1948).

6 For a summary of the now extensive literature on Chesapeake population history in the seventeenth century, see John J. McCusker and Russell R. Menard, *The Economy of British America, 1607–1789* (Chapel Hill, N.C., 1985): 133–43, 236–57, and writings cited there; Gloria Main, *Tobacco Colony: Life in Early Maryland, 1650–1720* (Princeton, 1982); and Darrett B. Rutman and Anita H. Rutman, *A Place in Time: Middlesex County, Virginia, 1650–1750* (New York, 1984). See also Edmund S. Morgan, *American Slavery, American Freedom* (New York, 1975): chaps. 7–15, and Paul G. Clemens, *The Atlantic Economy and Colonial Maryland's Eastern Shore* (Ithaca, N.Y., 1980): chaps. 1–3. The shift in the composition of the labor force is analyzed in David W. Galenson, *White Servitude in Colonial America: An Economic Analysis* (Cambridge, 1981): chaps. 8, 9; for the figures cited, see Main, *Tobacco Colony*: 100, and Main, "Maryland and the Chesapeake Economy, 1670–1720," in *Law, Society, and Politics in Early Maryland*, eds. Aubrey C. Land *et al.* (Baltimore, 1977): 134–5.

7 *The Prose Works of William Byrd of Westover*, ed. Louis B. Wright (Cambridge, Mass., 1966): intro.; Ivor Noël Hume, *Here Lies Virginia* (New York, 1963): 139–42; Thomas T. Waterman and John A. Barrows, *Domestic Colonial Architecture of Tidewater Virginia* (New York, 1968): 12–13.

8 Louis B. Wright, *The First Gentlemen of Virginia* (San Marino, Calif., 1940): 191 and chap. 6; Rutman and Rutman, *Place in Time*: 153–6, 211–14, 220; *William Fitzhugh and his Chesapeake World, 1676–1701*, ed. Richard B. David (Chapel Hill, N.C., 1963): 18, 14–15, 175–6; Henry Hartwell, James Blair, and Edward Chilton, *The Present State of Virginia, and the College [1697]*, ed. Hunter D. Farish (Williamsburg, Va., 1940): 8; Main, *Tobacco Colony*: 261, 153, 141.

9   ibid.: 140; Hartwell *et al.*, *Present State*: 14.

10 Elizabeth C. Vann and Margaret C. Dixon, *Virginia's First German Colony* (Richmond, Va., 1961); John W. Wayland, *Germanna ... 1714–1956* (Staunton, Va., 1956): 10–21.

11 Thomas J. Wertenbaker, *The Planters of Colonial Virginia* (Princeton, 1922): 57 and appendix; *Memoirs of a Huguenot Family*, ed. Ann Maury (New York, 1972): 264.

12 Hugh T. Lefler and William S. Powell, *Colonial North Carolina* (New York, 1973): chaps. 2, 3.

13 Peter H. Wood, *Black Majority* (New York, 1974): chaps. 1, 2, 4, p. 106; *The Carolina Chronicle of Dr. Francis Le Jau, 1706–1717*, ed. Frank T. Klingberg (Berkeley, 1956): 55; Mary Stafford to [?] [South Carolina], Aug. 23, 1711, in *South Carolina Historical Magazine*, 81 (1980): 4.

14 Verner W. Crane, *The Southern Frontier, 1670–1732* (Durham, N.C., 1928): chaps. 5, 6 (figures at p. 111).

15 Denys Hay, "England, Scotland and Europe: The Problem of the Frontier," *Transactions of the Royal Historical Society*, 5th ser., 25 (1975): 77–91, quotation at p. 82.

16 William Blackstone, *Commentaries on the Laws of England*, 3rd ed. (Oxford, 1768): bk. I, chap. 14, i; *The Eighteenth-Century Constitution, 1688–1815*, ed. E. Neville Williams (Cambridge, 1960): 387–8.

17 Alonzo Quint, ed., "Journal of the Rev. John Pike," *Proceedings of the Massachusetts Historical Society*, 14 (1875–6): 149, 131; *Puritans among the Indians: Accounts of Captivity and Redemption, 1676–1724*, ed. Alden T. Vaughan and Edward W. Clark (Cambridge, Mass., 1981): 163; James Axtell, *The European and the Indian* (Oxford, 1981): chaps. 2, 8.

18 *The Colonial and State Records of North Carolina*, eds. William L. Saunders *et al.* (Raleigh, etc., 1886–1914): I, 827; Richard M. Brown, *The South Carolina Regulators* (Cambridge, Mass., 1963): 7, 12.

19 Alden T. Vaughan and Daniel K. Richter, "Crossing the Cultural Divide: Indians and New Englanders, 1605–1763," *Proceedings of the American Antiquarian Society*, 90, pt. I (1980): 53–95, traces the fates of 1,641 New England prisoners of the Indians and French, only 754 of whom are known to have seen their homes again.

20 The literature on the captivity narratives is extensive. See esp. the introduction to the excellent collection *Puritans among the Indians*; Roy H. Pearce, "The Significances of the Captivity Narratives," *American Literature*, 19 (1947): 1–20; and David L. Minter, "By Dens of Lions ...," ibid.: 45 (1973): 335–47. The psychological impact of these writings is extremely difficult to grasp. For one attempt to penetrate these inner experiences, see Richard Slotkin, *Regeneration through Violence: The Mythology of the American Frontier, 1600–1860* (Middletown, Conn., 1977): chaps. 4–6.

21 Gov. Gabriel Johnston to Lord Wilmington, Brompton, on Cape Fear River, Feb. 10, 1737, W. R. Coe Papers, South Carolina Historical Society (Charleston, S.C.); Bernard Romans, *A Concise Natural History of East and West Florida ...* [1775], reprint ed. (New Orleans, 1961): 41 (cf. Romans's "An Attempt towards a Short Description of West Florida," in *Publications of the Mississippi Historical Society*, V [1925]: 180: a

"vile race ... the very savages are scandalized at the lives of those brutes in human shapes"); James Habersham to James Wright, Aug. 20, 1772, *Letters of Hon. James Habersham, 1756–1775 (Collections of the Georgia Historical Society,* VI, Savannah, 1904): 203–4; *Belfast [Ireland] News Letter,* Feb. 12, 1768; Marc B. Fried, *The Early History of Kingston & Ulster County, N.Y.* (Kingston, N.Y., 1975); "De Graffenried's Manuscript ...," in *Colonial and State Records of North Carolina:* I, 905ff.; Richard J. Hooker, ed., *The Carolina Backcountry on the Eve of the Revolution* (Chapel Hill, N.C., 1953); Brown, *South Carolina Regulators,* chap. 2; Albert T. Volwiler, *George Croghan and the Westward Movement, 1741–1782* (Cleveland, 1926): 214. For a vivid account of disorder and violence on the Kentucky frontier associated through kinship with Jefferson, see Boynton Merrill, Jr., *Jefferson's Nephews* (Princeton, 1976).

22   *The Secret Diary of William Byrd of Westover, 1709–1712,* ed. Louis B. Wright and Marion Tinling (Richmond, Va., 1941): 2, 15, 46, 79, 84, 112, 113, 127, 192, 205, 307, 419, 494, 551, 564.

23   Wright, *First Gentlemen,* chap. 11; *The Carolina Chronicle of Dr. Francis Le Jau:* 78, 55, 129, 130, 108, 61; *The Diary of Colonel Landon Carter of Sabine Hall, 1752–1778,* ed. Jack P. Greene (Charlottesville, Va., 1965).

24   Stephen S. Webb, *The Governors-General: The English Army and the Definition of the Empire, 1569–1681* (Chapel Hill, N.C., 1979): esp. chap. 1, Conclusion, and Epilogue; *Calendar of State Papers, Colonial Series, 1574–1660,* ed. W. Noel Sainsbury (London, 1860): 12, cited in David Konig, "Criminal Justice in the New World: English Anticipations and the Virginia Experience in the Sixteenth and Seventeenth Centuries," forthcoming in *American Journal of Legal History.* On the transportation of convicts, see in general Abbot E. Smith, *Colonists in Bondage* (Chapel Hill, N.C., 1947): part II; for a close look at the processes involved and the latest estimate of overall figures, see the articles by A. Roger Ekirch and Kenneth Morgan in *William and Mary Quarterly,* 3rd ser., 42 (1985): 184–227.

25   *The Statutes at Large; Being a Collection of All the Laws of Virginia ...,* ed. William W. Hening, II (New York, 1823): 510; William Stith, *The History of the First Discovery and Settlement of Virginia ...* [1747], facsimile ed. (Spartanburg, S.C., 1965): 168; Hugh Jones, *The Present State of Virginia ...* [1724], ed. Richard L. Morton (Chapel Hill, N.C., 1956): 135 (cf. 87–8); William Livingston *et al., The Independent Reflector ...* [1752–3], ed. Milton M. Klein (Cambridge, Mass., 1963): 166, 165; Franklin's "Petition" to exchange American rattlesnakes for British convicts, in *Papers of Benjamin Franklin,* eds. Leonard W. Labaree *et al.* (New Haven, 1959–1977): XIII, 240–2.

26   Of the vast literature on New England Puritanism, Edmund Morgan's *Visible Saints: The History of a Puritan Idea* (New York, 1963) is crucial to this point. It traces out the New England Puritans' idea of the true church, based on earlier views but fully articulated and fulfilled only on these shores; it shaped all aspects of the Puritans' lives.

27   Two excellent articles have recently made the first serious entries into this fascinating and little-known subject: Jon Butler, "Magic, Astrology, and the Early American Religious Heritage, 1600–1760," *American Historical Review,* 84 (April 1979): 317–46; and Elizabeth W. Fisher,

" 'Prophesies and Revelations': German Cabbalists in Early Pennsylvania," *Pennsylvania Magazine of History and Biography*, 109 (1985): 299–333.

28 On Kelpius, see Julius F. Sachse's old and heavily documented but chaotic *The German Pietists of Provincial Pennsylvania* (Philadelphia, 1895), especially pp. 219–50, and the Butler and Fisher articles cited above. I have also used details in Ernest L. Lashlee, "Johannes Kelpius and his Woman in the Wilderness: A Chapter in the History of Colonial Pennsylvania Religious Thought," in *Glaube, Geist, Geschichte: Festschrift für Ernst Benz ...*, ed. Gerhard Müller and Winfried Zeller (Leiden, 1967): 327–38.

29 Sachse, *German Pietists*: 196, 335–40, 388–401.

30 The fullest account of Ephrata and its context is E. G. Alderfer, *The Ephrata Commune: An Early American Counterculture* (Pittsburgh, 1985), a sympathetic treatment which contains excellent sections of the German background and on the bizarre training Beissel's singers endured.

31 Walter C. Klein, *Johann Conrad Beissel, Mystic and Martinet, 1690–1768* (Philadelphia, Pa., 1942): chaps. 3, 4, p. 100; Sachse, *German Sectarians*: I, 73–8; Gillian L. Gollin, *Moravians in Two Worlds* (New York, 1967); Jacob J. Sessler, *Communal Pietism among Early American Moravians* (New York, 1933); Hopple, "Spatial Development of the Southeastern Pennsylvania Plain Dutch Community to 1970," *Pennsylvania Folklife*, 21, no. 2 (1971–2): 18–20; 21, no. 3 (1972): 36–45.

32 "Report of the Journey of Francis Louis Michel from Berne, Switzerland, to Virginia [1701–2]," *Virginia Magazine of History and Biography*, 24 (1916): 295; Milton W. Hamilton, *Sir William Johnson: Colonial American, 1715–1763* (Port Washington, N.Y., 1976): 33–5, 304–5, 306–10; Lord Adam Gordon, "Journal of an Officer ... in 1764 and 1765," in *Travels in the American Colonies*, ed. Newton D. Mereness (New York, 1916): 417.

33 Crane, *Southern Frontier*, chap. 5; James Axtell, "The White Indians of Colonial America," *William and Mary Quarterly*, 32 (1975): 55–88; Vaughan and Richter, "Crossing the Cultural Divide": 60–72; *Life, Letters and Papers of William Dunbar of Elgin, Morayshire, Scotland, and Natchez, Mississippi, Pioneer Scientist of the Southern United States*, ed. Eron Rowland (Jackson, Miss., 1930).

34 E. P. Panagopoulos, *New Smyrna: An Eighteenth Century Greek Odyssey* (Gainesville, Fla., 1966); Bernard Bailyn, *Voyagers to the West: A Passage in the Peopling of America on the Eve of the Revolution* (New York, 1986): chap. 12.

2

CONVERGENCE: DEVELOPMENT OF AN AMERICAN SOCIETY, 1720–80

Jack P. Greene

Like Bailyn, Jack P. Greene is impressed by the regional diversity of British America. In the larger work, of which this essay is a part, Greene explores the same four mainland regions as Bailyn, but also encompasses the Atlantic and Caribbean islands, as well as Ireland. Greene believes that "each of the major regions of the early modern colonial British world quickly developed its own distinctive socioeconomic and cultural configurations." Nevertheless, also like Bailyn, Greene perceives the emergence of a distinctive American culture out of these several regional cultures. What for Bailyn was inchoate and plastic in 1700 is for Greene considerably more well-defined and fixed by 1750.

Greene and Bailyn also agree on some central features of this emergent culture. For example, both stress the exploitation at the core of eighteenth-century American society. Nevertheless, while Bailyn's portrait is rather dark and grim, Greene's is somewhat more sunny and optimistic. Thus Greene is most impressed by the expansiveness of eighteenth-century mainland America and particularly the "conception of America as a place in which free people could pursue their own individual happiness in safety and with a fair prospect that they might be successful in their several quests." Whether these different emphases can be attributed to contrasting perspectives, chronological foci, or even individual temperaments may be a question worth pondering.

More generally, the reader should explore Greene's argument concerning the convergence of various parts of America. Consider, for example, the "socioeconomic trajectory" of slavery. Was it not becoming more entrenched in the plantation colonies but weakening in the farm colonies? Similarly, were not the northern colonies becoming more commercial and the southern colonies more agricultural over time? Was not New England with its college-educated clergy and literate laity far removed from the

predominantly illiterate southern colonies? In these and other respects,
might not divergence rather than convergence be more plausible?

* * *

As between 1660 and 1760 each of the regions of colonial British
America became both more creole[a] and more metropolitan, as they
increasingly assimilated to a common American social and behavioral
pattern and to British cultural models, they became more and more
alike, and this powerful social convergence resulted in the emergence and articulation of a common cultural pattern that, though
present to some degree throughout the British American world, was
especially evident among the continental colonies. If the central
features of this pattern were most powerfully manifest at the center
of British North America, in the Chesapeake and Middle Colonies,
they were also present to a conspicuous degree in the peripheries,
in the Lower South and New England. This pattern can be discussed under three rubrics: growth, differentiation, and values.

The growth of the colonies was genuinely impressive, and in
each colonial region demographic growth was particularly dramatic. Every region, even the island colonies, showed a sustained
increase in population during the century beginning in 1660, the
continental colonies growing at about 2.6 percent per annum and
the island colonies at about 1.5 percent.

This growth resulted from both immigration and natural increase. Perhaps as many as one out of five new whites were
immigrants; a much higher proportion of new blacks, especially in
the islands, derived from slave imports. By far the largest source of
this vigorous demographic rise on the continent, however, was
natural increase. This increase was primarily the result of three
factors: declining mortality, younger ages at marriage of from four
to five years for women than in Europe, and a bountiful food
supply and high nutrition that already by the 1750s had operated
to make male residents of the continental colonies three to three-
and-a-half inches taller than their British counterparts.

Natural growth was, however, lower in cities and in coastal
areas of the Chesapeake and Lower South, where, as in the West
Indies, mortality was significantly higher. Nevertheless, in overall
population trends, the mortality differential between northern and
southern colonies may have been at least partly offset by a more
plentiful food and protein supply in the South, one indication of

44

which was that the average height of militiamen during the Revolution increased from North to South. The special demographic vigor demonstrated by the continental colonies was no doubt also stimulated by the continuing availability of land and the high levels of economic opportunity to meet the demands of both the growing population and an expanding overseas commerce. Although the island colonies had about the same number of whites per household as in contemporary England, those on the continent averaged between five and seven people, the largest in the entire British world.[1]

The psychology of expansiveness implied by the demographic performance of the populations of colonial British America, especially on the continent, was also reflected in the extent of territorial expansion and the mobility of the population. At the conclusion of Queen Anne's War in 1713, the continental settlers were still clustered in a series of noncontiguous nuclei close to the Atlantic seaboard. There were two large centers of settlement, one in the Chesapeake and another covering the coastal regions of eastern and southern New England and reaching up the Connecticut River valley. Two smaller concentrations of population fanned out from Philadelphia and New York, and there were isolated groups of settlement on the central Maine coast, in the upper Connecticut River valley in what is now southeastern Vermont, around Albany on the Hudson River, on the upper Delaware River in the vicinity of Easton, Pennsylvania, on the lower Delaware, at three widely dispersed points in Tidewater North Carolina, and at Charleston and Port Royal in South Carolina.

During the next fifty years, population spilled out in all possible directions from these nuclei until by the 1760s and 1770s there was one long continuum of settlement stretching from Georgia to Maine and reaching inland for more than 150 miles, and new nuclei were building in East and West Florida and Nova Scotia. This rapid spread of settlement was one sign of the high levels of geographical mobility among settlers in all regions on the continent. Although southerners were somewhat more mobile than New Englanders, no region had a persistence rate much above 60 percent during the third quarter of the eighteenth century, and farmers everywhere showed an especially strong propensity to move. Residents from New York north tended to move longer distances north into upper New York and New England; those from Pennsylvania south tended to move west and south into the broad upland areas between the seacoast and the Appalachian Mountains.[2]

But the most impressive evidence of growth lies in the economic realm. "Led by a growing demand for colonial exports, linked to an expanding commercial empire, protected and promoted by a strong imperial system, and endowed with an abundance of natural resources," the economy of colonial British America, John McCusker and Russell Menard have observed, "became increasingly successful" between 1607 and 1775. There were marked differences between the economies of the plantation colonies of the Chesapeake, the Lower South, and the West Indies and those of the farm colonies from Pennsylvania north. Those of the latter were less highly specialized, much less capital- and labor-intensive, less dependent on servile labor, especially the use of slaves, and somewhat less tied to external markets. At the same time, the economies of all the continental colonies were somewhat more complex and better balanced than those in the West Indies. Yet the economic performance of every region over time was impressive. Growth seems not to have been especially rapid before 1740, but every available indicator – numbers of slaves, rising levels of personal wealth, volume of agricultural production, amount of exports, value of imports from Britain, quantities shipped in the coastal trade – suggests extraordinary growth thereafter. McCusker and Menard estimate that the gross national product (GNP) multiplied about twenty-five times between 1650 and 1770, increasing at an annual average rate of 2.7 percent for British America as a whole and 3.2 percent for British North America. This increase, they posit, may have represented a real per capita growth rate of 0.6 percent, which was twice that of Britain and was "sufficient to double income" over that period.[3]

By the time of the American Revolution, this vigorous economic growth had produced a standard of living that may have been "the highest achieved for the great bulk of the [free] population in any country up to that time." In her massive study of the wealth of the continental colonies, Alice Hanson Jones has found that for the continental colonies as a whole in 1774 average per capita wealth – composed of land, slaves, livestock, nonagricultural productive goods, and consumer goods – was £60.20 This figure may have been lower than that of England and Wales, for which there is no reliable estimate of per capita wealth after 1688, the date for which Gregory King estimated that it was already about £55. But Jones concludes that it must nevertheless have been "of a very respectable order of magnitude in comparison" with that of the metropolis. There were, of course, marked regional variations. As McCusker and Menard have revised Jones's figures, New England with a net worth per free white person of £33 was the poorest region, followed by the Middle Colonies with a figure of £51 and the southern colonies – the Chesapeake and Lower South combined – with the striking amount of £132. No comparable figures are available for the island colonies, although McCusker and Menard cite the astounding figure of £1,200 per capita for the relatively small slave-owning white population of Jamaica in the early 1770s.[4]

The sources of this remarkable prosperity lay in a combination of the demands for food and other commodities on the part of the burgeoning population and in growing overseas markets for colonial products. Though the proportion of income gained through exports declined over time, it was still substantial in 1770. Exports of all varieties, including ships and shipping services and those vended in both overseas and coastal trades, may have contributed from 17 to 19 percent of total income. The annual average worth of the six highest-valued commodities exported over the five years 1768–72 were as follows: tobacco, £766,000; shipping earnings, £610,000; bread and flour, £412,000; rice, £312,000; dried fish, £287,000; and indigo, £117,000. The Chesapeake was responsible for 42 percent of total exports, twice the figure for the Lower South and the Middle Colonies and more than two and a half times that for New England. The value of exports per capita and per free white resident increased from North to South, reflecting the greater per capita wealth of the free white populations of those regions.[5]

A substantial rise in colonial buying power occurred on the eve of the American Revolution. The Middle Colonies, the Chesapeake, and New England all took somewhat less than a third and the Lower South somewhat more than a tenth of total commodity imports into the continental colonies. The Chesapeake had the highest average value of imports per free white resident, followed by the Lower South, New England, and the Middle Colonies in that order. The Chesapeake and the Lower South still had a favorable balance of exports over imports, but the Middle Colonies imported commodities worth more than twice as much as those they exported, and New England, which displayed a substantial deficit in food production during the late colonial period, imported nearly three times as much as it exported. Yet both the Middle Colonies and New England seem to have made up a considerable proportion of these deficits, perhaps as much as 60 percent, by invisible earnings derived from the sale of ships and shipping and other merchandizing services. Both import and export figures reflect the development of a considerable coastwise trade among the colonies. Though all four regions participated in this trade, it was dominated by New England and the Middle Colonies, and it marked the early stages in the articulation of an integrated "American" economy through which products from all regions were widely distributed for domestic consumption on a continental scale.[6]

As McCusker and Menard have remarked, these figures "describe a strong, flexible, and diverse economy ... able to operate without a considerable metropolitan subsidy," at least in peace time. In stark contrast to the situation during the first generations of settlement, none of these continental regions relied heavily on foreign investment. Rather, they "accumulated most of their capital on their own" through the productivity of their inhabitants, savings, and capital improvements, developments that were also reflected in the emergence of a resident and highly skilled commercial sector. The impressive performance of the economies of every one of these regions in turn probably also heralded, to one degree or another, increased specialization of production and a consequent lowering of production costs; improvements in transportation and a resulting decline in distribution costs; advances in human capital, including rising technical expertise; improvements in economic organization; and at least some technological advances such as occurred in shipbuilding and shipping.[7]

This impressive demographic, territorial, and economic growth supported an increasingly complex society with an ever larger range, more dense distribution, and more deeply established agglomeration of social institutions. These included families and kinship groups; neighborhoods and hamlets; stores and artisanal establishments; local judicial and administrative institutions; churches; transportation facilities, including roads, bridges, ferries, and a few canals; and a variety of cultural institutions, including schools, libraries, clubs, and other social organizations. Although many of these institutions were well represented in the countryside, others, including especially commercial and artisanal establishments and cultural institutions, were most fully developed in the towns.

The extensive spread of population and the continuing rustication process it represented meant that as the eighteenth century proceeded, a declining proportion of the population lived in towns. Yet substantial urbanization occurred in all of the older settled areas, especially after 1720. Boston was the largest colonial town into the 1740s, when its population leveled off to between 15,000 and 16,000, where it remained for the rest of the colonial period. At some point between 1745 and 1760, the populations of both Philadelphia and New York passed that of Boston. By 1775 the population of Philadelphia was perhaps as high as 40,000, that of New York 25,000. Also by 1775, Charleston and Newport had populations ranging between 9,000 and 12,000; Baltimore and Norfolk, both of which had developed primarily after 1750 in the Chesapeake, traditionally the least urbanized area of continental America, had around 6,000; a dozen towns – New Haven, Norwich, New London, Salem, Lancaster, Hartford, Middletown, Portsmouth, Marblehead, Providence, Albany, Annapolis, and Savannah – had between 3,000 and 5,000; and perhaps as many as fifty other places had between 500 and 3,000 people.

To an important extent, all of these towns, even those that doubled as provincial capitals, were trading centers. The largest served as general trading marts and processing, communications, and financial centers for an extensive hinterland. Others were mere collection, distribution, and shipping points. But all provided a greater or lesser range of services to surrounding areas. In the largest cities, roughly half of the adult male population was employed in the service sector, offering a wide variety of professional, commercial, building, transport, and other skills. Of the remaining half of the adult male working population, only around 2 percent were in a very small public sector; about a quarter in the industrial sector, including textile and leather trades, food and drink processing, shipbuilding and fitting crafts, and metal and furniture trades; and just over a fifth in maritime commerce and fisheries, including mariners and merchants and supporting personnel.[8]

The increasingly complex occupational structure of the towns, a trend that was also evident, if to a much less impressive extent, in the countryside, was one powerful indication of the results of the steady process of social differentiation that had been occurring in all the major regions of colonial British America during the century after 1660. For instance, the resident commercial sector of the population had developed during these years into an increasingly complex group ranging from petty retailers, peddlers, and hawkers at the lowest level up through primary traders composed mostly of country storekeepers and urban retailers, to secondary traders or wholesalers who collected local products from and distributed finished goods to retailers, to tertiary traders or large merchants who presided over the overseas trade and offered more and more sophisticated financial and insurance services to the commercial economy.

A similar development can be followed with regard to the professions, including the ministry, medicine, and the law. To an important extent, the law remained an unspecialized activity, though by mid-century in several colonies an important distinction had developed between those who practiced before provincial courts and those whose business was primarily local. Everywhere, however, the law became an increasingly self-conscious profession with a concern for maintaining standards, growing sophistication and expertise reflected in a large number of impressive legal libraries, and enhanced social status and respectability. The large volume of litigation over land and mercantile property made the law an especially lucrative activity that by the 1740s and 1750s was attracting not just, as earlier, immigrants but also native sons of the creole elites and middle orders.[9]

The process of social differentiation can also be observed in the development of a much more sharply articulated social structure. To be sure, even at the end of the colonial period, the emerging social hierarchies in the several regions of colonial British America were all much less finely developed and more open than in metropolitan Britain. Nowhere was there anything remotely resembling a legally privileged aristocracy. Indeed, colonial society was not yet divided into well-defined social classes but consisted of two broad and not always discrete social categories, independents and dependents. *Independents* were those with sufficient property in land, tools, or personal goods to make them theoretically free from external control by any other person; *dependents* were those whose wills, in Sir William Blackstone's phrase, were subject to the control of the people on whom they depended.[10]

By contemporary standards, the independent proportion of the population was very large. At the top of this category, the most successful planters, merchants, landlords, and lawyers were, by the 1720s and 1730s in the oldest colonies and by the 1740s and 1750s in the newer ones, a self-conscious and conspicuous elite that, though consisting of no more than 2 to 3 percent of colonial families, was distinguished from the rest of society by its substantially greater wealth and affluent and refined lifestyles. Manifest in their clothing, consumption patterns, housing, modes of transportation, education, cosmopolitan outlook, prominence in both public office and the emerging cultural infrastructures, and cultivation of the traditional values of the British rural and urban gentries, including liberality, civility, and stewardship, the superior social status of these developing elites was also evident in the large number of dependents their members could command and by the passive deference usually accorded them by other independent members of society. Yet this largely self-made group, as Richard Hofstadter has remarked, had "only a slender sense of the personal prerogative, the code of honor, or the grand extravagance" usually associated with its equivalents in Europe. Rather, it exhibited "the disciplined ethic of work, the individual assertiveness, the progressive outlook … and the calculating and materialistic way of life" associated with the burgeoning middle classes of contemporary Britain.[11]

Some scholars have linked the growing concentrations of property that sustained the several regional colonial elites and the increasing density of population in older settled areas with a decrease in opportunities for upward social mobility beginning during the middle decades of the eighteenth century. In support of these claims, they have cited the appearance of a considerable body of agricultural tenants in several colonies, an increase in the number of people of both sexes among the landless free laboring population, and a rise in the number of people on the poor rolls, especially in the larger cities. Yet it is by no means clear that the increase in poverty, which, even in the cities, still remained far below that in Britain, either was a linear process or was yet leading to the creation of a substantial underclass of residual poor among the free population. Several studies have shown that both tenancy and employment as free labor were very often merely stages in the life cycle, a way for young men to gather the resources necessary to achieve later in life an independent status as landowners or in nonagricultural employment. Similarly, for young women, a period in the labor market was frequently a temporary phase between leaving home and marriage. Moreover, if opportunities to acquire land were declining in long-occupied areas, they were still present in the many new settlements that after 1720 were formed at a phenomenal rate in every region of continental British America. A combination of the demands stimulated by a burgeoning population and the steady development of a more complex occupational structure created vast new and, for some people, obviously preferable opportunities for employment in service, industrial, and mercantile activities.[12]

Certainly in the 1760s and 1770s, as earlier, the most impressive aspect of the free population of Britain's American colonies was the extraordinarily large number of families of independent middling status, which was proportionately substantially more numerous than in any other contemporary Western society. Situated immediately below the elite and, like their counterparts in England, sharing, in many cases, the values and the orientations of those just above them, this vast and increasingly differentiated body of yeoman farmers, artisans, smaller traders, and lesser professionals included the great bulk of independent people in the colonies. In every region of continental colonial British America, their sheer numbers meant that the emerging American society would be "a preponderantly middle-class world" in which "the simpler agencies of the middle class" would be "in strong evidence: the little churches of the dissenting sects, the taverns ... the societies for [social and] self-improvement and 'philosophical' inquiry, the increasingly eclectic little colleges, the contumacious newspapers, the county court houses and town halls, the how-to-do books, the *Poor Richard's Almanack*[b]."[13]

In the developing American social schema, agricultural tenants and people employed with contracts in the service, industrial, and commercial sectors constituted an ambiguous intermediate group who, though they in many cases enjoyed sufficient resources in the form of their own skills and property to function and be regarded by the rest of society as independent people, were at least technically dependent on their landlords or employers. But such people formed only a small part of the social category of dependents. Because they were defined in the early modern British world as extensions of their husbands' and fathers' legal and social personalities, wives and children together were certainly the largest groups of dependents in colonial America. At least within the confines of the free population, however, most, if not the vast majority, of women and children were members of families whose male head was independent. As a consequence, they assumed his independent social status.[14]

When colonial Americans referred to *social* dependents, they were talking largely about people who fell into one or the other of three groups of laborers, all of whom were employed to provide a substantial amount of the extraordinary effort required to produce the food and the vendible commodities necessary to sustain this rapidly expanding and still highly exploitive society: free laborers, servants, and slaves. Although much of the labor in the farm colonies, especially in New England, where the pace of economic development was slower and the labor requirements much lower, had been supplied by family members, the demand for labor was a persistent problem in the land- and resource-rich but labor-poor colonies from New York south to Barbados. Over time, first in New England and then in the Chesapeake and Middle Colonies, an expanding pool of free laborers, mostly younger men and women just getting started in life, slowly developed into a significant, if notoriously expensive, component of the labor market. By the mid-eighteenth century, male laborers in this category may have constituted as much as 10 percent of the adult male population of large towns and an even larger percentage of the inhabitants of smaller towns and long-established rural districts.[15]

From the Middle Colonies south, however, servitude, which was also present in New England, especially before 1720, had almost certainly been a more important means of supplying the demand for labor beyond what could be provided by family members, and the predominant form of servant labor was provided through indentured servitude, a new institution developed in the first half of the seventeenth century to meet the heavy labor requirements of the West Indian and Chesapeake colonies. Servitude was a transitional status that enabled people to secure passage to the colonies in return for selling their labor for a set period of time, at the end of which they hoped to move into a position from which they could acquire land and an independent status. With the substitution of blacks for whites as plantation laborers, beginning in the West Indies and extending to the continent during the closing decades of the seventeenth century, servitude changed from an institution that supplied primarily unskilled labor to one that furnished considerable amounts of skilled labor, albeit by the mid-eighteenth century throughout the colonies slaves were more and more being trained to perform skilled tasks formerly assigned to servants. Notwithstanding these changes in the institution and use of white servitude, however, the demand for unskilled servant labor remained high in all regions of continental British America except New England. The especially high demand for such labor in the Chesapeake and Middle Colonies was evidenced by the eagerness with which buyers snapped up as many as 40,000 to 50,000 largely young, male, and minimally skilled convicts transported from Britain between 1718 and 1775.[16]

Life was no picnic for servants, who had traditionally been and still in the mid-eighteenth century were often worked hard, but servitude at least held out an eventual promise of freedom and independence for the more ambitious and fortunate of those who survived their terms; the same could not be said for slaves. Blacks – of whom all except perhaps 1 to 2 percent were slaves – constituted the largest single category of the dependent population, over a third of the population of colonial British America as a whole and more than 20 percent in the continental colonies in 1760. These substantial numbers remind us of the extraordinary extent to which the growth and prosperity of the emerging society of free colonial British America as well as the high incidence of independent individuals who lived there were achieved as a result of slave labor, of the forced emigration from their widely dispersed homelands of thousands of people of African descent and their systematic subjugation to an intrinsically harsh and virtually inescapable labor regime based on racial discrimination and enforced by the full power of the law.[17]

To be sure, except in some rural parishes in low-country South Carolina and Georgia, slaves were nowhere nearly so numerous in any of the continental colonies as they were in the West Indies, where, in 1760, for the region as a whole, they outnumbered whites by about 7 to 1, ranging from 5 to 1 in Barbados up to almost 10 to 1 in Antigua and Jamaica. At the same time, among the continental colonies, whites exceeded blacks in every region, but there were striking differences between the regions heavily engaged in plantation agriculture and the farm colonies of the North. Thus, though the Lower South had only 1.3 and the Chesapeake colonies 1.7 whites for every slave, whites in the Middle Colonies outnumbered blacks by 14 to 1 and in New England by 35 to 1. Moreover, the percentage of slaves in the population was only one of several important variables that produced substantial temporal and spatial variations in the nature of slavery and its impact upon those who were subjected to it. Others included the ways slaves were employed, the social distance between whites and slaves, and the proportion of newly imported Africans in the slave population.

Everywhere on the continent, however, the institution of slavery

seems to have gone through a similar cycle. More open, less op-
pressive, and often more conducive to the formation of a stable
family life among slaves during its earliest decades, it became more
rigid, more differentiated, and often less congenial for slaves as
they became more numerous and more integral to the culture and
as the proportion of new male slaves imported directly from Africa
increased.

No region displayed a manifest reluctance to employ slaves
before the 1760s and 1770s. If only those colonies from New York
south "had fairly elaborate slave codes," they all still "sanctioned
slaveholding on the eve of the American Revolution" and "had at
least the rudiments of a statutory law of slavery or race" that
"defined slavery as a lifetime condition," made slave status "her-
editable through the mother," identified it racially with people of
African descent, defined slaves as property, and established a
system of "racial etiquette" designed to maintain a clear and permanent distinction between the free white inhabitants and their
black slaves. Everywhere, this well-established system of racial
slavery was thus based on "the permanent, violent domination of
natally alienated and generally dishonored persons" defined primarily on the basis of color and without "social existence" outside
the persons of their free owners. Along with the continuing importance of the institution of servitude, the powerful presence, wide
diffusion, and - except in Nova Scotia and New Hampshire -
expanding use of slavery in the 1760s and 1770s throughout colonial
British America provides a vivid reminder of just how fundamentally
exploitive that society was.[18]

If the emerging society of late colonial British America was at once
expansive, mobile, prosperous, increasingly more differentiated,
and exploitive of its least fortunate members, it fulfilled many of
the most sanguine hopes of the first settlers. The extraordinary
outpouring of people from the British Isles and continental Europe
into the British colonies was the result not of "discontent and
persecution at home," not of a determination "to enlarge the realm
of English power," not of a desire "to reach the glories of the other
world," and not even of "visions of liberty." Rather, what "stirred
people into these extraordinary activities," as G. R. Elton has written, was "a drive for land and fortune." Lured to America by
"promises of riches," they were primarily moved by "the common
and acceptable human emotions of greed and the search for greater

wealth." Except for the New England puritans, Perry Miller has noted, most immigrants "came for better advantage and for less danger, and to give their posterity the opportunity of success."[19]

Given this orientation among immigrants and settlers, the establishment and development of Britain's overseas empire rapidly turned into what D. A. Farnie has described as "a revolutionary cultural expansion wherein the energies of the littoral communities" in Ireland and America "were increasingly diverted into economic fields." As the "successive emergence of staple after staple made the Atlantic basin the sphere of a commercial empire unparalleled in the past in its nature" and "as a common economic civilization" emerged in which consumption became an increasingly powerful motor among people "in both transatlantic and cisatlantic lands" and "commerce became the great bond of unity in societies otherwise divided," these littoral societies increasingly became one of the most vivid "manifestation[s] of the efflorescent secular culture of western Europe," and the " 'Great Tradition' " of the "emerging Atlantic civilizations became a secular rather than a sacred tradition, and in particular an economic, a commercial, a 'sensate' tradition" in which the major focus of the people who shared in it was upon production, profit, trade, and consumption.[20]

Notwithstanding the "serene rustic image of self-sufficient communities" invoked by some historians to characterize colonial British America, no group of colonists, as Carole Shammas has shown, were "commercial primitives" in the sense that they were entirely cut off from the secular market society of this broader Atlantic commercial world. Very few households had the resources necessary to be self-sufficient and therefore had both to supplement "homegrown products with textiles, flour, butter, and meat bought from tradesmen, peddlars, and neighboring producers" and to function in an environment in which the prices that were almost always "attached to their labor and goods" were invariably "affected by regional, continental, and international markets." Even in the most isolated areas of colonial New England, Shammas has found, colonial Americans "fully participate[d] in" this emerging commercial world. Although the extent of that participation varied according to wealth and accessibility to markets, there was no dual economic system as has been posited by some historians and "no stark dichotomy of market versus nonmarket activity" from one area or one social group to the next. Rather, there was only a "gradual reduction occurring as one moved from major seaport areas to minor, from coast to interior, from older settlements to the frontier." Indeed, not only did most households usually have to spend about "a quarter of per capita income on goods imported from outside the *colony*" in which they lived, but over time they also exhibited that same "voracious appetite ... for new market commodities" manifested by consumers throughout the Atlantic world during the century after 1660. Indeed, the social depth and extent of British–American involvement in this consumer revolution provided a remarkable testimony to the breadth of economic well-being among colonists in all regions: the top two-thirds of the population participated in it, whereas only the top quarter did so in Britain.[21]

In this emerging secular and commercial culture, the central orientation of people in the littoral became the achievement of personal independence, a state in which a man and his family and broader dependents could live "at ease" rather than in anxiety, in contentment rather than in want, in respectability rather than in meanness, and, perhaps most important, in freedom from the will and control of other men. On the eastern side of the Atlantic, in Britain and in Ireland, and in the confined spaces of the small Atlantic and Caribbean island colonies, the proportion of independent men in the total male population was small. But in the continental colonies, the opportunity to acquire land, an independent trade, or both, was so wide as to put the achievement of independence within the grasp of most able-bodied, active, and enterprising free men. The prospect for "a very comfortable and independent subsistence" held out by promotional writers, land developers, and government authorities contributed throughout the colonial era to act as a powerful magnet in attracting settlers to new colonies and newly opening areas.[22]

Moreover, although the achievement of genuine affluence and a gentle status was confined to a relatively small number of people, as it was in contemporary Britain, the comparatively widespread realization of independence by people whose beginnings were modest, a realization achieved mostly by the disciplined application of industry to the mastery of the soil, contributed to an equally broad diffusion of an expansive sense of self-worth throughout the independent, mostly landowning adult male population. In J. R. Pole's words, this expansive psychology in turn gave rise to "the very rapid advance of the more egocentric type of individualism" in which the ideal of the masterless man became associated with a variety of other values of "an individualising character." These values included a jealous regard for personal autonomy; "a hearty confidence in the individual['s] ... ability to manage his own affairs"; a growing "respect for the integrity of individual character" and individual choice in such fundamental matters as decisions about when and whom to marry, what career to pursue, and where and what religious beliefs to profess; "a profound attachment to private property"; a deep "suspicion of government"; and high expectations for one's children.[23]

In this situation, the achievement and peaceful enjoyment of personal independence, the objective that had initially drawn so many of both the first settlers and later immigrants to the colonies, continued to be the most visible and powerful imperative in the emerging American culture, the principal aspiration and animating drive in the lives of colonists in all regions. The most popular cultural image in eighteenth-century British America was the biblical image of the independent farmer sitting contentedly and safely under his own shade trees in front of his own home in full view of his fields, his flocks, and his dependents, including slaves if he had them. This was precisely the image Thomas Jefferson evoked in the Declaration of Independence when he included among the inalienable rights of man not merely life and liberty but also the "pursuit of happiness," a phrase that had been defined more specifically three weeks earlier by Jefferson's fellow Virginian George Mason[c] in the first article of the Virginia Declaration of Rights as "the enjoyment of life and liberty, with the means of acquiring and possessing property, and pursuing and obtaining happiness and safety."[24]

The pursuit of happiness and the expansive individualism that lay behind it have often been associated with the profit motive. "*The love of gain*," Samuel Miller noted in 1800 in his retrospective commentary on developments in America during the previous century, "particularly characterizes the inhabitants of the *United States*." But the considerable individuality Americans "were able to cultivate in their personal lives" and their devotion to personal independence should not be confused with "either the drive for profit maximization or the individualism of economic competition." If the "manifold opportunities for individualistic economic enterprise" everywhere fostered a social order that "was shot through with a restless mobility" and "a pervasive materialism," James Henretta is certainly correct to emphasize both the extent to which "the 'calculus of advantage' for these men and women was not mere pecuniary gain, but encompassed a much wider range of social and cultural goals." He is also right to stress the degree to which the expression of individual desires was mitigated by a prior concern with "meeting ... household needs" and "maintaining ... established social relationships within the community." Henretta does not deny that "economic gain was important to these men and women," but he correctly insists that it was usually "subordinate to (or encompassed by) two other goals: the yearly subsistence and the long-run financial security of the family unit." Indeed, it might be argued that precisely because "the family persisted as the basic unit of ... production, capital formation, and property trans-mission," virtually all early Americans associated the drive for personal independence and the pursuit of happiness with the promotion and perpetuation of the welfare of the lineal family. For most colonial Americans the pursuit of self by definition also involved the fulfillment of family obligations.[25]

Certainly, the individual pursuit of happiness, the quest for personal independence, emphatically did not "whittle away at the foundations of the family, community, church, and other institu-tions of the social order." The people who created and perpetuated the new societies of colonial British America sought not merely personal independence as individuals and the welfare of their families but also the social goal of improved societies that would both guarantee the independence they hoped to achieve and enable them to enjoy its fruits. Indeed, demands and aspirations for im-provement were nearly as prominent among settlers in these new societies as were those for independence and affluence.[26]

Ubiquitous in the economic writings of early modern Britain, the language of improvement as it took shape in Britain primarily referred to schemes, devices, or projects through which the econ-omic position of the nation might be advanced, the estates or fortunes of individuals might be bettered, or existing resources might be made more productive. In the new societies of colonial British America, the term *improvement* carried similar connotations. Settlers sought to "improve" their situation by securing the neces-sary capital and labor to develop their lands and fortunes; towns that would provide them with local markets in which they could exchange the produce of their lands for finished goods; bounties that would encourage them to experiment with new crops; and roads, bridges, and ferries that would provide them with better access to wider markets and link them more closely to economic and administrative centers.[27]

In the new and relatively undeveloped societies of colonial British America, however, the term *improvement* acquired a much wider meaning: it was used to describe a state of society that was far removed from the savagery associated with the native Indians. An *improved* society was one defined by a series of positive and negative juxtapositions. Not wild, barbaric, irregular, rustic, or crude, it was settled, cultivated, civilized, orderly, developed, and polite. The primary model for an improved society was the emerging and more settled, orderly, and coherent society of contemporary Britain. For new frontier settlements within the colonies, it was the older occupied areas along the seacoast. With re-creation and not innovation as their aim, colonial British Americans generally aspired to a fully developed market society with credit, commercial agriculture, slavery, and a rapid circulation of money and goods. They wanted a settled and hierarchical social structure with social distinctions ranging from the genteel down to the vulgar. In particular, they wanted a social structure that would enable successful independent and affluent people, in conformity with the long-standing traditions of Western civilization (and probably all other highly developed civilizations), to exploit dependent people. They desired authoritative, if not very obtrusive, political institutions that could facilitate their socioeconomic and cultural development and would be presided over by people whose very success in the private realm testified to their merit and capacity and gave them a legitimate claim to political leadership. They wanted vital traditional social institutions that would contribute to and stand as visible symbols of their improvement, including churches, schools, and towns.[28]

If the concept of improvement thus enabled colonial British Americans to think of their societies in developmental terms and if their demographic vigor and material prosperity provided two impressive measures of the degree to which they were moving rapidly toward the achievement of an improved state, the changing character of public life offered still a third such measure. For during the century after 1660 all of the older colonies underwent a profound transformation in the political sphere. Because the colony, and not the region, was the unit of political organization, a regional framework is inappropriate for an analysis of political developments. Indeed, each colony constituted an almost wholly discrete political environment with its own distinctive configurations of political activity, and this distinctiveness was reinforced because at least until the Seven Years' War and really until the crises that preceded the American Revolution there was virtually no common political life among the colonies. By the mid-eighteenth century, however, all but the very newest colonies of Georgia and Nova Scotia, in the islands as well as on the continent, had experienced a major expansion of political resources, which contributed to a significant increase in the capabilities of provincial political systems.

By the 1730s and 1740s in older colonies and by the 1740s and 1750s in the newer ones, both provincial and, except in the most recently settled areas, local politics were dominated by coherent, effective, acknowledged, and authoritative political elites with considerable social and economic power, extensive political experience, confidence in their capacity to govern, and – what crucially distinguished them from their European counterparts – broad public support. Second, they had viable governing institutions at both the local and provincial levels most of which were becoming more and more assimilated to those in metropolitan Britain, vigorous traditions of internal self-government, and extensive experience in coping with the socioeconomic and other problems peculiar to their own societies. Third, even though political participation was limited to white, independent, adult males, their political systems were almost certainly more inclusive and more responsive to public opinion than those of any other societies in the world at that time, and they were becoming more and more capable of permitting the resolution of conflict, absorbing new and diverse groups, and, as their recent histories had so amply attested, providing political stability in periods of rapid demographic, economic, and territorial expansion.

If the several colonial polities were becoming more expert, they were also becoming far more settled. By the mid-eighteenth century, levels of collective violence and civil disorder were ordinarily low, few colonies had outstanding issues that deeply divided the polity, society routinely accepted existing institutional and leadership structures, relations among the several branches and levels of government had been thoroughly regularized, rates of turnover among elected officials were low, changes in leadership followed an orderly process through regular constitutional channels without serious disruption of the polity, and factional and party strife was either being routinized or reduced to levels at which it was not dysfunctional within the political system. As was manifest in declining turnover among elected representatives to the colonial assemblies in most colonies, the electorate increasingly exhibited a passive and uncoerced deference toward the governing elite. With their attentions firmly concentrated on their own individual and family goals in the private realm, the vast bulk of the electorate seems, in ordinary times, to have had little interest in taking an active role in public life. Together, these developments brought a new stability and regularity to colonial political life in the three or four decades before 1760.

Notwithstanding these developments, the public realm everywhere remained small. Citizens expected little from government; budgets and taxes were low; paid officials were few; civil and judicial establishments were small, part-time, and unprofessional; and the maintenance of order devolved very largely upon local units of government, which had few coercive resources *vis-à-vis* the free population. Thus, despite efforts by elites to enforce stricter moral standards in communities during the mid-eighteenth century and attempts by provincial governments to deal with a possible rise in crime by adopting more severe penal measures during the last half of the century, local governments, bowing to local opinion, remained relatively permissive in dealing with minor offenses involving violations of morality and punished all but the most heinous crimes with whippings and fines rather than imprisonment, banishment, or execution. Indeed, possessing limited powers, colonial governments necessarily exerted only weak authority and were heavily dependent upon public opinion, which sharply limited the scope for action among political leaders. Government in these always potentially highly participatory polities was necessarily consensual. Always open to challenge from dissatisfied elements among the free population, the several polities of late colonial British America invariably contained a latent potential for widespread popular mobilization.[29]

If many of the features of these emerging American political systems revealed a growing capacity for accommodation among increasingly differentiated and complex social populations within the several colonial polities, the same can be said for developments in other areas of cultural life. The societies of all regions of colonial British America remained predominantly English. But the substantial immigration of non-English groups after 1713 and, notwithstanding the strong predisposition of people from many of these groups to settle in communities of their own kind, the consequent inter-mingling of peoples of diverse cultural and national backgrounds and competing religious persuasions slowly edged people toward a habit of compromise and an enhanced capacity for the toleration and acceptance of ethnic, cultural, and religious diversity. At the same time, the overwhelming cultural preoccupation with the pursuit of individual and family happiness in the socioeconomic area seems everywhere to have weakened the impulse to try to enforce a coercive religious uniformity.

But this is not to suggest that pluralism was necessarily pushing people in the direction of ever greater secularism. Using New England as a surrogate for the whole of colonial America, many historians have interpreted the weakening of the puritan religious synthesis as an indication of growing secularism. Although they have admitted that this process was temporarily reversed by the series of mid-eighteenth-century religious revivals known as the Great Awakening, they have argued that it accelerated after mid-century and that by the 1770s and 1780s, British America, as Hofstadter has remarked, may well have been one of "the most unchurched regions in all of Christendom."[30]

But this interpretation seems to have the process of religious development backward. Except for the early puritan settlers of New England and, to a considerably lesser extent, the Quaker founders of Pennsylvania, the vast majority of early colonists seem to have had a profoundly secular orientation from the beginning. If they were almost all nominally Protestant, they seem to have had neither a deep religiosity nor, perhaps, even very strong attach-ments to any specific doctrine or form of religion. So pervasive and powerful, in fact, was the secular bias of the early settlers outside New England that it is highly probable that, contrary to the tra-ditional interpretation, the inhabitants of British America were becoming, if not less secular, at least no less and possibly even somewhat more religious during the last century of the colonial period.

Although it is difficult to sustain the argument that any of the several regions of colonial British America south of New England had yet become deeply religious before the so-called second Great Awakening at the end of the eighteenth century, it is also true that interest in religion was substantial throughout the first eight de-cades of the eighteenth century and that, as Patricia Bonomi has argued, the trend toward social consolidation during the same period everywhere resulted in the emergence of religious organizations "as significant centers of stability and influence" and in the enhancement of religious authority. In short supply in many colonies as late as the 1720s and 1730s, ministers by the mid-eighteenth century "were visibly present in every section except the far frontier, and ecclesiastical consolidation was well under way in all denominations." As Bonomi and Peter Eisenstadt have shown, the number of churches in the seven largest Protestant denominations increased more than seven times between 1700 and 1780, an overall rate of congregation formation that rose in much closer ratio to population growth than has commonly been supposed. Whereas the white population increased 888 percent between 1700 and 1780, the number of churches rose by 632 percent, and one suspects that the gap would have been even smaller if the authors had used an earlier baseline of 1660 or 1680. With one church for every 467 whites, the Middle Colonies had the highest ratio of churches to population in 1750. New England came next with one church for every 606 whites, and the southern colonies – the Chesapeake and the Lower South combined – were last with only one church for every 1,046 whites. Bonomi and Eisenstadt also show that church adherence as measured by estimated church attendance declined relatively steadily from 80 percent of the white population in 1700 to 78 percent in 1720, around 75 percent in the 1740s and 1750s, 69 percent in 1765, and 59 percent in 1780. But they argue that everywhere in continental British North America during the eighteenth century, the churched population, which ranged from about 80 percent of whites in New England down to about 56 percent in the Chesapeake, considerably exceeded the unchurched.[31]

If, however, most people were both nominally Christian and occasional church attendants, if the religious needs of the population were not nearly so badly served as historians have often suggested, if the changing religious landscape outside New England contains "little that accords with the notion of declension," and if, perhaps, by the late colonial period interest in religion may even have been considerably more extensive than during the earliest generations of settlement in all regions except New England, still religious life remained in many respects fragile and unsettled. Church hierarchies in the colonies were undeveloped, clerical authority in most major denominations was weak, lay control over religious matters was extensive and relations between ministers and congregations often conflicted, anticlericalism was wide-spread, and a shortage of trained ministers among several denom-inations left many newly settled areas without ministers.

These conditions may not have been sufficiently severe to create the "breakdown of church religion" that some historians have suggested was responsible for making people "unusually suscep-tible" to the evangelical revivals that swept so many congregations at various times during the middle decades of the eighteenth century. As Jon Butler has persuasively argued, moreover, those revivals were probably far too heterogeneous, too disconnected in time and space, and insufficiently general to constitute a continent-wide "Great" Awakening of the sort invented by modern his-torians. Nevertheless, the widespread appeal of evangelical religion represented by those revivals strongly suggests that existing religious institutions were failing in important respects to meet the spiritual needs of colonial populations, who in significant numbers turned to an alternative and, for them, more emotionally satisfying form of religious belief that emphasized the importance of conver-sion, the centrality of the individual in the conversion experience, and the primacy of religious beliefs in daily life.[32]

For New England, the attraction of evangelicalism, as several scholars have suggested, may well have represented a reaction to the rapid assimilation of the region to the dominant patterns of behavior in the rest of colonial British America. As New Englanders became more and more preoccupied with the worldly concerns involved in the individual pursuit of happiness, as they became less attentive to religion and more materialistic, more consumption-oriented, and less deferential to authority in both the religious and civil realms, they also seem to have longed for a return to the older, simpler, and more pious and coherent communal social order that by the 1730s and 1740s mostly survived only in the region's collective memory. In other regions, the appeal of evan-gelicalism may have been rooted in a profound disquiet arising out of an inability of many people to adjust to the extreme good fortune and prosperity they enjoyed and a corresponding sense of their own unworthiness.

Whatever their source, these many spiritual awakenings have been seen by some historians as occasions and vehicles for the revival and intensification within New England of the "special themes of New England providential thought" and their "spread ... to other sections of America." The idea of national election, of the chosenness of the American people, has certainly been a highly visible and at times powerful component of American culture. Indeed, as Sacvan Bercovitch has argued, the idea that *"In the beginning was the word, and the word was with the New England Way, and the word became 'America'"* may well have been the most important ingredient in what he calls "the myth of America." As his formulation suggests, however, notwithstanding efforts by Cotton Mather[d] and other Congregational clergymen to generalize and promote this conception of America as "sacred space," the idea that any segment of colonial British America had a special relationship with God and a providential destiny was almost wholly confined to New England before the second half of the eighteenth century. The inhabitants of all regions of colonial British America "believed in an absolute, intervening deity who controlled and directed all the natural and human developments within the universe." Yet, as John Berens has emphasized, "no ... section outside New England [ever] considered itself to be the New Israel or to have a world-affecting divine mission to perform."[33]

By the 1770s, however, this ancient New England theme, the intellectual roots of which – in America – may be found in the puritans' ambition of erecting a city upon a hill and in their conception of themselves as God's chosen people, was becoming an American theme. Bercovitch may well be correct in arguing that the puritans "provided the scriptural basis for what we have come to call the myth of America." But it is far less certain that the concept of America as an elect nation that became so powerfully evident during the era of the American Revolution can be traced so directly and so completely to "the influence of New Englanders on other sections of America in the course of the Awakening" and later. If it obviously owed something to the conception, articulated especially strongly by New England clergymen, of the Seven Years' War[e] as a providential struggle against popery and absolutism, it certainly also had important secular roots. Indeed, an important element in the emerging idea of Americans as a chosen people was the optimistic prediction, set forth by American writers from all regions, including John Trumbull, Hugh Henry Brackenridge, and Philip Freneau, that America not only might have a special place in secular history but also might soon be transformed "into a new Athens."

As Joseph Ellis has contended, this "effusive vision" was to an important degree "the result of a straightforward and conscious extrapolation from the visible and much discussed maturation of colonial society," particularly from its phenomenal demographic and economic performance over the previous century. Attributing that performance less to the special regard of the Almighty than to the favorable effects of the weakness of traditional economic, social, political, and religious constraints in America, exponents of this vision linked America's special future role to the expected further development "of a liberal mentality that exalted the untapped power that would be generated within individuals and society at large when [all] traditional impediments to thought and action were obliterated." Not Providence *per se* but the manifold, undirected, and unfettered actions of free individuals each pursuing his or her own happiness and operating in an unrestrained field of action would propel America to its special destiny. During the era of the Revolution, this idea was infused with ever more power by an emerging sense of the possibility of national greatness deriving out of the successful prosecution of the War for Independence and the creation of the American republic.[34]

EDITOR'S NOTES

a   Creole, deriving from the Spanish *criollo*, meaning born in or native to, and thereby suggesting a committed settler. In this context, it suggests growing local identity.

b   From 1731 to 1758 Benjamin Franklin published annual editions of *Poor Richard's Almanack*, which was part calendar, part weather chart, part diary, and part epigrams and proverbs designed to amuse. It sold more than a quarter of million copies overall.

c   George Mason (1725–92) was primarily responsible for drafting the Virginia Declaration, the first bill of rights adopted by any state (on June 12, 1776).

d   Cotton Mather (1663–1728), New England's most prominent third-generation Puritan minister.

e   The Seven Years' War actually lasted nine years, not seven, in the New World (1754–63), and is otherwise known as the French and Indian War but more accurately as the Great War for Empire.

NOTES

Reprinted from Jack P. Greene, *Pursuits of Happiness: The Social Development of Early Modern British Colonies and the Formation of American Culture* (Chapel Hill N.C., 1988). © 1988 The University of North Carolina Press. Used by permission of the author and publisher.

1 Jim Potter, "Demographic Development and Family Structure," in J. P. Greene and J. R. Pole, eds., *Colonial British America: Essays in the New History of the Early Modern Era* (Baltimore, Md., 1984): 123–56; and "The Growth of Population in America, 1700–1860," in D. V. Glass and D. E. C. Eversley, eds., *Population in History* (London, 1965): 631–88; Robert V. Wells, *Population of the British Colonies in America before 1776: A Survey of Census Data* (Princeton, 1975):45–333, and "Household Size and Composition in the British Colonies in America, 1675–1775," *Journal of Interdisciplinary History*, 4 (1974): 543–70; John J. McCusker and Russell R. Menard, *The Economy of British America, 1607–1789* (Chapel Hill, N.C., 1985): 212–35; Henry A. Gemery, "European Emigration to North America, 1700–1820: Numbers and Quasi-Numbers," *Perspectives in American History*, n.s., I (1984): 283–342; Kenneth L. Sokoloff and Georgia C. Villaflor, "The Early Achievement of Modern Stature in America," *Social Science History*, 4 (1982): 453–81. Bernard Bailyn's suggestive *The Peopling of British North America: An Introduction* (New York, 1986) and his masterful *Voyagers to the West: A Passage in the Peopling of America on the Eve of the American Revolution* (New York, 1986), came to hand after this chapter was written, but they are obviously relevant to this subject.

2 The statements about mobility are based on the excellent article by Georgia C. Villaflor and Kenneth L. Sokoloff, "Migration in Colonial America: Evidence from the Muster Rolls," *Social Science History*, 6 (1984): 539–70. See also Darrett B. Rutman, "People in Process: The New Hampshire Towns of the Eighteenth Century," *Journal of Urban History*, 1 (1975): 268–92, and D. W. Meinig, *The Shaping of America: A Geographical Perspective on 500 Years of History*, Vol. 1, *Atlantic America, 1492–1800* (New Haven, Conn., 1986): 91–109, 119–90, 213–54.

3 McCusker and Menard, *Economy of British America*: 51–60.

4 ibid.: 55, 59–61; Alice Hanson Jones, "Wealth Estimates for the American Middle Colonies, 1774," *Economic Development and Cultural Change*, 18 (1970): 130; *The Wealth of a Nation to Be: The American Colonies on the Eve of the Revolution* (New York, 1980): 302–3; and "Wealth and Growth of the Thirteen Colonies: Some Implications," *Journal of Economic History*, 44 (1984): 250–2. See also Jeffrey G. Williamson and Peter H. Lindert, *American Inequality: A Macroeconomic History* (New York, 1980): 9–31; and James A. Henretta, "Wealth and Social Structure," in Greene and Pole, eds., *Colonial British America*: 262–89.

5 McCusker and Menard, *Economy of British America*: 85–6; James F. Shepherd and Gary M. Walton, "Trade, Distribution, and Economic Growth in Colonial America," *Journal of Economic History*, 32 (1972): 130–1, 144.

6 McCusker and Menard, *Economy of British America*: 280–1; Shepherd and Walton, "Trade, Distribution, and Economic Growth": 136; and "Estimates of 'Invisible' Earnings in the Balance of Payments of the British North American Colonies, 1768–1772," *Journal of Economic History*, 29 (1969): 553–69; James F. Shepherd and Samuel H. Williamson, "The Coastal Trade of the British North American Colonies, 1768–1772," ibid., 32 (1972): 783–810; William S. Sachs, "Interurban Correspondents

and the Development of a National Economy before the Revolution: New York as a Case Study," *New York History*, 36 (1955): 320–35. On developments within the import–export sector of the economy of the continental colonies, see also Marc Egnal, "The Economic Development of the Thirteen Continental Colonies," *William and Mary Quarterly*, 3rd ser., 32 (1975): 191–222; John R. Hanson II, "The Economic Development of the Thirteen Colonies, 1720 to 1775: A Critique," ibid., 37 (1980): 165–75; James F. Shepherd, "Commodity Exports from the British North American Colonies to Overseas Areas, 1768–1772: Magnitudes and Patterns of Trade," *Explorations in Economic History*, 8 (1970): 5–76; David Klingaman, "Food Surpluses and Deficits in the American Colonies, 1768–1772," *Journal of Economic History*, 31 (1971): 553–69; Gary M. Walton and James F. Shepherd, *The Economic Rise of Early America* (Cambridge, 1979); and Edwin J. Perkins, *The Economy of Colonial America* (New York, 1980). On the emergence of an American domestic economy, see Richard B. Sheridan, "The Domestic Economy," in Greene and Pole, eds., *Colonial British America*: 43–85.

7 McCusker and Menard, *Economy of British America*: 84, 266, 270, 310–27; Gary M. Walton, "Sources of Productivity Change in American Colonial Shipping, 1675–1775," *Economic History Review*, 2nd ser., 20 (1967): 67–78; James F. Shepherd and Gary M. Walton, *Shipping, Maritime Trade, and Economic Development of Colonial North America* (Cambridge, 1972), 158–9, 166, and "Trade, Distribution, and Economic Growth": 128–9, 144. See also Jacob M. Price, "The Transatlantic Economy," in Greene and Pole, eds., *Colonial British America*: 18–42.

8 Jacob M. Price, "Economic Function and the Growth of American Port Towns in the Eighteenth Century," *Perspectives in American History*, 8 (1974): 123–86; Carl Bridenbaugh, *Cities in the Wilderness: The First Century of Urban Life in America, 1625–1742* (New York, 1938), and *Cities in Revolt: Urban Life in America, 1743–1776* (New York, 1955); James T. Lemon, "Urbanization and the Development of Eighteenth-Century Southeastern Pennsylvania and Adjacent Delaware," *William and Mary Quarterly*, 3rd ser., 24 (1967): 501–42; Joseph A. Ernst and H. Roy Merrens, " 'Camden's turrets pierce the skies!': The Urban Process in the Southern Colonies during the Eighteenth Century," ibid., 30 (1973): 549–74; Hermann Wellenreuther, "Urbanization in the Colonial South: A Critique," ibid., 31 (1974): 653–71. See also Gary B. Nash, *The Urban Crucible: Social Change, Political Consciousness, and the Origins of the American Revolution* (Cambridge, Mass., 1979), for information on the changing distribution of wealth in Boston, New York, and Philadelphia.

9 Price, "Economic Function and Growth of American Port Towns": 138–9, 177–83; Daniel J. Boorstin, *The Americans: The Colonial Experience* (New York, 1958): 189–239; Stephen Botein, "The Legal Profession in Colonial North America," in Wilfrid Prest, ed., *Lawyers in Early Modern Europe and America* (London, 1981): 129–46; John M. Murrin, "The Legal Transformation: The Bench and Bar of Eighteenth-Century Massachusetts," in Stanley N. Katz, ed., *Colonial America: Essays in Politics and Social Development* (Boston, 1971): 415–49; Alan F. Day, "A Social

Study of Lawyers in Maryland, 1660–1775," 3 vols. (Ph.D. dissertation, Johns Hopkins University, 1976); A. G. Roeber, *Faithful Magistrates and Republican Lawyers: Creators of Virginia Legal Culture, 1680–1810* (Chapel Hill, N.C., 1981): 32–137; Milton M. Klein, "From Community to Status: The Development of the Legal Profession in Colonial New York," *New York History*, 60 (1979): 133–56.

10 A fuller discussion of the nature and meaning of these social categories may be found in Jack P. Greene, *All Men Are Created Equal: Some Reflections on the Meaning of the American Revolution* (Oxford, 1976). See also Richard Bushman, " 'This New Man': Dependence and Independence, 1776," in Bushman, *et al.*, eds., *Uprooted Americans: Essays in Honor of Oscar Handlin* (Boston, 1979): 77–96.

11 See Jackson Turner Main, *The Social Structure of Revolutionary America* (Princeton, 1965); Philip Greven, *The Protestant Temperament: Patterns of Child-Rearing, Religious Experience, and the Self in Early America* (New York, 1977): 265–334; Bushman, "American High-Style and Vernacular Cultures" in Jack P. Greene and J. R. Pole, eds., *Colonial British America: Essays on the New History of the Early Modern Era* (Baltimore, 1984): 345–83; Richard Hofstadter, *America at 1750: A Social Portrait* (New York, 1971): 131–79.

12 The case for constricting society is put most forcefully by Kenneth A. Lockridge, "Social Change and the Meaning of the American Revolution," *Journal of Social History*, 6 (1972–3): 403–39; James A. Henretta, *The Evolution of American Society, 1700–1815* (Lexington, Mass., 1973); and Nash, *Urban Crucible*. But see also Jack P. Greene, "The Social Origins of the American Revolution: An Evaluation and an Interpretation," *Political Science Quarterly*, 58 (1973): 1–22. Evidence in support of the contrary view, which is put forward here, may be found in Jackson Turner Main, *Society and Economy in Colonial Connecticut* (Princeton, 1985); Sung Bok Kim, *Landlord and Tenant in Colonial New York: Manorial Society, 1664–1775* (Chapel Hill, N.C., 1978); Lucy Simler, "Tenancy in Colonial Pennsylvania: The Case of Chester County," *William and Mary Quarterly*, 3rd ser., 43 (1986): 542–69; and Hermann Wellenreuther, "Labor in the Era of the American Revolution: A Discussion of Recent Concepts and Theories," *Labor History*, 22 (1981): 573–600.

13 Hofstadter, *America at 1750*, 131–79.

14 Simler, "Tenancy in Colonial Pennsylvania": 542–69; Mary Beth Norton, "The Evolution of White Women's Experience in Early America," *American Historical Review*, 89 (1984): 593–614.

15 Wellenreuther, "Labor in the Era of the American Revolution": 579–83; Simler, "Tenancy in Colonial Pennsylvania": 562–9; Richard S. Dunn, "Servants and Slaves: The Recruitment and Employment of Labor," in Greene and Pole, eds., *Colonial British America*: 180–8.

16 David W. Galenson, *White Servitude in America: An Economic Analysis* (Cambridge, 1981), "White Servitude and the Growth of Black Slavery in Colonial America," *Journal of Economic History*, 41 (1981): 39–47, and "The Rise and Fall of Indentured Servitude in the Americas: An Economic Analysis," ibid., 44 (1984): 1–13; Farley Grubb, "Immigrant

Servant Labor: Their Occupational and Geographic Distribution in the Late Eighteenth-Century Mid-Atlantic Economy," *Social Science History*, 9 (1985): 249–75, and "The Market for Indentured Immigrants: Evidence on the Efficiency of Forward-Labor Contracting in Philadelphia, 1745–1773," *Journal of Economic History*, 45 (1985): 855–68; Dunn, "Servants and Slaves": 157–72; Wellenreuther, "Labor in the Era of the American Revolution": 585; A. Roger Ekirch, "Bound for America: A Profile of British Convicts Transported to the Colonies, 1718–1775," *William and Mary Quarterly*, 3rd ser., 42 (1985): 184–200.

17 See Philip D. Curtin, *The Atlantic Slave Trade: A Census* (Madison, 1969).

18 William M. Wiecek, "The Statutory Law of Slavery and Race in the Thirteen Mainland Colonies of British America," *William and Mary Quarterly*, 3rd ser., 34 (1977): 258–80; Rhett S. Jones, "Structural Differentiation and the Status of Blacks in British Colonial America, 1630–1755," *Journal of Human Relations*, 3 (1971): 322–46; Orlando Patterson, *Slavery and Social Death: A Comparative Study* (Cambridge, Mass., 1982): 13, 38.

19 G. R. Elton, "Contentment and Discontent," in David B. Quinn, ed., *Early Maryland in a Wider World* (Detroit, 1982): 114–15; Perry Miller, *Errand into the Wilderness* (Cambridge, Mass., 1956): 4; Hofstadter, *America at 1750*.

20 D. A. Farnie, "The Commercial Empire of the Atlantic, 1607–1783," *Economic History Review*, 2nd ser., 15 (1962): 212–13.

21 Carole Shammas, "How Self-Sufficient was Early America?," *Journal of Interdisciplinary History*, 13 (1982): 252, 258, 263, 267–8, "The Domestic Environment in Early Modern England and America," *Journal of Social History*, 14 (1980): 18, "Consumer Behavior in Colonial America," *Social Science History*, 6 (1982): 68, 79–80, 83.

22 Samuel Williams, *Natural and Civil History of Vermont*, 2 vols. (Walpole, N. H., 1794): 2: 354.

23 J. R. Pole, *American Individualism and the Promise of Progress* (Oxford, 1980): 6, 8, 12–14, 17.

24 The Virginia Declaration of Rights is conveniently reprinted in Jack P. Greene, ed., *Colonies to Nation, 1763–1789: A Documentary History of the American Revolution* (New York, 1975): 333.

25 Samuel Miller, *A Brief Retrospect of the Eighteenth Century*, 2 vols. (New York, 1803): 2: 407; Pole, *American Individualism*: 13–14; Rowland Berthoff, *An Unsettled People: Social Order and Disorder in American History* (New York, 1971): 124; James A. Henretta, "Families and Farms: *Mentalité* in Pre-Industrial America," *William and Mary Quarterly*, 3rd ser., 35 (1978): 5, 14–16, 18–19, 25–6.

26 Berthoff, *Unsettled People*: 124; Peter H. Wood, " 'I did the Best I Could for My Day': The Study of Early Black History during the Second Reconstruction, 1960 to 1976," *William and Mary Quarterly*, 3rd ser., 35 (1978):187.

27 See esp. Joan Thirsk, *Economic Policy and Projects: The Development of a Consumer Society in Early Modern England* (Oxford, 1978); Joyce Appleby, *Economic Thought and Ideology in Seventeenth-Century England* (Princeton, 1978); and Robert D. Mitchell, *Commercialism and Frontier:*

Perspectives on the Early Shenandoah Valley (Charlottesville, Va., 1977): 133–240; Harry Roy Merrens, *Colonial North Carolina in the Eighteenth Century: A Study in Historical Geography* (Chapel Hill, N.C., 1964): 85–172.

28 See Roy Harvey Pearce, *The Savages of America: A Study of the Indian and the Idea of Civilization* (Baltimore, 1953); Louis B. Wright, *Culture on the Moving Frontier* (Bloomington, 1955): 11–45; Leo Marx, *The Machine in the Garden: Technology and the Pastoral Ideal in America* (New York, 1964): 75–144; Kenneth S. Lynn, *Mark Twain and Southwestern Humor* (Boston, 1959): 3–22; and Jack P. Greene, "Search for Identity: An Interpretation of the Meaning of Selected Patterns of Social Response in Eighteenth-Century America," *Journal of Social History*, 3 (1970): 189–220.

29 See Jack P. Greene, "The Growth of Political Stability: An Interpretation of Colonial Political Development in the Anglo-American Colonies, 1660–1760," in John Parker and Carol Urness, eds., *The American Revolution: A Heritage of Change* (Minneapolis, 1975): 26–72, and "Legislative Turnover in British America, 1696 to 1775: A Quantitative Analysis," *William and Mary Quarterly*, 3rd ser., 38 (1981): 442–63; John M. Murrin, "Political Development," in Greene and Pole, eds., *Colonial British America*: 408–56; Katherine Preyer, "Penal Measures in the American Colonies: An Overview," *American Journal of Legal History*, 26 (1982): 326–53; Douglas Greenberg, "Crime, Law Enforcement, and Social Control in Colonial America," ibid.: 293–325.

30 David D. Hall, "Religion and Society: Problems and Reconsiderations," in Greene and Pole, eds., *Colonial British America*: 317–44; Hofstadter, *America at 1750*: 3–32, 180–216, 217–92.

31 Patricia U. Bonomi, *Under the Cope of Heaven: Religion, Society, and Politics in Colonial America* (New York, 1986): 1–27; Bonomi and Peter B. Eisenstadt, "Church Adherence in the Eighteenth-Century British American Colonies," *William and Mary Quarterly*, 3rd ser., 39 (1982): 245–86.

32 Among a vast literature on this subject, see Bonomi, *Under the Cope of Heaven*: 131–60; Martin E. Lodge, "The Crisis of the Churches in the Middle Colonies, 1720–1750," *Pennsylvania Magazine of History and Biography*, 95 (1971): 195–220; Jon Butler, "Enthusiasm Described and Decried: The Great Awakening as Interpretive Fiction," *Journal of American History*, 69 (1982): 305–25; and Hall, "Religion and Society": 317–38.

33 John F. Berens, *Providence and Patriotism in Early America, 1640–1815* (Charlottesville, Va., 1978): 29; Sacvan Bercovitch, "Rhetoric as Authority: Puritanism, the Bible, and the Myth of America," *Social Science Information*, 21 (1982): 5–6, "Colonial Puritan Rhetoric and the Discovery of American Identity," *Canadian Review of American Studies*, 6 (1975), and *The American Jeremiad* (Madison, Wis., 1978).

34 Berens, *Providence and Patriotism*: 29; Bercovitch, "Rhetoric as Authority": 5; Nathan O. Hatch, *The Sacred Cause of Liberty: Republican Thought and the Millennium in Revolutionary New England* (New Haven, Conn.,1977); Joseph J. Ellis, "Culture and Capitalism in Pre-Revolutionary America," *American Quarterly*, 31 (1979): 176–7, 180, 184; Jack P. Greene, "Paine, America, and the 'Modernization' of Political Consciousness," *Political Science Quarterly*, 93 (1978): 73–92.

Part II

ETHNIC ENCOUNTERS

The history of early America is not merely the story of European settlers but the complex interaction of three major groups: white, red, and black. By focusing upon Indians and Afro-Americans respectively, James Merrell and Ira Berlin offer ways of understanding ethnic encounters. Both, for example, emphasize spatial variations: a bipolar division in Merrell's analysis and a tripartite division in Berlin's. Both are sensitive to changes over time: ethnic encounters were never timeless but rather extremely dynamic. Both examine their subjects as active participants in the cultural process; neither Indians nor Afro-Americans were simply victims. Both peoples adapted to the ways of Europeans but both developed strategies of survival and resistance.

3

"THE CUSTOMES OF OUR COUNTREY": INDIANS AND COLONISTS IN EARLY AMERICA

James H. Merrell

In assessing the relations of natives and newcomers in North America, James H. Merrell argues that the most vital consideration was the specific location of Indians either side of a moving boundary – a cultural frontier – running longitudinally (north–south) throughout the continent. On one flank, native Americans set many of the terms of cultural contact; on the other, colonists did. Rather than the regional categorizations employed by Bailyn and Greene, Merrell posits a simpler and – for his purposes – compelling bipolar division that makes sense of the myriad encounters between Indians and colonists in early America.

Merrell's account is also notable for his retrieval of the human dimensions of the encounters between Indian and colonists. Merrell eschews the standard formulas for addressing Indian–white relations: Old World vs. New World, savagery vs. civilization, wilderness vs. settlement. He also avoids lifeless abstractions like assimilation or acculturation with their too easy assumptions of a unilinear transfer of culture from whites to Indians. Rather, he attends to everyday interactions in many different spheres – language, trade, diplomacy, and religion. He listens to Indian voices, hears them laughing and swearing, sees them gesturing, drinking, dressing up, and building houses that betoken intimate contacts between Indians and colonists. He confronts cultural conquest, but insists that the process was always complicated. Indians, for example, were not just victims but eager and discriminating participants in the new economic system that ultimately did so much to destroy their way of life.

As sensitive as Merrell is to the face-to-face contacts among Indians and whites, does he go too far in placing Indians center stage in colonial America? Were there not many places in colonial America, even as early as the mid-seventeenth century, where the land was all but empty of its original inhabitants? By the early eighteenth century, might many colonists never see an Indian? At the same time, were there not other ways in

*which the Indians influenced colonial development? Even without inti-
mate contact, might not Indians intrude on colonial consciousness? Is it
true, as another historian of Indians has argued, that "While all peoples
to some extent define themselves by contrast with other peoples, the
English colonists forged their particular American identity more on an
Indian anvil than upon other European colonists or Africans" [James
Axtell,* The European and the Indian: Essays in the Ethnohistory of
Colonial North America *(New York, 1981: 308]?*

* * *

It was 1634, Maryland's first year, and already there was trouble
on the colony's northern border. At William Claiborne's Chesapeake Bay trading outpost on Kent Island a Susquehannock Indian
had injured a Wicomiss while both were doing business there, and
some of Claiborne's men thought it funny. Soon five Sus-
quehannocks and three of Claiborne's people lay dead, ambushed
by angry Wicomiss warriors. Now, two months later, the
Wicomisses sent a messenger to Governor Leonard Calvert with
word that they wanted to make amends for the actions of their
young men. "What will give you content," the envoy asked Calvert.
The governor's answer was simple: turn over the culprits "unto me,
to do with them as I shall thinke fit."

There was "a little pause." Then the Wicomiss spokesman tried
to set the governor straight. "It is the manner amongst us Indians,"
he said, "that if any such like accident happen, wee doe redeeme
the life of a man that is so slaine, with a 100. armes length of
*Roanoke*ᵃ... and since that you are heere strangers, and come into
our Countrey, you should rather conforme your selves to the
Customes of our Countrey, then impose yours upon us." If Calvert
understood, he did not let on. "It seems you come not sufficiently
instructed in the business which wee have with the Wicomesses,"
he replied; "therefore tell them what I have said; and that I expect
a speedy answere; and so dismist him."[1]

Calvert's conversation with the Wicomiss was part of a continuing debate in colonial times as native Americans and Anglo-Americans tried to establish whose country this was and whose customs
ought to hold sway. Their exchange was more explicit than most,
however, because in 1634 both natives and newcomers could at
least claim to rule the Chesapeake. Elsewhere the issue was not in
doubt, and conformity was not up for debate. When John Lawsonᵇ

left Charleston, South Carolina, in 1700 to head inland through "a Country inhabited by none but Savages," for example, he was careful to behave in a manner "acceptable to those sort of Creatures." He relied on Indian guides, said nothing when his Key-auwee hosts served such delicacies as "Fawns, taken out of the Doe's Bellies, and boil'd in the same slimy Bags Nature had plac'd them in," and sat patiently through the night in a Waxhaw council house as old men sang and young people danced.[2]

Compare this with Dr. Alexander Hamilton's[c] journey from Maryland to Maine and back again more than forty years later. Hamilton, too, met many native Americans in his travels, enjoyed the hospitality of a local headman, and sat with Indians at a sacred ceremony. Yet here any resemblance to Lawson's journey ends, for Hamilton never left the familiar Anglo-American confines of taverns and clubs, concerts and churches, enthusiastic New Lights and impertinent social upstarts. Along the coast colonists were many, natives few, and it was Indians who had to fit in. Instead of fawns, Hamilton's Indian host (who "lives after the English mode") served him a glass of excellent wine. Instead of joining the "confused Rabble" in the Waxhaw council house, Hamilton took a pew near some Indians during a service in a Boston church.[3]

Between Hamilton's journey and Lawson's lay a barrier that scholars have labeled a frontier, a cultural divide, or a marchland. On one side of this line native Americans set the conditions under which intercultural encounters occurred; on the other, colonists did. Frederick Jackson Turner's Eurocentric version of the American frontier has given the concept a bad name, but there can be no doubt that a frontier existed in colonial times.[d] Certainly English colonists had no doubts. "Wee are here att the end of the world," wrote William Byrd I in 1690 from his plantation at the falls of the James River. And Byrd was right: it was the end of his world, the English world, and the beginning of another – called "Indian Country" – where different rules applied.[4]

Different sorts of Indian peoples lived on opposite sides of this frontier. The natives Hamilton and other coastal travelers encountered, a common sight even late in the eighteenth century, were variously termed "neighbour-Indians," "little Tribes," "domestic Indians," "resident Indians," "plantation Indians," "Settlement Indians." Those Lawson and other explorers visited were "remoter Indians," "wilder Indians," "Inland Indians," "back nations," "strange Indians," "foreign Indians."[5] Within each category there was considerable variety. "Remoter Indians" ranged from the Santees of South Carolina, "very tractable" because of their heavy involvement in colonial trade, to Tomahittans in the Virginia mountains, who were so unaccustomed to seeing Europeans that they raised a scaffold when the first Englishmen arrived in 1670 so "theire people might stand and gaze at them and not offend them by theire throng." Similarly, the "neighbour-Indians" Hamilton met included not only the Boston churchgoers but also a band of Indian oysterers wading naked through the shallows alongside the road.[6] Nonetheless, this spectrum of native cultures broke down into two basic types: those inhabiting Byrd's world and those from Indian Country.

The invisible barrier between the Santees and the oysterers was crucial in shaping the life of an Indian people. A tribe's population, its economy, and its political life – indeed, its entire culture – depended less on whether it lived in New England, New York, or North Carolina than on whether it was located among the English. Thus "plantation Indians" in Massachusetts and Virginia had more in common with one another than with some "back nation" nearby. North or south, their numbers were small, their subsistence routine disrupted, their political autonomy compromised, their customs under indirect influence from colonial neighbors if not direct attack from Christian missionaries.

Not the least of the differences between resident and inland groups was the way they interacted with the English. While hardly a precise gauge, laughter helps draw this distinction, because in intercultural contacts whoever made fun of the other generally was in control of the situation. In Indian Country the joke was on the colonist. Lawson's hosts often "laugh'd their Sides sore" at his antics, and he was not alone. Natives made fun of the Anglo-American because his fingernails were too short and his spoons too small. They laughed at his attempts to speak their language, laughed at his prayers, laughed at his beard.[7] Where a man like Hamilton felt at home, on the other hand, Indians tended to be the butt of the jokes. When the "queen" of a local tribe performed a ceremonial dance in Williamsburg in 1702, the audience burst out laughing, and the laughter never stopped. Colonists mocked Indian efforts to speak English or ride a horse, dress in English clothing or understand English law.[8]

"Above all things," wrote one colonist of the Massachusett Indians, they "loved not to be laughed at."[9] The Massachusetts –

and, eventually, Indians throughout the East – would have to get used to it. When English colonists first arrived in America, virtually all of the land between the Atlantic and the Mississippi was Indian Country; by the end of the colonial era virtually none of it was. The history of Indian–English relations in early America is the story of how this dramatic change in the country and its "Customes" came about. It is no laughing matter, but listening for laughter is one way of retracing the steps that led from "remoter Indians" to "neighbor-Indians," from "wild" to "domestic." To tell that story we must try to grasp what forces turned Tomahittans tractable, pulled Santees across that invisible line, and put clothes on those naked oysterers.

I

The place to begin is with that border between Anglo-America and Indian America, a border as difficult to pinpoint on a map as it was real. Sometimes its location was obvious. In 1524, when Abenakis on the Maine coast refused even to allow Giovanni de Verrazano's exploring party to come ashore, it reached right down to the water's edge. Plotting its position thereafter can be more complicated. For one thing, there was no inexorable advance across the continent; the English push into the interior could quickly reverse itself when Indians fought back. During King Philip's War of 1675-6, for example, native warriors destroyed thirteen New England towns, and it was 1700 before colonists reoccupied the lands they had held at the war's beginning.[10] Even when the boundary did move west, its progress was uneven. Much depended on when the English arrived in a particular area: Carolinians in 1670 (not to mention Georgians in 1732) were clinging to the beaches at a time when their fellow colonists to the north had conquered the entire coastal plain. To complicate matters further, navigable rivers helped some colonists get ahead in the race for land. Thus the Connecticut River valley boasted a thriving English population one hundred miles from the coast at a time when most towns were little more than a day's walk from Boston or Plymouth, and this pattern of settlement was followed later along the Hudson, the Potomac, and the Savannah.

Whatever its twists and turns, its distortions and detours on the way west, the frontier did move across the continent, and the principal forces behind it were warfare, disease, and colonial settlement. Each was crucial in tipping the scales from what John Winthrop called a land "full of Indians" to one dominated by European immigrants. The familiar roster of names representing Indian warfare in colonial times – from Powhatan and Opechancanough[e] in the Chesapeake, to Pequots and King Philip in New England, to Tuscaroras and Yamasees in the Carolinas – testifies to war's prominent role in the conquest of America. In Virginia, battles with colonists during the first half of the seventeenth century reduced the Powhatan Confederacy to a "harmless curiosity." The natives of New England lost some 10,000 people in wars with colonists between 1600 and 1750, and in North Carolina 1,000 Tuscaroras were killed or enslaved during a single campaign in 1712. And these were only a fraction of the Indians' combat losses; violence along the edges of the colonial world was endemic, and untold numbers of natives perished in forgotten skirmishes.[11]

The casualties suffered in wars with Anglo-America were certainly appalling; the Indians' losses from exposure to alien diseases – conservatively estimated at 75 percent in New England alone – almost defy comprehension. Yet noting that demographic disaster formed a grim backdrop to all of colonial history is one thing, coming up with reliable population estimates for Indians quite another. A best guess for the number of natives east of the Mississippi River on the eve of permanent English settlement might be close to 1,000,000; a century earlier the total would have been higher still, for by the time the English set foot on these shores, Indians were well acquainted with imported diseases.[12] Whatever the earlier figures, after Anglo-Americans arrived native numbers plummeted with frightening speed. In 1674, inquiries among New England tribes elicited similar answers: from 4,000 warriors to 300, from 5,000 to 1,000, from 3,000 to 300, from 3,000 to 250, on and on the roll call of death went as memory called forth the world Indians had lost. Some thirty years later another curious colonist took a census of natives in Virginia, and again the response was a litany of loss: "much decreased of late"; "reduc'd to very few Men"; "a small number yet living"; "almost wasted"; "Wasting"; "but three men living, which yet keep up their Kingdom, and retain their Fashion."[13]

Sickness did its terrible work in different ways. It wiped out the Patuxets in a single stroke in 1616–17 while the nearby Narragansetts, who escaped that particular scourge, watched tuberculosis and pneumonia steadily reduce their numbers during the rest of the seventeenth century. In the Carolina piedmont epidemics came once a generation – in 1698, 1718, 1738, and 1759 – cutting the Catawbas's population from perhaps 5,000 to a mere 500. Whether disease struck in one fatal blow or over several generations, the end result was the same. At the close of the colonial period there were only 150,000 Indians left in the East. Survivors of the devastation understood neither its cause nor its cure, but they knew who was to blame. "They have a superstition," wrote one Pennsylvania colonist, "that as many Indians must die each year, as the number of Europeans that newly arrive."[14]

English colonists considered the Indians' catastrophic losses a sign of God's favor. It was, wrote one colonial governor, "as if Heaven designed by the Diminution of these Indian Neighbours, to make room for our growing Settlements," and indeed disease often did clear the way for colonial farmers.[15] But the farmers helped. Natives still around when the English moved into an area found that their new neighbors were "like pidgeons": "where one of those people settled, ... a thousand more would settle." A generation or so after the first pioneers arrived, the colonial population would reach a critical mass, the pressure on Indians would increase, and many tribes would retreat.[16] Within twenty years of Pennsylvania's founding, Indians near Philadelphia talked of heading into the hinterlands, and near Charleston in 1710 local native groups had "gone further up in the Country Thro' badd usage they received from some of Our People." In 1755 Edmond Atkin, soon to be the crown's superintendent of Indian affairs for the Southern Department, blamed it less on "badd usage" than a simple "difference of manners and way of life" between Indian and English. Whatever the reason, history taught him that "the Indians generally chuse to withdraw, as white People draw near to them." "Will not it be impossible for Indians and White people to live together?" wondered a Pennsylvanian. "Will not there be ... a perpetual Scene of quarreling?" The answer, throughout England's mainland provinces, was often yes.[17]

War, disease, settlement – these three horsemen of the Indian apocalypse are essential to an understanding of English contacts with native America. But they are more the story's beginning than its end, for they cannot capture the substance and subtlety of the American encounter. The conquest of the continent was not as swift as the emphasis on depopulation and displacement implies; Indians did not surrender or disappear overnight. Without belittling the devastation wrought by smallpox, militias, or settlers, we need to remember that Indians survived. While some abandoned traditional burial rituals in the aftermath of an epidemic, most continued to inter their dead in customary fashion.[18] While warfare or sickness utterly destroyed some groups, others constructed new societies from fragments of the old. While many did retreat when faced with the prospect of being hemmed in by farms and fences, many others did not.

To understand how the Indians lost America and the English won it, we must look past the grand events – warfare, epidemics, the frontier's advance – to examine the less celebrated but no less important meetings between peoples. The real (and still largely untold) story is less dramatic than invasions and battles, less drastic than sickness and settlement; more intimate, more human in scale, it is also harder to uncover. These long-forgotten encounters lie in scraps of evidence, mere snatches of conversations that took place in several different contact arenas – linguistic, economic, diplomatic, legal, and religious – where Indian met colonist. The conversations, taken together, speak of a shift in patterns of interaction as face-to-face contacts slowly became more Anglo-American than native American, more like Alexander Hamilton's journey than John Lawson's. If that shift, that frontier, is often hard to pin down precisely, the overall trend is unmistakable: Indians slowly gave way and colonists slowly took over, until the line between one world and another was not Verrazano's shore or Byrd's plantation but the Appalachians and then beyond.

II

American Indians and English colonists brought to their encounter considerable experience with exotic peoples. For native Americans the English were only the latest in a series of European intruders, while those English colonists had a fund of knowledge about alien cultures derived from books about America and contacts with Ireland.[19] Yet if neither were novices in dealing with foreigners, they had a hard time making sense of one another once sustained interaction began at the end of the sixteenth century. Indians in New England called "every thing which they cannot comprehend" *Manitóo*, and they used the term frequently when talking among themselves about the English. Indians, whose cultures emphasized personal restraint, were appalled by the colonists' "excited chattering,

... the haste and rashness to do something," and some wondered aloud why, if "the *Europeans* are always rangling and uneasy, ... they do not go out of this World, since they are so uneasy and discontented in it."[20] Colonists were no better at comprehending natives. "Uncivil and stupid as garden poles," noted one. "A very strange kind of People," wrote another. "An odd sort of People," agreed a third. "Their way of Living is so contrary to ours," concluded John Lawson in 1709, after studying Carolina Indians for eight years, "that neither we nor they can fathom one anothers Designs and Methods."[21]

True understanding of the other would remain elusive. But the quest for that elusive goal started immediately, with a search for some way to cross the linguistic barrier. Thus began a tug-of-war between English and Indian as each tried to impose its modes of communication on the other. Natives expected colonists to follow local custom, which dictated that "the most powerful Nation of these Savages scorns to treat or trade with any others (of fewer Numbers and less Power) in any other Tongue but their own." The English agreed in principle, but insisted that they, not Indians, had the numbers and the power. Moreover, colonists felt that the English language should prevail not only because England *should* rule; it would actually *help* England rule, because "changing of the language of a barbarous people, into the speech of a more civil and potent nation" was a way "to reduce such a people unto the civility and religion of the prevailing nation."[22]

Colonists expecting Indians to welcome the chance to learn "the treasure of our tongue" were disappointed.[23] The intruders did eventually win the war of words, but it was a long struggle, waged against stiff opposition. At first an elaborate pantomime was probably the most common means of conversing, no doubt accompanied by wild swinging of arms, exaggerated facial expressions, and whatever sounds might help get the gist of the message across. Crude, perhaps, but it worked. It was not hard to guess that Indians waving furs on the end of a stick at a passing ship were interested in trade or that an Englishman piling beads into an Indian's canoe wanted to make friends. Nor was it easy to mistake the meaning behind "stern-look'd Countenances" or a "scornefull posture."[24]

In the early stages of contact, aboriginal symbol systems expanded the mime's repertoire, and colonists had to read a foreign text. Seventeenth-century Virginians learned when to head west into Indian Country by counting the pebbles, knots in a string, or kernels of corn sent from native traders in the interior. Those same colonists could tell the tribe of the Indian bringing the message by a glance at his tattoo or paint: a serpent meant Occaneechi, a terrapin Susquehannock, three arrows Nahyssan. Crown officials went along with the traders: South Carolina sent knotted strings as messages to distant Indians, and New York authorities demanded that the Iroquois not only receive but give belts of wampum beads. Even colonists who still used pen and paper might go out of their way to accommodate Indians. One Albany trader recorded his transactions with natives by drawing in an account book "crude sketches of each beaver so that at a future date the customer would be able to look in the book and see for himself the amount owed."[25]

Useful as they were, pictographs and pantomime had their limits, and attempts to talk to one another followed close on the heels of contact. The conversations that ensued were easy prey to misinterpretation, however. Philip Amadas and Arthur Barlowe returned from their 1584 voyage to the Carolina coast certain that the Indian name for the area was "Wingandacoia." Sir Walter Raleigh, their sponsor, was equally certain that they were wrong: the word actually meant "you wear good clothes, or gay clothes." Modern linguists have suggested that both were mistaken, that in fact the Indians were talking about some trees in which they thought the visitors were interested. Those more fluent in the local language could also be fooled. On one occasion when the Virginia colonist William Strachey informed his native companion that he was hungry and the Indian replied "I will give you food," Strachey thought he was being called a beggar.[26]

Despite the pitfalls, the need to discuss more complex matters encouraged the two cultures to break through the language barrier. The first halting steps were probably secondary to the sign language in common currency: a verbal exchange between the explorer William Hilton and a tribe of Carolina Indians, for example, consisted of many gestures but only two words, "Bonny" and "Skerry." Far more useful were pidgin languages[f] – English as well as several different Indian versions – that developed. Impatient colonists, who called these inventions "a broken language," "a made-up, childish language," were always trying to learn more, but Indians held back.[27] In New Netherland, where the linguistic battle has been studied most thoroughly, natives clearly sought to establish and then maintain the upper hand. One frustrated colonial student claimed "that they rather try to conceal their language from us than to properly communicate it, except in things that have to do with everyday trade, saying that it is sufficient for us to understand them to this extent." The Indians' purpose was obvious: "Even those [colonists] who can best of all speak with the savages, and get along well in trade, are nevertheless altogether in the dark and as bewildered, when they hear the savages talking among themselves." Another "Indian grammarian" trying to crack this code became hopelessly confused by the different tenses and pronunciations: "I stand oftentimes and look, but do not know how to put it down." His efforts to sort out the confusion failed, for Indians, he concluded, were "very stupid" and his fellow colonists ignorant. One supposed expert, consulted about variable pronunciations, explained the mystery by claiming that local tribes altered their entire language every few years.[28]

The "Indian grammarians" did not give up easily. Their persistence, coupled with the growing need to communicate as contacts became more frequent, overcame the Indians' reluctance to train capable linguists. Most early interpreters were colonists who mastered a native language, not Indians speaking English, for despite claims that some natives were delighted to learn and then show off their English, most colonists agreed that the local tribe's speech "is the first thing to be employed with them."[29] Over time, however, Indians were the ones expected to learn a foreign language. Not surprisingly, neighboring groups were the first to face this language requirement; indeed, a pledge to learn English could be part of formal submission to colonial rule. In Maryland, the Piscataway tayac (chief) began English lessons at the same time that he gave up polygamy, began dressing in English clothes, and converted to Christianity. Across the Potomac River in Virginia, colonial authorities during the 1670s encouraged the shift to English by insisting that tributary Indians provide their own interpreter at official meetings. More often, Settlement Indians simply picked up the language by imitating the English around them. In 1710, only forty years after South Carolina's founding, a colonist noticed that "the Young Indians born since we inhabited these parts and that converse with us ... speak good English."[30]

Even as they lost linguistic predominance, Indians resisted by refusing whenever possible to speak an alien tongue. "If you ask them a question," one Virginian complained of the tributary Indians in the 1680s, "unlesse they be made three parts drunk they will not answer, tho they can speake English." "Notwithstanding some of them could speak good English," reported another visitor to the colony's tributaries three decades later, "yet when they treat of any thing that concerns their nation, they will not treat but in their own language, ... nor will not answer to any question made to them without it be in their own tongue." Such stubbornness only slowed the spread of linguistic imperialism, however. In 1734, "seeing the tributary Indians understand and can speak the English language very well," Virginia removed the natives' facade of superiority by discharging its official interpreters.[31]

A similar shift from Indian to English occurred in nonverbal modes of discourse. Not content to deal solely in wampum and tattoos, Anglo-Americans introduced competing symbols that eventually supplanted those devised by Indians. During the seventeenth century the Virginia assembly, impressed by the native custom of tribal identification, "took up the humour" and began issuing medals to friendly Indians. But there was an important difference: with medals, colonists no longer had to decipher tribal markings, or even tell one tribe from another, since from the English point of view the only important distinction was medal or no medal, friend or foe. In the eighteenth century, New Jersey made the same distinction by using red ribbons that the colony's Indians were to wear at all times.[32]

Along with their ribbons, New Jersey's native friends carried another mark of their loyalty, a "Registration Certificate," and ultimately it was pieces of paper like these that replaced the pictographs and pebbles. Natives themselves helped hasten the spread of writing. Awed by this new means of conversing and eager to capture its power, Indians copied the figures John Lawson jotted down, asked that their initials be carved into a tree alongside those of colonial explorers in order to "be an Englishman," and pestered Roger Williams,[8] "Make me a paper."[33] Even native diplomats who protested against "that Pen and Ink work" began demanding copies of the treaties to take home.[34]

Indian and English forms coexisted well into the eighteenth century. In 1758, messengers sent from Philadelphia to the Ohio country carried belts of wampum that were keyed to a written speech, so that the talk could be read and the belts delivered simultaneously. To Indians this marked a real improvement, for it "was like two tongues": the letter "confirmed what the Messenger said to them" through the belts. Even so, the direction – from the rattle of wampum beads to the scratch of pen on paper – was clear.

A few Indians learned to read and write, either in English or in their own language.[35] But the vast majority remained illiterate, inhabitants of a symbolic universe they were unable to decipher.

III

Much of the impetus for communication between peoples – that march from gesture through jargon to fluency – came from a shared eagerness for trade. It was trade that prompted Indians to hoist furs on sticks, trade that gave birth to the pidgin languages, trade that trained most interpreters. The lists of Indian words colonists compiled reveal how closely talking was tied to trading. Each phrase book had Indian equivalents for all sorts of merchandise, numbers for counting these items, and handy phrases every enterprising salesman should know, like "How d'ye do," "Have you got anything to eat," "Englishman is thirsty," "What price," "I will sell you Goods very cheap," "I will pay you well," "My money is very good," and "It is worth it."[36]

The colonists' concern with price serves as a reminder that, while Indian and English were both experienced traders and each had products the other wanted, they were schooled in different classrooms. Hence handing over one object in return for another was not as simple or as easy as it looked. Among Indians, exchange was embedded in a ceremonial code designed to cement relations between peoples; in these rituals the giving itself was as important as the gift. Colonists, on the other hand, tended to think more of prices and profits. Intercultural trade in colonial America combined both traditions at first; eventually, however, commerce went the way of speech, and natives ended up living by the economic rules of the Atlantic world.

Indians unacquainted with European ways were a colonial trader's favorite customers. These people, still operating within the context of aboriginal exchange, cared little about sampling the entire range of trade goods and less about prices. They sought wares that fitted established norms – glass instead of shell beads, for instance, or mirrors that substituted for crystal – and in return they gave whatever the colonist considered fair. It did not take Indians long to catch on, however. In New England they had "already" in 1634 "learned much subtiltie and cunning by bargaining with the *English*," and Roger Williams agreed that "they are marvellous subtle in their Bargaines." Experience made natives discriminating consumers: instead of accepting whatever was offered, they began to shop more carefully. "The Indians wilbe very long and teadeous in viewing" a trader's merchandise, complained one colonist, "and doe tumble it and tosse it and mingle it a hundred times over."[37] They were looking not just for beads or mirrors but cloth, tools, and weapons. Moreover, that cloth had to be "a sad colour," that iron hoe a certain weight, that gun a light flintlock instead of a cumbersome matchlock.[38] And all – cloth, hoe, gun – had to be for sale at a fair price, for the more Indians traded with colonists, the fewer qualms they had about haggling over rates of exchange.[39]

Indians, though soon enough "wise in trade and traffic" with colonists, did not immediately become slaves to European habits of exchange or pawns in the Atlantic economic system. In fact, during the early years of intercultural trade the colonist who hoped to succeed tried to meet his customers' needs and obey their rules. In putting together a cargo he selected the right color, the right weight, and the right price. Upon arriving in a village he gave gifts to the proper people and accepted their offer of adoption, even marriage, into a kinship network. Once the bargaining began, he said nothing about the Indians' preference for bartering, "not by any certeyne measure or by our English waightes and measures," but by an arm's length instead of a yard and a mouthful instead of a pint. He went along because competition for Indian customers was fierce – not only between England and France but between Pennsylvania and New York, Albany and Schenectady, even within (especially within) Albany itself – and Indians could afford to be selective. "If any traders will not suffer the Indians soe to doe [examine the goods for sale]," one colonist lamented, "they wilbe distasted with the said traders and fall out with them and refuse to have any trade."[40]

As time went on, however, few Indians could simply refuse to trade. While natives did not become dependent on European wares overnight, within a generation or two of their entry into regular trade relations they did become dependent. The early shift from comity to competition and from passive acceptance to active haggling was only the beginning. The next stage removed the production of goods from its traditional context. Deer once put to many different uses were now left to rot as the hunter stripped the skin from the carcass and moved on. Prisoners of war once adopted to replace dead kinfolk or tortured to assuage a mourner's grief were now sold. Wampum once restricted to persons of high status was now mass-produced by coastal communities that interrupted their seasonal subsistence routine to concentrate on the shells.[41] The final step was more obvious, as people less able to remember and to replicate traditional craft skills found they simply could not get along without European commodities.

Settlement Indians were the first to pass through these three stages. But even peoples well removed from colonial settlements found that a generation or so of colonial trade had taken its toll and "they cannot live without the assistance of the English." "What are we red People?" a Cherokee asked in 1753. "The Cloaths we wear, we cannot make ourselves, they are made to us.... We cannot make our Guns, they are made to us. Every necessary Thing in Life we must have from the white People." Lest any Indians forget this harsh truth, colonists reminded them: "We can live without you, but you cannot live without us." " 'Tis in vain for you to stand out [against us]," a South Carolinian informed the Creeks in 1728. "What can you do without the English?"[42]

If trade could reach beyond the frontier to control distant natives, its effect on those living amid colonists can be imagined. Among neighbor Indians the appetite for English goods remained; the accepted means of acquiring them did not. The spread of colonial farms accelerated the depletion of game begun by the fur trade, and colonists frowned on native hunters traipsing across fenced fields in pursuit of what animals were left. Other ways of earning a living would have to be found.

Many put old skills to new uses. Indian priests cured a Maryland planter, and they ended the drought ruining William Byrd's crops. Indian warriors defended a colony against other Indians, fought the French or Spanish, and captured runaway slaves. Indian farmers found a ready market for their produce in the cities and among colonists recently arrived in an area. And Indian hunters were still at work, despite colonial resistance. When, in 1759, Pamunkeys paddled off into the Virginia marshes to hunt birds that were then peddled to local planters, they followed a routine common all along the eastern seaboard for generations.[43] Indians generally sold the same kinds of game they had always eaten themselves; but if deer and turkey were scarce, enterprising hunters still found a way to make a sale. On Long Island they killed colonists' livestock, advertised it as venison, and vended it to unsuspecting customers in New York City; another hunter in

New England sold beef as moose meat to the president of Harvard.[44]

Aboriginal craft skills proved equally adaptable. Indian woodworkers, from the obscure Virginia native John the Bowlmaker to the celebrated Mohegan preacher Samson Occom,[h] carved not only the traditional bowls and spoons but also a flat-bottomed vessel specifically designed for Anglo-American tables. Potters, too, catered to consumer tastes, developing shapes aimed at the colonial market.[45] Among those who made containers out of fiber rather than wood or clay, the step from aboriginal practices to production for Anglo-America may have been bigger. Indians managed to sell their aboriginal cane or hemp baskets at first, but at the end of the seventeenth century they apparently began to adopt from colonists not only new styles but new materials, fashioning woodsplint basketry modeled after patterns Swedish and German emigrants brought to the Delaware Valley.

The line between fitting old skills to new circumstances and developing wholly new abilities is blurred. Were the Cherokees making woodsplint baskets the same ones who knew split-cane weaving? Was Edward Gunstocker merely trying his hand at a different form? Were the New England Indians who fashioned shingles and clapboards for sale in Boston already accomplished woodworkers? The answers are unclear. But often the boundary between old and new was more obvious, for many plantation Indians learned to work at novel tasks. They became wheelwrights and tailors, blacksmiths and shoemakers, experts at building stone walls and adepts at chasing the whale on the open sea.

The work resident Indians took up to make a living in the Anglo-American world lends credence to colonial claims that they could "soon learne any mechanicall trades, having quicke wits, understanding apprehensions, strong memories, with nimble inventions, and a quicke hand."[46] Their "apprehensions" enabled them to discern the best means of earning an income using what they already knew; their "inventions" facilitated imitation of alien forms when that became necessary. But while the skills and the products were much the same for all natives living among the English colonists, the terms on which they worked were not. Some were more fortunate than others. The luckiest were those like the Pamunkeys or the "venison" merchants in New York and Boston, peddlers hawking their merchandise from place to place. Next came those who hired themselves out to a colonist or local government for a task or a season, whether it be to help a farmer in North Carolina plant his crops or a Dutchman along the Hudson harvest his, to build a stone wall for a town in Rhode Island or to hunt wolves for a county in Virginia.[47]

Many Indians could only dream of such freedom, for they were trapped in one form of bound labor or another, from debt peonage to indentured servitude to outright enslavement. Among Settlement Indians the road from free to forced labor was wide, slippery, and all downhill, with colonists often pushing from behind. Indian debtors, Indian criminals, Indian paupers, even Indian students who received poor marks – all might wind up in servitude. War captives might also be made servants, but the more common fate for them was enslavement. In 1708, South Carolina planters held no fewer than 1,400 Indians in bondage, and countless other natives ended their days on a Chesapeake tobacco quarter, a West Indian sugar plantation, or a New England farm. Whether slave or servant, in Rhode Island unfree Indian labor was so common that, when Dr. Alexander Hamilton rode through in 1744, children fled at the sight of his black slave, "for here negroe slaves are not so much in use as with us, their servants being chiefly bound or indentured Indians."[48] There might seem to be little resemblance between remote Indians admiring a trader's glass beads and the native workers Hamilton saw. But all occupied a single spectrum of economic activity; they were at once participants in and victims of a world market.

IV

Following the native Americans' entry into an alien economic system obscures how far trade remained what it had been in aboriginal America, an arm of diplomacy. Certainly Indians and colonists were aware that swapping merchandise was more than a way to make a living. Natives often spoke of peace and trade as one and the same thing, and colonists were quick to agree. In 1736, after giving some of the credit to God and the king, the South Carolina legislature asserted that the colony's "Security and Welfare ... hath been owing to nothing more than the Regulations ... with regard to the Trade and Commerce carryed on from hence with the several Nations of Indians almost surrounding us.... [I]t is by these means alone that We have been able to preserve a general Peace and Friendship with them."[49] For trade to serve as a vital cog in any diplomatic machine, however, that machine had to be built; learning to communicate and working out rules of exchange were essential to successful diplomacy, but without a mutually agreed-upon body of protocol for conducting a formal conversation they were just talking and trading.

Confusion reigned at first, in part because many early colonial leaders – Ralph Lane at Roanoke, John Smith in Virginia, Miles Standish of Plymouth – were by training and temperament about as far from diplomats as they could be. The conquistador was their model, and they came to America fresh from service among alien peoples where the sword was the first rather than the last resort. But even colonists who put more stock in negotiation often fared little better. Faced with a political world that bore little resemblance to their own, they tried to conjure up emperors, kings, and nations that were not there.[50] However comfortably the word "Emperor" may have fitted Powhatan, it was ill suited to a Piscataway tayac or a Tuscarora headman, who were also awarded the title.[51] In fact, most eastern Indian chiefs led by persuasion and example, custom and council. Whatever authority a headman did wield generally was limited to a narrow sphere of face-to-face relations; few ruled an extensive territory. Nonetheless, Anglo-Americans looked for, and thought they found, not only emperors but also vast nations of Tuscaroras, Cherokees, Creeks, and Iroquois, when what they actually saw were independent villages linked (if at all) by kinship, language, ethnicity, or crisis. Reality inevitably intruded, leaving many English diplomats feeling as Carolina authorities did in 1682 as they cast about for an alliance with a people "whose Government is lesse Anarchicall" than the colony's current friends.[52]

Experience taught colonists the limitations of kingly power and the narrow definition of nationhood in native America. With time came more invitations to the king *and* headmen, stricter insistence on speaking with representatives of every town in a nation, and greater concern that each of those villages receive gifts. In 1755 Edmond Atkin knew enough to write of "the Cherokee Nations," and he went on to explain that these entities were not only politically independent but different in character. "The Indians ... have no such titles or persons, as emperors, or kings," wrote the trader James Adair at the close of the colonial era. "The power of their chiefs, is an empty sound... . Every town is independent of another."[53]

Colonists sorting out Indian political reality also had to undergo a crash course in native diplomacy, for, once diplomatic relations opened, Indian rules prevailed. The Covenant Chain,[i] forged in the late seventeenth century to connect the Iroquois and other Indians with New York and other colonies, was only the most famous example of how native diplomacy shaped formal intercultural contacts. From Creeks and Cherokees to Delawares and Shawnees, natives set the tempo and tenor of diplomatic encounters. They came when they pleased, and in delegations larger than cost-conscious crown officials liked. They insisted on preliminary rituals ("the usual Salutation of Shaking of hands" in the Southeast, "the usual Compliments of Condolence" in Iroquoia) and punctuated their talks with wampum belts and gifts. The talks themselves sounded strange to colonial ears, for native ambassadors spoke in a rich, metaphorical language of elder brothers and nephews, paths clear or bloody, hatchets taken up or thrown down, a language that invested kinship terms and everyday objects with deeper meaning.[54]

"Indian Business" often tested the colonists' patience. First they had to sit through "a long and tedious Relation using all the Indian Ceremonies and Phrases." Then, knowing from experience that "the manner of saying things to Indians depends ... on Forms and a narrow Observation of them," they had to respond in the same fashion, even while "thinking it most proper to deliver it according to our own way of speech than to conform ourselves to the Indian dialect." A colonial official might consider wampum only shells and presents mere bribes, but before starting negotiations with native leaders, he made sure he had both on hand and that all proceeded "according to the custum of the Indians."[55]

Anglo-American diplomats went along initially because they had to: their pretensions to conquest aside, the English simply lacked the power to dictate forms, much less terms. But they continued to play the diplomatic game by Indian rules, because treaty protocol became a tool for exerting influence. Wherever the fall in native numbers and the Indians' dependence on trade tipped the balance of power toward the English, native diplomatic formulas became a means of wielding that power. Skillfully employed, diplomacy was a vehicle not only for contracting alliances and settling differences but also for issuing threats, acquiring land, and, as one governor phrased it, putting "a Bridle in the Mouths of our Indians." It is true that for the Five Nations[j] treaty councils were "a species of drama in which the Iroquois were the playwrights, the directors and the teaching actors"; but with Indians along the coast in the seventeenth century, Anglo-Americans had begun to direct the play themselves, and, before 1800, more distant groups also found that the path between peoples was becoming a one-way street, the chain was becoming fetters.[56]

With even the pretense of equality stripped away, function followed form; diplomatic relations became less negotiation than protection and, finally, less protection than subjection. The time devoted to hearing a tributary's complaints and the energy spent redressing grievances dwindled with the years, and enforcement of treaty rights, never very rigorous, fell still lower on the public agenda. In the end, diplomacy was a way to build a paper prison. Treaties stipulated that the selection of headmen be supervised, contacts with other native groups curtailed, and the tribe confined to certain lands. Some of these clauses were difficult to enforce in the backwaters where Settlement Indians commonly lived, and old habits proved hard to break. Nonetheless, even where traditional chiefs still held sway and people still slipped off to fight old enemies or visit old friends, they did so knowing that they could be called to account through the same diplomatic channels that once had brought English crown and Indian tribe together as equals on a stage arranged according to native custom.

V

It was a fundamental tenet of the faith English colonists brought to America that belief and behavior were two sides of the same coin, that civilization must accompany – indeed, it must precede – Christianity. The law could not dictate belief, but it could do something about behavior. In 1646, a week after skeptical Indians heckled a Puritan minister during a sermon, Massachusetts Bay passed a law against blasphemy by anyone, Christian or pagan. Six years later, Plymouth legislators forbade Indians from working on the Sabbath, and in 1675 Connecticut went even further, not only insisting that natives honor the Sabbath but requiring their "ready and comely attendance" whenever preachers held services for them.[57] Once the law had stopped Indians from working or heckling and got them to pay attention, it was up to missionaries to do the rest.

The missionary's ability to win an Indian audience for Christ depended largely on where that audience was. Tribes beyond the frontier were for the most part indifferent to the Christian message as translated by the English, in part because English clergymen, unlike the Jesuits operating in New France, rarely visited Indian Country to spread the word.[58] In New England, every minister was tied to a particular congregation and therefore could not venture too far away in search of converts. But even men recruited to do the Lord's work among remote tribes tended to hug the coast. Clergymen sent to South Carolina in the early eighteenth century by the Society for the Propagation of the Gospel in Foreign Parts to "propagate Christianity ... among the wild Indians in the woods" found some excuse – rumblings of war among those distant peoples, plenty of pagans close at hand among the colonial population – to postpone their mission. Few went beyond asking traders about the best tribes to approach and having the Lord's Prayer translated into Yamasee or Shawnee for future use. In Virginia the story was much the same. "The missionaries that are now sent," reported the Anglican cleric Hugh Jones in 1724, "generally keep among the English, and rarely see an Indian."[59]

Reluctance to head into the interior may have stemmed from a lack of nerve, but it also could have arisen from a sense that Indians there were not very fertile soil for sowing the English version of Christianity. Jesuits with a tolerance for native ways, a gift for languages, and a religion rich in symbol and ritual enjoyed considerable success. English Protestants, on the other hand, usually lacked the delicate touch needed to convert distant Indians. They "know but little how to manage them [Indians]," Jones remarked; "for you may as well talk reason, philosophy, or divinity to a block, as to them, unless you perfectly understand their temper, and know how to humour them." If a missionary did make the effort, he discovered that natives beyond the frontier were uninterested in the gospel according to the English, especially when they found out that conversion entailed political subjection and cultural suicide. Some reacted with open scorn, laughing or going so far as "flatly to say, that our Lord God was not God, since hee suffered us to sustaine much hunger, and also to be killed of the Renapoaks." Others listened politely and walked away. Still others were ready to grant that Christianity was fine for the English but not for Indians, who preferred a different way.[60] "We are Indians," they would say when pressed, "and don't wish to be transformed into white men.... As little as we desire the preacher to become Indian, so little ought he to desire the Indians to become preachers."[61]

Settlement Indians were more susceptible to the missionary's message. Confidence in their own cultural traditions had been badly shaken by demographic disaster; who could doubt the power of the Englishman's God when Indians mysteriously died by the score and colonists did not even become ill? The awe an epidemic could inspire was clear from the very beginning of the English colonial venture. At Roanoke, where disease visited every native town that opposed the English beachhead and "the people began to die very fast," colonists reported that survivors were "perswaded that it was the worke of our God through our meanes, and that wee by him might kil and slai whom wee would without weapons and not come neere them." Once the colonists' more conventional weapons had defeated Indians in battle, the newcomers further sapped native commitment to ancient deities and added to the growing evidence of the Christian God's power.[62]

Defeated and surrounded, these internal colonies were reminded of the weakness of their spiritual powers in incidents less dramatic but perhaps no less significant than losses to disease or combat. Take, for example, a confrontation in Stonington, Connecticut, between an English colonist named Thomas Stanton and an Indian shaman from Long Island who had come over to bewitch a local native. When Stanton defended the Indian, the shaman "grew still more high and positive in his language, until he told Mr. Stanton he could immediately tare his house in pieces, and himself flye out at the top of the chimney." Unimpressed, Stanton grabbed the shaman, tied him up, and "whipped him until he promised to desist and go home." Local Indians who had gathered outside to watch now waited expectantly for the house to be torn apart by the forces the shaman could summon. Nothing happened, and at last they "went away much Surprised."[63] In such surprises lay the seeds of doubt, and they left conquered natives more ready to listen and more likely to be convinced.

But if practically all Christian Indians were Settlement Indians, not all Settlement Indians were Christian. Many lived among colonists for years without being approached and offered the opportunity to convert. In New England, where English missionaries were most active, no more than twenty Congregational clergymen attempted to spread the gospel among the Indians even on a part-time basis. Connecticut was particularly slow to act; its 1675 law requiring polite attention to any minister who visited the natives was a dead letter, for few if any ministers bothered. A traveler passing through the colony in 1704 found "every where in the Towns as I passed, a Number of Indians …, the most salvage of all the salvages of that kind [Settlement Indians] that I had ever Seen: little or no care taken (as I heard upon enquiry) to make them otherwise."[64]

Those neighboring Indians who *were* offered the chance to convert sometimes turned it down. Narragansetts, Mohegans, and other groups defeated in King Philip's War wanted nothing to do with the religion of the victors, and well into the eighteenth century they spurned missionary overtures. In South Carolina, clergymen in coastal parishes conversed regularly with "Neighbouring Indians," but found these remnant groups unlikely candidates for conversion. They "are a moving People," one reported, "often changing their place of habitation so that I can give no account of their Number" – much less the state of their souls. Prodding them did no good, for they seemed "wholy addicted to their own barbarous and Sloathful Customs and will only give a laugh w[he]n pleased or a grin w[he]n displeas'd for an Answer." "It must be the work of time and power that must have any happy Influence upon em," one would-be savior concluded glumly.[65]

Some were willing to spend more time and wield more power in the crusade for Christ, but even they found it difficult to exert much influence. The least successful tended to be those who expected the most, who insisted that civility and Christianity go hand in hand. John Eliot's Massachusetts praying towns were the classic example. Here, Eliot predicted, natives seeking Christ would be isolated from the corrupting influence of other Indians or of colonists, here they could be instructed in the finer points of faith and civility, and here carefully watched to ensure that the lessons – from length of hair to cut of coat to knowledge of Christ's teachings – had been learned. In the third quarter of the seventeenth century, Eliot established fourteen of these villages, brought more than 1,000 Indians to live in them, and translated the Bible into Algonquian. By his own admission, however, few praying Indians actually mastered his difficult course of instruction well enough to pass the stringent requirements for church membership in Puritan New England. His hopes that the future would yield a more abundant harvest of souls were dashed when many of his charges joined King Philip's war parties and many of the rest ended up imprisoned on an island in Boston Harbor, kept there by a populace convinced that Eliot's experiment was a failure.[66]

Plans to isolate and educate individual Indians rather than

whole towns enjoyed still less success. Harvard's Indian College, built in the mid-1650s, housed only a handful of native students (more of whom died at the school than graduated from it) before being torn down four decades later. Its counterpart at William and Mary, the Brafferton building, housed many more pupils, but none lived up to expectations. Upon completing the course of instruction and going home, wrote William Byrd II, "instead of civilizing and converting the rest, they have immediately relapsed into infidelity and barbarism themselves." Similarly, Eleazar Wheelock's grand schemes for schooling Indians ended up as Dartmouth, a college for colonial boys, after a series of failures that left its founder deeply embittered. "It grieves and breaks my heart," Wheelock wrote in 1768 after fourteen years of trying, "that while I am wearing my life out to do good to the poor Indians, they themselves have no more Desire to help forward the great Design of their Happiness... . [There] are so many of them pulling the other way and as fast as they can undoing all I have done." From John Eliot onward, others who adopted a strict approach to Indian conversion felt the same sense of frustration.[67]

A few missionaries took a different tack among Settlement Indians and were better rewarded. The work of the Mayhew family on Martha's Vineyard offers the best contrast in both method and result. The Mayhews were unusually well versed in native culture, and rather than demand immediate, sweeping changes in Indian habits, they were willing to accept slow progress toward English notions of civility. Upon their arrival in the 1640s they encountered a native population still relatively intact but well aware that English colonists had just destroyed the Pequots not far away on the mainland. Added to these promising ingredients were certain fortuitous (Mayhew called them providential) events – diseases spared Christian Indians, lightning struck a sachem[k] who had mocked a convert – that made skeptics into believers. The result was a swift, widespread, and deeply rooted commitment to Christianity, a commitment that Eliot, laboring away on the mainland, could only envy and try to claim for himself.[68]

The Mayhews' formula also worked elsewhere. In 1714 Virginia lieutenant governor Alexander Spotswood set up a mission at a frontier fort that was as promising as it was undemanding. Children of tributary Indians trooped into Charles Griffin's classroom by day and returned to their nearby village at night. In school they learned to recite prayers; at home they mastered the war dance, complete with "antic motions, and hideous cries." Whether Griffin could have become another Mayhew will never be known; after a few years, political squabbles in Williamsburg dismantled Spotswood's school. More impressive and more enduring results came during the Great Awakening, when New England Indians long resistant to any strain of the Christian faith changed their minds. These holdouts responded enthusiastically to preachers who had the oratorical skill, the emotional performance, the disdain for doctrinal detail, and the tolerance of congregational participation that corresponded to the natives' own religious traditions.[69]

After more than a century, the missionary campaign had enjoyed mixed results. On the one hand, signs of progress were clear: in New England at one time or another more than a score of Indian churches had been built, nearly one hundred praying towns or reservations organized, and even more natives had become teachers or preachers. On the other hand, however, those bent on wiping out every stain of paganism were disappointed. Too many Indians remained outside the fold, and those within it had entered on their own terms, shaping the new religion to serve their spiritual and cultural needs. Far from making Indians English, the new faith (where natives embraced it) proved to be a powerful revitalizing force, helping people to cope with defeat and dispossession, to rebuild their aboriginal communities on a new foundation.[70]

VI

In the end it proved easier to kill Indians than convert them, easier to make them speak English than make them listen to a sermon, easier to get them into a courtroom than into a church, easier to bring them to acknowledge the English king than the English God. The missionary's failure to see his dreams become reality is a useful reminder that natives were neither the "Indian dust" one early New Englander envisioned nor the "soft Wax, ready to take any Impression" that a Virginian described.[71] Far from crumbling and being swept aside or passively receiving everything the English handed them, Indians learned to conform to the new "Customes of the Countrey" without surrendering unconditionally to the country's new rulers.

It was not easy. Some tribes fought, some fled. Others stayed behind and protested the invasion of America in their own way, stealing a colonial school's Latin and Greek books or burning a planter's fences, acts some have termed "purely whimsical" but that may have had symbolic significance.[72] Still others made their feelings known by refusing to abide by colonial customs. The problem in the Massachusetts praying town of Natick was as simple as saying "Hello." Waban, the community's first headman and one of John Eliot's converts, won praise for greeting colonists "with English salutations." But some inhabitants of Natick would not follow Waban's lead. In 1680 they were "refusing to take notice of an Englishman if they meet him in the street," and decades later one holdout, Hannah Pittimee, still "past by ... with a great deal of scorn ... with her face turned right from us."[73]

Pittimee and every other Settlement Indian had reason to be scornful, for those natives living behind the frontier faced a future of poverty and oppression. As their resources disappeared and their skills eroded, natives searched desperately for ways to put food in their mouths and a roof over their heads. The search sometimes led to an ancestor's grave, which Indians ransacked for the valuable wampum it contained. Not everyone was driven to such lengths, but almost all struggled to scrape together the necessities of life, and they did so amid the insults, the laughter, the abuses spawned by the conquerors' hatred. Sometimes that hatred was disclosed only by a slip of the pen: a clerk in a Massachusetts court referred to an Indian as "it," and a Philadelphia scribe wrote that the spectators at a council consisted of "many other People and Indians."[74] More often the colonists' feelings were easier to detect. Young Indian apprentices discovered that "their fellow Prentices viz. English Boys will dispise them and treat them as Slaves." The colonial youths picked up this attitude from their parents, who openly doubted that anything besides "Powder and Ball" would convert the natives, and, acting on that belief, placed only "a Bullet and Flynt" in a missionary's collection plate. Even colonists with good intentions inflicted their own kind of pain. When the evangelist George Whitefield's colleague Benjamin Ingham built a schoolhouse for Indians atop an ancient temple mound near Savannah, Georgia, he dismissed the local Creeks' spiritual attachment to the site and insisted that it now serve a different deity.[75]

But if neighboring Indians did not prosper, they did survive. One secret of their survival was the ability they had to make themselves inconspicuous. When drinking, for example, they aped their English neighbors. "It rent my heart as well as ears," wrote one Virginian in the 1680s, "when once passing by a company of Indians in James City, that drinking in a ring were deplorably drunk ... one cried to another swear swear, you be Englishman swear, w[i]th that he made a horrid yelling, imperfectly vomited up oaths, whereupon the other cryd, oh! now your [sic] be Englishman."[76]

Natives learning to drink and curse like an Englishman were also learning to dress like one, and this camouflage, too, was crucial to their survival. Simply putting on English clothes was not enough; one had to know how to wear them. A century after John Smith, Virginia Indians had not yet mastered the art. "They were ridiculously dressed," a colonist noted in 1702. "One had a shirt on with a crown on his head, another a coat and neither trousers, stockings nor shoes." The Indian "queen" was better dressed, in "nice clothes of a French pattern," but still "they were not put on right. One thing was too large, another too small, hence it did not fit." By the end of the colonial period Virginia Indians had conformed to what colonists considered "right." "They commonly dress like the Virginians," the traveler Andrew Burnaby observed in 1759, and in fact they were so well disguised that Burnaby admitted he had "sometimes mistaken them for the lower sort of that people." Four years later, Indians living near Braintree, Massachusetts, had also perfected their disguise and were said to be "actually very often mistaken for English."[77]

As important as this mimetic talent was the ability to retain a distinctly Indian identity. Natives imitating colonists still stood out in subtle ways in every sphere of contact. For most, English was a second language, imperfectly mastered and used only for talking with colonists and slaves. In the mid-eighteenth century, one Rhode Island native woman's English vocabulary consisted of a single word – "broom" – and in Massachusetts confused colonists learned that the Braintree Indians' English disguise held up only "till you come to converse with them."[78] In material culture and economic pursuits, too, their conversion was less than complete. Many led a peripatetic life modeled on traditional habits of seasonal migration. From Etiwans in South Carolina to Naticks in Massachusetts, they were "strangely disposed and addicted to wander from place to place." If they did come to lead what colonists considered a settled existence, Indians still might depart from colonial norms. One built an English frame house but no chimney, preferring to rely on an open fire; others put brick fireplaces into their wigwams; still others bought tea tables, dressers, chairs, and other articles commonly found in colonial households, then placed the furniture in the domed dwellings they made out of bark and saplings.[79]

The same habit of blending into the landscape of English America without becoming wholly invisible can be seen in diplomacy, law, and religion. Though native enclaves might be "little Tribes," tribes they were, not mere aggregates of individuals or a vaguely defined ethnic group. However unequal the terms of diplomacy had become, Indians with their own corporate identity and cadre of leaders were equipped to deal with colonial politicians on a diplomatic footing. They were also in a position to police themselves, and many continued to settle their own disputes. In 1704, some Settlement Indians in New England were "Govern'd by Law's of their own making." "If the natives committt any crime on their own precincts among themselves, the English takes no Cognezens of it," and the same was true of South Carolina's Indians more than a century later.[80] Finally, and perhaps most important, the Christianity that some remnant groups used as the new foundation for an ancient identity remained distinct from its English progenitor. The sharing of tobacco during services on Martha's Vineyard incorporated old rituals into a new ceremonial context, and in Rhode Island the Narragansetts's August Meeting – several days of services, feasts, and dances – harked back to a traditional harvest festival.[81] In all of these ways, Indians managed to pacify the powerful without losing all sense of a unique past – and a separate future.

This adaptive talent was present from the first. In 1634 – the very year Calvert and the Wicomiss were meeting along the Chesapeake – it was already on display in New England, where William Wood and two companions got lost on the way to Plymouth, "being deluded by a misleading path." It was, the travelers thought, too wide to be an Indian trail, but they were wrong. They had been fooled because "the dayly concourse of *Indians* from the *Naragansets* who traded for shooes, wearing them homewards had made this *Indian* tract like an *English* walke, and had rear'd up great stickes against the trees, and marked the rest with their hatchets in the *English* fashion, which begat in us a security of our wrong way to be right."[82] Like Narragansetts, Indians throughout the East who might look English were in fact following, indeed carving, paths that took them toward another destination. Learning to survive as a conquered people by combining European and aboriginal ways: this was the fate in store for every native group as the English and other migrants from the Old World pushed deeper into the heart of the American continent.

EDITOR'S NOTES

a *Roanoke* is the local name for what is more generally known as wampum, i.e. strings of shell beads, which were highly valued by all coastal Indians and served as a medium of exchange.

b John Lawson was an English explorer, who was killed by the Tuscaroras in 1711.

c Dr. Alexander Hamilton, a Scottish physician resident in Annapolis, Maryland, toured the northern colonies in 1744.

d The "Turner thesis" argues the "free land" of the western frontier encouraged the growth of democracy, capitalism, and individualism in America.

e Powhatan (1540s?–1618), chief of the Pamunkeys, named for his main fortified village near the James River falls, created a Confederacy of Virginia Indians. His brother and successor, Opechancanough (fl. 1607–44), was responsible for the famous 1622 and 1644 uprisings which killed many Virginia colonists.

f Pidgin languages were rudimentary trade languages that arose between peoples who were otherwise unintelligible to one another.

g Roger Williams (1603–83), founder of Rhode Island.

h Samson Occom (1723–92) played a leading role in obtaining support in England for the Indian Charity School which evolved into Dartmouth College.

i In 1677 the Iroquois League of Five Nations allied themselves to the British in a multiparty confederation known as the Covenant Chain. They also affiliated other tribes directly to their League and thus indirectly to the Chain.

j The Five Iroquois Nations were the Senecas, Cayugas, Onondagas, Oneidas, and Mohawks.

k A sachem was a leader or representative responsible for carrying out or coordinating group rather than family or individual concerns.

NOTES

Reprinted from *Strangers Within the Realm: Cultural Margins of the First British Empire*, edited by Bernard Bailyn and Philip D. Morgan (Chapel Hill, N.C., 1991). © 1991 The University of North Carolina Press. Used by permission of the author and publisher.

1 "A Relation of Maryland, 1635," in Clayton Colman Hall, ed., *Narratives of Early Maryland, 1633–1684* (New York, 1925): 88–90.

2 John Lawson, *A New Voyage to Carolina*, ed. Hugh Talmage Lefler (Chapel Hill, N.C., 1967): 6, 22, 39, 43–5, 58.

3 Carl Bridenbaugh, ed., *Gentleman's Progress: The Itinerarium of Dr. Alexander Hamilton,* 1744 (Chapel Hill, N.C., 1948): 98, 110.
4 Marion Tinling, ed., *The Correspondence of the Three William Byrds of Westover, Virginia, 1684–1776* (Charlottesville, Va., 1977): I, 136; *Minutes of the Provincial Council of Pennsylvania, from the Organization to the Termination of the Proprietary Government,* 10 vols. (Philadelphia, Harrisburg, Pa., 1851–2): V, 119, 122; VII, 6.
5 William P. Cumming, ed., *The Discoveries of John Lederer* .... (Charlottesville, Va., 1958): 41, 42 ("remoter"). Joseph Ewan and Nesta Ewan, eds., *John Banister and his Natural History of Virginia, 1678–1692* (Urbana, Ill., 1970): 385 ("neighbor"). James Axtell, *The Invasion Within: The Contest of Cultures in Colonial North America* (New York, 1985): 206 ("little Tribes" and "back nations"). Jane Henry, "The Choptank Indians of Maryland under the Proprietary Government," *Maryland Historical Magazine,* LXV (1970): 179; Samuel Cole Williams, ed., *Adair's History of the American Indians* (New York, 1974 [orig. pub. 1930]): 369 ("domestic"). Kathleen Joan Bragdon, "Crime and Punishment among the Indians of Massachusetts, 1675–1750," *Ethnohistory,* XXVIII (1981): 23 ("plantation"), 25 ("strange"). Yasuhide Kawashima, "Indians and Southern Colonial Statutes," *Indian Historian,* VII (1974): 11 ("resident"). Chapman J. Milling, *Red Carolinians* (Columbia, S.C., 1969 [orig. pub. 1940]): 62 ("Settlement"). Robert Maule to Mr. Chamberlaine, Aug. 2, 1711, Great Britain, Society for the Propagation of the Gospel in Foreign Parts, ser. A, VII, 364 (microfilm, Library of Congress). Edward McM. Larrabee, *Recurrent Themes and Sequences in North American Indian–European Culture Contact,* APS, *Transactions,* n.s., LXVI, pt. 7 (Philadelphia, 1976): 11 ("wilder"). Daniel Gookin, "Historical Collections of the Indians in New England ... ," Massachusetts Historical Society, *Collections,* 1st ser., I (Boston, 1806 [orig. pub. 1792]): 156 ("Inland"). Wesley Frank Craven, *White, Red, and Black: The Seventeenth-Century Virginian* (New York, 1977): 60 ("foreign").
6 Lawson, *New Voyage:* 23; "Letter of Abraham Wood to John Richards, August 22, 1674," in Clarence Walworth Alvord and Lee Bidgood, eds., *The First Explorations of the Trans-Allegheny Region by the Virginians, 1650–1674* (Cleveland, Ohio, 1912): 213; Bridenbaugh, *Gentleman's Progress:* 34, 172.
7 Lawson, *New Voyage:* 46, 47, 62, 176; Ewan and Ewan, eds., *Banister and his Natural History:* 382; and Robert Beverley, *The History and Present State of Virginia,* ed. Louis B. Wright (Chapel Hill, N.C., 1947): 182 (spoons); Allen W. Trelease, *Indian Affairs in Colonial New York: The Seventeenth Century* (Ithaca, N.Y., 1960): 169–70 (prayers); William Wood, *Wood's New-England's Prospect,* Burt Franklin, Research and Source Works Series, no. 131 (New York, 1967 [orig. pub. Boston, 1865, Publications of the Prince Society, III]): 72.
8 William J. Hinke, trans. and ed., "Report of the Journey of Francis Louis Michel from Berne, Switzerland, to Virginia, October 2, 1701–December 1, 1702," *Virginia Magazine of History and Biography,* XXIV (1916): 132–4 (speech and dress); William Byrd, *The Prose Works of William Byrd of Westover: Narratives of a Colonial Virginian,* ed. Louis B. Wright (Cam-

bridge, Mass., 1966): 316; and Edward Porter Alexander, ed., *The Journal of John Fontaine: An Irish Huguenot Son in Spain and Virginia, 1710–1719* (Williamsburg, Va., 1972): 99 (horses); Bragdon, "Crime and Punishment": 24; and Francis Jennings, *The Invasion of America: Indians, Colonialism, and the Cant of Conquest* (Chapel Hill, N.C., 1975): 241 (laws).

9 Quoted in Kathleen J. Bragdon, " 'Emphaticall Speech and Great Action': An Analysis of Seventeenth-Century Native Speech Events Described in Early Sources," *Man in the Northeast*, no. 33 (Spring 1987): 106.

10 Neal Salisbury, *Manitou and Providence: Indians, Europeans, and the Making of New England, 1500–1643* (New York, 1982): 52; Douglas Edward Leach, *Flintlock and Tomahawk: New England in King Philip's War* (New York, 1966 [orig. pub. 1958]): 243, 247.

11 Quotations in Jennings, *Invasion of America*: 28; and Craven, *White, Red, and Black*: 65. For warfare, see Sherburne F. Cook, "Interracial Warfare and Population Decline among the New England Indians," *Ethnohistory*, XX (1973): 1–24; Hugh T. Lefler and William S. Powell, *Colonial North Carolina: A History* (New York, 1973): 78.

12 On Indian deaths: Sherburne F. Cook, "The Significance of Disease in the Extinction of the New England Indians," *Human Biology*, XLV (1973): 501. Alden Vaughan places the figure of combat losses at 15–20 percent of the population (*New England Frontier: Puritans and Indians, 1620–1675*, rev. ed. [New York, 1979]: 329). For a general discussion of disease, see Jennings, *Invasion of America*: chap. 2; J. Leitch Wright, Jr., *The Only Land They Knew: The Tragic Story of the American Indians in the Old South* (New York, 1981): 22–6; James Axtell, "The English Colonial Impact on Indian Culture," in Axtell, *The European and the Indian: Essays in the Ethnohistory of Colonial North America* (New York, 1981): 248–53; Alfred W. Crosby, "Virgin Soil Epidemics as a Factor in the Aboriginal Depopulation in America," *William and Mary Quarterly*, 3rd ser., XXXIII (1976): 289–99.

13 Jennings, *Invasion of America*: 26; Beverley, *History*: 232–3.

14 J. Leitch Wright, Jr., *Britain and the American Frontier, 1783–1815* (Athens, Ga., 1975): 3; Francis Daniel Pastorius, "Circumstantial Geographical Description of Pennsylvania" (1700), in Albert Cook Myers, ed., *Narratives of Early Pennsylvania, West New Jersey, and Delaware, 1630–1707* (New York, 1912): 410–11.

15 Alexander Spotswood to the Board of Trade, Dec. 22, 1718, PRO, CO 5/1318, 590–1 (Lib. of Cong. transcripts: 488).

16 Samuel Hazard, comp., *Pennsylvania Archives: Selected and Arranged from Original Documents in the Office of the Secretary of the Commonwealth*, 1st ser., 12 vols. (Philadelphia, 1852–6): III, 548. I estimate the timing from my own work (James H. Merrell, *The Indians' New World: Catawbas and their Neighbors from European Contact through the Era of Removal* [Chapel Hill, N.C., 1989]: chaps. 2–4); and from Peter A. Thomas, "Cultural Change on the Southern New England Frontier, 1630–1665," in William H. Fitzhugh, ed., *Cultures in Contact: The Impact of European Contacts on Native American Cultural Institutions,*

A.D. 1000–1800, Anthropological Society of Washington Series (Washington, D.C., 1985): 131–61.

17 Pastorius, "Geographical Description," *Narratives of Pennsylvania*: 410; Frank J. Klingberg, ed., *The Carolina Chronicle of Dr. Francis Le Jau, 1706–1717*, University of California Publications in History, no. 53 (Berkeley, Calif., 1956): 78; Wilbur R. Jacobs, ed., *Indians of the Southern Colonial Frontier: The Edmond Atkin Report and Plan of 1755* (Columbia, S.C., 1954): 47; Hazard, comp., *Penn. Arch.*, 1st ser., II, 214. For general discussions of settlers, see William Cronon, *Changes in the Land: Indians, Colonists, and the Ecology of New England* (New York, 1983); Merrell, *Indians' New World*: chaps. 5–6.

18 Salisbury, *Manitou and Providence*: 106; James Axtell, "Last Rights: The Acculturation of Native Funerals in Colonial North America," in Axtell, *European and Indian*: 110–28; James H. Merrell, "Cultural Continuity among the Piscataway Indians of Colonial Maryland," *William and Mary Quarterly*, 3rd ser., XXXVI (1979): 561; Robinson *et al.*, "Narragansett Cemetery," *Cultures in Contact*: 108–9, 122–4.

19 For Ireland, see Nicholas P. Canny, "The Ideology of Colonization: From Ireland to America," *William and Mary Quarterly*, 3rd ser., XXX (1973): 575–95.

20 Roger Williams, *A Key into the Language of America; or, An Help to the Language of the Natives in That Part of America Called New-England ... ,* Rhode Island Historical Society, *Collections*, I (Providence, R.I., 1827): 95, III; Charles T. Gehring and Robert S. Grumet, eds., "Observations of the Indians from Jasper Danckaerts's Journal, 1679–1680," *William and Mary Quarterly*, 3rd ser., XLIV (1987): 109; Lawson, *New Voyage*: 184.

21 Quoted in Trelease, *Indian Affairs*: 39; Robert Maule to Mr. Chamberlaine, Aug. 2, 1711, SPG, ser. A, VII, 363 (microfilm, Lib. of Cong.); Lawson, *New Voyage*: 239, 240.

22 Lawson, *New Voyage*: 233; Gookin, "Historical Collections": 221–2.

23 Quoted in Stephen J. Greenblatt, "Learning to Curse: Aspects of Linguistic Colonialism in the Sixteenth Century," in Fredi Chiappelli, ed., *First Images of America: The Impact of the New World on the Old* (Berkeley, Calif., 1976): II, 561.

24 See Salisbury, *Manitou and Providence*: 53; and J. Frederick Fausz, "Present at the 'Creation': The Chesapeake World that Greeted the Maryland Colonists," *Maryland Historical Magazine*, LXXIX (1984): 17; "The Discovery of New Brittaine, 1650," *Narratives of Carolina*: 9; "Relation of Hilton," ibid.: 41, 51.

25 Ewan and Ewan, eds., *Banister and his Natural History*: 384; Beverley, *History*: 160–1, 190; *Discoveries of Lederer*: 13; Lawson, *New Voyage*: 48; Mary A. Druke, "Iroquois Treaties: Common Forms, Varying Interpretations," in Francis Jennings *et al.*, eds., *The History and Culture of Iroquois Diplomacy: An Interdisciplinary Guide to the Treaties of the Six Nations and their League* (Syracuse, N.Y., 1985): 89; Thomas Elliot Norton, *The Fur Trade in Colonial New York, 1686–1776* (Madison, Wis., 1974): 29–30.

26 Karen Ordahl Kupperman, *Roanoke: The Abandoned Colony* (Totowa, N.J., 1984): 17; Frank T. Siebert, Jr., "Resurrecting Virginia Algonquian from the Dead: The Reconstituted and Historical Phonology of

Powhatan," in James M. Crawford, ed., *Studies in Southeastern Indian Languages* (Athens, Ga., 1975): 292.

27 "Relation of Hilton," *Narratives of Carolina*: 50–1.

28 Quoted in Lois M. Feister, "Linguistic Communication between the Dutch and Indians in New Netherland, 1609–1664" *Ethnohistory*, XX (1973): 32–3.

29 ibid.: 33–7; J. Frederick Fausz, "Middlemen in Peace and War: Virginia's Earliest Indian Interpreters, 1608–1632," *Virginia Magazine of History and Biography*, XCV (1987): 41–64; Wood, *New-England's Prospect*: 103; quoted in Feister, "Linguistic Communication": 31.

30 Merrell, "Cultural Continuity": 557; "Virginia Colonial Records: Commissions, Bacon's Rebellion, etc.," *Virginia Magazine of History and Biography*, XIV (1906–1907): 294; Klingberg, ed., *Carolina Chronicle*: 68.

31 Edmund Berkeley and Dorothy S. Berkeley, eds., "Another 'Account of Virginia,' by the Reverend John Clayton," *Virginia Magazine of History and Biography*, LXXVI (1968): 434; Alexander, ed., *Journal of Fontaine*: 93; William Waller Hening, ed., *The Statutes at Large: Being a Collection of the Laws of Virginia ...*, IV (Richmond, Va., 1820): 461.

32 Beverley, *History*: 190; Larrabee, *Recurrent Themes*, APS, Trans., n.s., XVI, pt. 7, 7.

33 Lawson, *New Voyage*: 57; "John Clayton's Transcript of the Journal of Robert Fallam," *First Explorations*: 191; Williams, *Key into the Language*: 66.

34 *Penn. Ccl. Minutes*, IV, 708; William N. Fenton, "Structure, Continuity, and Change in the Process of Iroquois Treaty Making," *Iroquois Diplomacy*: 26; Druke, "Iroquois Treaties": 86–8.

35 *Penn. Ccl. Minutes*, III, 189, VIII, 212; Gookin, "Historical Collections," 197–8; Laurie Weinstein, " 'We're Still Living on our Traditional Homeland': The Wampanoag Legacy in New England," in Frank W. Porter III, ed., *Strategies for Survival: American Indians in the Eastern United States*, Contributions in Ethnic Studies, no. 15 (Westport, Conn., 1986): 92; Bragdon, "Native Speech Events," *Man in the Northeast*, no. 33 (Spring 1987): 107–8.

36 Lawson, *New Voyage*: 233–9; Edward P. Alexander, "An Indian Vocabulary from Fort Christanna, 1716," *Virginia Magazine of History and Biography*, LXXIX (1971): 309–10; Wood, *New-England's Prospect*: 111–16; Williams, *Key into the Language*, esp. chap. 25. The following analysis of trade is indebted to Axtell, "English Colonial Impact," in Axtell, *European and Indian*: 253–65; Jennings, *Invasion of America*: chap. 6; Salisbury, *Manitou and Providence*: chaps. 2, 5; Cronon, *Changes in the Land*: chap. 5; Richard White, *The Roots of Dependency: Subsistence, Environment, and Social Change among the Choctaws, Pawnees, and Navajos* (Lincoln, Nebr., 1983): pt. I; Christopher L. Miller and George R. Hamell, "A New Perspective on Indian–White Contact: Cultural Symbols and Colonial Trade," *Journal of American History*, LXXIII (1986–7): 311–28.

37 Salisbury, *Manitou and Providence*: 52–3; Cronon, *Changes in the Land*: 83; Cumming, ed., *Discoveries of Lederer*: 42; Miller and Hamell, "Cultural Symbols": 315–18. Quotations from Wood, *New-England's Prospect*: 88; Williams, *Key into the Language*: 135; Albright G. Zimmerman,

"European Trade Relations in the Seventeenth and Eighteenth Centuries," *Delaware Indian Symposium*: 66.

38 Williams, *Key into the Language*: 134; Merrell, "Indians' New World," *William and Mary Quarterly*, 3rd ser., XLI (1984): 549; Norton, *Fur Trade in New York*: 31; Trelease, *Indian Affairs*: 49; Axtell, "English Colonial Impact," *European and Indian*: 254–5; Ted J. Brasser, *Riding on the Frontier's Crest: Mahican Indian Culture and Culture Change*, National Museum of Man, Mercury Series, Ethnology Division, paper no. 13 (Ottawa, 1974): 16; Vaughan, *New England Frontier*: 220; John Phillip Reid, *A Better Kind of Hatchet: Law, Trade, and Diplomacy in the Cherokee Nation during the Early Years of European Contact* (University Park, Pa., 1976): 38, 84; Patrick M. Malone, "Changing Military Technology among the Indians of Southern New England, 1600–77," *American Quarterly*, XXV (1973): 52.

39 Salisbury, *Manitou and Providence*, 52–4; Cronon, *Changes in the Land*: 83; Cumming, ed., *Discoveries of Lederer*: 42.

40 Quoted in Zimmerman, "European Trade Relations": 62, 66.

41 John Brickell, *The Natural History of North-Carolina* (Dublin, 1737; rpt. 1911): 119–20; Hinke, trans. and ed., "Journey of Michel," *Virginia Magazine of History and Biography*, XXIV (1916): 42 (deer). Theda Perdue, *Slavery and the Evolution of Cherokee Society, 1540–1866* (Knoxville, Tenn., 1979): chaps. 1–2; Wright, *Only Land They Knew*: chap. 6, and 221 (slaves). Cronon, *Changes in the Land*: 95–7, 102–3; Salisbury, *Manitou and Providence*: 147–52 (wampum).

42 Quoted in Merrell, "Indians' New World," *William and Mary Quarterly*, 3rd ser., XLI (1984): 553; William L. McDowell, Jr., ed., *Documents Relating to Indian Affairs, May 21, 1750–August 7, 1754* (Columbia, S.C., 1958): 453; Cadwallader Colden, *The History of the Five Indian Nations Depending on the Province of New-York in America* (Ithaca, N.Y., 1958): 66; W. Noel Sainsbury, comp., Records in the British Public Record Office Relating to South Carolina, 1663–1782, 36 vols. (microfilm, Columbia, S.C., 1955): XXIII, 125.

43 Priests: Lawson, *New Voyage*: 227–8; Beverley, *History*: 204–5. See also Ted J. Brasser, *A Basketful of Indian Culture Change*, National Museum of Man, Canadian Ethnology Service, Mercury Series, paper no. 22 (Ottawa, 1975): 15; Brasser, *Frontier's Crest*: 40.

Warriors: Richard R. Johnson, "The Search for a Usable Indian: An Aspect of the Defense of Colonial New England," *Journal of American History*, LXIV (1977–8): 623–51; Wright, *Only Land They Knew*: 87–8, 124, 166.

Farmers: Hinke, trans. and ed., "Journey of Michel": 122; Peter A. Thomas, "The Fur Trade, Indian Land, and the Need to Define Adequate 'Environmental' Parameters," *Ethnohistory*, XXVIII (1981): 359–79; Trelease, *Indian Affairs*: 44, 68, 189.

Hunters: Andrew Burnaby, *Travels through the Middle Settlements of North America, in the Years 1759 and 1760*, 3rd ed. (London, 1798), in Rufus Rockwell Wilson, ed., *Burnaby's Travels through North America* (New York, 1904): 62–3.

44 Trelease, *Indian Affairs*: 89–90; Vaughan, *New England Frontier*: 199–200.

45 See Brasser, *Basketful of Change*: 15–16, 21; Brasser, *Frontier's Crest*, 40; Porter, "Behind the Frontier," *Maryland Historical Magazine*, LXXV (1980): 46. For Samson Occom, see Axtell, *Invasion Within*: 204. John the Bowlmaker is mentioned in Wright, *Only Land They Knew*: 98, 162.

46 Wood, *New-England's Prospect*: 88

47 Brasser, *Frontier's Crest*: 33; John A. Sainsbury, "Indian Labor in Early Rhode Island," *New England Quarterly*, XLVIII (1975): 380–1; Wright, *Only Land They Knew*: 157–8; Trelease, *Indian Affairs*: 179.

48 Bridenbaugh, ed., *Gentleman's Progress*: 167–8.

49 Merrell, "Indians' New World": 553; Peter Wraxall, *An Abridgement of the Indian Affairs ... Transacted in the Colony of New York, from the Year 1678 to the Year 1751*, ed. Charles Howard McIlwain (Cambridge, Mass., 1915): 195; Sainsbury, comp., BPRO Recs. Relating to So. Car., XVIII, 85–6 (see also VII, 77–8; and Hazard, comp., *Penn. Arch.*, 1st ser., III, 486).

50 Kupperman, *Roanoke*; Philip L. Barbour, *The Three Worlds of Captain John Smith* (Boston, 1964); Salisbury, *Manitou and Providence*: chap. 4.

51 Merrell, "Cultural Continuity": 550; Cumming, ed., *Discoveries of Lederer*: 33. See also Hinke, trans. and ed., "Journey of Michel,": 129.

52 T. J. C. Brasser, "The Coastal Algonkians: People of the First Frontiers," in Eleanor Burke Leacock and Nancy Oestreich Lurie, eds., *North American Indians in Historical Perspective* (New York, 1971): 65; Jennings, *Invasion of America*: 115; Salisbury, *Manitou and Providence*: 42–7; Cronon, *Changes in the Land*: 59–60; John Phillip Reid, *A Law of Blood: The Primitive Law of the Cherokee Nation* (New York, 1970): chaps. 1–7; Douglas W. Boyce, "Did a Tuscarora Confederacy Exist?" in Charles M. Hudson, ed., *Four Centuries of Southern Indians* (Athens, Ga., 1975): 28–45. Quotation from A. S. Salley, Jr., indexer, *Records in the British Public Record Office Relating to South Carolina*, 5 vols. (Atlanta, Columbia, S.C., 1928–47): I, 117.

53 H. R. McIlwaine *et al.*, eds., *Executive Journals of the Council of Colonial Virginia*, 6 vols. (Richmond, Va., 1925–66): III, 412, 422; Lawson, *New Voyage*: 48–9; William L. McDowell, Jr., ed., *Documents Relating to Indian Affairs, 1754–1765* (Columbia, S.C., 1970): 35; Jacobs, ed., *Atkin Plan*: 49, 53; Williams, ed., *Adair's History*: 459–60.

54 Fenton, "Iroquois Treaty Making," *Iroquois Diplomacy*: 6; Francis Jennings, *The Ambiguous Iroquois Empire: The Covenant Chain Confederation of Indian Tribes with English Colonies from its Beginning to the Lancaster Treaty of 1744* (New York, 1984); Druke, "Iroquois Treaties," *Iroquois Diplomacy*: 85–98; Fenton, "Iroquois Treaty Making," *Iroquois Diplomacy*: 3–36; Michael K. Foster, "Another Look at the Function of Wampum in Iroquois–White Councils," *Iroquois Diplomacy*: 99–114; Reid, *Better Hatchet*: 135; Merrell, *Indians' New World*: 145–50. Quotations are from Merrell: 147; *Penn. Ccl. Minutes*: VI, 275.

55 *Penn Ccl. Minutes*: II, 606, VI, 284, VII, 48, 53, 226; South Carolina Upper House Journal, Feb. 3, 1722, in William Sumner Jenkins, comp., Records of the States of the United States (microfilm, Washington, D.C., 1949): S.C. A.1a, reel 1, unit 1, 166.

56 Sainsbury, comp., BPRO Recs. Relating to So. Car., XXIV, 74; Fenton,

"Iroquois Treaty Making," *Iroquois Diplomacy*: 7; Jennings, *Ambiguous Empire*: chap. 17. Dorothy V. Jones, *License for Empire: Colonialism by Treaty in Early America* (Chicago, 1982), dates this shift to the years after 1763.

57 Jennings, *Invasion of America*: 241; Ronda, "Red and White at the Bench: Indians and the Law in Plymouth Colony, 1620–1691," Essex Institute, *Historical Collections*, CX (1974): 209; Axtell, *Invasion Within*: 221.

58 Gary B. Nash, "Notes on the History of Seventeenth-Century Mission-ization in Colonial America," *American Indian Culture and Research Journal*, II, no. 2 (1978): 3–8; William S. Simmons, "The Great Awaken-ing and Indian Conversion in Southern New England," in William Cowan, ed., *Papers of the Tenth Algonquian Conference* (Ottawa, 1979): 26; Axtell, *Invasion Within*, 138–9, 220–1, 242.

59 "Documents concerning Rev. Samuel Thomas, 1702–1707," *South Carolina Historical and Genealogical Magazine*, V (1904): 43; Hugh Jones, *The Present State of Virginia ...*, ed. Richard L. Morton (Chapel Hill, N.C., 1956): 62.

60 Quotations in Jones, *Present State of Virginia*: 62; and Craven, *White, Red, and Black*: 53. For the Indian response, see James P. Ronda, " 'We Are Well as We Are': An Indian Critique of Seventeenth-Century Missions," *William and Mary Quarterly*, 3rd ser., XXXIV (1977): 66–82; Axtell, *Invasion Within*: 266, 284–5.

61 Quoted in Porter, "A Century of Accommodation," *Maryland Historical Magazine*, LXXIV (1979): 179.

62 Thomas Harriot, *A Briefe and True Report of the New Found Land of Virginia: The Complete 1590 Theodor De Bry Edition* (New York, 1972): 28.

63 William S. Simmons, "Southern New England Shamanism: An Ethno-graphic Reconstruction," in William Cowan, ed., *Papers of the Seventh Algonquian Conference* (Ottawa, 1976): 245–6; Axtell, *Invasion Within*: 229.

64 Henry W. Bowden and James P. Ronda, eds., *John Eliot's Indian Dia-logues: A Study in Cultural Interaction*, Contributions in American His-tory, no. 88 (Westport, Conn., 1980): 22–3, 26; "The Journal of Madam Knight," in Perry Miller and Thomas H. Johnson, eds., *The Puritans* (New York, 1938): 437. See Axtell, *Invasion Within*: 186–7, 220–1.

65 For New England, see Simmons, "Awakening and Indian Conver-sion," in Cowan, ed., *Papers of Tenth Conference*: 26–7; Simmons, "Red Yankees," *American Ethnologist*, X (1983): 260; Bowden and Ronda, eds., *Eliot's Dialogues*: 33, 40; Axtell, *Invasion Within*: 243–7. For South Caro-lina, see in SPG, Ser. A: Thomas Hasell to the Secretary, Apr. 15, 1724, XVIII, 72; Benjamin Dennis to the Secretary, Mar. 21, 1714, X, 83–4; Richard Ludlam to the Secretary, Mar. 22, 1725, XIX, 62.

66 See Vaughan, *New England Frontier*: chaps. 9–11; Jennings, *Invasion of America*: 232–53; Axtell, *Invasion Within*: chaps. 7, 9; R. Pierce Beaver, "Methods in American Missions to the Indians in the Seventeenth and Eighteenth Centuries: Calvinist Models for Protestant Foreign Missions," *Journal of Presbyterian History*, XLVII (1969): 134–6; Salisbury, "Red Puritans," *William and Mary Quarterly*, 3rd ser., XXXI (1974): 27–54; Salisbury, "Prospero in New England: The Puritan Missionary as

Colonist," in William Cowan, ed., *Papers of the Sixth Algonquian Conference, 1974* (Ottawa, 1975): 254–61; Morrison, "Coyning Christians," *Ethnohistory*, XXI (1974): 77–92.

67 Vaughan, *New England Frontier*: 281–4; Jennings, *Invasion of America*: 247–8; Axtell, *Invasion Within*: 182–3; Salisbury, "Red Puritans": 46–7; Beaver, "Methods in American Missions": 141 (Harvard). Wright, *Only Land They Knew*: 180, 185–7; Axtell, *Invasion Within*, 190–6; Byrd, *Prose Works*: 220–1 (quotation on 220); Jones, *Present State of Virginia*: 114; Gregory A. Stiverson and Patrick H. Butler III. eds., "Virginia in 1732: The Travel Journal of William Hugh Grove," *Virginia Magazine of History and Biography*, LXXXV (1977): 25 (William and Mary). The Wheelock quotation is in Margaret Connell Szasz, " 'Poor Richard' Meets the Native American: Schooling for Young Indian Women in Eighteenth-Century Connecticut," *Pacific Historical Review*, XLIX (1980): 235. See also Axtell, *Invasion Within*, 206–7.

68 William S. Simmons, "Conversion from Indian to Puritan," *New England Quarterly*, LII (1979): 197–218. See also Vaughan, *New England Frontier*: 242–4, 295–8; Jennings, *Invasion of America*: 230–1, 245–7; Salisbury, "Prospero in New England," in Cowan, ed., *Papers of Sixth Conference*: 261–6; James P. Ronda, "Generations of Faith: The Christian Indians of Martha's Vineyard," *William and Mary Quarterly*, 3rd ser., XXXVIII (1981): 369–94.

69 On Virginia: Alexander, ed., *Journal of Fontaine*: 90–8 (quotation on 98): Jones, *Present State of Virginia*: 59. For more pessimistic views of this experiment, see Wright, *Only Land They Knew*: 187–8; Axtell, *Invasion Within*: 192–3.
   On Great Awakening: Simmons, "Awakening and Indian Conversions," in Cowan, ed., *Papers of Tenth Conference*: 27–33; Simmons, "Red Yankees": 261–7.

70 Axtell, *Invasion Within*: 273; Axtell, "Some Thoughts on the Ethnohistory of Missions," *Ethnohistory*, XXIX (1982): 35–40.

71 Quoted in Salisbury, *Manitou and Providence*: 153; Beverley, *History*: 16 (Beverley was imagining the views of earlier colonists).

72 Bragdon, "Crime and Punishment": 27 (books); Inhabitants of the Waxhaws to Samuel Wyly, Apr. 16, 1759, encl. in Wyly to Gov. William Henry Lyttelton, Apr. 26, 1759, Lyttelton Papers, William Clements Library, Ann Arbor, Mich. (fences). The comment is Bragdon's, on the theft of the books.

73 Quoted in Morrison, "Coyning Christians": 81–2; and in Bragdon, "Crime and Punishment": 27.

74 John Witthoft, "Archaeology as a Key to the Colonial Fur Trade," in *Aspects of the Fur Trade: Selected Papers of the 1965 North American Fur Trade Conference* (St. Paul, Minn., 1967): 61; Yasuhide Kawashima, *Puritan Justice and the Indian: White Man's Law in Massachusetts, 1630–1763* (Middletown, Conn., 1986): 109; *Penn. Ccl. Minutes*: III, 167.

75 Axtell, *Invasion Within*: 210 (quotation); Wright, *Only Land They Knew*: 208–9.

76 Berkeley and Berkeley, eds., "Another 'Account of Virginia,' by Clayton": 436.

77 Hinke, trans. and ed., "Journey of Michel": 132–3; Burnaby, *Travels*: 62; Kawashima, *Puritan Justice*: 121 (quotation).
78 Simmons, "Red Yankees": 262; Kawashima, *Puritan Justice*: 121.
79 Bragdon, "Probate Records": 138 (quotation); William S. Simmons, *Spirit of the New England Tribes: Indian History and Folklore, 1620-1984* (Hanover, N.H., 1986): 19; Laurie Weinstein, "'We're Still Living on Our Traditional Homeland': The Wampanoag Legacy in New England," in Frank W. Porter III, ed., *Strategies for Survival: American Indians in the Eastern United States*, Contributions in Ethnic Studies, no. 15 (Westport, Conn., 1986): 91–2; Bragdon, "Probate Records": 137–8; Alden T. Vaughan and Daniel K. Richter, "Crossing the Cultural Divide: Indians and New Englanders, 1605–1763," American Antiquarian Society, *Proceedings*, XC (1980): 36–7; William C. Sturtevant, "Two 1761 Wigwams at Niantic, Connecticut," *American Antiquity*, XL (1975): 437–44.
80 "Journal of Knight," *The Puritans*: 437; Merrell, *Indians' New World*: 235–6.
81 Bragdon, "Native Speech Events," *Man in the Northeast*, no. 33 (Spring 1987): 108; Simmons, "Red Yankees": 263–4. See also James P. Ronda, "Generations of Faith: The Christian Indians of Martha's Vineyard," *WMQ*, 3rd ser., XXXVIII (1981): 369–94.
82 Wood, *New-England's Prospect*: 79.

4

TIME, SPACE, AND THE EVOLUTION OF AFRO-AMERICAN SOCIETY ON BRITISH MAINLAND NORTH AMERICA

Ira Berlin

In exploring the development of black life in British North America, Ira Berlin offers yet another way of characterizing its regional diversity. He identifies three provincial slave societies, grouping New England and the Mid-Atlantic into one Northern farm system, and then locating two Southern plantation systems, one in the Chesapeake and the other in the Lower South. In addition to spatial variations, Berlin emphasizes temporal change. Black life in early America was not static but rather thoroughly dynamic. Most significant in shaping Afro-American cultures, Berlin argues, were the dimensions and pace of the slave trade, the varying proportions of whites and blacks, and the type of work in which slaves engaged. By the eve of the American Revolution, the differential effects of these three factors, particularly evident in contrasting balances of creoles and Africans, had created contrasting Afro-American cultures: heavily influenced by whites in the North; thoroughly creole in the Chesapeake; and most African in the Lower South.

There is much that is thought-provoking about these arguments. Incorporating the North into his analysis, Berlin reminds the reader that slavery was a continental, not just a Southern, institution. Perhaps the North was not monolithic – slavery was more deeply rooted in the Mid-Atlantic than in New England, for example – but it unquestionably contained many slaves, even after the Revolution. Nevertheless, focusing upon the chronology of slavery may force a rethinking of its geography. A major watershed in the history of slavery occurred when slave-owning societies became slave societies, when, in other words, slavery became the dominant labor system and thereby influenced all other social relations. This fateful transition occurred at the end of the seventeenth and beginning of the eighteenth centuries in the two Southern slave systems, but it never happened in the North. From this perspective, the North was diverging from the South even before the Revolution.

* * *

Recent interest in the beginnings of slavery on the mainland of British North America has revealed a striking diversity in Afro-American life. During the seventeenth and eighteenth centuries, three distinct slave systems evolved: a Northern nonplantation system and two Southern plantation systems, one around Chesapeake Bay and the other in the Carolina and Georgia low-country. Slavery took shape differently in each with important consequences for the growth of black culture and society. The development of these slave societies depended upon the nature of the slave trade and the demographic configurations of blacks and whites as well as upon the diverse character of colonial economy. Thus, while cultural differences between newly arrived Africans and second and third generation Afro-Americans or creoles[a] everywhere provided the basis for social stratification within black society, African–creole differences emerged at different times with different force and even different meaning in the North, the Chesapeake region, and the low-country. A careful examination of the diverse development of Afro-American culture in the colonial era yields important clues for an understanding of the full complexity of black society in the centuries that followed.

The nature of slavery and the demographic balance of whites and blacks during the seventeenth and first decades of the eighteenth centuries tended to incorporate Northern blacks into the emerging Euro-American culture, even as whites denied them a place in Northern society. But changes in the character of the slave trade during the middle third of the eighteenth century gave new impetus to African culture and institutions in the Northern colonies. By the American Revolution, Afro-American culture had been integrated into the larger Euro-American one, but black people remained acutely conscious of their African inheritance and freely drew on it in shaping their lives.

Throughout the colonial years, blacks composed a small fraction of the population of New England and the Middle Colonies. Only in New York and Rhode Island did they reach 15 percent of the population. In most Northern colonies the proportion was considerably smaller. At its height, the black population totaled 8 percent of the population of New Jersey and less than 4 percent in Massachusetts and Connecticut. But these colony-wide enumerations dilute the presence of blacks and underestimate the importance of slave labor. In some of the most productive agricultural regions and in the cities, blacks composed a larger share of the population, sometimes constituting as much as one-third of the whole and perhaps one-half of the work force.[1] Although many Northern whites never saw a black slave, others had daily, intimate contact with them. And, although some blacks found it difficult to join together with their former countrymen, others lived in close contact.

The vast majority of Northern blacks lived and worked in the countryside. A few labored in highly capitalized rural industries – tanneries, salt works, and iron furnaces – where they often composed the bulk of the work force, skilled and unskilled. Iron masters, the largest employers of industrial slaves, also were often the largest slaveholders in the North. Pennsylvania iron masters manifested their dependence on slave labor when, in 1727, they petitioned for a reduction in the tariff on slaves so they might keep their furnaces in operation. Bloomeries and forges in other colonies similarly relied on slave labor.[2] But in an overwhelmingly agrarian society only a small proportion of the slave population engaged in industrial labor.

Like most rural whites, most rural blacks toiled as agricultural workers. In southern New England, on Long Island, and in northern New Jersey, which contained the North's densest black populations, slaves tended stock and raised crops for export to the sugar islands. Farmers engaged in provisioning the West Indies with draft animals and foodstuffs were familiar with slavery and had easy access to slaves. Some, like the Barbadian *émigrés* in northern New Jersey, had migrated from the sugar islands. Others, particularly those around Narragansett Bay, styled themselves planters in the West Indian manner. They built great houses, bred race horses, and accumulated slaves, sometimes holding twenty or more bondsmen. But, whatever the aspirations of this commercial gentry, the provisioning trade could not support a plantation regime. Most slaves lived on farms (not plantations), worked at a variety of tasks, and never labored in large gangs. No one in the North suggested that agricultural labor could be done only by black people, a common assertion in the sugar islands and the Carolina low-country. In northern New England, the Hudson Valley, and Pennsylvania, the seasonal demands of cereal farming undermined the viability of slavery. For most wheat farmers, as Peter Kalm[b] shrewdly observed, "a Negro or black slave requires too much money at one time," and they relied instead on white indentured servants and free workers to supplement their own labor. Throughout the North's bread basket, even those members of the gentry who could afford the larger capital investment and the concomitant risk that slave ownership entailed generally depended on the labor of indentured servants more than on that of slaves. Fully two-thirds of the bond servants held by the wealthiest farmers in Lancaster and Chester counties, Pennsylvania, were indentured whites rather than chattel blacks. These farmers tended to view their slaves more as status symbols than as agricultural workers. While slaves labored in the fields part of the year, as did nearly everyone, they also spent a large portion of their time working in and around their masters' houses as domestic servants, stable keepers, and gardeners. Significantly, the wills and inventories of Northern slaveholders listed their slaves with other high-status objects like clocks and carriages rather than with land or agricultural implements.[3]

The distinct demands of Northern agriculture shaped black life in the countryside. Where the provisioning trade predominated, black men worked as stock minders and herdsmen while black women labored as dairy maids as well as domestics of various kinds. The large number of slaves demanded by the provisioning trade and the ready access to horses and mules it allowed placed black companionship within easy reach of most bondsmen. Such was not always true in the cereal region. Living scattered throughout the countryside on the largest farms and working in the house as often as in the field, blacks enjoyed neither the mobility nor the autonomy of slaves employed in the provisioning trade. But, if the demands of Northern agriculture affected black life in different ways, almost all rural blacks lived and worked in close proximity to whites. Slaves quickly learned the rudiments of the English language, the Christian religion, the white man's ways. In the North, few rural blacks remained untouched by the larger forces of Euro-American life.

Northern slaves were also disproportionately urban. During the eighteenth century, a fifth to a quarter of the blacks in New York lived in New York City. Portsmouth and Boston contained fully a third of the blacks in New Hampshire and Massachusetts, and nearly half of Rhode Island's black population resided in Newport. Ownership of slaves was almost universal among the urban elite and commonplace among the middling classes as well. On the eve of the Revolution, nearly three-fourths of Boston's wealthiest quartile of propertyholders ranked in the slaveholding class. Fragmentary evidence from earlier in the century suggests that urban slave-ownership had been even more widespread but contracted with the growth of a free working class. Viewed from the top of colonial society, the observation of one visitor that there was "not a house in Boston" that did "not have one or two" slaves might be applied to every Northern city with but slight exaggeration.[4]

Urban slaves generally worked as house servants – cooking, cleaning, tending gardens and stables, and running errands. They lived in back rooms, lofts, closets, and, occasionally, makeshift alley shacks. Under these cramped conditions, few masters held more than one or two slaves. However they might cherish a large retinue of retainers, urban slaveholders rarely had the room to lodge them. Because of the general shortage of space, masters discouraged their slaves from establishing families in the cities. Women with reputations for fecundity found few buyers, and some slaveholders sold their domestics at the first sign of pregnancy. A New York master candidly announced the sale of his cook "because she breeds too fast for her owners to put up with such inconvenience," and others gave away children because they were an unwarranted expense. As a result, black women had few children, and their fertility ratio was generally lower than that of whites. The inability or unwillingness of urban masters to support large households placed a severe strain on black family life.[5] But it also encouraged masters to allow their slaves to live out, hire their own time, and thereby gain a measure of independence and freedom.

In the cities as in the countryside, blacks tended to live and work in close proximity to whites. Northern slaves not only gained first-hand knowledge of their masters' world, but they also rubbed elbows with lower-class whites in taverns, cock fights, and fairs where poor people of varying status mingled.[6] If urban life allowed slaves to meet more frequently and enjoy a larger degree of social autonomy than did slavery in the countryside, the cosmopolitan nature of cities speeded the transformation of Africans to Afro-Americans. Acculturation in the cities of the North was a matter of years, not generations.[c]

Newly arrived blacks, most already experienced in the New World and familiar with their proscribed status, turned Northern bondage to their advantage where they could. They quickly established a stable family life and, unlike newly imported Africans elsewhere on the continent, increased their numbers by natural means during the first generation. By 1708, the governor of Rhode Island observed that the colony's slaves were "supplied by the offspring of those they have already, which increase daily...." The transplanted creoles also seized the opportunities provided by the complex Northern economy, the relatively close ties of master and slave, and, for many, the independence afforded by urban life. In New Amsterdam, for example, the diverse needs of the Dutch mercantile economy induced the West India Company, the largest slaveholder in the colony, to allow its slaves to live out and work on their own in return for a stipulated amount of labor and an annual tribute.[d] "Half-freedom," as this system came to be called, enlarged black opportunities and allowed for the development of a strong black community. When the West India Company refused to make these privileges hereditary, "half-free" slaves organized and protested, demanding that they be allowed to pass their rights to their children. Failing that, New Amsterdam slaves pressed their masters in other ways to elevate their children's status. Some, hearing rumors that baptism meant freedom, tried to gain church membership. A Dutch prelate complained that these blacks "wanted nothing else than to deliver their children from bodily slavery, without striving for piety and Christian virtues." Even after the conquering English abolished "half-freedom" and instituted a more rigorous system of racial servitude, blacks continued to use the leverage gained by their prominent role in the city's economy to set standards of treatment well above those in the plantation colonies. Into the eighteenth century, New York slaves informally enjoyed the rights of an earlier era, including the right to hold property of their own. "The Custome of this Country," bristled a frustrated New York master to a West Indian friend, "will not allow us to use our Negroes as you doe in Barbados."[7]

Throughout the North, the same factors that mitigated the harshest features of bondage in New York strengthened the position of slaves in dealing with their masters. Small holdings, close living conditions, and the absence of gang labor drew masters and slaves together. A visitor to Connecticut noted in disgust that slaveowners were "too Indulgent (especially the farmers) to their Slaves, suffering too great a familiarity from them, permitting them to sit at Table and eat with them (as they say to save time) and into the dish goes the black hoof as freely as the white hand." Slaves used knowledge gained at their masters' tables to press for additional privileges: the right to visit friends, live with their families, or hire their own time. One slaveholder reluctantly cancelled the sale of his slaves because of "an invariable indulgence here to permit Slaves of any kind of worth or Character who must change Masters, to choose those Masters," and he could not persuade his slaves "to leave their Country (if I may call it so), their acquaintances & friends."[8] Such indulgences originated not only in the ability of slaves to manipulate their masters to their own benefit, but also from the confidence of slaveholders in their own hegemony. Surety of white dominance, derived from white numerical superiority, complemented the blacks' understanding of how best to bend bondage to their own advantage and to maximize black opportunities within slavery.

During the middle decades of the eighteenth century, the nature of Northern slavery changed dramatically. Growing demand for labor, especially when European wars limited the supply of white indentured servants and when depression sent free workers west in search of new opportunities, increased the importance of slaves in the work force. Between 1732 and 1754, blacks composed fully a third of the immigrants (forced and voluntary) arriving in New York. The new importance of slave labor changed the nature of the slave trade. Merchants who previously took black slaves only on consignment now began to import them directly from Africa, often in large numbers. Before 1741, for example, 70 percent of the slaves arriving in New York originated in the West Indies and other mainland sources and only 30 percent came directly from Africa. After that date, the proportions were reversed. Specializing in the slave trade, African slavers carried many times more slaves than did West Indian traders. Whereas slaves had earlier arrived in small parcels rarely numbering more than a half-dozen, direct shipments from Africa at times now totaled over a hundred and, occasionally, several times that. Slaves increasingly replaced white indentured servants as the chief source of unfree labor not only in the areas that had produced for the provisioning trade, where their pre-eminence had been established earlier in the century, but in the cities as well. In the 1760s, when slave importation into Pennsylvania peaked, blacks composed more than three-quarters of Philadelphia's servant population.[9]

The transformation of Northern slavery had a lasting influence on the development of Afro-American culture. Although the Northern black population remained predominantly Afro-American after nearly a century of slow importation from the West Indies and steady natural increase, the direct entry of Africans into Northern society reoriented black culture.

Even before the redirection of the Northern slave trade, those few Africans in the Northern colonies often stood apart from the creole majority. While Afro-American slaves established precedents and customs, which they then drew upon to improve their condition, Africans tended to stake all to recapture the world they had lost. Significantly, Africans, many of whom did not yet speak English and still carried tribal names, composed the majority of the participants in the New York slave insurrection of 1712, even though most of the city's blacks were creoles.[10] The division between Africans and Afro-Americans became more visible as the number of Africans increased after mid-century. Not only did creoles and Africans evince different aspirations, but their life-chances – as reflected in their resistance to disease and their likelihood of establishing a family – also diverged sharply. Greater visibility may have sharpened differences between creoles and Africans, but Africans were too few in number to stand apart for long. Whatever conflicts different life-chances and beliefs created, whites paid such distinctions little heed in incorporating the African minority into their slaveholdings. The propensity of Northern whites to lump blacks together mitigated intraracial differences. Rather than permanently dividing blacks, the entry of Africans into Northern society gave a new direction to Afro-American culture.[11]

Newly arrived Africans reawakened Afro-Americans to their African past by providing direct knowledge of West African society. Creole blacks began to combine their African inheritance into their own evolving culture. In some measure, the easy confidence of Northern whites in their own dominance speeded the syncretization of African and creole culture by allowing blacks to act far more openly than slaves in the plantation colonies. Northern blacks incorporated African culture into their own Afro-American culture not only in the common-place and unconscious way that generally characterizes the transit of culture but also with a high degree of consciousness and deliberateness. They designated their churches "African," and they called themselves "Sons of Africa."[12] They adopted African forms to maximize their freedom, to choose their leaders, and, in general, to give shape to their lives. This new African influence was manifested most fully in Negro election day, a ritual festival of role reversal common throughout West Africa and celebrated openly by blacks in New England and a scattering of places in the Middle Colonies.

The celebration of Negro election day took a variety of forms, but everywhere it was a day of great merrymaking that drew blacks from all over the countryside. "All the various languages of Africa, mixed with broken and ludicrous English, filled the air, accompanied with the music of the fiddle, tambourine, the banjo, [and] drum," recalled an observer of the festival in Newport. Negro election day culminated with the selection of black kings, governors, and judges. These officials sometimes held symbolic power over the whole community and real power over the black community. While the black governors held court, adjudicating minor disputes, the blacks paraded and partied, dressed in their masters' clothes and mounted on their masters' horses. Such role reversal, like similar status inversions in Africa and elsewhere, confirmed rather than challenged the existing order, but it also gave blacks an opportunity to express themselves more fully than the narrow boundaries of slavery ordinarily allowed. Negro election day permitted a seeming release from bondage, and it also provided a mechanism for blacks to recognize and honor their own notables. Most important, it established a framework for the development of black politics. In the places where Negro election day survived into the nineteenth century, its politics shaped the politics within the black community and merged with partisan divisions of American society. Slaves elsewhere in the New World also celebrated this holiday, but whites in the plantation colonies found the implications of role reversal too frightening to allow even symbolically. Northern whites, on the other hand, not only aided election day materially but sometimes joined in themselves. Still, white cooperation was an important but not the crucial element in the rise of Negro election day. Its origin in the 1740s and 1750s suggests how the entry of Africans reoriented Afro-American culture at a formative point in its development.[13]

African acculturation in the Northern colonies at once incorporated blacks into American society and sharpened the memory of their African past and their desire to preserve it. While small numbers and close proximity to whites forced blacks to conform to the forms of the dominant Euro-American culture, the confidence of whites in their own hegemony allowed black slaves a good measure of autonomy. In this context it is not surprising that a black New England sea captain established the first back-to-Africa movement in mainland North America.[14]

Unlike African acculturation in the Northern colonies, the transformation of Africans into Afro-Americans in the Carolina and Georgia low-country was a slow, halting process whose effects resonated differently within black society. While creolization created a unified Afro-American population in the North, it left low-country blacks deeply divided. A minority lived and worked in close proximity to whites in the cities that lined the rice coast, fully conversant with the most cosmopolitan sector of lowland society. A portion of this urban elite, increasingly light-skinned, pressed for further incorporation into white society, confident they could compete as equals. The mass of black people, however, remained physically separated and psychologically estranged from the Anglo-American world and culturally closer to Africa than any other blacks on continental North America.

The sharp division was not immediately apparent. At first it seemed that African acculturation in the Lower South would follow the Northern pattern. The first blacks arrived in the low-country in small groups from the West Indies. Often they accompanied their owners and, like them, frequently immigrated in small family groups. Many had already spent considerable time on the sugar islands, and some had doubtless been born there. Most spoke English, understood European customs and manners, and, as their language skills and family ties suggest, had made the difficult adjustment to the conditions of black life in the New World.

As in the Northern colonies, whites dominated the population of the pioneer Carolina settlement. Until the end of the seventeenth century, they composed better than two-thirds of the settlers. During this period and into the first years of the eighteenth century, most white slaveholders engaged in mixed farming and stock raising for export to the West Indian islands where they had originated. Generally, they lived on small farms, held few slaves, and worked closely with their bond servants. Even when they hated and feared blacks and yearned for the prerogatives of West

Indian slave masters, the demands of the primitive, labor-scarce economy frequently placed master and slave face-to-face on opposite sides of a sawbuck.[15] Such direct, equalitarian confrontations tempered white domination and curbed slavery's harshest features.

White dependence on blacks to defend their valuable lowland beachhead reinforced this "sawbuck equality." The threat of invasion by the Spanish and French to the south and Indians to the west hung ominously over the low-country during its formative years. To bolster colonial defenses, officials not only drafted slaves in time of war but also regularly enlisted them into the militia.

The unsettled conditions that made the low-country vulnerable to external enemies strengthened the slave's hand in other ways. Confronted by an overbearing master or a particularly onerous assignment, many blacks took to the woods. Truancy was an easy alternative in the thinly settled, heavily forested low-country. Forest dangers generally sent truant slaves back to their owners, but the possibility of another flight induced slaveholders to accept them with few questions asked. Some bondsmen, however, took advantage of these circumstances to escape permanently. Maroon colonies existed throughout the lowland swamps and into the backcountry.[e] Maroons lived a hard life, perhaps more difficult than slaves, and few blacks chose to join these outlaw bands. But the ease of escape and the existence of a maroon alternative made masters chary about abusing their slaves.[16]

The transplanted African's intimate knowledge of the subtropical lowland environment – especially when compared to the Englishman's dense ignorance – magnified white dependence on blacks and enlarged black opportunities within the slave regime. Since the geography, climate, and topography of the low-country more closely resembled the West African than the English countryside, African not European technology and agronomy often guided lowland development. From the first, whites depended on blacks to identify useful flora and fauna and to define the appropriate methods of production. Blacks, adapting African techniques to the circumstances of the Carolina wilderness, shaped the lowland cattle industry and played a central role in the introduction and development of the region's leading staple. In short, transplanted Englishmen learned as much or more from transplanted Africans as did the former Africans from them.[17] While whites eventually appropriated this knowledge and turned it against black people to

123

rivet tighter the bonds of servitude, white dependence on African know-how operated during those first years to place blacks in managerial as well as menial positions and thereby permitted blacks to gain a larger share of the fruits of the new land than whites might otherwise allow. In such circumstances, white domination made itself felt, but both whites and blacks incorporated much of West African culture into their new way of life.

If the distinction between white and black culture remained small in the low-country, so too did differences within black society. The absence of direct importation of African slaves prevented the emergence of African–creole differences; and, since few blacks gained their liberty during those years, differences in status within the black community were almost nonexistent. The small radius of settlement and the ease of water transportation, moreover, placed most blacks within easy reach of Charles Town. A "city" of several dozen rude buildings where the colonial legislature met in a tavern could hardly have impressed slaves as radically different from their own primitive quarters. Town slaves, for their part, doubtless had first-hand familiarity with farm work as few masters could afford the luxury of placing their slaves in livery.[18]

Thus, during the first years of settlement, black life in the low-country, like black life in the North, evolved toward a unified Afro-American culture. Although their numbers combined with other circumstances to allow Carolina blacks a larger role in shaping their culture than that enjoyed by blacks in the North, there remained striking similarities in the early development of Afro-American life in both regions. During the last few years of the seventeenth century, however, changes in economy and society undermined these commonalities and set the development of low-country Afro-American life on a distinctive course.

The discovery of exportable staples, first naval stores and then rice and indigo, transformed the low-country as surely as the sugar revolution transformed the West Indies. Under the pressure of the riches that staple production provided, planters banished the white yeomanry to the hinterland, consolidated small farms into large plantations, and carved new plantations out of the malaria-ridden swamps. Before long, black slaves began pouring into the region and, sometime during the first decade of the eighteenth century, white numerical superiority gave way to the low-country's distinguishing demographic characteristic: the black majority.

Black numerical dominance grew rapidly during the eighteenth century. By the 1720s, blacks outnumbered whites by more than two to one in South Carolina. In the heavily settled plantation parishes surrounding Charles Town, blacks enjoyed a three-to-one majority. That margin grew steadily until the disruptions of the Revolutionary era, but it again increased thereafter. Georgia, where metropolitan policies reined planter ambition, remained slaveless until mid-century. Once restrictions on slavery were removed, planters imported blacks in large numbers, giving lowland Georgia counties considerable black majorities.[19]

Direct importation of slaves from Africa provided the impetus to the growth of the black majority. Some West Indian Afro-Americans continued to enter the low-country, but they shrank to a small fraction of the whole.[20] As African importation increased, Charles Town took its place as the largest mainland slave mart and the center of the lowland slave trade. Almost all of the slaves in Carolina and later in Georgia – indeed, fully 40 percent of all pre-Revolutionary black arrivals in mainland North America – entered at Charles Town. The enormous number of slaves allowed slave masters a wide range of choices. Low-country planters developed preferences far beyond the usual demands for healthy adult and adolescent males and concerned themselves with the regional and tribal origins of their purchases. Some planters may have based their choices on long experience and a considered understanding of the physical and social character of various African nations. But, for the most part, these preferences were shallow ethnic stereotypes. Coromantees revolted; Angolans ran away; Iboes destroyed themselves. At other times, lowland planters apparently preferred just those slaves they did not get, perhaps because all Africans made unsatisfactory slaves and the unobtainable ones looked better at a distance. Although low-country slave masters desired Gambian people above all others, Angolans composed a far larger proportion of the African arrivals. But, however confused or mistaken in their beliefs, planters held them firmly and, in some measure, put them into practice. "Gold Coast and Gambia's are the best, next to them the Windward Coast are prefer'd to Angola's," observed a Charles Town merchant in describing the most salable mixture. "There must not be a Callabar[f] amongst them."[21] Planter preferences informed low-country slave traders and, to a considerable degree, determined the tribal origins of lowland blacks.

Whatever their origins, rice cultivation shaped the destiny of

African people arriving at Charles Town. Although the production of pitch and tar played a pivotal role in the early development of the staple-based economy in South Carolina, rice quickly became the dominant plantation crop. Rice cultivation evolved slowly during the late seventeenth and early eighteenth centuries as planters, aided by knowledgeable blacks, mastered the complex techniques necessary for commercial production. During the first half of the eighteenth century, rice culture was limited to the inland swamps, where slave-built dikes controlled the irrigation of low-lying rice fields. But by mid-century planters had discovered how to regulate the tidal floods to irrigate and drain their fields. Rice production moved to the tidal swamps that lined the region's many rivers and expanded greatly. By the beginning of the nineteenth century, the rice coast stretched from Cape Fear in North Carolina to the Satilla River in Georgia.[22] Throughout the low-country, rice was king.

The relatively mild slave regime of the pioneer years disappeared as rice cultivation expanded. Slaves increasingly lived in large units, and they worked in field gangs rather than at a variety of tasks. The strict requirements of rice production set the course of their work. And rice was a hard master. For a large portion of the year, slaves labored knee-deep in brackish muck under the hot tropical sun; and, even after the fields were drained, the crops laid-by, and the grain threshed, there were canals to clear and dams to repair. By mid-century planters had also begun to grow indigo on the upland sections of their estates. Indigo complemented rice in its seasonal requirements, and it made even heavier labor demands. The ready availability of African imports compounded the new harsh realities of plantation slavery by cheapening black life in the eyes of many masters. As long as the slave trade remained open, they skimped on food, clothing, and medical attention for their slaves, knowing full well that substitutes could be easily had. With the planters' reliance on male African imports, slaves found it increasingly difficult to establish and maintain a normal family life. Brutal working conditions, the disease-ridden, lowland environment, and the open slave trade made for a deadly combination. Slave birth rates fell steadily during the middle years of the eighteenth century and mortality rates rose sharply. Between 1730 and 1760, deaths outnumbered births among blacks and only African importation allowed for continued population growth. Not until the eve of the Revolution did the black population begin again to reproduce naturally.

The low-country plantation system with its urban centers, its black majority, its dependence on "salt-water" slaves transformed black culture and society just as it reshaped the white world. The unified Afro-American culture and society that had evolved during the pioneer years disappeared as rice cultivation spread. In its place a sharp division developed between an increasingly urban creole and a plantation-based African population. The growth of plantation slavery not only set blacks further apart from whites, it also sharply divided blacks.

One branch of black society took shape within the bounds of the region's cities and towns. If planters lived removed from most slaves, they maintained close, intimate relations with some. The masters' great wealth, transient life, and seasonal urban residence placed them in close contact with house servants who kept their estates, boatmen who carried messages and supplies back and forth to their plantations, and urban artisans who made city life not only possible but comfortable. In addition, coastal cities needed large numbers of workers to transport and process the plantation staples, to serve the hundreds of ships that annually visited the low-country, and to satisfy the planters' newly acquired taste for luxury goods. Blacks did most of this work. Throughout the eighteenth century they composed more than half the population of Charles Town and other low-country ports. Probably nothing arrived or left these cities without some black handling it. Black artisans also played a large role in urban life. Master craftsmen employed them in every variety of work. A visitor to Charles Town found that even barbers "are supported in idleness & ease by their negroes ...; & in fact many of the mechaniks bear nothing more of their trade than the name." Although most black artisans labored along the waterfront as shipwrights, ropemakers, and coopers, low-country blacks – unlike blacks in Northern cities – also entered the higher trades, working as gold beaters, silversmiths, and cabinetmakers. In addition, black women gained control over much of the marketing in the low-country ports, mediating between slave-grown produce in the countryside and urban consumption. White tradesmen and journeymen periodically protested against slave competition, but planters, master craftsmen, and urban consumers who benefited from black labor and services easily brushed aside these objections.[23]

Mobile, often skilled, and occasionally literate, urban slaves understood the white world. They used their knowledge to improve their position within low-country society even while the condition of the mass of black people deteriorated in the wake of the rice revolution. Many urban creoles not only retained the independence of the earlier years but enlarged upon it. They hired their own time, earned wages from "overwork," kept market stalls, and sometimes even opened shops. Some lived apart from their masters and rented houses of their own, paying their owners a portion of their earnings in return for *de facto* freedom. Such liberty enabled a few black people to keep their families intact and perhaps even accumulate property for themselves. The small black communities that developed below the Bluff in Savannah and in Charles Town's Neck confirm the growing independence of urban creoles.[24]

The incongruous prosperity of urban bondsmen jarred whites. By hiring their own time, living apart from their masters, and controlling their own family life, these blacks forcibly and visibly claimed the white man's privileges. Perhaps no aspect of their behavior was as obvious and, hence, as galling as their elaborate dress. While plantation slaves – men and women – worked stripped to the waist wearing no more than loin cloths (thereby confirming the white man's image of savagery), urban slaves appropriated their masters' taste for fine clothes and often the clothes themselves. Low-country legislators enacted various sumptuary regulations to restrain the slaves' penchant for dressing above their station. The South Carolina Assembly once even considered prohibiting masters from giving their old clothes to their slaves. But hand-me-downs were clearly not the problem as long as slaves earned wages and had easy access to the urban marketplace. Frustrated by the realities of urban slavery, lawmakers passed and re-passed the old regulations to little effect. On the eve of the Revolution, a Charles Town Grand Jury continued to bemoan the fact that the "Law for preventing the excessive and costly Apparel of Negroes and other Slaves in this province (especially in *Charles Town*) [was] not being put into Force."[25]

Increasingly during the eighteenth century, blacks gained privileged positions within low-country society as a result of intimate, usually sexual, relations with white slave masters. Like slaveholders everywhere, lowland planters assumed that sexual access to slave women was simply another of the master's prerogatives. Perhaps because their origin was West Indian or perhaps because their dual residence separated them from their white wives part of the year, white men established sexual liaisons with black women

128

frequently and openly. Some white men and black women formed stable, long-lasting unions, legitimate in everything but law. More often than other slaveholders on continental British North America, low-country planters recognized and provided for their mulatto offspring, and, occasionally, extended legal freedom. South Carolina's small free Negro population, almost totally confined to Charles Town, was largely the product of such relations. Light-skinned people of color enjoyed special standing in the low-country ports, as they did in the West Indies, and whites occasionally looked the other way when such creoles passed into the dominant caste. But even when the planters did not grant legal freedom, they usually assured the elevated standing of their mulatto scions by training them for artisan trades or placing them in household positions. If the countryside was "blackened" by African imports, Charles Town and the other low-country ports exhibited a mélange of "colored" peoples.[26]

While one branch of black society stood so close to whites that its members sometimes disappeared into the white population, most plantation slaves remained alienated from the world of their master, physically and culturally. Living in large units often numbering in the hundreds on plantations that they had carved out of the malarial swamps and working under the direction of black drivers, the black majority gained only fleeting knowledge of Anglo-American culture. What they knew did not encourage them to learn more. Instead, they strove to widen the distance between themselves and their captors. In doing so, they too built upon the large degree of autonomy black people had earlier enjoyed.

In the pioneer period, many masters required slaves to raise their own provisions. Slaves regularly kept small gardens and tended barnyard fowl to maintain themselves, and they often marketed their surplus. Blacks kept these prerogatives with the development of the plantation system. In fact, the growth of low-country towns, the increasing specialization in staple production, and the comparative absence of nonslaveholding whites enlarged the market for slave-grown produce. Planters, of course, disliked the independence truck gardening afforded plantation blacks and the tendency of slaves to confuse their owners' produce with their own, but the ease of water transportation and the absence of white supervision made it difficult to prevent.

The task system, a mode of work organization peculiar to the low-country, further strengthened black autonomy. Under the task system, a slave's daily routine was sharply defined: so many rows of rice to be sowed, so much grain to be threshed, or so many lines of canal to be cleared. Such a precise definition of work suggests that city-bound planters found it almost impossible to keep their slaves in the fields from sunup to sundown. With little direct white supervision, slaves and their black foremen conspired to preserve a large portion of the day for their own use, while meeting their masters' minimum work requirements. Struggle over the definition of a task doubtless continued throughout the formative years of the low-country plantation system and after, but by the end of the century certain lines had been drawn. Slaves generally left the field sometime in the early afternoon, a practice that protected them from the harsh afternoon sun and allowed them time to tend their own gardens and stock. Like participation in the low-country's internal economy, the task system provided slaves with a large measure of control over their own lives.

The autonomy generated by both the task system and truck gardening provided the material basis for lowland black culture. Within the confines of the overwhelmingly black countryside, African culture survived well. The continual arrival of Africans into the low-country renewed and refreshed slave knowledge of West African life. In such a setting blacks could hardly lose their past. The distinctive pattern of the lowland slave trade, moreover, heightened the impact of the newly arrived Africans on the evolution of black culture. While slaves dribbled into the North through a multiplicity of ports, they poured into the low-country through a single city. The large, unicentered slave trade and the large slaveholding units assured the survival not only of the common denominators of West African culture but also many of its particular tribal and national forms. Planter preferences or perhaps the chance ascendancy of one group sometimes allowed specific African cultures to reconstitute themselves within the plantation setting. To be sure, Africans changed in the low-country. Even where blacks enjoyed numerical superiority and a considerable degree of autonomy, they could no more transport their culture unchanged than could their masters. But low-country blacks incorporated more of West African culture – as reflected in their language, religion, work patterns, and much else – into their new lives than did other black Americans. Throughout the eighteenth century and into the nineteenth, low-country blacks continued to work the land, name their children, and communicate through word and song in a manner that openly combined African traditions with the circumstances of plantation life.[27]

The new pattern of creolization that developed following the rice revolution smashed the emerging homogeneity of black life in the first years of settlement and left low-country blacks deeply divided. One branch of black culture evolved in close proximity to whites. Urban, often skilled, well-traveled, and increasingly American-born, creoles knew white society well, and they used their knowledge to better themselves. Some, clearly a well-connected minority, pressed for incorporation into the white world. They urged missionary groups to admit their children to school and later petitioned lawmakers to allow their testimony in court, carefully adding that they did not expect full equality with whites.[28] Plantation slaves shared few of the assimilationist aspirations of urban creoles. By their dress, language, and work routine, they lived in a world apart. Rather than demand incorporation into white society, they yearned only to be left alone. Within the quarter, aided by their numerical dominance, their plantation-based social hierarchy, and their continued contact with Africa, they developed their own distinctive culture, different not only from that of whites but also from the cosmopolitan world of their Afro-American brethren. To be sure, there were connections between the black majority and the urban creoles. Many – market women, jobbing artisans, and boatmen – moved easily between these two worlds, and most blacks undoubtedly learned something of the other world through chance encounters, occasional visits, and word of mouth.[29] Common white oppression continually shrank the social distance that the distinctive experience created, but by the eve of the Revolution, deep cultural differences separated those blacks who sought to improve their lives through incorporation into the white world and those who determined to disregard the white man's ways. If the movement from African to creole obliterated cultural differences among Northern blacks, creolization fractured black society in the low-country.

Cultural distinctions between Africans and Afro-Americans developed in the Chesapeake as well, although the dimension of differences between African and creole tended to be time rather than space. Unlike in the low-country, white planters did not promote the creation of a distinctive group whose origins, function, and physical appearance distinguished them from the mass of plantation slaves and offered them hope, however faint, of eventual incorporation into white society. And, compared to the North, African immigration into the Chesapeake came relatively early in the process of cultural transformation. As a result, African–creole differences disappeared with time and a single, unified Afro-American culture slowly emerged in the Chesapeake.

As in the low-country, little distinguished black and white laborers during the early years of settlement. Most of the first blacks brought into the Chesapeake region were West Indian creoles who bore English or Spanish surnames and carried records of baptism. Along the River James, as along the Cooper, the demands of pioneer life at times operated to strengthen the slaves' bargaining position. Some blacks set the condition of their labor, secured their family life, participated in the region's internal economy, and occasionally bartered for their liberty. This, of course, did not save most black people from the brutal exploitation that almost all propertyless men and women faced as planters squeezed the last pound of profit from the tobacco economy. The blacks' treatment at the hands of planters differed little from that of white bound labor in large measure because it was difficult to treat people more brutally.[30] While the advantages of this peculiar brand of equality may have been lost on its beneficiaries, those blacks who were able to complete their terms of servitude quickly joined whites in the mad scramble for land, servants, and status.

Many did well. During the seventeenth century, black freemen could be found throughout the region owning land, holding servants, and occasionally attaining minor offices. Like whites, they accumulated property, sued their neighbors, and passed their estates to their children. In 1651, Anthony Johnson, the best known of these early Negro freemen, received a 250-acre headright for importing five persons into Virginia. John Johnson, a neighbor and probably a relative, did even better, earning 550 acres for bringing eleven persons into the colony. Both men owned substantial farms on the Eastern Shore, held servants, and left their heirs sizable estates. As established members of their communities, they enjoyed the rights of citizens. When a servant claiming his freedom fled Anthony Johnson's plantation and took refuge with a nearby white farmer, Johnson took his neighbor to court and won the return of his servant along with damages against the white man.[31]

The class rather than racial basis of early Chesapeake society enabled many black men to compete successfully for that scarcest of all New World commodities: the affection of white women. Bastardy lists indicate that white female servants ignored the strictures against what white lawmakers labeled "shameful" and "unnatural" acts and joined together with men of their own condition regardless of color. Fragmentary evidence from various parts of seventeenth-century Virginia reveals that approximately one-quarter to one-third of the bastard children born to white women were mulattoes. The commonplace nature of these interracial unions might have been the reason why one justice legally sanctified the marriage of Hester, an English servant woman, to James Tate, a black slave. Some successful, property-owning whites and blacks also intermarried. In Virginia's Northampton county, Francis Payne, a Negro freeman, married a white woman, who later remarried a white man after Payne's death. William Greensted, a white attorney who represented Elizabeth Key, a mulatto woman, in her successful suit for her freedom, later married her. In 1691, when the Virginia General Assembly finally ruled against the practice, some propertied whites found the legislation novel and obnoxious enough to muster a protest.[32]

By the middle of the seventeenth century, Negro freemen sharing and fulfilling the same ideals and aspirations that whites held were no anomaly in the Chesapeake region. An Eastern Shore tax list of 1668 counted nearly a third of black tithables free. If most blacks did not escape the tightening noose of enslavement, they continued to live and work under conditions not much different from white servants. Throughout the seventeenth and into the first decades of the eighteenth century, black and white servants ran away together, slept together, and, upon occasion, stood shoulder to shoulder against the weighty champions of established authority. Thus viewed from the first years of settlement – the relatively small number of blacks, their creole origins, and the initial success of some in establishing a place in society – black acculturation in the Chesapeake appeared to be following the nonplantation pattern of the Northern colonies and the pioneer low-country.[33]

The emergence of a planter class and its consolidation of power during a series of political crises in the middle years of the seventeenth century transformed black life in the Chesapeake and threatened this pattern of cultural change. Following the legalization of slavery in the 1660s, black slaves slowly but steadily replaced white indentured servants as the main source of plantation labor.

By 1700, blacks made up more than half the agricultural work force in Virginia and, since the great planters could best afford to purchase slaves, blacks composed an even larger share of the workers on the largest estates. Increased reliance on slave labor quickly outstripped West Indian supplies. Beginning in the 1680s, Africans entered the region in increasingly large numbers. The proportion of blacks born in Africa grew steadily throughout the waning years of the seventeenth century, so that by the first decade of the eighteenth century, Africans composed some three-quarters of the region's blacks.[34] Unlike the low-country, African imports never threatened the Chesapeake's overall white numerical superiority, but by the beginning of the eighteenth century they dominated black society. Some eighty years after the first blacks arrived at Jamestown and some forty years after the legalization of slavery, African importation profoundly transformed black life.

Slave conditions deteriorated as their numbers increased. With an eye for a quick profit, planters in the Chesapeake imported males disproportionately. Generally men outnumbered women more than two to one on Chesapeake slavers. Wildly imbalanced sex ratios undermined black family life. Physically spent and emotionally drained by the rigors of the Middle Passage, African women had few children. Thus, as in the North and the Carolina lowlands, the black birth rate fell and mortality rate surged upward with the commencement of direct African importation.[35]

The hard facts of life and death in the Chesapeake region distinguished creoles and Africans at the beginning of the eighteenth century. The demands of the tobacco economy enlarged these differences in several ways. Generally, planters placed little trust in newly arrived Africans with their strange tongues and alien customs. While they assigned creoles to artisanal duties on their plantations and to service within their households, they sent Africans to the distant, upland quarters where the slaves did the dull, backbreaking work of clearing the land and tending tobacco. The small size of these specialized upcountry units, their isolation from the mainstream of Chesapeake life, and their rude frontier conditions made these largely male compounds lonely, unhealthy places that narrowed men's vision. The dynamics of creole life, however, broadened black understanding of life in the New World. Traveling freely through the countryside as artisans, watermen, and domestic servants, creoles gained in confidence as they mastered the terrain, perfected their English, and learned about

134

Christianity and other cultural modes that whites equated with civilization. Knowledge of the white world enabled black creoles to manipulate their masters to their own advantage. If Afro-Americans became increasingly knowledgeable about their circumstances and confident of their ability to deal with them, Africans remained provincials, limited by the narrow alternatives of plantation life.[36]

As in the low-country and the Northern colonies, Africans in the Chesapeake strove to escape whites, while creoles used their knowledge of white society for their own benefit. These cultural differences, which were reflected in all aspects of black life, can be seen most clearly in the diverse patterns of resistance. Africans ran away toward the backcountry and isolated swamps. They generally moved in groups that included women and children, despite the hazards such groups entailed for a successful escape. Their purpose was to recreate the only society they knew free from white domination. In 1727, Governor William Gooch of Virginia reported that about a dozen slaves had left a new plantation near the falls of the James River. They headed west and settled near Lexington, built houses, and planted a crop before being retaken. But Afro-Americans ran away alone, usually with the hope of escaping into American society. Moving toward the areas of heaviest settlement, they found refuge in the thick network of black kinship that covered the countryside and sold their labor to white yeomen with few questions asked. While the possibility of passing as free remained small in the years before the Revolution, the creoles' obvious confidence in their ability to integrate themselves into American society stands in stark contrast to that of Africans, who sought first to flee it.[37]

During the middle years of the eighteenth century, changes in the Chesapeake economy and society diminished differences within black society and created a unified Afro-American culture. The success of the tobacco economy enlarged the area of settlement and allowed planters to increase their holdings. The most successful planters, anxious to protect themselves from the rigors of the world marketplace, strove for plantation self-sufficiency. The great estates of the Chesapeake became self-contained enterprises with slaves taking positions as artisans, tradesmen, wagoners, and, sometimes, managers; the plantation was "like a Town," as a tutor on Robert Carter's estate observed, "but most of the Inhabitants are black."[8] The increased sophistication of the Chesapeake economy propelled many more blacks into artisanal positions and the larger units of production, tighter pattern of settlement, and the greater mobility allowed by the growing network of roads ended the deadening isolation of the upcountry quarter. Bondsmen increasingly lived in large groups, and those who did not could generally find black companionship within a few miles' walk. Finally, better food, clothing, and shelter and, perhaps, the development of immunities to New World diseases enabled blacks to live longer, healthier lives.[38]

As part of their drive for self-sufficiency, Chesapeake slaveholders encouraged the development of an indigenous slave population. Spurred by the proven ability of Africans to survive and reproduce and pressed in the international slave market by the superior resources of West Indian sugar magnates and lowland rice growers, Chesapeake planters strove to correct the sexual imbalance within the black population, perhaps by importing a large proportion of women or lessening the burden of female slaves. Blacks quickly took advantage of this new circumstance and placed their family life on a firmer footing. Husbands and wives petitioned their owners to allow them to reside together on the same quarter and saw to it that their families were fed, beyond their masters' rations. Planters, for their part, were usually receptive to slaves' demands for a secure family life, both because it reflected their own values and because they profited mightily from the addition of slave children. Thomas Jefferson frankly considered "a woman who brings a child every two years as more profitable than the best man on the farm [for] what she produces is an addition to capital, while his labor disappears in mere consumption." Under these circumstances, the black population increased rapidly. Planters relied less and less on African importation and, by the 1740s, most of the growth of the black population came from natural increase. Within a generation, African importation was, for all practical purposes, no longer a significant source of slave labor. In the early 1770s, the period of the greatest importation into the low-country, only 500 of the 5,000 slaves added annually to the black population of Virginia derived directly from Africa.[39]

The establishment of the black family marked the re-emergence of Afro-American culture in the Chesapeake. Although Africans continued to enter the region, albeit at a slower pace, the nature of the slave trade minimized their impact on the development of black society in the region. Unlike those in the low-country, newly

EVOLUTION OF AFRO-AMERICAN SOCIETY

arrived Africans could rarely hope to remain together. Rather than funnel their cargo through a single port, Chesapeake slavers peddled it in small lots at the many tobacco landings that lined the bay's extensive perimeter. Planters rarely bought more than a few slaves at a time, and larger purchasers, usually the great planter-merchants, often acted as jobbers, quickly reselling these slaves to back country freeholders.[40] The resulting fragmentation sent newly arrived Africans in all directions and prevented the maintenance of tribal or shipboard ties. Chesapeake slaveholders cared little about the origins of their slaves. In their eyes, newly arrived Africans were not Iboes, Coromantees, or Angolans, but "new Negroes." While the unicentered slave trade sustained and strengthened African culture in the low-country, the Chesapeake slave trade facilitated the absorption of Africans into the evolving creole society.

Differences between creoles and Africans did not disappear with the creation of a self-sustaining Afro-American population. The creoles' advantages – language skills, familiarity with the countryside, artisanal standing, and knowledge of the plantation routine – continued to propel them into positions of authority within the slave hierarchy. In some ways, the growing complexity of the Chesapeake economy widened the distance between Africans and creoles, at least at first. Most of the skilled and managerial positions within the region's expanding iron industry went to creole blacks as did the artisanal work in flour mills and weaving houses. On some plantations, moreover, artisan and house status became lodged in particular families with parents passing privileged positions on to their children. Increasingly, skilled slaves entered the market economy by selling their own time and earning money from "overwork," thereby gaining a large measure of freedom. For the most part, Africans remained on rude, backwoods plantations tending the broad-leaf weed. Since creole slaves sold at a premium price and most great planters had already established self-sustaining slave forces, small planters purchased nearly all of the newly arrived Africans after mid-century. These upward-striving men generally owned the least developed, most distant farms. Their labor requirements remained primitive compared to the sophisticated division of labor on the self-contained plantation-towns.[41]

Over the long term, however, economic changes sped the integration of Africans into Afro-American society. Under the pressure

137

of a world-wide food shortage, Chesapeake planters turned from the production of tobacco to that of foodstuff, especially wheat. The demands of wheat cultivation transformed the nature of labor in the region. Whereas tobacco farming required season-long labor, wheat farming employed workers steadily only during planting and harvesting. The remainder of the year, laborers had little to do with the crop. At the same time, however, wheat required a larger and more skilled labor force to transport the grain to market and to store it, mill it, and reship it as flour, bread, or bulk grain. Economic changes encouraged masters to teach their slaves skills and to hire them out during the slack season. At first, these opportunities went mostly to creoles, but as the wheat economy grew, spurring urbanization and manufacturing, the demands for artisans and hirelings outstripped the creole population.[42] An increasing number of Africans were placed in positions previously reserved for creoles. The process of cultural transformation that earlier in the eighteenth century had taken a generation or more was considerably shorter at mid-century. Africans became Afro-Americans with increasing rapidity as the century wore on, eliminating the differences within black society that African importation had created.

Chesapeake blacks enjoyed considerably less autonomy than their low-country counterparts. Resident planters, small units of production, and the presence of large numbers of whites meant that most blacks lived and worked in close proximity to whites. While low-country planters fled to coastal cities for a large part of the year, the resident planter was a fixture of Chesapeake life. Small freeholders labored alongside slaves, and great planters prided themselves on regulating all aspects of their far-flung estates through a combination of direct personal supervision and plantation-based overseers. The latter were usually white, drawn from the region's white majority. Those few blacks who achieved managerial positions, moreover, enjoyed considerably less authority than lowland drivers. The presence of numerous nonslaveholding whites circumscribed black opportunities in other ways as well. While Chesapeake slaves commonly kept gardens and flocks of barnyard animals, white competitors limited their market and created a variety of social tensions. If low-country masters sometimes encouraged their slaves to produce nonstaple garden crops, whites in the Chesapeake – slaveholders and nonslaveholders alike – complained that blacks stole more than they raised and worked to

curb the practice. Thus, at every turn, economy and society conspired to constrain black autonomy.

The requirements of tobacco cultivation reinforced the planters'
concern about daily work routine. Whereas the task system insu-
lated low-country blacks against white intervention and
maximized black control over their work, the constant attention
demanded by tobacco impelled Chesapeake planters to oversee the
tedious process of cultivating, topping, worming, suckering, and
curing tobacco. The desire of Chesapeake masters to control their
slaves went beyond the supervision of labor. Believing that slaves
depended on them "for every necessity of life," they intervened in
the most intimate aspects of black life. "I hope you will take care
that the Negroes both men and women I sent you up last always
go by the names we gave them," Robert "King" Carter reminded
his steward.[h] "I am sure we repeated them so often ... that everyone
knew their names & would readily answer to them." Chesapeake
planters sought to shape domestic relations, cure physical mal-
adies, and form personalities. However miserably they failed to
ensure black domestic tranquility and reform slave drunkards,
paternalism at close quarters in the Chesapeake had a far more
potent influence on black life than the distant paternalism that
developed in the low-country. Chesapeake blacks developed no
distinct language and rarely utilized African day names for their
children.[43] Afro-American culture in the Chesapeake evolved parallel with Anglo-American culture and with a considerable
measure of congruence.

The diverse development of Afro-American culture during the
seventeenth and eighteenth centuries reveals the importance of
time and place in the study of American slavery. Black people in
colonial America shared many things: a common African lineage,
a common racial oppressor, a common desire to create the richest
life possible for themselves and their posterity in the most difficult
of circumstances. But these commonalities took different shape and
meaning within the diverse circumstances of the North American
mainland. The nature of the slave trade, the various demographic
configurations of whites and blacks, and the demands of particular
staples – to name some of the factors influencing the development
of slave society – created at least three distinctive patterns of
Afro-American life.

EDITOR'S NOTES

a Creole and Afro-American are used synonymously and refer to black people of native American birth.

b Peter Kalm was a Swedish traveler in mid-eighteenth-century North America.

c Acculturation or creolization refers to the transformation of Africans into Afro-Americans. This process entailed the consolidation of a variety of distinctive African cultures as well as the compounding of those cultures with various European and native American ones to create a new cultural type.

d In 1621 the States General of the Netherlands established the Dutch West India Company which three years later founded an outpost, the New Netherland. Its main settlement was New Amsterdam, which became New York City in 1664 after the English conquest.

e Maroons were bands or communities of runaway slaves; the term derived from the Spanish *cimarron*, originally referring to domestic cattle that had taken to the hills.

f From north-west to south-east, Gambians were from Senegambia, the Windward Coast encompassed the present-day Ivory Coast and Liberia, Coromantees were Akan people from the Gold Coast (present-day Ghana), Iboes and Callabars were from the Bight of Biafra (centered on the Niger Delta, or present-day Nigeria), and Angolans were from Central Africa.

g Robert Carter of Nomini Hall (1728–1804), Virginia planter.

h Robert "King" Carter of Corotoman (1663–1732), one of the wealthiest Americans of his generation and a prominent Virginia planter.

NOTES

Reprinted from *American Historical Review*, LXXXV (1980): 44–78, by permission of the author.

1 For a collection of the relevant censuses, see William S. Rossiter, *A Century of Population Growth* (Washington, D.C., 1909): 149–84. Also see Robert V. Wells, *The Population of the British Colonies in America before 1776: A Survey of Census Data* (Princeton, 1975): 69–143, and Wells's correction of the 1731 enumeration, "The New York Census of 1731," *New York Historical Society Quarterly*, 57 (1973): 255–9. For estimates of the Northern black population predating these censuses, see U.S. Bureau of the Census, *Historical Statistics of the United States, Colonial Times to 1957* (Washington, D.C., 1960): 756.

2 Edgar J. McManus, *Black Bondage in the North* (Syracuse, N.Y., 1973): 42–3; Charles S. Boyer, *Early Forges and Furnaces in New Jersey* (Philadelphia, 1963): 30–1, 149, 166, 194–9, 239; Frances D. Pingeon, "Slavery in New Jersey on the Eve of the Revolution," in Williams C. Wright, ed., *New Jersey in the American Revolution* (rev. ed., Trenton, N.J. 1974): 51–2, 57; Darold D. Wax, "The Demand for Slave Labor in Colonial

Pennsylvania," *Pennsylvania History*, 34 (1967): 334–5; and William Binning, *Pennsylvania Iron Manufacture in the Eighteenth Century* (Harrisburg, Pa., 1931): 122–5.

3 Kalm, *Peter Kalm's Travels in North America*, ed. and trans A. B. Benson, 1 (New York, 1937): 205, as quoted in Alan Tully, "Patterns of Slaveholding in Colonial Pennsylvania: Chester and Lancaster Counties, 1729–1758," *Journal of Social History*, 6 (1973): 286; Lorenzo J. Greene, *The Negro in Colonial New England* (New York, 1942): 103–12; McManus, *Black Bondage in the North*: 40–1; Pingeon, "Slavery in New Jersey": 51; William D. Miller, "The Narragansett Planters," *American Antiquarian Society Proceedings*, 43 (1933): 67–71; Tully,"Patterns of Slaveholding in Colonial Pennsylvania": 284–303; Steven B. Frankt, "Patterns of Slave-Holding in Somerset County, N.J.," seminar paper, 1967, in Special Collections, Rutgers University Library, New Brunswick, N.J.; Wax, "The Demand for Slave Labor in Colonial Pennsylvania": 332–40; and Jerome H. Woods, Jr., "The Negro in Early Pennsylvania: The Lancaster Experience, 1730 –1790," in Elinor Miller and Eugene D. Genovese, eds., *Plantation, Town, and County: Essays on the Local History of American Slave Society* (Urbana, Ill., 1974): 447–8.

4 N. B. Shurtleff *et al.*, eds. *Records of the Governor and Company of Massachusetts Bay in New England* (1628–1698), 1 (Boston, 1853): 79, as quoted in Carl Bridenbaugh, *Cities in the Wilderness*, 1625–1742 (New York, 1938): 49; Rossiter, *A Century of Population Growth*: 149–84; Greene, *The Negro in Colonial New England*: 78, 81–2, 84–8, 92–3: Gary B. Nash, "Slaves and Slaveowners in Colonial Philadelphia," *William and Mary Quarterly*, 3rd ser., 30 (1973): 226–52; and Thomas Archdeacon, *New York City*, 1664–1710: *Conquest and Change* (Ithaca, N.Y. 1976): 46–7.

5 New York *Weekly Post-Boy*, May 17, 1756, as quoted in McManus, *Black Bondage in the North*: 38; Carl Bridenbaugh, *Cities in Revolt, 1743–1776* (New York, 1955): 88, 285–6, and *Cities in the Wilderness*: 163, 200–1; Nash, "Slaves and Slaveowners in Colonial Pennsylvania": 243–4; Archdeacon, *New York City*: 89–90; Rossiter, *A Century of Population Growth*: 170–80; Edgar J. McManus, *A History of Slavery in New York* (Syracuse, N.Y., 1966): 44–45, and *Black Bondage in the North*: 37–9; and Wells, *The Population in the British Colonies of America before 1776*: 116–23.

6 Eric Foner, *Tom Paine and Revolutionary America* (New York, 1976): 48–56.

7 Governor Samuel Cranston to the Board of Trade, December 5, 1708, in J. R. Bartlett, ed., *Records of the Colony of Rhode Island and Providence Plantations*, 4 (1860): 55, as quoted in Miller, "Narragansett Planters": 68 n. 2; and Cadwallader Colden to Mr. Jordan, March 26, 1717, in *Letters and Papers of Cadwallader Colden*, 1 (New York, 1917): 39, as quoted in Arthur Zilversmit, *The First Emancipation: The Abolition of Negro Slavery in the North* (Chicago, 1967): 22. Joyce D. Goodfriend, "Burghers and Blacks: The Evolution of a Slave Society at New Amsterdam," *New York History*, 59 (1978): 125–44; McManus, *Slavery in New York*: 2–22; and Gerald F. DeJong, "The Dutch Reformed Church

and Negro Slavery in Colonial America," *Church History*, 40 (1971): 430.

8   Sara Kemble Knight, as quoted in Ralph F. Weld, *Slavery in Connecticut* (New Haven, 1935): 8–9; John Watts, *Letterbook of John Watts*, New York Historical Society Collections, no. 61 (New York, 1938): 151; and McManus, *Black Bondage in the North, passim*.

9   Nash, "Slaves and Slaveowners in Colonial Philadelphia": 226–37; James G. Lydon, "New York and the Slave Trade 1700 to 1774," *William and Mary Quarterly*, 3rd ser., 35 (1978): 387–8; and Darold D. Wax, "Quaker Merchants and the Slave Trade in Colonial Pennsylvania," *Pennsylvania Magazine of History and Biography*, 86 (1962): 145, and "Negro Imports into Pennsylvania": 256–7, 280–7.

10   Kenneth Scott, "The Slave Insurrection in New York in 1712," *New York Historical Society Quarterly*, 45 (1961): 43–74, esp. 62–7.

11   The shortage of African women and a sexual balance among Indians and, to a lesser extent, whites that favored women encouraged black men to marry Indian and, occasionally, white women, especially in New England; Winthrop D. Jordan, "American Chiaroscuro: The Status and Definition of Mulattoes in the British Colonies," *William and Mary Quarterly*, 3rd ser., 19 (1962): 197–8, esp. n. 28.

12   For petitions by blacks, see Robert C. Twombly, "Black Resistance to Slavery in Massachusetts," in William L. O'Neill, ed., *Insights and Parallels* (Minneapolis, 1973): 13–16; and, for various association names, see Dorothy Porter, ed., *Early Negro Writings*, 1760–1837 (Boston, 1971).

13   Henry Bull, "Memoir of Rhode Island," Newport *Rhode-Island Republican*, April 19, 1837, as quoted in William D. Pierson, "Afro-American Culture in Eighteenth-Century New England" (Ph.D. dissertation, Indiana University, 1975): 181; Joseph P. Reidy, " 'Negro Election Day' and Black Community Life in New England, 1750–1860," *Marxist Perspectives*, 1 (1978): 102–17; Alice M. Earle, *Colonial Days in Old New York* (5th ed., New York, 1922); Woods, "The Negro in Early Pennsylvania": 451; and Pierson, "Afro-American Culture in Eighteenth-Century New England": 181–313.

14   Peter Williams, *A Discourse, Delivered in the Death of Capt. Paul Cuffee* (New York, 1817).

15   Peter H. Wood, *Black Majority: Negroes in Colonial South Carolina from 1670 through the Stono Rebellion* (New York, 1974): 13–24, 94–7.

16   John D. Duncan, "Servitude and Slavery in Colonial South Carolina, 1670–1776" (Ph.D. dissertation, Emory University, 1971): 587–601; and Herbert Aptheker, "Maroons within the Present Limits of the United States," *Journal of Negro History*, 24 (1939): 167–84.

17   Wood, *Black Majority: Negroes in Colonial South Carolina*: 35–62, 119–30.

18   ibid: 99–103, 157, 159.

19   Peter H. Wood, " 'More like a Negro Country': Demographic Patterns in Colonial South Carolina, 1670–1740," in Stanley L. Engerman and Eugene D. Genovese, eds., *Race and Slavery in the Western Hemisphere: Quantitative Studies* (Princeton, 1975): 131–45; Julian J. Petty, *The Growth and Distribution of Population in South Carolina* (Columbia, S.C.

1943): 15–58, 220–7, Bureau of the Census, *Historical Statistics of the United States*: 756; and *Returns of the Whole Number of Persons within the ... United States [1790]* (Philadelphia, 1791).

20 W. Robert Higgins, "Charleston: Terminus and Entrepôt of the Colonial Slave Trade," in Martin L. Kilson and Robert I. Rotberg, eds., *The African Diaspora* (Cambridge, Mass., 1976): 115.

21 Wood, *Black Majority: Negroes in Colonial South Carolina*, xiv, and " 'More like a Negro Country' ": 149–54; Higgins, "Charleston: Terminus and Entrepôt of the Colonial Slave Trade": 118–27; Darold D. Wax, "Preferences for Slaves in Colonial America," *Journal of Negro History* 58 (1973): 388–99; Curtin, *The Atlantic Slave Trade*: 143, 156–7; and Henry Laurens, *The Papers of Henry Laurens*, ed. Philip M. Hamer, George C. Rogers, Jr., and David R. Chesnutt, 7 vols. (Columbia, S.C., 1970–), 1: 294–5.

22 Converse D. Clowse, *Economic Beginnings of Colonial South Carolina, 1670–1730* (Columbia, S.C., 1971): 122–33, 167–71, 220–1, 231–5, 256–8: Wood, *Black Majority: Negroes in Colonial South Carolina*: 35–62; Lewis C. Gray, *History of Agriculture in the Southern United States to 1860*, 2 vols. (Washington, 1933), 1: 277–89; James M. Clifton, "Golden Grains of White: Rice Planting on the Lower Cape Fear," *North Carolina Historical Review*, 50 (1973): 368–78; Douglas C. Wilms, "The Development of Rice Culture in 18th-Century Georgia," *Southeastern Geographer*, 12 (1972): 45–57; and David L. Coon, "The Development of Market Agriculture in South Carolina, 1670–1785" (Ph.D. dissertation, University of Illinois, Urbana-Champaign, 1972): 126–7, 168–9, 178–86, 215–68.

23 Joseph W. Barnwell, ed., "The Diary of Timothy Ford," *South Carolina Historical Magazine*, 13 (1914): 142; Alexander Hewatt, *An Historical Account of the Rise and Progress of the Colonies of South Carolina and Georgia*, 2 (London, 1779): 97; Alan Candler, ed., *The Colonial Records of the State of Georgia*, 18 (Atlanta, 1912): 277–82; Charles S. Henry, comp., *A Digest of all the Ordinances of Savannah* (Savannah, Ga., 1854): 94–7; Petition from Charleston Carpenters and Bricklayers, 1783, and Petition from Charleston Coopers, 1793, Legislative Papers, South Carolina Department of Archives and History, Columbia; Thomas Cooper and David J. McCord, *The Statutes at Large of South Carolina*, 10 vols. (Columbia, S.C., 1836–41) 2: 22–3, 7: 385–7, 9: 692–7; Donald R. Lennon and Ida B. Kellam, eds., *The Wilmington Town Book, 1743–1778* (Raleigh, N.C., 1973): 165–6; Petition from Newberne, 1785, North Carolina Legislative Papers, North Carolina State Archives, Raleigh; Carl Bridenbaugh, *Colonial Craftsmen* (New York, 1950): 139–41, and *Cities in Revolt*: 88–9, 244, 274, 285–6; Leila Sellers, *Charleston Business on the Eve of the America Revolution* (Chapel Hill, N.C., 1934): 99–108; Duncan, "Servitude and Slavery in Colonial South Carolina": 439–46; and Kenneth Coleman, *Colonial Georgia, A History* (New York, 1976): 229–30.

24 Candler, *Colonial Records of the State of Georgia*: 23–30, 252–62; Henry, *Ordinances of Savannah*: 95–7; Alexander Edwards, comp., *Ordinances of the City Council of Charleston* (Charleston, S.C. 1802): 65–8, Cooper and McCord, *Statutes at Large of South Carolina*, 7: 363, 380–1, 393; Lennon and Kellam, *The Wilmington Town Book*: xxx–xxxi, 165–8, 204–5;

Duncan, "Servitude and Slavery in Colonial South Carolina": 467–9, 481–4; and Sellers, *Charleston Business on the Eve of the American Revolution*: 99–102, 106–8.

25 *South Carolina Gazette*, May 24, 1773, as quoted in Duncan, "Servitude and Slavery in Colonial South Carolina": Leowald *et al.*, "Bolzius Answers a Questionnaire on Carolina and Georgia": 236; Cooper and McCord, *Statutes at Large of South Carolina*, 7: 396–412; and Duncan, "Servitude and Slavery in Colonial South Carolina": 233–7.

26 Winthrop D. Jordan, *White over Black: American Attitudes toward the Negro* (Chapel Hill, N.C., 1968): 144–50, 167–78, and "American Chiaroscuro: The Status and Definition of Mulattoes in the British Colonies": 186–200; Wood, *Black Majority: Negroes in Colonial South Carolina*: 100–3; and General Tax, Receipts and Payments, 1761–69, Records of the Public Treasurers of South Carolina, South Carolina Department of Archives and History, Columbia.

27 Wood, *Black Majority: Negroes in Colonial South Carolina*, esp. chap. 6; Lorenzo D. Turner, *Africanisms in the Gullah Dialect* (Chicago, 1949); William R. Bascom, "Acculturation among the Gullah Negroes," *American Anthropologist*, 43 (1941): 43–50; Klingberg, *An Appraisal of the Negro in South Carolina*; and Hennig Cohen, "Slave Names in Colonial South Carolina," *American Speech*, 28 (1952): 102–7.

28 Frank J. Klingberg, *An Appraisal of the Negro in Colonial South Carolina* (Washington, 1941): 116–17; and Petition of John and William Morriss, 1791, and Petition from Camden Negroes, 1793, South Carolina Legislative Papers, South Carolina Department of Archives and History, Columbia.

29 For one planter's attempt to keep boatmen from mixing with his plantation hands, see Laurens, *Papers of Henry Laurens*, 4: 319, 633; and Sellers, *Charleston Business on the Eve of the American Revolution*: 108.

30 Edmund S. Morgan, *American Slavery, American Freedom: The Ordeal of Colonial Virginia* (New York, 1975): 108–79, 215–49; and Wesley Frank Craven, *White, Red, and Black: The Seventeenth-Century Virginian* (Charlottesville, Va., 1971): 75–99.

31 Ross M. Kimmel, "Free Blacks in Seventeenth-Century Maryland," *Maryland Historical Magazine*, 71 (1976): 19–25; John H. Russell, *The Free Negro in Virginia, 1619–1865* (Baltimore, 1913): 24–38, 88, 116, 119–20, 136–7; James H. Brewer, "Negro Property Owners in Seventeenth-Century Virginia," *William and Mary Quarterly*, 3rd ser., 12 (1955): 575–80; and Susie M. Ames, *Studies of the Virginia Eastern Shore in the Seventeenth Century* (Richmond, Va., 1940): 99–108.

32 Morgan, *American Slavery, American Freedom*: 329–37; Warren M. Billings, "The Cases of Fernando and Elizabeth Key: A Note on the Status of Blacks in the Seventeenth Century," *William and Mary Quarterly*, 3rd ser., 30 (1973): 467–74; and Kimmel, "Free Blacks in Seventeenth-Century Maryland": 20–1.

33 Edmund S. Morgan, "Slavery and Freedom: The American Paradox," *Journal of American History*, 59 (1972): 17–18; and T. H. Breen, "A Changing Labor Force and Race Relations in Virginia, 1660–1710," *Journal of Social History*, 7 (1973): 3–25.

34 Allan Kulikoff, "A 'Prolifick' People: Black Population Growth in the Chesapeake Colonies, 1700–1790," *Southern Studies*, 16 (1977): 391–6, 403–5, and "The Origins of Afro-American Society in Tidewater Maryland and Virginia, 1700 to 1790," *William and Mary Quarterly*, 3rd ser., 35 (1978): 229–31; Russell R. Menard, "The Maryland Slave Population, 1658 to 1730: A Demographic Profile of Blacks in Four Counties," ibid: 32 (1975): 30–2; and Craven, *White, Red, and Black*: 89–103.

35 Kulikoff, "A 'Prolifick' People: Black Population Growth": 392–406; Menard, "The Maryland Slave Population": 30–5, 38–49; and Craven, *White, Red, and Black*: 98–101.

36 Gerald W. Mullin, *Flight and Rebellion: Slave Resistance in Eighteenth-Century Virginia* (New York, 1972), esp. chaps. 2–3; Menard, "The Maryland Slave Population": 32–54; and Kulikoff, "Origins of Afro-American Society in Tidewater Maryland and Virginia": 236–49.

37 Mullin, *Flight and Rebellion: Slave Resistance in Eighteenth-Century Virginia*: 34–110, esp. table 3 (pp. 108–9); and Kulikoff, "Origins of Afro-American Society in Tidewater Maryland and Virginia": 253–4.

38 Philip V. Fithian, *The Journal and Letters of Philip Vickers Fithian*, 1773–1774, ed. Hunter D. Farish (Williamsburg, Va., 1943): 73; Mullin, *Flight and Resistance: Slave Resistance in Eighteenth-Century Virginia*: 19–32; Kulikoff, "Origins of Afro-American Society in Tidewater Maryland and Virginia": 240–2, 246–9; Louis Morton, *Robert Carter of Nomini Hall: A Virginia Tobacco Planter of the Eighteenth Century* (Charlottesville, Va., 1941); Michael Greenberg, "William Byrd II and the World of the Market," *Southern Studies*, 16 (1977): 429–56; and especially, Landon Carter, *The Diary of Colonel Landon Carter of Sabine Hall, 1752–1778*, ed. Jack P. Greene, 2 vols. (Charlottesville, Va., 1966), *passim*.

39 Allan Kulikoff, "The Beginnings of the Afro-American Family in Maryland," in Aubrey C. Land *et al.*, eds., *Law, Society and Politics in Early Maryland* (Baltimore, 1977): 177–96, "A 'Prolifick' People: Black Population Growth": 401–3, 405–14, and "Origins of Afro-American Society in Tidewater Maryland and Virginia": 246–53; Daniel Dulany to Robert Carter, December 18, 1768, Colonial Papers, Maryland Historical Society, Baltimore; Robert Carter to John Pound, March 16, 1779, to Fleet Cox, January 2, 1788, and to George Newman, December 29, 1789, typescript, Robert Carter Papers, Duke University, Durham, N.C.; John C. Fitzpatrick, ed., *The Writings of George Washington*, 39 vols. (Washington, 1931–44), 2: 526, 29: 154, 398; and Edwin M. Betts, ed., *Thomas Jefferson's Farm Book* (New York, 1953), pt. 2: 46, 12–13, 21, 24–6, 42–6.

40 Mullin, *Flight and Rebellion: Slave Resistance in Eighteenth-Century Virginia*: 14–16; Kulikoff, "Origins of Afro-American Society in Tidewater Maryland and Virginia": 230–5; Darold D. Wax, "Black Immigrants: The Slave Trade in Colonial Maryland," *Maryland Magazine of History*, 73 (1978): 30–45; and Winthrop D. Jordan, "Planter and Slave Identity Formation: Some Problems in the Comparative Approach," in Vera Rubin and Arthur Tuden, eds., *Comparative Perspectives on Slavery in New World Plantation Societies*, Annals of the New York Academy of Sciences, no. 292 (Washington, 1933): 38.

41 Kulikoff, "The Beginnings of the Afro-American Family in Maryland":

185–6; Jordan, *White over Black*: 405 n. 7; Mullin, *Flight and Rebellion: Slave Resistance in Eighteenth-Century Virginia*: 83–139; "Description of Servants, 1772," Northampton Furnace, Ridgely Account Books, Maryland Historical Society, Baltimore; and Ronald L. Lewis, *Coal, Iron, and Slaves: Industrial Slavery in Maryland and Virginia*, 1715–1865 (Westport, Conn., 1979): 82–4, 162–3.

42 Carville Earle and Ronald Hoffman, "The Urban South: The First Two Centuries," *Perspectives in American History*, 10 (1976): 26–76; Mullin, *Flight and Rebellion: Slave Resistance in Eighteenth-Century Virginia*: 87–8, 124–7; and Lewis C. Gray, *History of Agriculture in the Southern United States to 1860*, 2 vols., 2: 602–17. Although the best study of slave hiring in the Chesapeake region focuses on the post-Revolution years, the forces promoting slave hire after the war suggest that the practice predates the Revolution. See Sarah S. Hughes, "Slaves for Hire: The Allocation of Black Labor in Elizabeth City County, Virginia, 1782 to 1810," *William and Mary Quarterly*, 3rd ser., 35 (1978): 260–86.

43 Robert Carter to Robert Jones, Robert "King" Carter Letterbooks, Alderman Library, University of Virginia, Charlottesville; and Robert Carter to William Carr, March 15, 1785, Carter Papers, typescript, Duke University, Durham, N.C.

Part III

PRIVATE AND PUBLIC WORLDS

Linking private and public, interior experience and external event, is one of the great challenges facing contemporary historians. Jon Butler confronts it through an analysis of evangelicalism, which emphasized a personal and subjective relationship to God but which was also a communal movement. Rhys Isaac likewise treats religion – in his case Anglicanism – but moves beyond the church into the home in order to emphasize the permeability of public and private realms in mid-eighteenth-century Virginia. Laurel Ulrich focuses upon the home but demonstrates how one woman's life interacted with that of many others, leading her to identify a separate female economy in late eighteenth-century Maine. Finally, like both Isaac and Ulrich, Tim Breen takes his readers into ordinary colonial American households, but in his case to investigate what they purchased. He then shows how humdrum, personal, and individual consumer decisions could be transformed into broad-gauged, public, political statements. In these ways, these four historians reveal the promise of connecting the intimate details of everyday life to broader public concerns.

5

THE PLURAL ORIGINS OF AMERICAN REVIVALISM

Jon Butler

Exploring the relationship between internal states of mind and external circumstances comes naturally to scholars of American religion. In this stimulating essay, Jon Butler links these two concerns most directly in his discussion of the contrasting roles of the Tennent family and George Whitefield as evangelical leaders. Butler explores the careers of the Tennents and Whitefield in order to discover the different ways in which revivalist ministers appealed to lay audiences. More generally, Butler argues that early American religious life was astonishingly complex and diverse. His major revisions of received wisdom include: early American religion must be understood in a European context and not in isolation; the European pattern of state churches was renewed and reinvigorated in eighteenth-century America; Anglicanism was not moribund in the colonies; modest Christianization rather than deChristianization or declension (which an earlier overemphasis on the alleged waning of Puritanism decreed) best encapsulates religious trends in the eighteenth century. However, perhaps his most arresting claim is that the impact of the 1740s' revivals known as the Great Awakening has been exaggerated. Rather, Butler persuasively suggests that the rise of religious pluralism and episodic revivalism, which extended almost a century from the 1670s through the 1760s, is a far more impressive feature of colonial American religion than a single Awakening.

The reader might consider points of intersection between this essay and others, particularly those of Bailyn, Greene and Isaac. Do Bailyn and Butler treat the messianic pietist sects such as the Woman in the Wilderness in similar ways? Do Butler's arguments fit Greene's notion of convergence? Do Butler and Isaac agree about the strengths of Anglicanism in Virginia?

The logic of Butler's arguments also merits consideration. Is the astonishing variety of Christian expression that Butler documents easily squared with his conclusion of a general religious indifference? Is his argument for the growth of religious authority, both among the state churches and the evangelical denominations, fully satisfactory? Some of the defining characteristics of eighteenth-century American religion, it has often been argued, were the relative power of the laity, the relative weakness of the ministry, and the decentralization of state church authority. If these are all true, can eighteenth-century American religion, particularly evangelicalism, be so easily severed from an association with the American Revolution, which was after all a crisis of authority?

* * *

A broadening stream of Christian spiritual expression overran European settlement in the eighteenth-century colonies. This widening diversity forever altered the European religious configuration of colonial America. Two such streams were especially important: the establishmentarian Anglican and Congregationalist traditions and the explosion of efforts at religious renewal and revival. Neither of these traditions produced church adherence or membership rates equal to twentieth-century American practice. But they laid out new and powerful forms of religious practice and activity that influenced organized Christian endeavor for more than a century after their first appearance in the colonies.

Historians usually focus on the "Great Awakening" of the 1740s as the principal religious occurrence of prerevolutionary American society. Since its first elucidation in Joseph Tracy's *The Great Awakening*, which was published in 1841 to provide historical support for America's nineteenth-century revivals, its interpretative significance has multiplied a thousandfold. In the 1970s and 1980s, various historians have seen in it nothing less than the first unifying event of the colonial experience, the origins of the American evangelical tradition, and a major source of revolutionary antiauthoritarian and republican rhetoric.

This emphasis on the "Great Awakening" may say more about subsequent times than about its own. The term was not contemporary, nor was it known to the historians of the revolutionary and early national periods. Internal descriptive and analytical inconsistencies belie the event's importance and even its existence; it is difficult to date, for example, because revivals linked to it started in New England long before 1730 yet did not appear with force in Virginia until the 1760s. Its supporters questioned only certain kinds of authority, not authority itself, and they usually strengthened rather than weakened denominational and clerical institutions. It missed most colonies, and even in New England its long-term effects have been greatly exaggerated. On reflection, it might better be thought of as an interpretive fiction and as an American equivalent of the Roman Empire's Donation of Constantine, the medieval forgery that the papacy used to justify its subsequent claims to political authority. More important, an obsessive concern with it distorts important historical subtleties and obscures other crucial realities of eighteenth-century American religious development.[1]

For better or worse, the state church tradition,[a] rather than Dissenting evangelicalism or voluntaryism, gave Christianity its primary shape in eighteenth-century colonial American society, at least through 1740. The state church tradition took its power from three major characteristics: coercion, territoriality, and public ceremonialism. Different varieties in different colonies used these means in very different ways. But they produced a remarkably similar product, especially when viewed from the perspective of the laity whose religious needs and desires they sought to direct.

The principal task of congregations enjoying the benefits of legal establishment was to construct an effective parish life. This was true of all the colonial state church systems, whether in the Anglican middle and southern colonies or the Congregationalist commonwealths of Massachusetts and Connecticut. The territorial parish designated the physical boundaries within which clergymen exercised their ministry. The parish minister assumed responsibility for propagating and maintaining Christian practice and belief among the entire population, not just among a few knowledgeable and loyal believers. Indeed, the state church minister rightly assumed that evangelism – spreading the Christian gospel – was the major obligation of his ministry. Even where the state church minister might reach for saints, he ministered to everyone.

In the main, legal establishment turned Anglican parish churches into vital centers of colonial community life. In Virginia especially, but also in other colonies with Anglican establishment, the Sabbath emerged as a day of intense and quickly mingled sacred and secular ceremonies – the gathering of the laity for worship, the reading of the ceremonies prescribed for worship in the *Book of Common Prayer*, the spreading out of the worshipers across the church lawns as listeners broke up into small knots of conversation after the service, and sometimes more social activities, such as horse racing, which might continue into the afternoon. Vestry meetings followed parallel patterns. The vestrymen often met on court days, in part because some also served as magistrates, and the collection of so many prestigious and economically active men together in a single place provided a common focus for the conduct of secular business. Before and after the vestry had decided on building maintenance, ministers' salaries, or poor relief, they and other parish residents were busy with transactions of many kinds – land, goods, and increasingly after 1700, slaves.[2]

Anglican parish life upheld the modern social structure by honoring establishmentarian concepts of deference and social prestige. The South Carolina commissary, Gideon Johnston, always placed the most prominent communicant at the top of his communicant list at St. Philip's Church in Charleston in 1711 and 1712: Judge Nicholas Trott, on Whitsunday, May 20, 1711; Colonel William Rhett and Madame Rhett, followed by the customs official Colonel Robert Quarry, on August 5; Governor Charles Craven on Easter Sunday, April 20, 1712. When prestigious men's wives took communion alone, as Madame Rhett frequently did, Johnston always placed their names ahead of less prestigious male communicants.[3]

Anglican ceremonialism accompanied a rising secular ceremonialism in eighteenth-century America. For elites rising out of an expanding colonial economy came installation ceremonies for public offices, silver maces for magistrates' courts, engraved seals for commissions, and duplication of English court and legal ceremonies. Anglicans frequently occupied center stage in these rituals. As early as the 1680s and certainly by 1710, Anglican clergymen regularly preached before the assemblies in colonies where the Church of England was established. They heard confessions from convicted murderers and preached public execution sermons for the condemned containing messages – rhetorical and ritual – designed for the living.[4]

The Anglican laity always included a wide spectrum of contemporary social classes. The church enjoyed strong aristocratic support, in part because it was established by law, in part because Crown officials were at least tacit Anglicans, and in part because it was the king's church. But modest men and women formed its adherents in most parishes. Though Johnston began his communicant lists with the names of the socially prestigious, he concluded them with the names of the unknown and the obscure. "Mr. and Mrs. Hitchcock" appeared last on all but one of Johnston's lists; they were Johnston's most loyal communicants, and at least one of them appeared at each communion between September 1711 and May 1712.[5]

Parish life and ministry in New England's state church establishment simultaneously paralleled and differed from its Anglican counterparts. The perception and reality of decline was one major difference. Unlike Anglicans, who could look upon growth and expanding institutional vitality in the eighteenth century, most New England Puritans viewed the century at best with equanimity, at worst with fear. Declension that reduced church membership to no more than 10 to 15 percent of the adults in towns like Salem before 1700 was accompanied by expanding denominational pluralism after 1700. Competition from Quakers, Baptists, and Presbyterians escalated even as many potential listeners drifted away from churches altogether. Adherence patterns also became more complex. Gender was the most striking point of difference. Between 1680 and 1740 a new spiritual couple emerged in New England, the member wife and the nonmember, or delayed-member, husband. Women made up the majority of members in most New England established churches in the 1680s. By the 1720s women dominated membership in virtually all known New England congregations. In one regard, this development was a product of the seventeenth-century Puritan emphasis on the woman's role in family religion. In another, however, it reflected a shift in the timing and, perhaps, in the substance of male spiritual awakening. Women continued to join churches in their twenties, just before or just after marriage. Men increasingly delayed church membership until their thirties or forties. Single men seldom became full members at all, and married men often undertook full membership only before assuming local political office, something that usually happened after they passed their fortieth birthday.[6]

Towns reacted to these changes in a variety of ways. Before 1740 not a single New England town, parish, or provincial leader called for abolishing the state church system, despite New England's increasing religious and social complexity. In the "peaceable kingdoms" Michael Zuckerman describes, a religious majoritarianism defined orthodoxy at the expense of any vocal minority. But given the lack of a centralizing church power, these peaceable kingdoms varied widely from one town to another. Some churches adhered to the Half-Way Covenant,[b] some did not; some required religious testimonials for full membership, some did not; some held to Congregational principles, some to "Presbyterian" or even Baptist ones. Other towns and parishes quietly gave in to the increasing variety of opinion and, as in Salem, grudgingly accepted the inevitability of Dissenting worship in their communities. It must be added, however, that the variety present in eighteenth-century New England can be exaggerated. It constituted only a shallow preview of modern American pluralism because most of it, Quakerism aside, circled a narrow Calvinist[c] orbit.[7]

Town and parish concern about ministerial matters bespoke the clergyman's central role in the religious life of the community. Although the law allowed civil officials to perform marriages and allowed the laity, including midwives, to perform baptisms, ministers performed most such ceremonies in New England. But many parish and town ministers baptized only children born to members, though some indeed baptized more widely. Ministers also conducted funeral ceremonies and preached constantly when cycles of sickness produced deaths in large numbers. And of course ministers buried the dead in the consecrated and fenced burial grounds found in most New England towns, but relatively uncommon in the middle and southern colonies even after the rise of Anglican worship in the eighteenth century.[8]

The principal ceremonial function of ministers in eighteenth-century New England towns was distinctive – delivering the sermon. Other regions knew what sermons were, of course. But they did not experience them with the frequency common in New England. Sabbath sermons were most important for those New Englanders who patronized their town and parish churches. There listeners learned about Scripture and salvation. As Harry Stout explains, early eighteenth-century New England Sabbath sermons "signaled [an] enduring loyalty to *Sola Scriptura*."[d] Listeners were told again and again to return to God's word as the primary instrument of their faith. That they were subsequently instructed on what those words really said and meant only confirmed the intent, if not the practice, of depending on the Bible as the source of Christian doctrine. Salvation was the object of that endeavor. What was typical of its discussion in New England sermons between

1690 and 1730 was its commonplace exposition. Preachers did not terrorize. Nor did they ignore. They simply assumed that their listeners should hear about the necessity of salvation and proceeded to tell them in thoroughly mundane ways.[9]

For popular evangelizing, weekday sermons were even more important. They might be preached on fast days, declared to proclaim public humiliation or to seek divine blessing for New England society, on thanksgiving days, on election days, and on military occasions, such as sermons delivered before militia units or to confirm election of militia officers, and, most ominously, at executions. The occasions held immense ceremonial importance. Here were unparalleled opportunities to speak to a broad range of men and women in local society, not just church members. Not surprisingly, town and parish ministers whose position to speak was sanctioned by the state in both theory and practice frequently used weekday sermons to comment on public as well as religious affairs.[10]

A striking pluralism of Christian expression soon supplemented the state churches of eighteenth-century America. This pluralism provided an astonishing variety of European religious traditions in a maturing, increasingly complex society. Although eighteenth-century American religious pluralism most likely did not exceed that found throughout Europe as a whole, by 1760 it probably had no equal in any single European society. As important as its existence was its effect. It soon underwrote a wide variety of ways to support religious renewal in prerevolutionary society and laid down complex patterns of revival that would persist into the nineteenth and even twentieth centuries.

Institutional proliferation became a major sign of eighteenth-century colonial religious pluralism. The diversity of individual opinion long characteristic of English settlement from Boston to Virginia in the seventeenth century took on institutional expression after 1680. This was most obvious, of course, in the rise of the great Dissenting denominational institutions organized in and around Philadelphia between 1685 and 1710 and extending into other colonies in later decades of the eighteenth century. Baptists, Presbyterians, and Quakers all had appeared in New England by the 1670s but gained significance through their persistence across the next half-century. In the case of the Quakers, this occurred despite the execution of three Public Friends from England in 1658 and jailings of Quaker leaders in Salem. Less well-known groups, de-

scended from the region's complex Puritan history, further complicated the New England mosaic. "Rogerenes," former Seventh Day
Baptists who followed John Rogers of Newport, Rhode Island,
combined Baptist and Quaker principles with a belief in miraculous healing and attracted adherents in both Rhode Island and
Connecticut, usually from among well-to-do rather than poor settlers. Seventh Day Baptists themselves sustained small but
persistent congregations in Rhode Island and Connecticut. Finally,
of course, Anglicans enjoyed the fruit of SPG[e] proselytization,
especially in Connecticut. As elsewhere, Anglican appeal was
broad, not narrow. Often they attracted poorer settlers squeezed
out of dominant parish and town churches. At the same time, by
mid-century, Anglicans enjoyed their own favor among new elites
in new and changing towns and began to hold public office in
numbers out of proportion to their numbers in society.[11]

The middle and southern colonies offered even broader examples
of Christian pluralism. As in New England, some of this pluralism
descended from English Baptist, Presbyterian, and Quaker sources.
Increasing ethnic pluralism soon engendered further religious
variety. French Protestants (Huguenots) and Sephardic Jews who
arrived in the 1680s and 1690s were joined in the next half-century
by settlers from Scotland, northern Ireland, a wide variety of German states and principalities, and Switzerland.

The new ethnic mix brought with it an even richer variety of
religious groups. This was first noticeable among Scots. The first
Scottish immigrants settled largely in West New Jersey and were
Quakers, but they were quickly followed by Scottish Anglicans
and, of course, by Presbyterians. German-speaking immigrants
settling in Pennsylvania provided even greater variety. The first
group, arriving in 1683 from the Rhine town of Krefeld, reflected
both the vibrancy and the complexity of late seventeenth- and early
eighteenth-century German pluralism. Most of the Krefeld immigrants had only recently become Mennonites, followers of the
sixteenth-century reformer Menno Simons, and though they expressed an interest in Quaker principles in indicating their desire
to emigrate to Pennsylvania, they had not yet joined the Quaker
movement. In fact, most never did. In Germantown, just outside
Philadelphia, they were joined by visionary Lutherans and more
than a few avowed sectarians, some led by the mysterious Johannes
Kelpius.[12]

Between 1695 and 1740 Christian pluralism exploded in the

middle colonies. The Keithian schism[f] among the Quakers stimulated a flurry of sectarian groups. Keithian Quakers became
Keithian Baptists who, in turn, became Calvinist or Particular
Baptists only to watch others become Anglicans and even Presbyterians. Kelpius's Wissahickon settlement disintegrated before
1710, after which a few followers traveled west. Near Lancaster, with
newly immigrating German Seventh Day Baptists, they formed
a new settlement at Ephrata (meaning "fruitful"), renowned for
its seeming prefigurement of nineteenth-century American
communitarianism. It was characterized by antiworldly sectarianism,
division into male and female segments, and a special musical
regimen that prompted Thomas Mann to model one of his principal
figures in *The Magic Mountain* after Ephrata's mid-eighteenth-
century leader, Conrad Beisel. "Dunkers," the derisive name
applied to the adherents of the Church of the Brethren, were
antipaedobaptists who believed in complete immersion during
adult baptism. Followers of the reformer Kaspar Schwenkfeld
arrived in Pennsylvania in 1734, and in 1741 Count Nicholas
Zinzendorf arrived in Philadelphia, bringing a major group of
Moravian settlers to the colony.[13]

Although the southern colonies could not compete with the
spiritual jangle heard in Pennsylvania, its landscape was by no
means silent. As in Pennsylvania, some of its pluralism came
through Continental sources. Followers of Jean de Labadie, a former Jesuit, formed a communitarian settlement in Maryland in
1683, and in 1728 Schwenkfeldian refugees who had fled Silesia
settled in Georgia, where they were followed in the 1730s by
Moravian immigrants. Older Quaker meetings persisted but did
not expand. More important was Dissenter activity. The Presbyterians experienced considerable growth in the 1750s as the result
of Scottish and Scots–Irish immigration. Especially in Virginia,
Baptists expanded after 1750, though usually at Anglican expense.
They challenged Anglican hegemony in the colony, both figura-
tively and literally, and lured Anglicans into foolish contests over
preaching and taxes that the Baptists could not lose.[14]

International cosmopolitanism accompanied this growing
eighteenth-century American religious pluralism. Cotton Mather
maintained an extensive European correspondence, particularly
with Pietists. Charleston's French Protestant minister, Paul L'Escot,
corresponded with two theologians in Neuchâtel and Geneva, Jean
Frederick Ostervald and Jean Alphonse Turrettini, sending

Turrettini rattlesnake skins. Henry Melchior Muhlenberg kept up an enormous correspondence with Lutheran leaders in Halle and elsewhere in Germany from the 1740s until his death in 1787. Quakers in Pennsylvania, New England, and the southern colonies used the "transatlantic connection" with traveling or Public Friends to keep the movement spiritually cohesive before 1750 and to promote religious change and reformation after 1750. English Seventh Day Baptists in New Jersey, Pennsylvania, and Rhode Island kept in close touch both through correspondence and through frequent emigration from one colony to the other. Even a settlement like Ephrata, physically far removed from the challenge of a city like Philadelphia, maintained a remarkably cosmopolitan theology, fusing together diverse elements of German pietism, anabaptism and social experimentation in its communitarian setting.[15]

This burgeoning pluralism and its broad public acceptance was perhaps best displayed in New York City in August 1763, when the governor proclaimed a day of thanksgiving to celebrate the British victory over France in the French and Indian War. The city's two Anglican clergymen were joined in their sermons by their Dutch, French, Presbyterian, Baptist, and Moravian counterparts. Even the "hazan," or prayer chanter, at Congregation Shearith Israel, Joseph Jesuron Pinto, delivered a thanksgiving sermon, taking for his text Zechariah 2:10: "Sing and rejoice, O daughter of Zion: for lo, I come, and I will dwell in the midst of thee, saith the Lord."[16]

The increase in religious pluralism provides an important clue to understanding the attempts at religious renewal in eighteenth-century America. It was the breadth and diversity of these efforts – not their cohesion or their limitation to the 1740s – that solidified their significance. They appeared as early as the 1670s, and reappeared in major forms in the 1680s, the 1730s, and the 1760s, with a major peak between 1740 and 1745. Middle colony religious renewal began tumultuously with the rise of "singing Quakers" on Long Island in the 1680s and continued with efforts to create a piety of suffering among French Huguenots in the 1690s, with Dutch revivals in the 1720s in New Jersey, and with Presbyterian and German revivals (the latter largely failures) in the 1740s in Pennsylvania. In the southern colonies efforts at religious renewal appeared for short periods in both South Carolina and Virginia in the 1740s, stimulated by the preaching of the Anglican itinerant, George

Whitefield, but met with more sustained growth there and in North Carolina after 1760, when Presbyterian and Baptist activity increased.[17]

Doctrinal diversity characterized eighteenth-century religious renewal. Calvinism clearly dominated New England revival. But it had been preceded in the 1710s by a major interest in German Pietist doctrines,[g] circulated through the writings of a Halle reformer, August Herman Francke, with whom Cotton Mather had begun an intensive correspondence in 1709. In the 1750s revivalism incorporated Wesleyan Arminianism,[h] brought to America through the example of John Wesley's English Methodists. In the middle colonies, not surprisingly, Calvinism was important in the Scottish Presbyterian revivals. But quite different doctrines spurred religious renewal among other communions. Frelinghuysen's[i] and Freeman's disciplinary revival among Dutch Reformed colonists was encouraged by a Dutch renewal tradition with strong seventeenth-century origins. Among Germans, efforts at religious renewal took root in reformed Lutheranism, in a distinct German Calvinist tradition quite unlike that found in New England, and in a Pietism of great breadth and eclecticism. As espoused by immigrants like Christopher Sauer, this Pietism could easily involve Lutheran sacramentalism, Hermetic Rosicrucianism, and universalist Freemasonry. And the spectacular growth of the Baptists in Virginia and North Carolina used Arminian doctrine as its fuel.[18]

Colonial revivals nearly always reflected regional and local conditions. In New England they flourished amid tensions stemming from religious, social, and economic maturation, which had brought increased disparities of wealth, social stratification, and sometimes incomprehensible social diversity. Middle colony revivalism was more narrowly circumscribed and often took root in efforts to articulate ethnic dimensions in religious observance, both Scottish and German. In Virginia, Baptist revivalism prospered alongside the inability and even the refusal of established Anglican churches to comprehend broadening religious needs in the colony, particularly among poorer, less literate settlers.[19]

The peculiar, seemingly contradictory, mix of provincialism, regionalism, and internationalism became especially obvious in the labor of revival and religious renewal. George Whitefield's colonial appeal fed on his English and Scottish success and on the news of that success spread by colonial newspapers and theological sympathizers. Private letters from ministers to each other, read at public occasions on both sides of the Atlantic, created a "concert of prayer" that made the revivals of the 1740s and 1750s seem even more momentous than they were. And the exchange was more than one-way. Thomas Prince's weekly newspaper, *The Christian History*, published in both Boston and Edinburgh in the 1740s, brought as much news of America to Europe as of Europe to America. George Whitefield, moreover, publicly acknowledged very early colonial models for his mid-century reform work. When he visited Northampton, Massachusetts, in 1740, he expressed more interest in Jonathan Edwards's grandfather than in Edwards[j] himself: "After a little refreshment, we crossed the ferry to Northampton, where no less than three hundred souls were saved about five years ago. Their pastor's name is Edwards, successor and grandson to the great [Solomon] Stoddard, whose memory will be always precious to my soul, and whose books entitled 'A Guide to Christ,' and 'Safety of Appearing in Christ's Righteousness,' I would recommend to all."[20]

In general, revivalism embraced conservative rather than radical or egalitarian approaches to the question of authority. It is true that revivals frequently produced schisms that threatened the old order. In New England, revivals in the 1740s produced more than 200 schismatic congregations that split away from old churches, and several "New Light" Congregationalist and "Separate" Baptist denominational organizations. In the middle colonies Presbyterian revivalists withdrew from the Synod of Philadelphia to form the Synod of New York. Yet these schisms usually occurred because proponents demanded more, not less, authority from their churches. This became particularly obvious during the Presbyterian schism of the 1740s. Usually interpreted as an attack on authority – as "antiauthoritarian" and as perhaps a preface to the American Revolution – it was actually proauthoritarian. Its instigators, Gilbert Tennent and the ministers of the evangelicals' so-called Log College, had long objected to disciplinary laxness in the old Synod of Philadelphia. When the synod refused to raise its disciplinary standards, the Log College ministers walked out, not into the heady air of antiauthoritarian freedom but to New York. There they created new presbyteries and finally another synod – the Synod of New York – to exercise effective coercive authority over "true" Presbyterian ministers, ministerial candidates, and congregations.[21]

Colonial revivals also raised, rather than lowered, the status of the ordained ministry and did little to increase lay authority within either local congregations or their denominational institutions. Revivalism prompted many ministers to change their style of preaching. Many turned to extemporaneous preaching more frequently than they had before, accelerating a tradition that can be dated back to at least the 1680s. Isaac Backus,[k] the New England Baptist leader, noted that revivalists used sermons to "Insinuate themselves into the affections" of the people and even induced opponents to incorporate more "emotion" and "sentiment" in their sermons. At the same time some sermons were clearly more "extemporaneous" than others. Some itinerant ministers, especially Whitefield, memorized sermons and interchanged sections to suit particular moments and audiences. Since they preached without notes their listeners believed these sermons to be products of immediate inspiration.[22]

Itinerancy likewise solidified ministerial authority. Although some itinerants lacked formal education, none of those who were active in the American colonies are known to have been illiterate. The century's most famous itinerant, George Whitefield, took an Oxford degree in 1736, and its most infamous, James Davenport,[l] stood at the top of his Yale class in 1732. Itinerants opposed settled ministers only selectively. They bypassed local churches when the minister opposed their work and preached in them when the minister was favorable. Nearly all itinerants wore the protective badge of clerical ordination. When he was charged in Virginia with being an unlicensed minister, the evangelical Presbyterian, Samuel Davies, defended his orthodoxy by pointing to his ordination by the Presbytery of New Castle. Only Davenport ventured into the colonial countryside lacking ordination, with just his high-flown spirituality and his Yale degree to protect him. But only Davenport was judged by a court to have been crazy.[23]

The complexities of religious renewal in eighteenth-century America are revealed with almost ironic fullness in the careers of the Tennents of New Jersey and Whitefield. The Tennents – the father, William Sr., and his four minister sons – Gilbert, John, William Jr., and Charles – were one of the best-known ministerial families in the colonies, and Whitefield, aside from Britain's monarchs, was arguably the best-known Englishman of the mid-eighteenth century. Yet the Tennents and Whitefield revealed the different means by which eighteenth-century revivalist clergymen probed lay religious understandings. These differences centered on the issue of charisma. In Max Weber's[m] definition, charisma involves three characteristics: leadership, demonstrations of supernatural intervention, and social validation of the leader's claims by followers. Hermits thus cannot exhibit charismatic leadership, because charisma is implicitly social; nor can atheists and humanists, because charisma takes root in supernatural belief and invocation. As another sociologist writes, charisma is "not a personality attribute" but "the social recognition of a [supernatural] claim."[24]

The Tennents emerged from a Scottish society redolent of intense popular supernatural expression, but by no means fully Christianized, much less Protestantized. Early modern Scotland exhibited magical expressions, including sacred places, healers, and amulets, as vivid as those found in England. And Scotland too was riven by strong regional differences, stark economic disparities, and major religious conflicts. Scottish Quaker, Anglican, and convenanting and nonconvenanting Presbyterian colonists to the Jerseys and Pennsylvania brought these divisions to the New World. William Tennent Sr. reflected this complexity in his own career. Sometimes called the father of American Presbyterianism, Tennent was a Scot who, living in northern Ireland, received Anglican ordination in the Church of Ireland in 1704 and served Anglican parishes there until he left for America. Only after applying for membership in the Presbytery of Philadelphia in 1718 did he recant his Anglican principles, before a suspicious presbytery.[25]

The Tennents cultivated community, Christianity, and Presbyterian adherence through long-term residential ministries. After ten years in New York, William Sr. served a fifteen-year residence with the "Scotch–Irish" community at Neshaminy in Bucks County, Pennsylvania. John and William Jr. monopolized Presbyterian preaching for forty years in the Scottish settlement at Freehold, New Jersey, where Joseph Morgan had earlier entertained and appalled the congregation with his astrological experiments. Gilbert Tennent served two congregations in thirty-eight years in his career at New Brunswick, New Jersey, and Philadelphia (the Second Presbyterian Church).[26]

Catechization and regeneration formed the Tennents' principal theological interests. William Sr.'s surviving manuscript sermons avoid millenarianism altogether, and Gilbert discussed it only perfunctorily during the French and Indian War, when many other

ministers turned to the theme as well. Instead, the Tennents cat-
echized. They stressed elemental Calvinist and Christian doctrine
to a heterogeneous and disputatious people. It was no accident that
Gilbert described his brother John as a "keen disputant" and "expert Casuist." The Tennents also stressed personal regeneration,
meaning spiritual rebirth occurring as a result of a conversion
experience. Their emphasis on regeneration was itself a proselytiz-
ing tool. Christian adherence would reshape the life of the
individual and, ultimately, of the community.[27]

Such evidence shows the Tennents to be evangelical – not charismatic. But though the Tennents Christianized and
Presbyterianized Scottish immigrants by emphasizing doctrine,
regeneration, and community, they also probed popular, quasi-
Christian Scottish supernaturalist sentiment. They did so by
manifesting supernatural power in their own bodies. Theirs was
not a cold, austere Calvinism that adamantly rejected popular
culture. Nor was it a Calvinism in which "ministers and their flocks
held a theology in common," as historians recently have described
New England. Rather, here was a Calvinism that simultaneously
tapped and disciplined yearnings for supernatural intervention,
through clergymen who were not only prophets of God's Word but
holy men.[28]

Three of the Tennent sons – Gilbert, John, and William Jr. – became
living exemplars of supernatural, even miraculous, intervention.
Their experiences took three principal forms: supernatural possession, apparition, and miracle. Supernatural possession occurred in
the form of God-induced sickness, radical personality shifts, and
ecstatic behavior. All of them attributed divine causes to the severe
sickness they endured in their early days as ministers. Gilbert
developed a debilitating illness that gave him an "affecting view of
eternity," and he likened his recovery to the raising of Lazarus, a
point he was not at all ashamed to make before his congregants:
"After I was raised up to health, I examined many about the
grounds of their hope of salvation." After John's own conversion
experience, he cast off his bitterness and anger, then began to
experience frequent weeping and sighing. "In his private Studies,"
Gilbert wrote, "he often took the *Bible* in his hand, and walked up
and down the room, *Weeping*, and *moaning* over it."[29]

Divine apparitions occurred in both religious and secular settings. John pleaded for and received visions of Christ during the
sickness that dogged him in his early ministry at Freehold. "O

brother, the Lord Jesus has come in mercy to my soul. I was begging for a crumb of mercy with the dogs, and Christ has told me that he will give me a crumb," he reportedly said. The apparitions increased as death approached a year later, and after John had been buried, Gilbert wrote of the perfect union of body and soul that death engendered. More mundane apparitions saved William Jr. from a perjury conviction. In a bizarre occurrence not unlike the early modern French episode recounted in Natalie Davis's *The Return of Martin Guerre*, which involved a clerical impostor, a stolen horse, and perjury charges, William Jr. was saved from conviction in part if not wholly by a Pennsylvania couple who dreamed he was in trouble and traveled to New Jersey. They corroborated Tennent's testimony in the case and freed him from the perjury charge.[30]

William Jr. also exemplified the miraculous both by being raised from the dead and by later losing all the toes on one foot for no known reason. The resurrection occurred during the illness he endured while taking his ordination examinations, a period during which his brother John, also ailing, received visions of Christ. William's condition worsened, and he died. His brother Gilbert came to comfort family and friends and to supervise the funeral arrangements. Three days later, however, after William had been "laid out on a board" and his funeral had been announced, his eyes opened, he groaned, and he was nursed back to health under Gilbert's guidance. Some years later, William awoke in the middle of the night to discover that the toes on one foot were missing. He could find neither the toes nor any instruments or animals that he could imagine might have effected their removal – knives, rats, even cats – and he traced the loss to the Devil: a miracle, to be sure, but one demonstrating God's power through the work of his nemesis.[31]

The Tennents explained what happened to them as demonstrations of God's direct intervention in human affairs, and their experiences set them apart as holy men, not mere expositors of God's written word. Such explanations were only reinforced by popular belief in supernaturalism. Gilbert acknowledged that his brother John eagerly evidenced his weeping and moaning "to almost all that came near him." His public spectacles validated his identity by affecting others: "Even some Strangers who came to see him, were much affected therewith; the *Tears* trickling down their Cheeks like *Hail*." In the 1740s Gilbert described his own God-induced sickness and Lazarus-like reprieve from death in a letter about religious revivals in the Presbyterian congregation at New Brunswick; it was circulated on both sides of the Atlantic in *The Christian History*.[32]

Not all evangelicals felt comfortable with claims of direct supernatural intervention, much less miracles. Jonathan Edwards distrusted them as Devil-induced and as easily mistaken for faith and grace itself. Presbyterian antirevivalists made the intriguing claim that the revivalists' pretenses about religious experiences crossed over into magic. David Evans, a conservative Presbyterian minister and reputed author of *The Querists*, likened Gilbert Tennent to an astrologer and fortune-teller. Could Tennent really ascertain "Men's *inward Feelings*"? If so, "Must not Mr. T have some cunning Art, beyond what is common to Man[?]" Pennsylvania wits joined in. A critique appearing in Benjamin Franklin's *General Magazine* compared both the Tennents and Whitefield to conjurers and "Holy Necromancers" and traced their lineage to Munster radicals and Commonwealth Ranters, some of whom claimed miraculous powers.[33]

George Whitefield's long public career reveals significant and surprising differences with that of the Tennents. Whitefield came closest to the Tennents' style in claiming parallels with Christ in his conversion experience. He unashamedly noted that both he and Christ had been born at inns (Whitefield did not claim a manger). His early religious struggles had produced bodily manifestations, including "unspeakable Pressure both of Body and Mind" and "an uncommon Drought and a disagreeable Claminess in my Mouth," which Whitefield compared to Christ's experience on the cross "when *Jesus Christ* cried out, 'I thirst.' " Whitefield also preached on miracles to considerable public effect. The manuscript diary of Daniel Rogers, a Massachusetts minister who followed Whitefield to New York in 1740, reveals that in his first New York sermon, Whitefield preached "upon the miracle of the woman healed of the bloody [flux]," all to "great power ... one or two women cryd out loud."[34]

But Whitefield stopped far short of the Tennents. He never claimed to have experienced apparitions or to have accomplished or benefited from miracles. He criticized John Wesley for tolerating trances and convulsions among listeners in England; there might be "something of God in it," but "the devil ... interposes." Like Edwards, he worried that such enthusiasm would "take people from the written word, and make them depend on visions, convulsions, etc., more than on the promises and precepts of the gospel." Whitefield had similar feelings about wonders and miracles. His journals reported wonders, such as deliverance from storms at sea and peculiar occurrences, with some frequency. But like the Mathers before him, Whitefield saw them as demonstrations of God's awesome powers in nature, not as miracles. The age of miracles had passed, and modern claims for their performance were fraudulent.[35]

Whitefield's evangelicalism also differed from that of the Tennents. Whitefield and the Tennents all preached on original sin, election, and regeneration. But Whitefield emphasized original sin and election while the Tennents emphasized regeneration. Whitefield made and sustained his reputation on his ability to convince men and women of God's sovereignty, the reality of original sin, and the doctrine of election. Listeners reported that their primary reaction to Whitefield lodged in their understanding of his great question, "Are you saved?" Since Whitefield usually convinced them that the answer was no, they took home an overwhelming sense of guilt and failure. Whitefield hoped that this guilt would result in their surrender of their lives to Christ. In contrast, the Tennents spoke about Christian regeneration and the creation, building, and sustaining of faith.[36]

This subtle difference in preaching intersected differences in pastoral labor. Whitefield traveled all his life and never labored in a settled ministry. In thirty-two years, between 1738 and 1770, he made seven tours of English America, the shortest lasting seven months (1738), the longest lasting three-and-a-half years (1744–8). Whitefield announced his grand themes to strangers. He made his reputation and exercised his ministry among people he had never met, quite unlike the Tennents, most of whose listeners knew them intimately. Whitefield's death dramatized the difference. In 1770 thousands of spectators crowded into Newburyport for Whitefield's funeral. No settled minister could have created such a stir. Even sympathizers thought the focus on the man, rather than on his message, was unseemly and excessive. Ezra Stiles, then Congregational minister at Newport, Rhode Island, carefully calculated the dimensions of Newburyport's Presbyterian church just to confirm his suspicion that the claims for the numbers of Whitefield's mourners were greatly exaggerated.[37]

The tumult at Whitefield's funeral points up the frequent

attempts of his followers to create a charismatic relationship despite Whitefield's careful reluctance about such matters. The public often interpreted his behavior charismatically and attempted to treat him as a holy man. Nathan Cole's description of Whitefield's appearance in Middletown, Connecticut, in 1740 offers one such instance: "When I see Mr. Whitfield come upon the Scaffold [at Middletown], he looked almost angellical – a young, slim, slender youth before some thousands of people, and with a bold, undaunted countenance. And my hearing how God was with him everywhere as he came along, it ... put me in a trembling fear before he began to preach, for he looked as if he was Cloathed with authority from the great God."[38]

Portraitists emphasized what was apparently a facial tic, which made Whitefield appear cross-eyed and which his followers associated with divine blessing. A satirical cartoon, published in London in 1760, lampooned their fascination with his problem. The cartoonist could not resist disparaging the sexual appetite of Whitefield's listeners – one says, "I wish his Spirit was in my Flesh" – and he also ridiculed the significance they attached to Whitefield's crossed eyes – "His poor Eye Sparkles with Holy Zeal," says another.[39]

Whitefield's corpse also became an object of attention. In 1775, a revolutionary chaplain, with a group of officers that included Benedict Arnold, entered Whitefield's tomb in Newburyport. They viewed the body, then removed the evangelist's clerical collar and wrist bands to pass among their soldiers. Such viewings, usually by evangelical ministers rather than military men, continued into the nineteenth century at a rate that suggests a kind of cult of Whitefield's body. In 1789 Jesse Lee and two other Methodist ministers entered Whitefield's tomb. "Removing the coffin lid, [we] beheld the awful ravages of 'the last enemy of man,' " Lee wrote. "How quiet the repose, how changed the features." In the 1820s Abel Stevens, also a Methodist minister, visited the tomb and "took his skull into my hands, and examined it with great interest." By the time David Marks, a Freewill Baptist minister, visited the tomb in 1834, "the coffin was about one third full of black earth, out of which projected a few bones. The skull bone was detached from the rest, and was turned over."[40]

George Whitefield probed popular culture, but not in the ways the Tennents did. Among other things, he probed it for questions, not answers. He used common concerns about life and death as a vehicle for demonstrating the truth of Christianity and the necessity of adherence to its doctrines. His constant preaching on God's sovereignty and original sin responded to yearnings for transcendent descriptions of the world even as it challenged contemporary cynicism and religious indifference. Although his message was often catechetical, he taught rudimentary Christian doctrine with drama and spectacle. Whitefield's performances were not charismatic, however. They focused attention on his figure, his face, his voice, his demeanor, and even his notoriety, as when a Delaware Anglican confronted Whitefield with the rumor that the orphan traveling with him was actually a concubine. But they did not involve claims to divine intervention either in his life or in his body.[41]

Ultimately the Tennents and Whitefield expressed two different evangelical styles common in American revivalism in the nineteenth and twentieth centuries. The Tennents were simultaneously more traditional and more radical. They were more traditional in their willingness to satisfy popular desires for direct supernatural intervention. They tapped a supernaturalist tradition deeply rooted in older times that continued to flower in America through figures who manifested direct supernatural intervention, such as Anne Lee at the end of the eighteenth century, Joseph Smith in the nineteenth century, and Father Divine, A. A. Allen, and Oral Roberts in the twentieth century. At the same time, the Tennents were more radical in their willingness to offer demonstrations of supernatural activity in the contemporary world. Through their very bodies, they revealed the power of supernatural authority and its capacity to change lives in ways that resembled nothing less than Christ's resurrection from the dead.[42]

In contrast, Whitefield proved to be more modern. He did not pursue people and their culture through charisma. He pursued them through popularity. In Whitefield, the self became an object of its own fascination rather than a vessel of supernatural exposition and intervention. Unlike the Tennents, Whitefield worked outside traditional denominational channels. He never abandoned the Church of England, though he criticized it bitterly. As a result his legacy was personal, rather than institutional. Followers sometimes established nondenominational congregations to promulgate Whitefield's message locally. Andrew Crosswell founded such a church in Boston in the 1740s, a Philadelphia meetinghouse opened to evangelical preachers of all kinds in that same decade, and a "Tabernacle" opened in Salem in 1770 after

Whitefield's death to carry his message into the next century. But all three had collapsed by the 1780s. Whitefield's nondenominational, noncharismatic revivals thus prefigured another tradition in American revivalism, exemplified in the careers of Charles Grandison Finney, Billy Sunday, Billy Graham, and Robert Schuller. Such evangelists thundered out the message of God's sovereignty and stressed their own popularity at the expense of any denominational loyalty, but they did not pursue claims to charismatic authority.[43]

The reinvigoration of the state church parishes in New England and in the southern colonies, the expansion of European religious diversity, and the rise of a pluralistic evangelical revivalism kept prerevolutionary rates of church adherence from sinking further in many places, if not everywhere, and improved them in some. At mid-century New England exhibited the greatest range in church adherence rates. Highs in rural membership rates varied from two-thirds of the adults to less than a fifth of the eligible adults, and in Boston Samuel Mather admitted in 1780 that "not one sixth" attended public worship. In New York some rural congregations contained between 40 and 60 percent of eligible adults, but others contained far less, and New York City's church adherence rate probably did not approach 15 percent.[44]

Anglican records suggest some gains early in the century followed by some losses after 1750. The well-known 1724 survey of Anglican congregations ordered by the Bishop of London exhibited large and suspicious gaps between attendance as reported by parish ministers and the record of actual communicants. Clergy frequently claimed congregations of between 100 and 200 at most Sabbath services but recorded only twenty to forty communicants. Statistics drawn from long series of yearly reports by SPG ministers in the middle colonies suggest both considerable variation in the ratio, depending on location, and in some places, a widening gap between the two figures as the century wore on. At Radnor, Pennsylvania, Anglican ministers reported about 20 percent of the areas's eligible nonsectarian, English-speaking residents as communicants; adding Quakers and Welsh Baptists probably brought the church adherence, attendance, or affiliation rate up to as much as 40 percent of the area's adults in this period. In contrast, at Apoquimminy in Delaware, where Anglicans were the largest single Christian group, communicants accounted for no more than

10 to 15 percent of the area's nonsectarian English-speaking residents between 1743 and 1752. At Newcastle, Delaware, the communication rate among potential Anglicans actually declined between 1744 and 1776, from between 15 and 20 percent of the eligible communicants in the 1740s and early 1750s to between 8 and 12 percent between 1760 and 1776, with no known increase in other Christian congregations to account for the difference.[45]

The result was a mixed record for both state churches and Dissenting evangelicals in eighteenth-century America. On the one hand, the renewal of state church activity in both the northern and the southern colonies, the rise of the Dissenting denominations and their vigorous efforts to promote ministerial labor and discipline, the increase of religious groups from the Continent, and the proliferation of a wide and sometimes surprising range of efforts at renewal all probably saved the public expression of Christianity from the kind of collapse that already seemed imminent in many colonies, led by Maryland and the Carolinas, in the 1680s. Without these new expressions of Christian activity and form, moreover, this weakened Christianity would also have been narrowly English and would have alternated between only middle-of-the-road Anglicanism and increasingly middle-of-the-road Dissenting groups. Instead the colonies were filled with astonishing varieties of Christian expression, which only increased as ethnic and national heterogeneity accelerated.

On the other hand, the statistics regarding church adherence, meager and frustrating as they are, provide little evidence to reject Hector St. John de Crèvecoeur's judgment that in later eighteenth-century America, "religious indifference is imperceptibly disseminated from one end of the continent to the other." Crèvecoeur put a happy face on this situation. He bypassed the suppression of African national religious systems in the colonies, and found persecution and "religious pride" all but absent from America. He eagerly traced American religious indifference to sectarian pluralism and wilderness spaciousness and ignored the European heritage of erratic lay adherence to institutional Christianity. "Zeal in Europe is confined; [but] here it evaporates in the great distance it has to travel; there it is a grain of powder inclosed; here it burns away in the open air and consumes without effect." Still, however poorly Crèvecoeur understood the causes of American religious indifference, his vivid, enduring metaphors rightly fixed its existence.[46]

EDITOR'S NOTES

a A state church is an established church, supported and maintained by the state.

b The Half-Way Covenant of 1662 was a response to the second-generation Puritans' failure to become church members. By creating "Halfway" members, their children could now be baptized.

c Puritan theology was heavily influenced by the writings of John Calvin, a French Protestant, who emphasized the Five Points – total depravity, limited atonement, unconditional election, irresistible grace, and final perseverence of the saints.

d Literally "Scriptures alone."

e The Society for the Propagation of the Gospel in Foreign Parts, founded in 1701, became the chief means of extending the Church of England or Anglicanism in America by supporting over 300 missionaries.

f The Keithian schism of the early 1690s took its name from George Keith, a Scottish Quaker (1639–1716), who charged that Pennsylvania Quakers were ill-disciplined and guilty of doctrinal heresy.

g Pietism was an effort to intensify Christian piety by stressing the feelings of the heart and protesting intellectualism, formalism, and rationalism.

h Arminianism took its name from the Dutch theologian Jacobus Arminius (1560–1609) and referred to a modification of the traditional doctrines of total depravity, limited atonement, and unconditional election. Used loosely, the term could be translated as "liberal" or "broad."

i Theodore Frelinghuysen (1691–1748) was a prominent Dutch Reformed minister in New Jersey.

j Jonathan Edwards (1703–58) was a prime mover in the revivals of the Connecticut Valley in the 1730s.

k Isaac Backus (1724–1806), born into a devout Congregational family, in the 1750s became a Baptist.

l In the early 1740s James Davenport (1716–57) was arrested in Connecticut and Massachusetts for his attacks on orthodoxy.

m Weber was a famous twentieth-century sociologist, who wrote about the Protestant Ethic and the Social Psychology of World Religions.

NOTES

Reprinted from Jon Butler, *Awash in a Sea of Faith: Christianizing the American People* (Cambridge, Mass., 1990). © 1990 the President and Fellows of Harvard College. Used by permission of Harvard University Press.

1 For a review of the problem of the "Great Awakening" as treated by modern historians and a general description of the important secondary works to 1982, see Jon Butler, "Enthusiasm Described and Decried: The Great Awakening as Interpretative Fiction," *Journal of American History*, 69 (1982–3): 305–25. The best general studies of the revivals are J. M. Bumsted and John E. Van de Wetering, *What Must I Do To Be*

Saved? The Great Awakening in Colonial America (Hinsdale, Ill., 1976), and relevant sections of David Lovejoy, *Religious Enthusiasm in the New World: Heresy to Revolution* (Cambridge, Mass., 1985); Christine Hyerman, *Commerce and Culture: The Maritime Communities of Colonial Massachusetts, 1690–1750* (New York, 1984); and Harry S. Stout, *The New England Soul: Preaching and Religious Culture in Colonial New England* (New York, 1986).

2 On the poor and on parish responsibilities for them, see Stephen E. Wiberley, Jr., "Four Cities: Public Poor Relief in Urban America, 1700–1775" (Ph.D. dissertation, Yale University, 1975), which discusses Anglican relief in Charleston; on parish life in Virginia, see Charles Sydnor, *Gentlemen Freeholders: Political Practices in Washington's Virginia* (Chapel Hill, N.C. 1952): 58–65, 88–94.

3 Frank J. Klingberg, ed., "Commissary Johnston's Notitia Parochialis," *South Carolina Historical and Genealogical Magazine*, 48 (1947): 26–34.

4 Evolving public ceremonialism in the colonies is in need of study, although some of its effects can be discerned through histories of early American art. For a discussion of this business among colonial Huguenot silversmiths, see my own book, *The Huguenots in America: A Refugee People in New World Society* (Cambridge, Mass., 1983): 131–2, 178–80.

5 Klingberg, ed., "Commissary Johnston's Notitia Parochialis."

6 Richard D. Shiels, "The Feminization of American Congregationalism, 1730–1835," *American Quarterly*, 33 (1981): 46–62; Paul R. Lucas, *Valley of Discord: Church and Society along the Connecticut River, 1636–1725* (Hanover, N.H., 1976): 141–2, 244–5; Laurel Thatcher Ulrich, *Good Wives: Image and Reality in the Lives of Women in Northern New England, 1650–1750* (New York, 1982); Edward M. Cook, Jr., *The Fathers of the Towns: Leadership and Community Structure in Eighteenth-Century New England* (Baltimore, 1976): 119–42.

7 Michael Zuckerman, *Peaceable Kingdoms: New England Towns in the Eighteenth Century* (New York, 1970): 112–13; Jonathan M. Chu, *Neighbors, Friends, or Madmen: The Puritan Adjustment to Quakerism in Seventeenth-Century Massachusetts Bay* (Westport, Conn., 1985); Christine Leigh Hyerman, "Specters of Subversion, Societies of Friends: Dissent and the Devil in Provincial Essex County, Massachusetts," in *Saints and Revolutionaries: Essays on Early American History*, ed. David D. Hall *et al.* (New York, 1984): 38–74.

8 Some notion of the humdrum of a minister's activity can be gained through *The Diary of Ebenezer Parkman*, ed. Francis G. Wallett (Worcester, Mass., 1982), as well as relevant portions of Patricia J. Tracy, *Jonathan Edwards, Pastor: Religion and Society in Eighteenth-Century Northampton* (New York, 1980); Stout, *New England Soul*; and J. William T. Youngs, *God's Messengers: Religious Leadership in Colonial New England, 1700–1750* (Baltimore, 1976).

9 Stout, *New England Soul*, offers the most thorough examination of the topic. See especially chap. 8.

10 ibid.: pp. 79–80, 82–3, 121–2, 167–74.

11 Richard Bushman, *From Puritan to Yankee: Character and the Social Order in Connecticut, 1690–1765* (Cambridge, Mass., 1967): 164–8; Bruce E.

Steiner, "New England Anglicanism, A Genteel Faith?" *William and Mary Quarterly*, 3rd ser., 27 (1970): 122–35; Bruce E. Steiner, "Anglican Officeholding in Pre-Revolutionary Connecticut: The Parameters of New England Community," ibid., 31 (1974): 369–406.

12 Ned Landsman, *Scotland and its First American Colony, 1683–1765* (Princeton, 1985); Bernard Bailyn, *The Peopling of British North America: An Introduction* (New York, 1986); Elizabeth W. Fisher, " 'Prophecies and Revelations': German Cabbalists in Early Pennsylvania," *Pennsylvania Magazine of History and Biography*, 109 (1985): 299–333; Ernest Lashlee, "Johannes Kelpius and his Woman in the Wilderness: A Chapter in the History of Colonial Pennsylvania Religious Thought," in *Glaube, Geist, Geschichte: Festschrift für Ernst Benz*, ed. Gerhard Muller and Winfried Zeller (Leiden, 1967): 327–38; Stephanie G. Wolf, *Urban Village: Population, Community, and Family Structure in Germantown, Pennsylvania, 1683–1800* (Princeton, 1976).

13 Dietmar Rothermund, *The Layman's Progress: Religious and Political Experience in Colonial Pennsylvania, 1740–1770* (Philadelphia, 1961): 1–16; Marianne Wokeck, "The Flow and Composition of German Immigration to Philadelphia, 1727–1775," *Pennsylvania Magazine of History and Biography*, 105 (1981): 249–78; Sally Schwartz, *"A Mixed Multitude": The Struggle for Toleration in Pennsylvania* (New York, 1987); and A. G. Roeber, "In German Ways? Problems and Potentials of Eighteenth-Century German Social and Emigration History," *William and Mary Quarterly*, 3rd ser. (1987): 750–74.

14 Lovejoy, *Religious Enthusiasm in the New World*: 156–8, 162–8; Rufus M. Jones, *The Quakers in the American Colonies* (New York, 1966): 265–353; Rhys Isaac, *The Transformation of Virginia, 1740–1790* (Chapel Hill, N.C., 1982): 161–205.

15 Jon Butler, "Into Pennsylvania's Spiritual Abyss: The Rise and Fall of the Later Keithians, 1694–1703," *Pennsylvania Magazine of History and Biography*, 101 (1977): 151–70; Butler, *The Huguenots in America*: 88, 111–13; Leo Schelbert, "From Reformed Preacher in the Palatinate to Pietist Monk in Pennsylvania: The Spiritual Path of Johann Peter Muller, 1709–1796," in *Germany and America: Essays on Problems of International Relations and Immigration*, ed. Hans L. Trefousse (New York, 1980): 139–50; *Die Korrespondenz Heinrich Melchior Muhlenbergs aus der Anfangszeit des deutschen Luthertums in Nordamerika*, ed. Kurt Aland (Berlin, 1986); Frederick B. Tolles, *Quakers and the Atlantic Culture* (New York, 1960); Jack D. Marietta, *The Reformation of American Quakerism, 1748–1783* (Philadelphia, 1984): 73–128.

16 John A. Dix, *History of the Parish of Trinity Church in the City of New York*, 6 vols. (New York, 1889–1950), I: 304.

17 Perry Miller, *The New England Mind: From Colony to Province* (Cambridge, Mass., 1953): 105–18. Miller's irony in entitling the chapter "Revivalism" is suggested in his title for the next chapter, "Intolerance." See also C. C. Goen, *Revivalism and Separatism in New England, 1740–1800: Strict Congregationalists and Separate Baptists in the Great Awakening* (New Haven, Conn., 1962): 6; Lucas, *Valley of Discord*: 199–202; Edwin Gaustad, *Great Awakening in New England* (New York,

1957): 16–20; Sydney Ahlstrom, *A Religious History of the American People* (New Haven, Conn., 1972): 314–29.

18 Gaustad, *Great Awakening in New England*: 111; John B. Frantz, "The Awakening of Religion among the German Settlers in the Middle Colonies," *William and Mary Quarterly*, 3rd ser., 33 (April 1976): 266–88; Charles H. Maxson, *The Great Awakening in the Middle Colonies* (Chicago, 1920): 1–10, 28, 32; Wesley M. Gewehr, *The Great Awakening in Virginia, 1740–1790* (Durham, N.C., 1930): 254.

19 Bushman, *From Puritan to Yankee*: 135–43, 183–220; Landsman, *Scotland and its First American Colony*: 227–55; Isaac, *Transformation of Virginia*: 161–205.

20 *George Whitefield's Journals* [ed. Iain Murray] (London, 1960): 476; Susan O'Brien, "A Transatlantic Community of Saints: The Great Awakening and the First Evangelical Network, 1735–1755," *American Historical Review*, 91 (1986): 811–32.

21 Leonard J. Trinterud, *The Forming of an American Tradition: A Re-Examination of Colonial Presbyterianism* (Philadelphia, 1949): 100–21, describes the formation of the New York Synod, though it ties the development too closely to Whitefield.

22 Backus quoted in Alan Heimert, *Religion and the American Mind from the Great Awakening to the Revolution* (Cambridge, Mass., 1966): 206; on Whitefield, see Stout, *New England Soul*: 192–4.

23 Harry S. Stout and Peter Onuf, "James Davenport and the Great Awakening in New London," *Journal of American History*, 70 (1983–4): 556–78.

24 *Max Weber on Charisma and Institution Building: Selected Papers*, ed. S. N. Eisenstadt (Chicago, 1968): esp. 18–27, 48. Weber sometimes confused issues by using the adjective "charismatic" as often as the noun "charisma." Also see Bryan R. Wilson, *The Noble Savages: The Primitive Origins of Charisma and its Contemporary Survival* (Berkeley, Calif., 1975): 2–3, 5, 110–11.

25 Christina Larner, *Enemies of God: The Witch-hunt in Scotland* (Baltimore, 1981): 157–74; Ned Landsman, "Revivalism and Nativism in the Middle Colonies: The Great Awakening and the Scots Community in East New Jersey," *American Quarterly*, 34 (1982): 149–64.

26 Landsman, "Revivalism and Nativism in the Middle Colonies": 155–6. I have not counted the mutually unsatisfactory one-year stay of Gilbert Tennent at New Castle, Delaware, where he began his ministry in 1726. Charles Tennent did not serve a predominantly Scottish congregation but did spend his entire career at White Clay Creek, Delaware. See De Benneville K. Ludwig, "Memorabilia of the Tennents," *Journal of Presbyterian History*, 1 (1902): 344–54.

27 William Tennent [Sr.], manuscript sermons, Presbyterian Historical Society, Philadelphia. One sermon has been published: Thomas C. Pears, Jr., ed., "William Tennent's Sacramental Sermon," *Journal of Presbyterian History*, 19 (1940): 76–84. On Gilbert Tennent's millennialist views, see the brief comments in James West Davidson, *The Logic of Millennial Thought: Eighteenth-Century New England* (New Haven, Conn., 1977): 149 n. Gilbert Tennent is notably absent from the discussion

in Christopher M. Beam, "Millennialism and American Nationalism, 1740–1800," *Journal of Presbyterian History*, 54 (1976): 182–99. In Heimert's *Religion and the American Mind*, Gilbert Tennent figures prominently as an evangelical but not as a millennialist.

28 George Selement, "The Meeting of Elite and Popular Minds at Cambridge, New England, 1638–1645," *William and Mary Quarterly*, 3rd ser., 41 (1984): 32–48; on the Log College, see Trinterud, *The Forming of an American Tradition*: 63–4, 74, 82, 169–95.

29 Gilbert Tennent, "Prefatory Discourse," in John Tennent, *The Nature of Regeneration Opened* (Boston, 1735): i–ix.

30 Thomas Henderson to Elias Boudinot, n.d. [1805], no. 11M7, ms. manuscript group I, New Jersey Historical Society, Trenton, N.J.; Archibald Alexander, *Biographical Sketches of the Founder and Principal Alumni of the Log College* (Philadelphia, 1851): 127–34; Carl Bridenbaugh, " 'The Famous Infamous Vagrant' Tom Bell," in Bridenbaugh, *Early Americans* (New York, 1981): 121–49.

31 Elias Boudinot, *Life of the Rev. William Tennent, late Pastor of the Presbyterian Church at Freehold, N.J.* (Trenton, N.J., 1833): 20–4; Boudinot's sketch, based on letters he received from members of Tennent's Freehold congregation, first appeared anonymously in the *Evangelical Intelligencer*, 2 (1806): 97–103, 145–66, 201–7, then as *Memoirs of the Life of William Tennent, … An Account of His Being Three Days in a Trance and Apparently Living* (Trenton, N.J., 1810); Alexander, *Biographical Sketches*: 150–2. Alexander offered a naturalistic explanation for the loss of Tennent's toes to deflate supernatural implications he found embarrassing. On missing body parts, see Douglas B. Price, "Miraculous Restoration of Lost Body Parts: Relationship to the Phantom Limb Phenomenon and to Limb-Burial Superstitions and Practices," in *American Folk Medicine: A Symposium*, ed. Wayland D. Hand (Berkeley, Calif., 1976): 49–72.

32 John Tennent, *The Nature of Regeneration Opened*: ii, iii; Jonathan Edwards, *Religious Affections*, ed. John E. Smith (New Haven, Conn., 1959): 21; Thomas Prince, *The Christian History Containing Accounts of the Revival and Propagation of Religion in Great-Britain and America for the Year 1744*, 5 (Boston, 1745): 292–3.

33 *The Querists, Part III* (Philadelphia, 1741): 91; "The Wonderful Wandering Spirit," in *The Great Awakening*, ed. Heimert and Miller: 147–51; also see *The Querists; or, An Extract of Sundry Passages Taken Out of Mr. Whitefield's Printed Sermons, Journals and Letters* (Philadelphia 1740): 44.

34 George Whitefield, *A Short Account of God's Dealings with the Reverend Mr. George Whitefield* (London, 1740): 8, 48–9; Daniel Rogers, diary, 1740–53, October 31, 1740, manuscript collection, New-York Historical Society, New York, N.Y. Compare Rogers's description with that in *Whitefield's Journals* [ed. Murray]: 484.

35 Whitefield quoted in Clarke Garrett, *Spirit Possession and Popular Religion from the Camisards to the Shakers* (Baltimore, 1987): 83.

36 Stuart C. Henry, *George Whitefield: Wayfaring Witness* (Nashville, Tenn., 1957): 95–114.

37 *The Literary Diary of Ezra Stiles*, ed. Franklin B. Dexter, 3 vols. (New York, 1910): I, 80.

38 "The Spiritual Travels of Nathan Cole," in *The Great Awakening: Event and Exegesis*, ed. Darrett B. Rutman (New York, 1970): 44.

39 See also the 1741 Whitefield portrait now in the National Portrait Gallery, London, and reproduced, among other places, in James Henretta and Gregory Nobles, *Evolution and Revolution: American Society, 1600–1820* (Lexington, Mass., 1987): 106, and the eighteenth-century portrait owned by the Ipswich Historical Society and pictured in Katherine Whiteside, "Early American Pleasure, The Whipple House ...," *House and Garden* (July 1987): 110–19.

40 Heimert, *Religion and the American Mind*: 48; Joel Headley, *The Chaplains and Clergy of the Revolution* (New York, 1864): 92–3; Leroy M. Lee, *The Life and Times of the Reverend Jesse Lee* (Louisville, Ky., 1948): 246; [Abel Stevens], *Sketches and Incidents; or, A Budget from the Saddle-Bags of a Superannuated Itinerant*, ed. George Peck (Cincinnati, 1848): 120; *Memoirs of the Life of David Marks, Minister of the Gospel*, ed. Marilla Marks (Dover, N.H., 1846): 335.

41 William Becket to George Whitefield, June 9, 1740, William Becket's Notices and Letters, manuscript collections, Historical Society of Pennsylvania, Philadelphia.

42 Howard C. Kee, *Miracle in the Early Christian World: A Study in Sociohistorical Method* (New Haven, Conn., 1983); Ramsay MacDonald, *Christianizing the Roman Empire, 100 A.D.–400 A.D.* (New Haven, Conn., 1984); *George Fox's "Book of Miracles,"* ed. Henry J. Cadbury (Cambridge, 1948); Richard Bushman, *Joseph Smith, and the Beginnings of Mormonism* (Urbana, Ill., 1984); David Harrell, Jr., *All Things are Possible: The Healing and Charismatic Revivals in Modern America* (Bloomington, Ind., 1975).

43 Historians generally homogenize evangelical revivalist style. For a general introduction to evangelicalism, see Leonard I. Sweet, "The Evangelical Tradition in America[: Introduction]," in *The Evangelical Tradition in America*, ed. Sweet (Macon, Ga., 1984): 1–86; on revivalism generally, see Whitney R. Cross, *The Burned-Over District: The Social and Intellectual History of Enthusiastic Religion in Western New York, 1800–1850* (New York, 1950); Timothy L. Smith, *Revivalism and Social Reform: American Protestantism on the Eve of the Civil War* (Nashville, Tenn., 1957); and William G. McLoughlin, *Revivals, Awakenings, and Reform: An Essay on Religion and Social Change in America, 1607–1977* (Chicago, 1978).

44 Two studies claim relatively high rates at mid-century: Patricia U. Bonomi and Peter R. Eisenstadt, "Church Adherence in the Eighteenth-Century British American Colonies," *William and Mary Quarterly*, 3rd ser., 39 (1982): 245–6; and Richard W. Pointer, *Protestant Pluralism and the New York Experience: A Study of Eighteenth-Century Religious Diversity* (Bloomington, Ind., 1987): 29–31, 151. On New England church adherence patterns, see Gerald F. Moran, "The Puritan Saint: Religious Experience, Church Membership, and Piety in Connecticut, 1636–1776" (Ph.D. dissertation, Rutgers University, 1973); and Richard P. Gildrie, *Salem, Massachusetts, 1626–1682: A Covenant Community* (Charlottesville, Va., 1975): 64, 163–4. Difficulties with the various estimates

center on the count of congregations, the "averages" used to indicate congregation size, and the differences that result from the fact that some historians count adults while others count adults and children. These technical problems are beyond the scope of the general study here, though I hope to address them in a subsequent publication.

45 The statistics from Radnor, Apoquimminy, and Newcastle have been collected from the "Notitia Parochialis" scattered through the voluminous reports of SPG ministers, contained in SPG manuscripts, ser. A, B, and C, United SPG Archives, London (microfilm, University of Minnesota, Minneapolis).

46 Hector St. John de Crèvecoeur, *Letters from an American Farmer and Sketches of Eighteenth-Century America*, ed. Albert E. Stone (New York, 1981): 76.

6

CHURCH AND HOME IN MID-EIGHTEENTH-CENTURY VIRGINIA

Rhys Isaac

In this highly imaginative foray into the public and private worlds of mid-eighteenth-century Virginians, Isaac takes the reader on a guided tour of an Anglican church, an important center of community life, and then of a gentry home, in many ways a public place. The boundary between private and public, sacred and profane, Isaac argues, was porous in early Virginia. Thus, Anglican churches were important places for reinforcing hierarchy and encouraging conviviality, and homes were important places for daily religious practices, important ceremonies, and displays of hospitality. Dance was a significant means of joining private and public worlds. Through dancing, Virginians expressed themselves about some of their most cherished values: self-assertion, display, competitiveness, and contest. Dancing also formed a significant bond, a common medium of expression, cementing together disparate social groups. While the lower orders imitated polite forms of dancing, the gentry in turn borrowed dance forms and musical accompaniments from their slaves.

Isaac's methods are especially noteworthy. Close attention to commonplace events provides access to an alien world. Isaac proceeds by searchlight, directing his shaft of light onto single places and events in order that each can render up their full cultural meaning, each can uncover further dimensions of the society's underlying set of values. He intensively scrutinizes not only words but gestures, demeanors, dress, architecture – in short, the total communications repertoire of a society – in the belief that a society's values will be evident in its use of space, ceremonies, rituals, and symbols.

The reader might speculate about the changes that Virginia homes and churches underwent as the eighteenth century proceeded. Isaac offers clues when he points to the restructuring of gentry houses and new domestic lifestyles, already evident by mid-century. The emergence of segregated,

178

private spaces, the increasing differentiation of domestic functions, the growth of refinement all indicate an intensifying emphasis on individual separateness. Elsewhere, Isaac has also explored the Baptist challenge to the inclusiveness of the Anglican Church. The Baptists, like other evangelicals, emphasized an individual's personal relationship to God, although allied to a highly disciplined and ordered social movement. Was individualism, then, soon to reign triumphant in late eighteenth-century Virginia? Or would new forms of community, perhaps less inclusive ones, also arise?

* * *

Churches were the important centers for community assembly, dispersed at the most frequent intervals in the countryside. The parishes of the established religion were sometimes, in the western part of the colony, coterminous with counties, but usually they were considerably smaller. In both cases the parish would have a number of houses of worship – churches and "chapels of ease." Each person, except those who formally dissented (and they were very few in the settled parts before mid-century), was deemed a member of "the Church of England as by law established." All were required to attend divine service at least once in four weeks, under penalty of a fine of five shillings or fifty pounds of tobacco, for failure to comply. It was important, therefore, that no part of the parish be too far from one or another of its churches. Central location and accessibility by road were the prime considerations for the siting of these edifices. Thus a church often stood alone in a cleared area near some crossroads at the center of its parish precinct.

The churches were generally plain structures. In the early eighteenth century they were oblong in form. Rarely did they have steeples or belfries. (In the absence of town or even village settlement too few of the parishioners would have lived within the sound of the bells.) Formerly churches had been constructed of wood, but by 1720 – as a further indication of the social consolidation that the great houses expressed – they were built of brick. The courses were sometimes elaborately contrived in such a way that blue-glazed "headers" alternated with light red "stretchers" in "Flemish bond" to form a checkerboard effect. Doors were handsomely picked out by the use of softer bricks rubbed into the pleasing forms of moldings that showed a contrasting deep, rich

179

color. The tall windows were elegantly arched and designed to let light freely into these temples of rational religion.

In the 1730s a new church design was introduced. Its rapid spread is a clear sign that those who dominated decision-making at the parish level thought it appropriate. The first of these new-fashioned edifices, Christ Church in Lancaster County, has somehow survived the triumph of the sectaries and escaped the ravages of three wars that have laid waste parts of Virginia. With nearly all of its woodwork and most of its original glass intact, it stands in its wall-enclosed green among the trees on the northern shore of the Rappahannock River, lovingly restored as a silent reminder of the religious observances and the social exchanges that it was built to contain.

As the churchgoers approached, they came upon the familiar bulk of this Greek-cross church, which presented from each side the face of one of its four tall gabled ends, carrying high the steep-pitched shingle roof. Fine rubbed brickwork dignified the plain lines of the great doors and windows. The common planters rode up, mounted astride; the gentry and their families came in coaches and six, with older sons and household retinue possibly riding escort. Before the start of the service the surroundings of the church "look'd like the Out-Skirts of a Country Horse Fair." The advance gathering was important. Philip Fithian,[a] whose Presbyterian upbringing in New Jersey filled him with Sabbatarian disapproval, noted that there were

> three grand divisions of time at the Church on Sundays, Viz. before Service giving & receiving letters of business, reading Advertisements, consulting about the price of Tobacco, Grain &c. & settling either the lineage, Age, or qualities of favourite Horses. 2. In the Church at Service, prayrs read over in haste, a Sermon seldom under & never over twenty minutes, but always made up of sound morality, or deep studied Metaphysicks. 3. After Service is over three quarters of an hour spent in strolling round the Church among the Crowd, … [when one might be] invited by several different Gentlemen home with them to dinner.

The combination of ordered service and animated conversation produced at the church a blend of formality and informality – of convivial engagement and structured relationship – that recurs in accounts of Virginia social gatherings.[1]

Those who were completely at ease on these community Sunday mornings, when the affairs of the world pressed in around the setting for divine service, have not left records of their untroubled feelings. Yet a note to Sir Peyton Skipwith from one of his agents shows how freely the very secular could be associated with the religious. Without revealing any sense of incongruity, the writer informed the baronet that a blood stallion of his had been taken to church so that the people might look over the proud creature with a view to having him cover their mares. Similarly, young Ben Carter, anxious to have Fithian take him to New Jersey, begged the tutor "to acquaint him with the manners of the People in regard to Religion, and he swears he can suit himself to any serious, or formal visage." It is evident that Virginians, whatever their rank, generally did not affect postures of grave piety and that on Sunday at church they took for granted the close proximity of the profane to the sacred.[2]

Concerns of the world, brought to the church door as a matter of course, were not so readily abandoned in order to cross its threshold into the more hallowed time and space set apart for worship. "It is not the Custom for Gentlemen to go into Church til Service is beginning, when they enter in a Body." Pride of rank accompanied the gentry even as they took their places within, so that we may picture them tramping booted to their pews at the front. Their exit was made "in the same manner"; women and humbler men waited to leave until the gentlemen had gone.[3]

Entering Christ Church, Lancaster County (and other churches following its design), one is suddenly in a lofty, light-filled, enclosed space. The high-vaulted interior would certainly be the largest "room" or hall that most parishioners ever entered. The intended effect was not – as with the form of Gothic churches – to channel the devotions of the faithful through the clergy and the sanctuary to the heavens, but rather, in the Protestant spirit, to make the community-congregation worshipfully present to itself.

The architectural plan maximized the visibility to the assembled community of a numerous emulative gentry. In the center the four arms of the Greek cross united to form a large focal space. Great oak-walled pews reserved for magistrates and leading families stood at the front of each arm of the church, delimiting the central area. High within the space thus defined stood the pulpit under its grand, ornately canopied sounding board, or "tester." The pulpit was the obvious point of attention in the design, symbolizing, again in the Protestant spirit, the central importance of the explication of the Word of God. Only a clergyman who had been examined, ordained, and licensed by a bishop, successor to the Apostles, could mount the elevated rostrum to unfold the divine mysteries. In tiered hierarchy beneath the pulpit were the desk from which the scriptural lessons were read, and the clerk's desk from which the parson's lay assistant "lined out" the psalms for communal intonation. Behind pulpit and desks, and hence symbolically and dramaturgically in the lowest position, was the gallery that a small number of slaves would enter by a steep narrow stairway just inside the south door.

On the far side of the central space stood the altar. Above it on the end wall, the words of the Ten Commandments and the Apostles' Creed shone out in gold lettering from black tablets, keeping the people mindful of the cosmic framework within which their community was contained and of the moral absolutes to which it was subject.

The seating plans of the Virginia churches – accentuated by the manner of entry and exit – exhibited the community to itself in ranked order. The form and tone of the liturgy reinforced the demonstration inherent in the physical setting. The services of the Book of Common Prayer had been given their vernacular shape in the sixteenth century and expressed strongly an ethos of English Christian gentility. The appointed set of words, read in the midst of a community ranged in order of precedence, continuously evoked postures of deference and submission. Liturgy and church plan thus readily combined to offer a powerful representation of a structured, hierarchical community. The ceremonial of the county court – as will be seen – asserted similar, complementary values and relationships. Church and courthouse, each in its proper way, exhibited symbols and formulas expressing the orientation of the local community to the larger social world.[4]

The words and forms of action at church clearly asserted the hierarchical nature of things, confirming definitions of authority within the rural community itself. The appeal of these proceedings for the gentry can readily be imagined. With a greater effort of the imagination it can be recognized that the services also offered satisfactions to humbler persons to the extent that they had internalized the view of the world that the liturgy and seating plan represented. Such persons might take pleasure in admiring the magnificence of the great and in deferentially receiving attentions bestowed on them from above. "Condescension" was, in the eighteenth century, a praiseworthy quality for persons of rank.

The institutional organization of the church also served to reinforce claims to authority from above and its acceptance from below. Each parish was ruled by a vestry of twelve gentlemen presided over by the minister. These worthies (who filled their own vacancies by cooption) regulated church affairs, annually imposing whatever taxes they considered necessary to pay the parson's salary, to meet incidental costs, and to repair, extend, or build *de novo* great and expensively furnished churches. The levies might occasion murmurings from parishioners, but the vestries also exercised patronage over lesser men, since the relief of the poor was entrusted to them. They could choose to ease – or not to ease – a person's declining years. It lay with them to decide whether to lighten the burden assumed by poor but self-sufficient householders who had to undertake the care of an aged or infirm relative.[5]

Christian formulas were scattered throughout the daily routines of Anglo-Virginians. Before dinner it was usual "to 'say Grace' as they call it; which is always express'd by the People in the following words, 'God bless us in what we are to receive' – & after Dinner, 'God make us thankful for his mercies.' " The best account we have of a child's growing up in a humble household before mid-century stresses the worthiness of the parents without suggesting unusual piety, yet it was recalled that "they taught ... short prayers" and made their children "very perfect in repeating the *Church Catechism*." Any child – perhaps a majority of white boys – who had instruction in reading, had the Bible for his reader. Landon Carter's[b] dependence for a good crop upon the contingencies of nature was reflected in a resigned, fatalistic supplication to God. The world of the Old Testament was one that eighteenth-century Virginians could readily identify with. In a famous passage, William Byrd compared himself to "one of the Patriarchs" with their "flocks ... Herds ... Bond-men and Bond-women." Similarly, the simple field-and-orchard metaphors of the New Testament parables referred to a recognizable world of immediate experience.[6]

Although all ranks of Anglo-Virginians subconsciously assumed a correspondence between Judaeo-Christian cosmology and the familiar rounds of daily life, they did not find it necessary to exhibit the assumption in pious routine. Family prayers were unusual in Chesapeake society. Custom and the law required attendance once in four weeks at church, but neither were strict concerning regularity, so that the cycle of the week – an important rhythm of life in Virginia – was marked more certainly by a seventh day of rest and conviviality than by prayerful devotions. "Generally ... by five o'clock on Saturday every Face (especially the Negroes) looks festive and cheerful – All the lower class of People, & the Servants, & the Slaves, consider [Sunday] ... as a Day of Pleasure & amusement, and spend it in such Diversions as they severally choose."[7]

Many slaves came or were sent to the religious observances of their masters. Yet the specific religious beliefs that prevailed at the quarters are difficult to ascertain. The fixed formalities of Anglican liturgical worship and the didacticism of much of the preaching could not readily be assimilated to African modes of proclaiming the meaning of life.[8]

The Reverend Mr. Hugh Jones gives a very revealing account of how the Christian religion was woven into the great events of the lives of Anglo-Virginians. As an Anglican of moderate temperament, Jones – unlike dissenting commentators – understood and accepted the customary forms and usages that prevailed in the Old Dominion. He reserved his occasional mild strictures for some of the colonial departures from English practice. Certainly he found the total absence of a bishop to be a serious truncation of the ritual forms of the Church. Since parishioners lacked means for "confirmation" as communicants, many were reluctant to present themselves for the sacrament, at least until the approach of death established a greater sense of urgency. The churches themselves could not be considered consecrated, and Jones proposed a substitute ceremony whereby there might be "some solemn dedication prescribed for setting ... [churches] apart for sacred uses; which would," he hoped, "make people behave themselves with greater reverence than they usually do, and have a greater value for the house of God and holy things."[9]

Hugh Jones noted also, significantly, that Virginians insisted on having certain rituals performed in their homes rather than in churches, as English usage would have required:

> It is customary to bury in gardens or orchards, where whole families lye interred together, in a spot generally handsomly enclosed, planted with evergreens, and the graves kept decently. Hence ... arises the occasion of preaching funeral sermons in houses, where at funerals are assembled a great

congregation of neighbours and friends; and if you insist upon having the sermon and ceremony at church, they'll say they will be without it, unless performed *after their usual custom*. In houses also there is occasion, from humour, custom sometimes, from necessity most frequently, to baptize children and *church* women ... . In houses also they most commonly marry, without regard to the time of day or season of the year.[10]

The definition of sacred space – its location at the church – had become confused, reaching almost the point of caricature with the removal of the churching of women to the home! It has been common to attribute these developments to the scattered settlement pattern and the distances arising from it, despite the notorious propensity of Virginians of all races and ranks to travel far to points of assembly when they were inclined to do so. As Jones noted, custom rather than expediency was already being argued in defense of the preference for services at the dwelling place. Custom, even when it arises originally from necessity, shapes experience. For colony-born Anglo-Virginians, rites of passage within the home were simply the taken-for-granted shape of things. Sacred significance attached to these rites, being no longer confined within the church, was transferred to the home and was there associated with the gathering of neighbors to share in the event. Christian forms were not set aside. The ceremonies of the Church were carried out as far as possible in the prescribed manner. (The law required marriage in all cases to be solemnized by a minister of the Established Church; custom dictated that "most of the middling people" would have a funeral sermon, though it cost them a very substantial forty-shilling fee.)

The transference of rites of passage from church to home meant, however, that specifically Christian ceremonies had come to be closely surrounded, and even overshadowed, by social rituals and forms of celebration that persons in the Anglo-Virginian tradition would have defined (if forced to distinguish) as secular rather than religious. Yet these social enactments were important and contributed powerfully to the aura of the house.

Afro-Virginians cannot have been caught in the subtle tensions between church-centered, "sacred" celebrations and home-centered, "profane" forms. For them the English Christian distinctions between the "religious" and the "secular" would probably have had little meaning. Although we can discover almost nothing of the symbols that the slaves used to represent ultimate value and meaning, we know that their primary modes of expression were song and dance, with exemplary tales perhaps playing a secondary role. A basic African cultural "grammar" appears to have transcended the great diversities of language and specific customs that confronted the captive migrants as they began to coalesce into a distinct society upon the North American seaboard. This is a case where the medium was indeed the essence of the message. Clearly, during the formative decades of the eighteenth century the slaves were able to keep alive distinctive African expressive styles and sensibilities. (In no other way could these features have survived strongly enough to be recorded by nineteenth- and twentieth-century folklorists and narrative collectors.) Spontaneous performances of song were the rule, invariably accompanied by rhythmic body movement and usually in the form of a litany between leaders and their communal choruses.[11]

Residences were highly significant places in the social landscape. The ideal of the home as a center of private domesticity was not familiar to Anglo-Virginians in the mid-eighteenth century. They lived or aspired to live in the constant presence of servants and guests. Their houses were the sacrosanct settings for hospitality and for the open celebration of the major events of life and death. Jones had lamented the absence of forms for the "solemn dedication" of churches; he could have gone on to note that an appropriate ritual did exist for homes. Early in his stay in Virginia Fithian became aware that "whenever any *person* or *Family* move into a House, or repair a house they have been living in before, they make a *Ball* & give a supper ... in compliance with Custom, to invite ... Neighbours, and dance, and be merry." Indeed, most of the dominant values of the culture were fused together in the display of hospitality, which was one of the supreme obligations that society laid upon heads of households. In 1705 Robert Beverley had written:

> The Inhabitants are very Courteous to Travellers ... . A Stranger has no more to do, but to inquire upon the Road, where any Gentleman or good House-keeper Lives, and there he may depend upon being received with Hospitality. This good Nature is so general ... that the Gentry when they go abroad, order their Principal Servant to entertain all Visitors

… . And the poor Planters, who have but one Bed, will very often sit up, or lie upon a Form or Couch all Night, to make room for a weary Traveller … . If there happen to be a Churl, that either out of Covetousness, or Ill-nature, won't comply with this generous Custom, he has a mark of Infamy set upon him, and is abhorr'd by all.

This observation was repeated in varied form throughout the colonial period, and often in a context that shows that the extending of hospitality was not only an obligation but also a source of intense gratification – almost an inner compulsion. The stress on hospitality arose from and contributed to the sacred importance attached to the house. A man's homeplace – his plantation and house – were special extensions of the self.[12]

Myths of southern hospitality at stately mansions must not be allowed to obscure the larger context in which the gentry's displays of magnificence occurred. The living quarters of the great majority of persons in the middle of the eighteenth century were still cramped and confined, yet changes were already taking place that had important long-term implications for the transformation of psyches, and so of religion and ideology. For this reason the evolution of household interiors from the turn of the seventeenth century to the 1750s will briefly be traced.

The seventeenth-century "Virginia house" (as documents of the period designated such structures) was a one-story frame dwelling with two rooms on the ground floor. The whole structure (very often including the roof) was covered with unpainted clapboards split out of four-foot lengths of oak. Chimneys were set outside the gables at one or both ends. In the roof, attics usually afforded additional space. They could be entered by a stair or ladder from one of the rooms below. Typically the entranceway led directly into the main living room with its focal hearth, so that the house was a comparatively open structure for both inhabitants and visitors. Even the great houses of the gentry were organized in such a way that access to the inner parts was through a "hall" in which most domestic activity was concentrated.[13]

Crowding people into a single room – sometimes as small as ten by twelve feet – made for a communal style of life. With so little specialization of space there could be only minimum differentiation of functions. Persons growing up in such an environment would not develop a sense of segregated self with a need for privacy. The physical congestion was further intensified by the extreme paucity of furniture. A recent analysis of inventories shows that more than half the households in the society owned personal property worth £60 or less. At this level of existence no more than one in four families had a table to sit at. About a third of the households had chairs or benches, but only one in seven of such families owned both. It is necessary to look well up the social scale before such possessions became the rule rather than the exception. Beds as we know them – let alone bedrooms – were not available to most households. In fewer than one-seventh of the inventories worth less than £60 did even a single bedstead raise the most privileged persons in the house off the floor. The small numbers of mattresses and blankets listed in inventories make it clear that most people shared sleeping space, lying two or three together. And nights were long, since most houses had no candles or lamps and could rely only on the light from the fire in the hearth after the day's end.[14]

Thus the inhabitants of the seventeenth-century Chesapeake world have been aptly characterized as "squatters or leaners." They rested slumped on the floor, or crouched on the boxes and chests that were the only ubiquitous items of furniture. They held their food bowls in one hand when they ate, using a spoon with the other. Nearly all persons, whatever their rank, lacked knives and forks until after 1700. Although the well-to-do had more space, more furniture, and greater quantities of superior equipment, as late as the 1680s their houses and possessions were not organized to sustain a life-style qualitatively different from that of their poorer neighbors.[15]

By the mid-eighteenth century an important series of changes had begun and was still continuing. First, distinct gentry families emerged and came to be more and more set apart by an increasingly refined way of life. This refinement was expressed in architecture, since the great houses had passageways with rooms opening off them to create segregated spaces for special persons and functions. Such movement away from communality was most dramatically signaled in the custom of "dining," with its reserved space, its linen-covered table, and its fashionably styled matching sets of plates, knives, forks, and other eating accoutrements. At regular times select companies gathered at this ritual center, and each member would be seated on a chair in a carefully defined social space.[16]

For the middling and lower orders in Virginia society, changes came later. Some poorer whites, together with the slaves, were still in a comparatively unmodified "seventeenth-century" condition of life at the end of the eighteenth century. The houses of common folk remained small, with little provision for segregation of persons and activities. By mid-century, for all save the very least fortunate, important modifications in household equipment had been made. Social space and the boundaries of the person were being redefined. Bedsteads, tables, and chairs came to be the rule rather than the exception. But even in the 1750s, the combination of tables and chairs was found in only one-third of households with inventories that were valued at less than £40 – households that constituted about 30 percent of the total. Knives and forks appeared in about the same proportion of inventories.[17]

Records have not been found that could support a direct analysis of customary behavior in the houses of humble tobacco growers. The patterns of ceremony-oriented, rule-bound life in the great houses, however, can be studied. They will be reviewed here through the detailed observations recorded in Philip Fithian's diary during the years 1773 and 1774.[18]

The young Fithian was greatly struck by the grandeur of Robert Carter's countryseat. The house stood on "a high spot of Ground," and being seventy-six by forty-four feet (with a height of more than forty feet), it could be seen "at the Distance of six Miles." It was not merely the size but the elegance that impressed him. A strong sense of authority is communicated in Fithian's description of the elaborate but controlled facades and the careful setting of the mansion itself in a great hundred-yard rectangle, with the corners defined by substantial one-and-a-half-story brick dependencies.[19]

Inside, the four principal rooms on the ground floor were "disposed of in the following manner. Below [the stairs?] is a dining Room ...; the second is a dining-Room for the Children; the third is Mr. Carters study; & the fourth is a Ball-Room thirty feet long." Significantly, Fithian omitted the hall from his count of rooms. The presence of the master in the hall when it was used to receive invited guests or as a cool summer living place might introduce an atmosphere of grave propriety, as on this occasion, noted by our diarist: "About ten [o'clock] an old Negro Man came with a complaint to Mr. Carter of the Overseer that he does not allow him his Peck of corn a Week ... . We were sitting in the passage, he sat himself down on the Floor clasp'd his Hands together, with his face directly to Mr.*Carter*, & then began his Narration." More generally, however, when it was not the scene of encounter between persons with a high sense of their dignity, the hall – significantly styled "the passage" – was the area of least formality in the house. Fithian gave two revealing glimpses of the comparative freedom of this space. In the first he showed "*Dennis*, a [slave] Boy of about twelve Years old, one of the Waiters at Table ... standing in the front Door" at the entrance to the hall, evidently taking his ease, when in a sudden gust, the door, "which is vastly huge & heavy," slammed to and took off the end of his middle finger. In the other scene children were bickering as Fithian "was passing through the Hall from Breakfast – [and] the Nurse, a short stump of a [white woman] ... call'd to [him], & begg'd [him] to close the Quarrel."[20]

The way in which the partitioning of interior spaces and the specialization of functions created greater refinement is clearly demonstrated in the use of the dining room that opened off the hall beneath the stairs. The dinner table was the center for the most highly formalized behavior in gentry houses. Decorum was enhanced by the setting aside of a separate chamber for the meals of young persons, who had not yet learned to conform to studied rituals. Fithian's note that the dining room was "where we usually sit" indicates some relaxation of strictness. Yet his whole account of the routines at Nomini Hall suggests that such use served less to vulgarize the room than to heighten the formality of social intercourse for those who were included in the circle that sat and conversed in this sanctum.[21]

Even more than the select seclusion of the room, the ceremonial character of the meals – especially dinner – marked off the table as sacrosanct within the time and space of daily domestic life. The dinner table was not only the center of ritual of the gentry household; it was also the very focus of that hospitality whose hallowed importance has already been stressed. (Guests were so much the expected thing that their absence would occasionally elicit a journal entry: "no company.") To the Honorable Robert Carter's table came not only the heads of neighboring houses and their families, "by particular invitation," but also, as they had cause to call on the master, a succession of persons in more or less client station, such as clerks, estate stewards, head overseers, and tobacco inspectors. A continual series of essential exchanges took place here – obligations incurred and returned. Tokens of social esteem, or simply of recognition, were given by the great and received by the less exalted. The tables of the honored guests would in turn be graced by the colonel himself; the patronized clients would be expected to make their returns in other, less honorific, ways.[22]

Bells, rung at stated hours, proclaimed the times of assembly at the highest table. Those who were eligible to attend were obligated to do so, as Fithian learned when, because his "Head was not dress'd, & [he] was too lazy to change ... clothes," he decided he would not go. "Mrs Carter ... in the evening lash'd [him] severely ... said [he] was rude, & censurable." The form of proceedings proclaimed the dominance of the master, whose role Fithian characterized as director of the "ceremonies at Table." He would "say Grace"; he "must carve – Drink the Health – and talk"; and he performed the offices of magnanimous hospitality: "Sir – This is a fine Sheeps-Head [fish], Mr Stadly shall I help you? – Or would you prefer a *Bass* or a *Perch*? – Or perhaps you will rather help yourself to some picked *Crab*." Since formality extended its constraints to the table talk, the master also conducted that, leading in with topics suitable for polite discourse. Thus on Wednesday, June 8, 1774, "Mr *Carter* ... introduced ... a conversation on Philosophy, on Eclipses; the manner of viewing them; Thence to Telescopes, & the information which they afforded us of the Solar System; Whether the planets be actually inhabited &c." On another occasion he opened with an observation "that many of the most just, & nervous [i.e., delicate] sentiments are contain'd in Songs & small Sketches of Poetry; but being attended with *Frippery Folly* or *Indecency* they are many times look'd over." Likewise the social awareness of the young was to be formed in a polite conversational mold. When they were being given orders "concerning their conduct" during the course of a great Christmas entertainment held at a neighboring gentleman's house, they were told to bring back "an Account of all the company at the Ball." The patriarch exercised less comprehensive control, however, when his peers were present. An analysis of the dinner table conversation topics reported in the diary shows that honored guests, less subject to the control of the grave gentleman, introduced a more trivial, anecdotal tone.[23]

At the conclusion of dinner (taken about three o'clock in the afternoon) came a series of toasts. It seems these were always loyal toasts – to the king, the governor, and in time the Continental Congress – sometimes followed by one to "absent Friends." (Even when the colonel and the tutor dined alone, this first group of toasts was *de rigueur*.) Then usually followed (after the ladies' withdrawal?) the gallantry of each gentleman "giving" the health of a lady whom he chose to name. Supper (taken at about nine o'clock) was also followed by toasts if there was company, and might be no less formal than dinner.

Two scenes depicted in Fithian's diary entries describe companies gathered for dancing at the hall: "Half after eight we were rung in to Supper; The room looked luminous and splendid; four very large candles burning on the table where we supp'd, three others in different parts of the Room; a gay, sociable Assembly, & four well instructed waiters!" On another occasion Fithian recorded that "the Company danced after candle-light a Minuet round, ... when we were Rung to Supper[.] after Supper we sit til twelve drinking loyal Toasts."[24]

The exclusive social authority that all this highly formal display was calculated to engender is revealed in the predicament of a man from a circle slightly below that of the gentry, who found himself patronized at the colonel's table twice during July 1774. According to Fithian he lacked refined style and became very self-conscious about it:

> Dined with us one – one – Mr. – Mr. – I forget his name – I know his trade tho': An Inspector [of Tobacco] – He is rather Dull, & seems unacquainted with company[,] for when he would, at Table, drink our Health, he held the Glass of Porter fast with both his Hands, and then gave an insignificant nod to each one at Table, in Hast, & with fear, & then drank like an Ox – The Good Inspector, at the second toast, after having seen a little our Manner[:] "Gentlemen & Ladies (but there was none in Womans Cloathing at Table except Mrs. Carter) The King" – I thought that during the Course of the Toasts he was better pleased with the Liquor than with the manner in which at this Time he was obliged to use it.

A few days later the inspector showed yet more unfamiliarity with bon ton when the company "had after Dinner, *Lime Punch & Madaira*; but he chose & had a Bowl of *Grogg* [rum and water]"![25]

When the house was the setting for a large-scale celebration of the greatness of its family and the magnanimity of its head, the precise lines of formality were inevitably trampled by the press of numbers gathered at the house. Unfortunately no grand rite of passage was celebrated at Nomini Hall while Fithian was there, but he was able to observe one day of a splendid four-day ball that

Squire Lee held at his family seat in January 1774. The tutor's account reveals how the festivities, which more than seventy guests attended, involved throwing open the whole ground floor of the great house. (It can be inferred from known custom that the bed-chambers upstairs and in the dependencies would have been reserved for those who had traveled the greatest distances.) The refinement of segregating different activities and functions could not be maintained, although an effort was made to retain polite tone in spite of irrepressible exuberance among many of the as-sembled visitors:

> As soon as I had handed the Ladies out, I was saluted by Parson *Smith*; I was introduced into a small Room where a number of Gentlemen were playing Cards ... to lay off my Boots[,] Riding-Coat &c – Next I was directed to the Dining-Room to see Young Mr. *Lee*; He introduced me to his Father ... . The Ladies dined first, when some Good order was pre-served; when they rose, each nimblest Fellow dined first – The Dinner was as elegant as could be well expected when so great an Assembly was to be kept for so long a time ... . About Seven the Ladies & Gentlemen begun to dance in the Ball-Room – first Minuets one Round; Second Giggs; third Reels, And last of All Country-Dances ... . The Music was a French-Horn and two Violins – The Ladies were Dressed Gay, and splendid, & when dancing their Silks & Brocades rustled and trailed behind them! – But all did not join in the Dance for there were parties in Rooms made up, some at Cards; some drinking for Pleasure; some toasting the Sons of america; some singing "Liberty Songs" as they call'd them, in which six, eight, ten or more would put their Heads near together and roar.[26]

Adaptation to climate and perhaps to the social leveling of a new settlement led to another manner of celebrating the hospitality of the head of the household and his homeplace – one that avoided encroaching on the formalities of the house or imposing the de-corum proper to domestic space upon the gathering. From late July until the end of summer the Carters of Nomini Hall and their gentleman tutor were frequently invited to attend "fish feasts" or "barbecues" upon the banks of the river. We shall see that outdoor entertainments might be even freer from restraint among common planters and slaves.[27]

The ceremonies that made the tobacco inspector feel so ill at ease were made possible by the leisured affluence that the ruling gentry enjoyed. Persons who had to work in the fields from dawn to dusk could not always sit at table for their dinner, let alone dress their heads. (In the earlier decades of the century many did not possess a table to sit at.) Of necessity, then, less formality prevailed at the common planters' houses and the slaves' quarters. This is not to say that there were no rules, no customary ritual forms – although no account has been found describing what these were. (Perhaps we get a hint of one in the inspector's way of drinking the health of the company, giving a "nod to each one at the Table" in a fashion that seemed "insignificant," or pointless, to the well-bred tutor from New Jersey.)

The humble "Virginia house," with its two rooms downstairs, was extremely restricted as to space for social gatherings. As described in one of the few accounts we have of festivities at a common planter's homeplace, entertainment necessarily flowed out of doors when it occurred on a large scale. A simple wooden Tidewater farmhouse, amid its orchards and outbuildings, was made ready for the celebration of the return visit of a younger brother who some two years before had gone west to teach school. Many years later that brother, Devereux Jarratt, remembered seeing, as he rode up, great "numbers, both within and without doors." Outside "the tankard [of hard cider] went briskly round, while the sound of music and dancing, was heard within."[28]

Little is known of the rituals with which slaves marked life's important moments. Uncomprehending white observers characterized the celebrations they saw among the slaves as completely informal – "Rude and uncultivated ... irregular and grotesque" were the words used by one traveler.[29]

When a householder opened the resources of his plantation to guests, the opportunities for self-assertion, display, and conviviality were at their greatest. For the gentry, a birthday, the Christmas season, or mere inclination provided sufficient reason to engage in lavish ostentation; for humbler people, cause for celebration was more likely to be a christening, a wedding, a homecoming, or a funeral.

The social circle was most complete at celebrations of house and of family rites of passage. Young and old, men and women, assembled together. Dancing was at the center of the action and was evidently one of the most meaningful expressions of the soul of this

194

entire people: "*Virginians* are of genuine Blood – They will dance or die!" It was inevitable, given the significance attached to this activity, and given the proud, self-assertive values of the society, that dancing should be vigorous and competitive. Performances were closely watched, and consensual judgments speedily became known.[30]

As one explores the dancing of Virginians of diverse ranks, and the passions and values it expressed, one has an opportunity to enter more deeply into the world of those whom historians have arrogantly called "the inarticulate." Most is known about activities in elite circles, but the evidence suggests that despite a self-conscious emphasis among the grandees on high, even courtly, styles, continuities connected the performances of the gentry with those of common farmers and slaves.

In the great houses attention was given to the formal instruction of young ladies and gentlemen in polite forms of dancing. Often lessons were conducted by teachers who came from Europe. The College of William and Mary was promoting such accomplishments well before its academic faculty was complete. The principal dances taught were the minuet and the by-then formalized and fashionable country dances and reels. Fithian noted the strictness of the teacher who held classes in the great houses of the Northern Neck on the eve of the Revolution, and the accuracy of the pupils' performances. Yet he saw the same pupils engage in more vigorous, less-refined plebeian dancing when they were out of school. Similarly, Andrew Burnaby, staying among the Virginians for a year in 1759–60, observed that they were

> immoderately fond of dancing, [but that] they discover great want of taste and elegance … . Towards the close of a evening, when the company are pretty well tired with country dances, it is usual to dance jiggs; a practice originally borrowed, I am informed, from the Negroes. These dances are without any method or regularity: a gentleman and lady stand up, and dance about the room, one of them retiring, the other pursuing, then perhaps meeting, in an irregular fantastical manner.

The jigs might not even be confined to the latter part of the evening. Nicholas Cresswell, describing a Twelfth Night ball in Alexandria in 1775, was struck by the aspirations to high style expressed in the dress and coiffure of the ladies. He also noted the general fondness for dancing, and the failure, as it seemed to him, to "perform it with the greatest elegance": "Betwixt the Country dances they have what I call everlasting jigs. A couple gets up and begins to dance ... (to some Negro tune) others comes and cuts them out, and these dances always last as long as the Fiddler can play. This is sociable, but I think it looks more like a Bacchanalian dance than one in a polite assembly."[31]

The form of the jig gives a strong sense of the consistency of the culture. Even in the most convivial activities a palpable element of contest was subtly incorporated. The company formed a circle, observing and informally adjudicating the performances in the center. A kind of challenge and response was rendered explicit (and extended to include females) in the "cutting out" ritual – which would certainly have been controlled by the judgment of the on-lookers. Even the pitting of the fiddler against dancers in a test of endurance carried intimations of contest.

Fithian had been impressed by the strict formality of gentry danc-ing lessons, but his diary also casts light on the processes by which African influences competed with European courtliness in giving expressive content to Virginia dancing. The New Jersey tutor recorded an episode involving the Honorable Robert Carter's son Benjamin and his nephew Harry: "This Evening [Sunday] the Negroes collected themselves into the School-Room & began to play the *Fiddle*, & dance ... . I went among them, *Ben* & *Harry* were of the company – *Harry* was dancing with his Coat off – I dispersed them however im-mediately." We see for an instant how the dance might function repeatedly as a common medium of expression, linking persons at opposite extremes of the social hierarchy. Such communication of tone and feeling was not confined to impromptu occasions. Slaves were present as attendants at the grandest balls, able to observe the performances of the gentry for later adaptation or satirization. The musicians at the assemblies in the great houses were usually blacks, who were thus certain to introduce in covert ways their own concep-tion of the dance into the most modish proceedings.[32]

An English traveler just off a ship on the Potomac observed the interaction of cultures in a situation where African traditions clearly predominated. On May 29, 1774, Nicholas Cresswell re-corded that he

went to see a Negro Ball. Sundays being the only days ... [they] have to themselves, they generally meet together and amuse themselves with Dancing to the Banjo ... a Gourd ...

with only four strings ... . Some of them sing to it ... . In their songs they generally relate the usage they have received from their Masters or Mistresses in a very satirical stile ... . Their dancing is most violent exercise ... . They all appear to be exceedingly happy at these merry-makings.[33]

Dancing certainly marked important entertainments at the homes of common planters, yet the records permit only tantalizing glimpses. The reminiscences of converts to radical evangelical religion make clear how significant this activity was as an intense form of social engagement and as an expression of attachment to worldly pleasure. Understandably, however, the pious memoirs do not describe carefully the sinful pastimes that they mention only to deplore. Travelers' reports of family entertainments have not been found, but we have vivid pen sketches of outdoor festivities. In July 1774 Nicholas Cresswell witnessed "what they call a reaping frolic" while he was ashore on the Maryland side of the Potomac. "This is a Harvest Feast," he noted. "The people [were] very merry, Dancing without either Shoes or Stockings and the Girls without stays." On another occasion he went to a barbecue, also on the shores of the Potomac: "These Barbecues are Hogs, roasted whole. This was under a large Tree. A great number of young people met together with a Fiddle and Banjo played by two Negroes, with Plenty of Toddy, which both Men and Women seem to be very fond of. I believe they have danced and drunk till there are few sober people amongst them." The fiddle and the banjo appearing together give a hint of cultural fusion. The "banjar" was still an African gourd instrument; for Anglo-Virginians "a sweet Fiddle," played by "a worthy good tempered Man," was an emblem of "distinguished ... social Virtues."[34]

Behind the "bacchanalian dance," and in the "irregular, fantastical manner" of the movements, was intensity of purpose. For many of the participants the stakes were high. In a comparatively open society, where land was plentiful and easily became exhausted and where much of the wealth, in the form of slaves, was mobile, the making of a good match was one of the surest ways to establish or secure a "fortune" (as it was called). A number of activities might enable young men to prove their prowess, but dancing was at the center of those community gatherings where men and women were most directly visible to each other and able to perform accordingly. Indeed, Virginia dancing – especially the jig, with its vigorous alternating pursuit and retreat – was a stylized representation of bold, active courtship on the part of both sexes. One visitor thought courtship, and others' keen observation of it, was "the principal business in Virginia."[35]

The workings of these processes can be seen most clearly in the reminiscences of another convert to strict evangelical piety. James Ireland was a penniless schoolmaster who emigrated from Scotland and had almost no family connections. He settled in a part of Frederick County where "balls, dancing and chanting to the sound of the violin, was the most prevailing practice." In his autobiography he recalled how, dancing being his "darling idol, and being esteemed by all who ever saw [him] perform upon the floor, a most complete dancer," he not only acquired "the confidence and esteem of ... young ladies" but also emerged as the protégé of a grand gentleman. In addition, he became the favorite companion of the "heads of tolerably numerous families" with whom he was actively engaged in "swearing, drinking and frolicking, [as well as] horse racing." Had he not suddenly become converted to evangelical religion, and so been led to renounce the conviviality at which he excelled, he would evidently have been on his way to a good marriage and advancement within gentry society. Small wonder, then, that performance in the dance was watched so intently and assessed so publicly – or that young men might vie to be designated leader of the ball. Activities, exciting in themselves and with such high stakes, could not but project compelling images of what the good life was about – images that would be internalized by young onlookers, and so, by entering powerfully into their socialization and character formation, be carried forward through their lives to sustain the pattern of cultural values.[36]

EDITOR'S NOTES

a In the early 1770s Fithian was a tutor in the home of Robert Carter of Nomini Hall.
b Landon Carter (1757–1820), a son of Robert "King" Carter, was a prominent Virginia planter, who lived at Sabine Hall.

NOTES

Reprinted from Rhys Isaac, *The Transformation of Virginia, 1740–1790* (Chapel Hill, N.C., 1982). © 1982 The University of North Carolina Press. Used by permission of the author and publisher.

1   [Edward Kimber], "Observations in Several Voyages and Travels in America," *William and Mary Quarterly*, 1st ser., XV (1906–7): 158; Hunter Dickinson Farish, ed., *Journal and Letters of Philip Vickers Fithian, 1773–1774: A Plantation Tutor of the Old Dominion* (Williamsburg, Va., 1957): 167.

2   Thomas Mutter to Sir Peyton Skipwith, March 20, 1775, Skipwith Papers, Box 1, p. 17, Earl Gregg Swem Library, The College of William and Mary, Williamsburg, Va.; Farish, ed., *Journal of Fithian*: 93.

3   ibid.: 29.

4   For a brief commentary on the tone of the liturgy, see Church of England, *The Book of Common Prayer, 1559: The Elizabethan Prayer Book*, ed. John E. Booty (Charlottesville, Va., 1976): 379–82.

5   On the functioning of the vestries, see William H. Seiler, "The Anglican Parish in Virginia," in James Morton Smith, ed., *Seventeenth-Century America: Essays in Colonial History* (Chapel Hill, N.C., 1959): 120–42.

6   Farish, ed., *Journal of Fithian*: 42; Devereux Jarratt, *The Life of the Reverend Devereux Jarratt, Rector of Bath Parish, Dinwiddie County, Virginia, Written by Himself, in a Series of Letters Addressed to the Rev. John Coleman* … (Baltimore, 1806; facsimile reprint, New York, 1969): 16; William Byrd II to Charles, Earl of Orrery, July 5, 1726, in "Virginia Council Journals, 1726–1753," *Virginia Magazine of History and Biography*, XXXII (1924): 27.

7   Farish, ed., *Journal of Fithian*: 137. See also p. 145.

8   Lawrence W. Levine, *Black Culture and Black Consciousness: Afro-American Folk Thought from Slavery to Freedom* (New York, 1977): 3–30.

9   Hugh Jones, *The Present State of Virginia, from Whence is Inferred a Short View of Maryland and North Carolina*, ed. Richard L. Morton (Chapel Hill, N.C., 1956): 97.

10   ibid.: 97 (emphasis added), 100.

11   Levine, *Black Culture*: 25–30.

12   Jones, *Present State of Virginia*: 97; Farish, ed., *Journal of Fithian*: 43; Robert Beverley, *The History and Present State of Virginia*, ed. Louis B. Wright (Chapel Hill, N.C., 1947): 312–13.

13   Cary Carson, "The 'Virginia House' in Maryland," *Maryland Historical Magazine*, LXIX (1974): 192–3.

14   Barbara Carson and Cary Carson, "Styles and Standards of Living in Southern Maryland, 1670–1752" (unpublished paper, 1976): table 2A, 34.

15   ibid.: 18; Lois Green Carr and Lorena S. Walsh, "Changing Life Styles in Colonial St. Mary's County," *Working Papers from the Regional Economic History Research Center* I, no. 3 (1978): 9–10.

16   ibid.: 23.

17   Carson and Carson, "Styles and Standards of Living": tables 1 and 2.

18   The journal dates from 1773–4. It reveals a refinement of genteel style that would be hard, if not impossible, to match in the second quarter of the eighteenth century. There also appears, with the man of "sensibility" in this later period, the beginnings of an ethos of domesticity in the Carter family that would not have been found earlier. See Jan Ellen Lewis Grimmelmann, "This World and the Next: Religion, Death, Success, and Love in Jefferson's Virginia" (Ph.D. dissertation, University

of Michigan, 1977): 259–99. See also Daniel Blake Smith, *Inside the Great House: Planter Family Life in Eighteenth-Century Chesapeake Society* (Ithaca, N.Y., 1980).

19 Farish, ed., *Journal of Fithian*: 80.
20 ibid.: 80, 129, 51, 133.
21 ibid.: 80, and *passim*.
22 ibid.: 158. See also pp. 93, 110, 129, 185. On social relations as calculated exchange, see Peter M. Blau, *Exchange and Power in Social Life* (New York, 1964).
23 Farish, ed., *Journal of Fithian*: 121, 67, 42, 40, 141, 117, 71, 56.
24 For examples of giving toasts, see ibid.: 47, 62, 64, 75, 77, 83, 84, 87, 95, 141, 191, 196, 198. The extended quotations are on pp. 34, 125.
25 ibid.: 138, 142.
26 ibid.: 56–7.
27 ibid.: 147, 150, 156, 172, 177, 183.
28 Jarratt, *Life*: 44.
29 *The Journal of Nicholas Cresswell, 1774–1777* (New York, 1924): 19.
30 Farish, ed., *Journal of Fithian*: 177.
31 ibid.: 33, 34; Burnaby, *Travels*: 26; *Cresswell Journal*: 53. On the college's attention to dancing lessons, see President James Blair's remark in 1705 on the hall as "the most useful place in the College for here we sometimes preach and pray [the chapel was not yet built], and sometimes we fiddle and dance; the one to edify, and the other to divert us." Quoted in Jones, *Present State of Virginia*: 11.
32 Farish, ed., *Journal of Fithian*: 61, 62. For an instance of slave parodying of the masters' dance movements, see Levine, *Black Culture*: 17.
33 *Cresswell Journal*: 18–19.
34 ibid.: 26, 30; *Virginia Gazette* (Purdie and Dixon), June 24, September 9, 1773.
35 Louis B. Wright and Marion Tinling, eds., *Quebec to Carolina in 1785–1786: Being the Travel Diary and Observations of Robert Hunter, Jr., a Young Merchant of London* (San Marino, Calif., 1943): 231.
36 James Ireland, *The Life of the Rev. James Ireland ...* (Winchester, Va., 1819): 49–50.

7

MARTHA BALLARD AND HER GIRLS: WOMEN'S WORK IN EIGHTEENTH-CENTURY MAINE

Laurel Thatcher Ulrich

Laurel Ulrich focuses upon an individual life, and a single diary, and yet manages to illumine a larger world. Family labor was central to the New England economy and to the early American economy more generally, but Ulrich demonstrates that family labor was far more complex than previously thought. In fact, she argues, there were two family economies, simultaneously independent and interdependent, one managed by women, and the other by men. Men and women worked together, but at the same time labor was divided along gender lines. The separate female economy was vibrant and varied and rested on the work of daughters, female relatives, and servant girls. The rhythms of an individual life were intimately bound up with larger concerns: Martha Ballard, for instance, could devote herself to the rigorous demands of midwifery only after her own childbearing years were over, and life became far more arduous for her after her own daughters had married. One woman's life intersected with that of many others. Indeed, a complex web of social and economic exchange enmeshed women and propelled them far beyond their own households. In this separate world of female exchange, work had a social as well as economic value and was more often cooperative than competitive. While men tended to work alone and focused more on profit, women tended to work in groups and focused more on neighborliness. In short, even though private and public worlds or inner and outer realms of experience were vastly different for the two sexes, the relationship was just as important for women as for men. Women may have had no formal political life but they had a rich community life.

Like Breen's and Isaac's essays, Ulrich's explores the ordinary details of everyday life. She recreates the texture of life in all its variety and complexity. Isaac's and Ulrich's depiction of family life might be considered complementary: one focusing on manly competition, the other on womanly cooperation. How Martha Ballard's life comports with Breen's depiction of a consumer revolution is worth considering. Clearly, the Ballard household, at least for a time, produced much that it consumed, including clothes, candles, and soap. The availability of labor may explain in large part the mix of household production and external consumption. Perhaps home production was cyclical in other households too. If Martha Ballard was typical, beautifying the domestic environment was a foreign concept to many early American women.

* * *

Near midnight on November 26, 1795, a sixty-year-old Maine woman named Martha Ballard sat writing in her diary. She had stayed up late waiting for Sarah Neal, her hired girl, to come home from watching with a sick neighbor. "I have been doing my house-work and Nursing my cow. Her bag is amazingly sweld," she wrote. "Sarah went to watch with Mary Densmore ... shee returnd and Sarah Densmore with her at 11 hour Evening. I have been picking wool till then. A womans work is never Done as the Song says and happy shee whose strength holds out to the end of the rais [race]." Then she added, "It is now the middle of the night and Mr Densmore calls me to his house."[1]

Because Martha Ballard was a midwife as well as a housewife, her regimen was somewhat unusual, yet her attitude toward women's work was not. The song she quoted was probably an American version of a seventeenth-century English ballad that begins, "There's never a day, from morn to night, / But I with work am tired quite." Each verse of this old song discusses some aspect of a housewife's duties, from textile production to feeding crying babies in the night, ending with the familiar proverb, "A woman's work is never done." Laments of overburdened housewives continued in the American folk repertoire well into the twentieth century.[2]

As yet, few historians have given serious attention to the actual structure of women's domestic burdens in early America or attempted to discover the particular conditions that may have given rise to their complaints. Nor has anyone considered working relations among women in the preindustrial female economy.

Martha Ballard's diary is a remarkably valuable source for such a study. Detailed daily entries for more than twenty-seven years not only document the full range of one woman's economic activities from maturity to old age but tell much about the lives of the young women who assisted her. These "girls" (she used the same collective term for them all) included her daughters Hannah and Dolly; her nieces Pamela, Parthena, and Clarissa Barton; and a succession of hired helpers like Sarah Neal. Martha Ballard's diary documents the genuine satisfactions that one woman derived from mastering her domestic environment. It shows both the variety and the social complexity of household labor, highlights the interdependence of mature women and young women within the family economy, and modifies earlier conceptions of patriarchy.

Although Martha Ballard lived almost to the era of industrialization, in education and in sensibility she belonged to the colonial period. Born in Oxford, Massachusetts, in 1735, she emigrated to the Kennebec River country of Maine in 1777 with her husband, Ephraim, and five children. Three other children had died in the diphtheria epidemic of 1769.[3] For the rest of their lives, the Ballards lived in that section of Hallowell, Maine, that separated in 1798 to become the town of Augusta. The extant diary opens in 1785, the year Mrs. Ballard turned fifty. It closes in May of 1812, about a month before her death. This essay will focus on the first fifteen years of the diary, 1785–1800, the period in which her two youngest daughters came of age and married.

The importance of such a document for our understanding of women's work in early America is clear. Martha Ballard's diary is the intact delft platter that allows us to identify and interpret the shattered fragments that are all that remain for so much of New England. The diary confirms, for example, the existence of a separate female economy existing beneath the level of traditional documentation. In Hallowell, as in other New England towns, male names predominate in surviving merchant accounts, while tax lists and town records give little, if any, evidence of female enterprise. Yet the diary makes quite clear not only that women were managing a rich and varied array of tasks within their own households but that they were trading with each other (and sometimes with men) independent of their husbands.

Martha Ballard's diary shifts our attention from the by now rather tired question of whether women shared men's work to far more interesting issues about how they interacted with each other within the female economy. We can now add detailed questions about the interaction of mothers and daughters, and mistresses and servants within the household. We can also begin to discuss changes in female consciousness, not as evidence of the emergence of women from patriarchal dominion, but as evidence of changing values within an already cohesive female realm.

Close study of such a document also shows the complexity of the family labor system. New Englanders may have preferred their own offspring to hired laborers, but no family gave birth to full-grown workers, nor could even the most powerful patriarch ensure an optimal balance of sons and daughters. By its very nature, a family labor system demanded a web of connections beyond the household. Households self-sufficient in land, livestock, and tools (and they were few) could never be perennially self-sufficient in labor. Furthermore, because mothers invested more heavily in childbearing and rearing than fathers, and because daughters married earlier than sons (and perhaps moved further away than their brothers), the transitions within the household were sharper for women and potentially more disruptive. This was particularly so in young towns where the sex ratio limited the number of single women available for household work.

Martha Ballard's diary is a record of a particular time and place, a Maine river town in the years just after the Revolution, but it is also a record of a particular kind of economy: one characterized by a clear gender division of labor, by reliance on family members and neighbors rather than bound servants, and by mixed enterprises (men engaged in lumbering and fishing as well as farming, women in small-scale textile production, poultry raising, and dairying). Exportable products were nonagricultural, and they were in the male domain. These conditions were not characteristic of every town in New England, but they were certainly typical of many from the seventeenth century forward.

Ephraim Ballard was one of the middling sort of Maine pioneers who opened up the river valleys in the years after the Revolution. According to the Hallowell tax list for 1784, he had three acres of tillage, eighty acres of "unimproved" and ten acres of "unimprovable" land. In addition, he had three cows and a pair of oxen, the latter as useful for lumbering as for farming. From 1779 to 1791, he and his sons operated saw- and gristmills, just as he and his father had done in Oxford and as his grandfather and great-grandfather had done a hundred years before in Andover, Massachusetts. Ephraim was also a surveyor. Into his eighties he continued to run lines for the Commonwealth of Massachusetts and for the wealthy

Kennebec Proprietors, who were attempting to assert control over squatter lands in the newly settled Maine interior.[4]

Equally important to an understanding of patterns of work in the diary is an appreciation for the composition of the Ballard family. When Martha Ballard began her diary in 1785, she was already a grandmother; her oldest daughter, Lucy Towne, lived upriver at Winslow. Yet, at the age of fifty, she still had five children living at home: Cyrus, twenty-nine (a quiet and dutiful son who alternately worked with his father and for other men and who never married); Jonathan, twenty-three; Hannah, fifteen; Dolly, twelve; and Ephraim, six. Martha Ballard's comment ten years later that "womans work is never Done," though formulaic, was grounded in the particular circumstances of her own life. She stayed up late picking wool on November 26, 1795, in an effort to sustain a system of household production established seven years before when her two youngest daughters were in their teens. Now both daughters were married. For a time, Martha Ballard had belonged to an unrecognized colonial elite, that corps of housewives who had not only health and energy but daughters. That she now sat alone waiting for her hired girl, Sarah Neal, marked a change in status. Close analysis of the diary not only reveals the variety, the social complexity, and the necessary autonomy of a mature woman's work; it shows, in striking detail, her close dependence on her girls.

At the most general level, Martha Ballard's diary simply confirms what we already know about the division of labor in northern New England and in other rural societies in the Western world: men worked "abroad," farming, surveying, lumbering, shipping, and milling; women worked in houses, gardens, and yards. Yet to see fifteen years of one woman's work pieced out through the pages of her diary is to understand more fully both the variety and the complexity of this work. Consider the vocabulary of textile production. The Ballard men sowed, turned, and broke flax; the women weeded, pulled, combed, spun, reeled, boiled, spooled, warped, quilled, wove, bucked, and bleached it. Slaughtering meant more than cutting, weighing, and salting meat; it also meant caring for the "orful" (offal) of the animal – cleaning ox tripe, dressing a calf's head or pig's feet, preparing sausage casings, or cooking the organ meats (or "harslet") of a veal. Candle and soapmaking meant trying tallow as well as spinning wicks and leaching wood ashes for lye.[5]

Even such an ordinary activity as knitting had multiple applications. Mrs. Ballard produced woolen "leggins" and "buskins" as well as stockings for her husband and sons; she knitted tow, linen, and cotton hose and even "footed" some pairs with "twine." Though the Ballards employed a tailor to make men's coats and breeches and called in a dressmaker to cut out women's gowns, Mrs. Ballard and her daughters made shifts, skirts, aprons, petticoats, night caps, trousers, jackets, and even a pair of "staise" (stays). They also hemmed sheets, stitched and filled mattresses, pieced quilts, and turned "raggs" into woven "coverlids."[6] Outdoor work was just as insistent. Martha Ballard milked cows, fed swine, set hens, and more than once trudged "up the Crik" looking for a wandering calf. When a sheep came in from the pasture wounded on the neck, she "drest it with Tarr." When a lamb was born with its "entrails hanging out," she sewed it up.[7]

Gardening chores stretched from the end of April, when Mr. Ballard plowed the various plots near the house, until late October, when the cabbages were brought into the cellar. Martha Ballard transplanted hundreds of seedlings every spring in addition to the usual sowing and weeding. In late summer and early autumn, she gathered seed for next year's garden as well as fresh vegetables for the table. She grew culinary herbs like sage, saffron, coriander, anise, mustard, and parsley as well as beans (in several varieties), cabbages, parsnips, turnips, beets, cucumbers, radishes, onions, garlic, peppers, carrots, "French turnips," lettuce, peppergrass, and melons.[8] She obviously was proud of being able to gather a milk pan full of "Poland King" beans as early as July 11, of having parsley "fresh and green from my gardin for to put in my gravy" on December 27, of bringing fresh cabbage from her cellar on March 13, and of cutting a "fine mess of greens from our cabbage stumps" on May 19.[9]

The three houses the Ballards inhabited during the years of the diary probably differed little in floor plan or space – each had two rooms on the first floor and two "chambers" above. All three houses, like many in Hallowell, were in some stage of incompleteness or disrepair. The upstairs rooms in the first could not be used in winter, though the kitchen had something that many lacked – an oven. Mrs. Forbes, Mrs. Savage, Mrs. Williams, and Mrs. Voce all baked in the Ballards's oven from time to time.[10] The second house had a "store" as well as the two rooms below and above, and it may have been more tightly built than the first, though the Ballards laid a hearth in the kitchen two years after they moved in and put new sashes in the chamber windows four years after that. The third house was new, but unfinished. The family moved in on October 27, 1799. On January 1, the men completed the clapboarding; on January 3, they put in partitions and built the cellar stairs. A year later, they were still caulking rooms, finishing doors, and building window sashes.[11]. On April 7, 1802, Ephraim put the lower casements into three windows and a "light" (or window) in the privy.

In such a setting, there was small occasion for housekeeping in the modern sense, though Martha Ballard was concerned about cleanliness. When the girls washed, they usually reused the water to scrub floors; on August 24, 1798, Mrs. Ballard spun yarn for a mop. Though the women occasionally "scoured pewter," there is no mention in the diary of window washing. "Housework" for Martha Ballard might just as well mean chopping wood, building fires, hauling water, pitching snow out of unsealed chambers, or chipping away ice from the platform around the well.[12] In the fall of 1800, she banked her new house with dirt, shoveling it away in the spring. On Bowman's Brook, where the family ran the mills, water was a continual problem. On one July day, after a heavy rainstorm, she carried no fewer than fifty pails of water from the cellar.[13]

Through all this, Martha Ballard pursued her own specialties – midwifery and healing. She delivered 797 babies in the twenty-seven years of the diary and practiced folk medicine as well. Like most female practitioners, she concentrated on diseases of women and children, though she was also adept at treating burns, rashes, or frozen toes and ears. She did not set bones, nor did she let blood – human blood, that is. On October 13, 1786, when Mr. Davis came to her house suffering from shingles, she noted, "We bled a cat and applied the blood which gave him relief." She occasionally opened an abscessed breast, though usually applied to doctors for anything approaching a surgical procedure.

Mrs. Ballard's patients came to her house seeking salves, pills, syrups, ointments, or, more often, simply advice. Forty to seventy times a year, she went to them, spending a few hours or several days administering clysters, dressing burns, or bathing inflamed throats, this in addition to the thirty to fifty deliveries she performed annually. Although she bought imported medicines like camphor or spermaceta and compounds like "elixir proprietas" from Dr. Samuel Colman, she grew or processed most of the medicines she used, sowing and harvesting herbs like chamomile, hyssop, and feverfew; gathering wild plants like burdock, Solomon's seal, or cold-water root; and transforming household staples like onions, tow, or soap into remedies for coughs, sore nipples, or the colic.[14]

Martha Ballard's obstetrical and medical specialties added to an already varied array of domestic tasks that shifted with the weather and the seasons, drawing upon a number of large- and small-muscle skills. To comprehend more fully both the variety and the social complexity of her work, it is helpful to compare her diary with a similar one by a New England male, Matthew Patten. Like Ephraim Ballard, Patten was a surveyor. He was also a carpenter, a farmer, and a public official in the town he had helped to pioneer, Bedford, New Hampshire.

Matthew Patten, from July 20 to 31, 1780, and Martha Ballard, from July 20 to 31, 1786, were both involved in several different kinds of work; both had contacts with neighbors; both used the labor of their children; both engaged in barter and trade. Yet Martha Ballard's work, at least as recorded in her diary, was not only more varied but more socially complex. Patten mentioned six specific tasks – mowing, hauling hay, sowing ("I sowed our Turnip seed in the Cow yards that we yarded Last summer"), taking depositions, attending court, and trading. Martha Ballard was herself involved in nine – carding, spinning, boiling warp, baking, cleaning cellar, gathering herbs, treating the sick, making fence ("I Cutt Alders and maid a Sort of a fence part round the yard by the mill Pond"), and trading. (There were no deliveries in this period.) In addition, she mentioned three other female tasks that her daughters performed independently – washing clothes, berrying, and brewing beer.

Matthew Patten had economic exchanges with six other persons, Martha Ballard with thirteen. There is a striking difference, however, in the way the two diarists recorded these transactions. In every case, Patten spelled out exactly what was given or expected on each side.[15] By comparison, Martha Ballard's accounts are indirect and vague. Although she includes some entries of the sort typical of Patten ("received a pair of shoes and 2/ from Mr Beeman for attending his wife and for medisen"), she has more entries like that for July 29, 1786: "I went afternoon to Mr Edsons Carried 32 skeins of Linning warp for her to weave 11½ skeins of Tow yarn and 8 of Cottne the girls went to Mr Savages for green Peas I let them have 1 lb of Butter." While it is quite clear from other entries in the diary that Martha Ballard had a long-standing economic relation with Mrs. Edson, only with great effort can the credits and debits in that account be extracted and arranged. Even more diffi-cult to define is the apparent trade of green peas for butter. Informal food exchanges were an integral part of life in rural New England, and they frequently appear in the Ballard diary, yet, in this case, it is entirely possible that a social event was implied. The girls may have been going to the Savages' to eat green peas, the butter being their contribution to the dinner.

There is an even stronger contrast between entries in the two diaries involving other family members. Matthew Patten clearly had help with the haying, since he wrote in the plural, "We began to mow," but only once in the ten days did he specifically mention another person, on July 31, recording that "David and I mowed in the meadow." In contrast, Martha Ballard included fifteen refer-ences to other workers. Two mention Mr. Ballard, six record specific activities of the girls (though only one mentions a daughter's name), two note the activities of a neighbor, and five acknowledge the arrival or departure of a male worker.

Male diarists, like Matthew Patten, are notorious for ignoring their wives. Not only are there no references to Elizabeth Patten in this section, I can find only two references to her in the entire year, the first on May 12, when she fell and "Strained" her ankle, and the second the next day when Patten went to Goffstown to get some rum to bathe it. In contrast, there are few weeks in Martha Ballard's diary when the reader does not know, at least in a general way, what Ephraim Ballard was doing. She also regularly noted the activities of her sons. Although Patten does give more attention in other parts of his diary to his sons, in 1780 he made only one reference to a daughter, that on November 30 when "Polly set out for Chester ... to stay and help her Uncle Majr Tolfords folks to Spin Wool."[16]

The differences in the two diaries cannot be explained simply in terms of personality. In her study of a commercial dairying region of New York in the late nineteenth century, Nancy Grey Osterud found a similar, though even more pronounced, contrast between the recording practices of men and women. Although both sexes were involved outside the market in labor exchanges of the sort common to the Ballard and Patten diaries, men tended to assign such transactions a monetary value even when no money was exchanged, while women "generally recorded their cooperative work as a direct, personal relationship, unmediated by market values." The blurring between sociability and trade that we have noted in the Ballard diary was even more pronounced in the records of the New York women. The contrasts between Patten and Ballard may reflect, then, larger gender differences within the northern rural economy.[17]

The comparison between the two diaries also suggests that the old adage that "woman's work is never done" derived not only from the large number of tasks for which women were responsible but from the complexity of the social relationships that structured their work. That a woman might more frequently note the activities of male workers than vice versa is hardly surprising, since (as Nancy Cott expressed it) women stood in "an adjunct and service relationship to men in economic activity." Matthew Patten's diary suggests that, unless his wife were absent or disabled, her activities really had little effect on his daily work. He simply took for granted that his meals would be ready and his clothes washed and mended. His wife, however, had to tune her work to his. But the point is larger than that. Martha Ballard's attentiveness to the work of the men in her household suggests that, even when their work did not directly affect her, as, for example, when the addition of another worker meant more food to prepare, she felt somehow connected to it. Some part of her duty was to be aware of the activities of others. In this respect, her behavior corroborates the importance of affiliation in the psychology of women.[18]

Martha Ballard's affiliations, however, extended to other women as well as to men. Certainly, she was a supportive wife, a "meet help" as a seventeenth-century housewife would have put it. She baked biscuit for sea journeys, fed and found beds for rafting crews, constructed packs for surveying trips, and washed the heavily soiled bedding and clothing when the men returned. Once in a while, she also took a direct part in the men's work, going into the field to rake hay or keeping account of mill transactions when Mr. Ballard was away. Her daughters also occasionally "rode horse to plough" or helped "drop corn."[19] Because their work was defined as supportive, women could more easily step across role boundaries to perform male work than vice versa. What is most striking about Martha Ballard's work in its totality, however, is not its relation to the work of the men, but its independence from it.

Some historians have assumed that the domestic labor of women was somehow subsumed in a patriarchal family economy. Martha

Ballard's diary, however, supports scattered evidence from earlier sources arguing that housewives managed the products of their own labor. "I medle not with the geese nor turke's," said one seventeenth-century New Englander, "for thay are hurs for she hath bene and is a good wife to me."[20] A domineering husband could, of course, "medle" in his wife's affairs, but a division of responsibility was encouraged not only by tradition but by the practical difficulties of minding his wife's business while sustaining his own. Ironically, the very dearth of evidence for women's work in male diaries and ledgers may in itself be presumptive evidence for a separate female economy. Ebenezer Parkman's[a] indifference to his wife's activities may be a consequence of "male chauvinism" (as Richard Dunn has suggested). It may also mean that Mrs. Parkman was managing quite well on her own.[21] Martha and Ephraim Ballard cooperated in providing for their family – he plowed her garden, she mended his packs – but, in large part, they worked independently, and they kept separate accounts; significantly, she paid her workers, he his.

What is equally apparent is that other Hallowell women did the same. The diary mentions male shoemakers, tailors, and carpenters as well as a pewterer, a printer, a tinker, and a clothier. But female dairywomen, nurses, spinners, weavers, dressmakers, a bonnet maker, a chair caner, and seven midwives other than Martha Ballard are noted also. Although the diary never mentions teachers, the town treasurer's accounts for the fall of 1787 record payments to three women for "keeping school."[22] Martha Ballard traded textiles and farm products with her female neighbors as well as physic and obstetrical services. She gave Mrs. Densmore three pounds of flax for cutting and fitting a gown, she traded Mrs. Porter tow yarn for blue-dyed yarn, and when Polly Savage helped with the washing, she paid her in flax and ashes.[23]

Martha Ballard's diary fills in blanks in women's lives left by traditional sources. Hallowell women did not just trade commodities that required visible tools, like spinning wheels or churns, objects that might be traced through probate inventories; they exchanged products that have left little trace in written records, things like ashes, herbs, seedlings, and baby chicks. On June 17, 1786, for example, Martha Ballard paid Mrs. Bolton one-half pound of tea for 400 plants she had received a few days before. Nor was their manufacturing confined to obvious products such as textiles or cheese. Mrs. Ballard herself, for a time, baked biscuit for Brook's

211

store. In this lumbering and shipping town, some of her neighbors also kept boarders.[24]

The diary helps us to recognize the selective nature of the evidence in male account books. In the handful of Hallowell records that survive, as in account books from other towns and from earlier periods, male names predominate. Even when female products appear, they are usually listed under men's names. One might assume that the sixteen-and-a-half pounds of butter credited to Ebenezer Farwell in a ledger kept by Samuel and William Howard was produced by his wife, or that the four pounds of spun yarn on James Burns's page came from the women of his family, but there is no way of knowing from the record whether the women personally profited from the transaction. Once in a while, the Howards mention a female worker, as in accounts with the shoemaker Samuel Welch which include references to "your wife's weaving"; but, in the Howard accounts as in all the others, most of the women of Hallowell are invisible.[25] Indeed, without the diary we would have no way of knowing anything about Martha Ballard's enterprises, including midwifery; the few references to the Ballards in extant account books are all listed under Ephraim's name.[26]

The Ballard diary gives ample evidence that the family economic system was based not only upon cooperation but upon a division of responsibility. Mrs. Ballard paid Mr. Savage, the blacksmith, for a spindle and for making irons for her loom, but she reckoned directly with Mrs. Savage, who offered not only her own labor in spinning but also a woolen wheel. Mr. Ballard negotiated with Mr. Densmore, the tailor; Mrs. Ballard dealt directly with Mrs. Densmore, the dressmaker. Mr. Ballard settled accounts for lumber with Mr. Weston, the merchant; Mrs. Ballard traded cabbages with Mrs. Weston for brandy and spices from their store.[27] Such evidence helps us to see the range of activity that may have lain behind the occasional entries in male ledgers, such as those of Thomas Chute of Marblehead, Massachusetts, who, in the 1730s, balanced an account "By you[r] wives accoumpt with mine."[28]

Thus, Martha Ballard's diary points to a world of women unrecorded in standard sources. That males dominated written records should not be taken as conclusive evidence that men dominated women. This is not to say, however, that women competed in the public economy on the same terms as men. Although it is difficult to develop precise comparisons because the two sexes not only performed different work but traded different products (how shall we measure the relative values of ashes and dung?), it is possible to derive rough wage differentials from the diary and other contemporary sources. Although men were, in general, paid more than women, the discrepancy varies considerably according to age and skill. In the 1790s, the Howards paid male laborers three shillings per day whether they were planting potatoes, reaping rye, or unloading the sloop. During the same period, Mrs. Ballard paid her household workers from one to two shillings. A weaver working full-time at her loom could earn four shillings a day, about the same as a skilled worker at the Howard mills. Yet few weavers could work full-time at their looms, women's work being subject to interruptions for cooking the meals and washing the clothes that millworkers and farmhands required.[29]

Martha Ballard could earn roughly six shillings per day as a midwife, about the same amount as her husband could claim for writing plans or for appraising an estate, though of course the time involved in a delivery was more variable and the hours less appealing. In all, Martha Ballard's earning capacity was probably considerably less than her husband's. In 1790, when her total cash income was twenty pounds, he earned thirty-eight pounds in three months' work for the Kennebec Proprietors.[30] Of course, such a comparison takes no account of the diversity of Ephraim Ballard's work or of the importance of barter transactions to the family economy. Nor does it consider the greater financial obligations of men. That Ephraim Ballard had cash to pay his taxes and buy meat and flour for the family strengthened Martha Ballard's ability to concentrate on her own enterprises.

The complexity of her economy is suggested in a matter-of-fact entry for July 2, 1791: "I went to Mr Weston Bot 3 lb pott ash at /6; went to Mr Burtuns Left four Dollars and an order on Mr Cogsill of Boston for 3,000 of shingles left by Hains Larned in Oct 88, which he is to purchase articles with for me in Boston." The next day, the six pennies' worth of potash she had purchased at Weston's store helped her complete a process begun almost a year before when her girls had spent four days harvesting flax. Parthena had recently finished the weaving, and now the cloth was ready to wash and "putt in ley." Thus, the cash transaction at Weston's store was a small link in a complex home production system.[31]

The exchange at Burton's store was also linked to the larger female economy. The four silver dollars plus the timber credit earned through unspecified services to the Learned family three years earlier brought eight yards of chintz home from Boston in September. Dolly picked up the cloth on September 14. On September 16, Mrs. Ballard went to the Densmores, to bring Lydia Densmore and her three children "home with me [to] cutt out my gown." On September 22, she closed accounts with Mrs. Densmore by delivering her of a daughter.

These July transactions suggest two quite different economic objectives. Martha Ballard labored not only to provide essentials for her family but to secure small pleasures for herself. Chintz from Boston was as much a part of her economic system as was homespun linen. Her ability to buy a new dress in the summer of 1791 is particularly interesting, given the disruption in the men's work that year. Mr. Ballard's relinquishment of the sawmills in March had no effect on Mrs. Ballard's ability to purchase a new dress in September. Martha Ballard was as independent as an eighteenth-century housewife could be.

Mrs. Ballard's economy was built upon the deft management of many resources, including the labor of the young women who worked with her. Early Americanists have given a great deal of attention to the intersection of economic history and family history, particularly to the passing of property from fathers to sons. There has been little, if anything, written about the relationship of mothers and daughters; nor have labor historians given much attention to the hired work of women in preindustrial New England. To explore these themes better, we must consider the chronological development of Martha Ballard's work.

Midwifery, like other female specialties, had to be integrated into a life span that typically included marriage in the early twenties and alternating periods of pregnancy and lactation for the next two decades. Martha Ballard performed her first delivery in July 1778, about a year after her migration to Maine.[32] She was then forty-one years old, near the end of childbearing. When she gave birth to her last child in 1779, her next oldest child was already six. Unfortunately, there is no detailed account of her midwifery practice between 1778 and 1785. The surviving diary makes quite clear, however, that the sort of obstetrical practice she sustained after 1785 would have been difficult for a woman who was herself giving birth every other year. This does not mean that young women were entirely excluded from the sort of experience that ultimately might lead to such a practice. Mothers – including nursing mothers –

assisted at births. At the Abiel Herrington house in June 1796, for example, "there are 22 in number slept under that roof the night."[33] Yet occasionally assisting at a birth was something less than routinely officiating as a midwife.

Midwifery was both time-consuming and unpredictable. Babies arrived in snowstorms, during harvest, and in the middle of the night. Labors could be frighteningly intense or annoyingly lackadaisical. After Mrs. Ballard had spent four days at James Caton's house in the spring of 1796, and then only after Mrs. Caton had consumed eleven glasses of wine in one day and "bisquit and wine at evening 3 times" were her twins finally born. (Even then, although Mrs. Ballard had been without sleep for three days, she "could not sleep for fleas.") A midwife sometimes spent two or three days at a delivery and sometimes did not make it at all. For Martha Ballard, the average time between "call" and delivery was ten hours. She usually spent another three to four hours in postpartum care, remaining through the night if the baby were born after dark. A pregnant woman might have managed such a schedule, but not a nursing mother. To carry an infant through stormy weather in the middle of the night on horseback or in a canoe would have been foolhardy.[34]

Freedom from childbearing, therefore, was one prerequisite for a midwife's work. A secure supply of household help was the other. If midwifery was dramatically episodic, housewifery was relentlessly regular. At home, day after day, there were meals to cook, cows to milk, fires to build, dishes and clothes to wash. The diary suggests a strong taboo against male involvement in such chores; if Martha Ballard was not at home to get her husband's breakfast, some other female had to be. After 1788, Martha Ballard consistently used a marginal notation "AH" to mark days spent entirely "at home." They were surprisingly few. Between 1790 and 1799, she left home, for some period of time, more than half of the days of the year. Midwifery does not account for all these excursions, of course, but it was responsible for a good many.

From 1785 until 1796, Martha Ballard relied upon her own daughters as well as upon a number of young women who lived temporarily in her house. "Girls washed" is a typical entry for these years. Martha Ballard was not the sort of woman to turn her growing daughters into household drudges, however, even if she could afford to. Hannah and Dolly needed skills to sustain their future families as well as to contribute to their own livelihood in the present. This, no doubt, explains why textile production accelerated in the Ballard household at exactly the same time as midwifery. We have long known that the late eighteenth century was an era of burgeoning household production. The Revolution and the nonimportation movements that preceded it gave new importance to textile skills. Judging from the Ballard diary, all of the weaving in Hallowell was done by women and girls. By expanding textile production, Martha Ballard provided household help for herself and an occupation for her girls. An entry for October 26, 1789, puts it succinctly: "My girls spun 23 double skeins and wove 27½ yds last weak and did the houswork besides."

The years between 1785 and 1795 were vintage ones for Martha Ballard. Her loom and wheels were busy, her garden flourishing, and even her poultry yard was booming. With the girls assuming routine household chores as well as the spinning and weaving, she was free to develop her own specialties. The system also seems to have worked well for the girls. There were quiltings, huskings, dances, and frequent visits to and from neighbors. By 1794 there was also a singing school that Sally Cox attended. Unfortunately, Mrs. Ballard was not systematic in recording wages. Her final reckoning with Pamela Barton and a fragment of an account with Parthena show that the base pay for the Barton girls was six pounds a year. In addition, of course, they received board and room and perhaps some basic clothing; Mrs. Ballard did not charge Pamela for the stockings she knitted for her in February 1787, but she did debit the apron "patren" she bought her in July.[35]

Even at the low rate of six pounds per annum, a young woman could, over the period of six or eight years that she worked, accumulate something toward her future. Parthena Barton and Sally Cox took not only quilts and bedding from their service with Mrs. Ballard but the skills to make more, having, for several years, shared both the equipment and the instruction Martha Ballard provided her daughters.[36] Although there is no reference in the diary to marriage "settlements" or "portions," some part of Mrs. Ballard's own income clearly went toward providing household goods for Hannah and Dolly. On June 3, 1795, as Dolly was preparing to set up housekeeping, her mother bought her a bureau, table, and bedstead as well as porringers, candlesticks, and canisters. Two weeks later, she added two sets of teacups and a teapot. Meanwhile, Dolly was herself purchasing crockery and furniture, and she and Sally were quilting.[37]

For the girls as well as for Martha Ballard, there was strength in cooperation. Such a system, however, carried the source of its own destruction. Preparing her helpers for marriage, Mrs. Ballard helped speed up their departure. The girls went by twos, Hannah and Parthena in 1792, Dolly and Sally in 1795. That is why, on November 26, 1795, we found her sitting, waiting for a hired girl, Sarah Neal, to come home. Sarah was gone within the month.

Not surprisingly, 1796 turned out to be a distressing year for Martha Ballard. So long as she had daughters at home, she had been able to count on at least one worker who would not quit, and for many years she had also been able to rely on her niece Parthena and Dolly's friend Sally Cox. Now she was at the mercy of her helpers. Her obstetrical practice was at its height, the work at home was as insistent as ever, and much of the time there was no one to help. In 1796 eight girls entered and left the Ballard house. In such a situation, a woman's work truly was "never done." On January 6, 1796, Mrs. Ballard began her washing, laying it aside when company came, then finishing it "except for rinsing" after they left. Such an interruption might have been a minor irritation had she not been called away early the next morning to a woman in labor. Not until three days later would she be able to write, "I finisht my washing." On June 4, 1796, she was busy cleaning the head and feet of a newly slaughtered calf, when Joseph Young called to say his wife was in labor. From Mrs. Young, she went to Mrs. Carter and then to Mrs. Staton. Having delivered three babies in twenty-four hours, she was ready for a rest. "I came home at Evening and do feel much fatgud," she wrote, "but was oblidged to sett up and cook the orful of my veal."[38]

The problem was not just in securing helpers, but in keeping them. Although the number of labor months available to Mrs. Ballard declined each year after Hannah's and Parthena's marriages, the crucial issue was how many workers she had to recruit and train in a year. One Sally Cox settling into the family was worth half a dozen short-term helpers. The persistence problem developed in 1796, and though it improved slightly in 1800, Martha Ballard's household never was quite the same. Between 1785 and 1795, eleven girls had lived and worked, for some period, in the Ballard house; in the six years from 1796 to 1802, there were twenty-nine. The effect on her morale – and on her diary – was marked. For the first time, Martha Ballard began to use her journal to plumb her frustrations. Crisp and confident entries gave way to long laments, and, in a few places, she even penned vignettes of women's oppression.

Captured by self-pity, Martha Ballard quarreled with her husband and with the girls on whom she depended. She dismissed Patty Easty for theft and Elizabeth Taylor for "ill manners." Sally Fletcher walked out on her own, returning to collect her "duds" and threatening to "sue us in a weak from this time if we did not pai her what was her due."[39] In May 1798, Mrs. Ballard sent her loom to her daughter Hannah. She seems to have recognized that she could no longer maintain the home production that had been so effective in the past. Fewer girls would now be needed, but, ironically, without the weaving, there may have been less reason for them to come and fewer yards of cloth with which to pay them.

It is too simple to conclude that Martha Ballard had grown irascible in her old age or the young women of the town less dependable. Surely some part of Mrs. Ballard's troubles can be attributed to the unusual demands she placed on the girls. It cannot have been easy for a sixteen-year-old to have taken total responsibility for a household when its mistress disappeared in the night, especially for one that contained no young persons at all, simply an old man and an aging bachelor. Yet Martha Ballard's troubles have wider significance. The problems she faced were both demographic and social, and they affected other women.

Laments over a shortage of servants have a long tradition in northern New England. The problem was both geographic and demographic. In frontier towns there were more males than females in the age groups from which servants came. Although the overall ratio in Augusta-Hallowell had evened out by 1800, as in many country towns, the earlier age at marriage of women than men still ensured that there would be fewer available female workers in the same age bracket. Only in coastal towns, where women strongly outnumbered men, was a supply of girls assured. Contemporaries recognized this geographic distinction. One of the liveliest pieces of satire from eighteenth-century New Hampshire is a poem composed sometime before 1782, presumably by Ruth Belknap, the wife of the Dover minister. Entitled "The Pleasures of a Country Life," it was written when Mrs. Belknap had "a true taste of them by having no *maid*."[40]

Martha Ballard was experiencing, then, the "peculiar pleasures" of a country life. She was also facing the realities of a sex-gender system that grounded women's work in the family and gave it less market value than men's. The most reliable servants were relatives, Mrs. Ballard's daughters, and her niece Parthena. From 1785 to 1795, Martha Ballard periodically employed short-term helpers to supplement the labor of her daughters. The girls who came to the house for short periods between 1795 and 1802 stayed about as long as did their predecessors, though now the helpers with deep personal commitments to the family were gone. There was no longer anyone who could be counted on to initiate short-term workers or to sustain the system on her own when needed.

Where genealogical information is unavailable, census data on family composition allow a conjecture of family affiliation for twenty-one of the twenty-nine girls. Most of the girls appear not to have been poor at all. The majority came from families whose assessed property fell just below Ephraim Ballard's $685. Like the New Hampshire girls who entered Lowell textile mills a generation later, Martha Ballard's helpers were from the middling ranks of property owners. Their work, like that of the millworkers, was also episodic. Although the persistence of Martha Ballard's workers can be more easily measured in weeks than in months, the pattern is strikingly similar.[41] Nineteenth-century workers probably followed patterns long established in the countryside from which they came.

We have already seen that much of women's work was in support of male workers and that women's wage labor was less lucrative than men's. This disparity, combined with a lower age at marriage, tended to concentrate the labor of women in the family. While a man of twenty-three might be rafting boards or splitting staves for Samuel Howard, a woman of the same age would probably be married, doing much the same work for her husband that she had earlier done for her father and brothers. Unless a family had an unusual number of daughters, it also made sense to let boys work outside the family while girls remained at home. The boys could earn more, and the girls could do some of the work they left behind, being able to perform tasks within the family setting that would have seemed inappropriate beyond it.

To say that women's work was concentrated in the family, however, is not to say that it was confined there. As we have seen, the female economy was characterized by both commodity and labor exchanges. A girl might help in the haying at home, then go out for a few weeks or months to work in another family, coming home again to help with the spinning, go out again when sought by another household, then move on to help a sister in childbed. Such a pattern is confirmed repeatedly in the diary.[42] Though Martha Ballard sometimes negotiated with mothers ("Mrs. Cypher says she may come again"), most of the time she appealed to and reckoned with the girls themselves.[43] The mobility of her helpers assured their independence.

European visitors commented frequently on the lack of deference shown by American servants. An English immigrant, Charles William Janson, observed: "The arrogance of domestics in the land of republican liberty and equality, is particularly calculated to excite the astonishment of strangers. To call persons of this description *servants* or to speak of their *master* or *mistress* is a grievous affront." He told of approaching the house of an American gentleman and asking the young woman who answered the door whether her master was home. "I have no master," she replied. "Don't you live here?" he responded. "I *stay* here," she answered.[44] The young woman understood that the source of her freedom was her ability to leave. Ironically, then, the very system that assured women's secondary status in the market economy allowed them a certain independence of it. Ruth Belknap put it this way in a letter to her daughter: "As to maid affairs they remain as you left them But I hourly Expect alterations as Madam says she is to Nurse Mrs. Kenny."[45] Ruth Belknap's sarcastic reference to "Madam" marked the limits of her own authority as a mistress.

The female labor supply was both fluid and, like the textile production system it sustained, widely dispersed. Both factors help explain why roughly 6 percent of the servant-age population of Hallowell passed through Martha Ballard's kitchen between 1795 and 1802. Although such conditions affected all women – the ceiling on home production being set by the availability of hands to spin, reel, weave, churn, or sew – the nature of Martha Ballard's occupation exaggerated the problem. Dressmakers or chair caners could schedule their excursions to other women's houses; weavers and dairywomen could do all their work at home. Furthermore, the low age at marriage, a condition that increased the burdens of housewifery, improved the market for midwifery. For a time in the 1790s, Martha Ballard was caught in a demographic squeeze.

In retrospect, what is surprising about this period is, not the stress, but the remarkable productivity. Martha Ballard delivered more babies in each of the two years after Dolly's marriage than in any other year in her career. Although deliveries declined in 1798 (the year she sent the loom to Hannah), they rose again in 1799. Commitment to her patients only partly accounts for her struggle to keep moving. In the fifteen years since her fiftieth birthday, she had built a rewarding career and had established a flourishing household system. She had no wish to retire.

In December 1799, Martha and Ephraim Ballard moved to a new house built on their son Jonathan's land. During construction, Mrs. Ballard always referred to it as "Mr. Ballard's house" or "his house," suggesting that she may not have entirely approved. The year 1800 indeed marked the end of an era for Martha Ballard. Although she never entirely gave up midwifery, her practice rapidly declined. Her illnesses during the next two years were undoubtedly organic, yet one cannot but wonder what role exhaustion and even periodic discouragement may have played. Still, illness brought minor triumphs. On November 28, 1800, when his wife was doubled over with a fit of "colic," Ephraim Ballard got out of bed, made her some tea, and warmed a brick for her stomach. In July 1802, during another bout of illness, Cyrus did the brewing, though she strained the wort and cooked him his supper.[46]

Eventually, determination conquered despair. "I have sufered much with my malladies in the coars of this weak," she wrote on October 30, 1802, "but God has held me up to perform for others." The story of Martha Ballard's last ten years belongs in another place, but it is appropriate to note here that in 1809, at the age of seventy-four, she delivered almost as many babies as she had in the year in which the diary began. She performed her last delivery on April 19, 1812, a month before her death at the age of seventy-seven. Her strength had held out to the end of the "rais."

The diary of Martha Moore Ballard is, above all else, a compelling record of a remarkable life; but, in telling her own story, Martha Ballard also recorded part of the larger history of early American women. Her diary documents the variety, the social complexity, and the considerable independence of women's work in late-eighteenth-century Maine, demonstrating the existence of a female economy that encompassed the activities of mothers, daughters, and neighbors. It shows how one group of women cooperated to build resources and to increase their own productivity. It suggests that the level of home production in individual households had as much to do with the availability of daughters as with the availability of flax. It demonstrates the importance of understanding the female life cycle in studying the family economy and of carefully delineating the sometimes very different obligations of women as wives, housewives, and village specialists. Finally, it vividly portrays the personal, and, to twentieth-century women, all too familiar complications of working "abroad" while continuing to work "at home."

Martha Ballard's diary demonstrates the existence of a richly nuanced world beneath the level of documentation available in standard sources. At the same time, it invites historians to make more creative use of such sources. As we learn to read the blanks in men's diaries and account books, to see tax lists and deeds for the partial records that they are, and to reformulate the questions we ask of our materials, we will discover the lives of women. Men's and women's lives were inextricably bound together in the family labor system of early New England, but the experiences of the two sexes were not identical. Nor can we make sense of the dramatic changes in the northern rural economy in the early nineteenth century if we fail to differentiate the experiences of young women, childbearing women, and "old wives" like Martha Ballard.

We need to recognize the ways in which small-scale home manufacturing and traditional specialties like midwifery sustained the female economy in early New England, tying women of various ages together through the exchange of goods and services, providing independent sources of income for wives, and giving mothers primary responsibility for the education and employment of daughters. Such an appreciation almost certainly will help us to ask better and more sophisticated questions about the nineteenth century. Obviously, the transition to factory production involved more than a move of young women from the household. It, potentially at least, disrupted a multitude of connections within the female economy.

Tracing that story is a task for another time – or person. History, like women's work, is never done.

EDITOR'S NOTE

a   Ebenezer Parkman served as the minister of Westborough, Massachusetts, from 1724 until his death in 1782.

NOTES

Reprinted from *Work and Labor in Early America*, edited by Stephen Innes (Chapel Hill, N.C., 1988). Copyright 1988 The University of North Carolina Press. Used by permission of the author and publisher.

1 Diary of Martha Moore Ballard, 1785–1812, MS, Maine State Library, Augusta, hereafter cited as MMB. Charles Elventon Nash included extensive excerpts from the Ballard diary in *The History of Augusta: First Settlements and Early Days as a Town* (a book printed in Augusta, 1904, but not published until 1961, when Edith Hary assembled the unbound signatures). The Nash abridgment, heavily biased toward genealogy, includes only about a third of the original, though it does suggest the range of material in it. Except for brief references in Nancy F. Cott, *The Bonds of Womanhood: "Woman's Sphere" in New England, 1780–1835* (New Haven, Conn., 1977): 19, 29; and in Richard W. Wertz and Dorothy C. Wertz, *Lying-In: A History of Childbirth in America* (New York, 1977): 9–12, 18, 20, the diary has been unused by scholars. I am writing a book-length study of the MS diary (published New York, 1990).

2 William Chappell, ed., *The Roxburghe Ballads* (Hertford, 1875), III: 301; Alan Lomax, *The Folk Songs of North America in the English Language* (Garden City, N.Y., 1975): 124, 133; Vance Randolph, ed., *Ozark Folksongs*, 4 vols. (Columbia, Mo., 1980), III: 69–70.

3 *Vital Records of Oxford, Massachusetts* (Worcester, Mass., 1905): 13, 14, 268; MMB: Feb. 20, Mar. 30, 1785, June 26, 1788, Oct. 7, 1789; Ernest Caulfield, "Some Common Diseases of Colonial Children," Colonial Society of Massachusetts, *Publications*, XXXV (1951): 23–4.

4 Charles Frederic Farlow, *Ballard Genealogy* (Boston, 1911): 82; James W. North, *The History of Augusta, Maine* (Somersworth, N.H., 1981 [orig. publ. 1870]): 185–9; MMB: Oct. 30, 1786, Aug. 23, 1790, Nov. 9, 1791, Dec. 14, 1795, Mar. 30, 1802; Nash, *History of Augusta*: 235, 301; North, *History of Augusta*: 819; Vincent York, *The Sandy River and its Valley* (Farmington, Maine, 1976): 66; Ephraim Ballard Depositions, Kennebec County Deeds, book 8, 461–3, book 9, 400–1, Kennebec County Court House, Augusta; Invoice of the Rateable Property in Possession of the Middle Parish in Hallowell, 1794, MS, Maine State Library.

5 MMB: Apr. 1, July 27, Nov. 28, 1785, Oct. 29, 1787, Nov. 1, 1788, Nov. 15, 1791.

6 MMB: Mar. 26, Apr. 15, May 19, Aug. 6, 1785, Mar. 28, Nov. 4, Dec. 6, Dec. 25, 1786, Dec. 25, 1789, Jan. 8, 30, 1790, July 9, Sept. 15, Nov. 19, 1791, Dec. 23, 1800.

7 MMB: June 5, 1785, July 12, 1788, Dec. 13, 1791, May 4, 1792, June 4, 1800.

8 MMB: May 25, 1785, May 5, 1787, May 13–14, 25–7, 1790, June 25–6, 1790, Apr. 14, June 17–18, July 28, Aug. 20, Oct. 14, 1791, Apr. 28, 1800.

9 MMB: Mar. 13, 1791, May 19, 1796, July 11, 1800, Dec. 27, 1800.

10 MMB: Mar. 15, 21, Apr. 27, 1785, Apr. 17, Oct. 21, Dec. 2, 1786, June 8,
    July 2, Oct. 15, Nov. 6, Dec. 19, 22, 1787, May 2, 1788, Jan. 11–12, July
    19, 20, 24, Aug. 12, Oct. 13, 18, 1797, June 2, 1799, Jan. 3, Dec. 20, 1800;
    William Allen, "Now and Then," Maine Historical Society, *Collections*,
    1st Ser., VII (1876): 275–6.
11 MMB: Nov. 27, 1793, May 18, 1797, Dec. 20, 1800, Jan. 6, 1801.
12 MMB: Jan. 12, 1790, Feb. 28, 1791, May 11, July 24, 1797, Nov. 22, 1798.
13 MMB: July 27, 1788, Apr. 7, Oct. 27, 1789.
14 For imported medicine, see MMB: Feb. 5, 1791, Oct. 5, 1793, Nov. 3,
    1795; homegrown herbs, Sept. 30, 1788, Apr. 5, 1790, Oct. 4, 1792, Sept.
    16, 1793; wild plants, July 28, 1787, July 12, 1792, June 5, 1794; and
    household staples, Mar. 4, 1789, Jan. 17, 1792, Mar. 29, 1797.
15 *The Diary of Matthew Patten of Bedford, N.H.* (Concord, N.H., 1903): 410, 417.
16 ibid.: 414, 423.
17 On rural New York (and for the quotation), see Nancy Grey Osterud,
    "Sharing and Exchanging Work: Cooperative Relationships among
    Women and among Men in an Upstate New York Dairying Commu-
    nity during the Late Nineteenth Century" (paper, based on "Strategies
    of Mutuality: Relations among Women and Men in an Agricultural
    Community" [Ph.D. dissertation, Brown University, 1984]). For sharply
    differing interpretations of the use of cash values in eighteenth-century
    account books, see Michael Merrill, "Cash is Good to Eat: Self-
    Sufficiency and Exchange in the Rural Economy of the United States,"
    Radical History Review, III (1977): 42–71; and Winifred B. Rothenberg,
    "The Market and Massachusetts Farmers, 1750–1855," *Journal of Econ-
    omic History*, XLI (1981): 283–314.
18 Cott, *Bonds of Womanhood*: 23. For the importance of affiliation to
    women, see, especially, Jean Baker Miller, *Toward a New Psychology of
    Women* (Boston, 1976).
19 MMB: July 26, Aug. 1, 1785, Apr. 25, 28, May 12, July 14, 1776, May 11,
    19, 1787, May 11, June 8, 9, Oct. 14, 1789.
20 George Francis Dow and Mary G. Thresher, eds., *Records and Files of
    the Quarterly Courts of Essex County, Massachusetts*, 9 vols. (Salem,
    Mass., 1911–75).
21 See Richard S. Dunn, "Servants and Slaves: The Recruitment and
    Employment of Labor," in Jack P. Greene and J. R. Pole, eds., *Colonial
    British America: Essays in the New History of the Early Modern Era*
    (Baltimore, 1984): 187.
22 MMB: Feb. 15, Dec. 23, 29, 1785, Mar. 10, June 6, Aug. 10, Sept. 28, Nov.
    15, 28, Dec. 6, 1786, Oct. 21, Nov. 23, 1787, Mar. 14, 1788, Feb. 25, June
    27, 1789, Mar. 6, 1790, Jan. 5, June 27, 1791, Dec. 9–11, 1801; Nash,
    History of Augusta: 525.
23 MMB: July 10, 1787, separate entry after Dec. 31, 1787, Mar. 6, 1788.
24 MMB: June 7, 1786: "Daniel Breakfasted here means to Bord at Boltons
    from this time." Martha Ballard may have been charging travelers and
    logging crews for the meals they ate with the family. There are 148
    entries regarding persons sleeping or eating at the Ballard house;
    though there is no mention of payment, this seems in excess of ordinary
    sociability.

25 Samuel and William Howard Account Book, 1773–1793, MS, Maine Historical Society: 126a, 141b, 116b.

26 ibid.: 117ab (mostly timber transactions) and Anonymous Account Book, Augusta, 1809, MS, Maine State Library, which lists mostly garden seeds in a period when Martha Ballard clearly was doing the gardening. Internal evidence suggests that the book was kept by Joseph North.

27 MMB: Mar. 11, 13, 1786, Jan. 16, 1787, Apr. 15, 1788, Sept. 1, 1789, Sept. 14, 1791.

28 Account Book of Thomas Chute, Maine Historical Society: 6.

29 Howard Accounts: 11b, 82b, 93b, 94b, 116b, 160b; MMB: Jan. 8, June 15–25, July 8, 1791, Oct. 15, 1792, Dec. 11, 1801. I arrived at daily rates for female workers by comparing piece rates with typical daily outputs.

30 Ephraim and William Richardson Accounts with Luke Barton Estate, 1787–1790, in Towne Papers, 3: 9, MS, Maine State Museum; Kennebec Purchase Company, Waste Book, 1754–1800, MS, Maine Historical Society: 169 (see also 185, 187, 467). Mr. Ballard received £31 in 1794, $145 in 1796, and $67 in 1798.

31 MMB: Aug. 4–7, 1790, June 17, 1791.

32 MMB: Jan. 15, 1796: "This is the 612 birth I have attended at since the year 1777 the first I assisted was the wife of Pelton Warrin in July 1778."

33 MMB: June 15, 1796, and see Nov. 26, 1790, July 25, 1798, Mar. 5, 1801.

34 MMB: Apr. 7–12, 1796.

35 MMB: Feb. 6, May 5, July 5, 1787.

36 MMB: Oct. 30, Nov. 20, 26, 27, 1792; Mrs. Ballard and Dolly helped Sally Cox quilt, Nov. 11, 1795.

37 MMB: Nov. 14, 1792, June 6, 17, Nov. 11, 1794, Mar. 21, June 4, 1795.

38 MMB: Jan. 6–9, June 4–5, 1796. This theme continues through the next five years: Jan. 15, 26, 1796, Jan. 18, 1797, Apr. 27, 1798, and May 13, 1800.

39 MMB: Dec. 19, 1795, Oct. 15, 1796, July 2, 1799, Oct. 1, 1801.

40 Elaine Crane is studying women's work in Philadelphia, Boston, Newport, Salem, and Portsmouth during the eighteenth century. She tells me that Elizabeth Drinker, the Philadelphia diarist, was much less concerned about the comings and goings of maids, a fact that undoubtedly had something to do with the availability of indentured servants. See Sharon V. Salinger, " 'Send No More Women': Female Servants in Eighteenth-Century Philadelphia," *Pennsylvania Magazine of History and Biography*, CVII (1983): 29–48. Mary Holyoke of Salem seems to have been equally indifferent, unless complaints have been edited out of her journals published in George Francis Dow, ed., *The Holyoke Diaries*, 1709–1856 (Salem, Mass., 1937). A woman of Portsmouth, New Hampshire, glibly told her daughter, in the 1760s: "Betty Tripe has Left me. I've got a better Maid." Mary Cochrane Rogers, *Glimpses of an Old Social Capital (Portsmouth, New Hampshire) as Illustrated by the Life of the Reverend Arthur Browne and His Circle* (Boston, 1923): 47. For the poem, see [Ruth Belknap?], "The Pleasures of a Country Life," Massachusetts Historical Society, *Collections*, 6th ser., IV (Boston, 1891): 228–9.

41 Thomas Dublin, *Women at Work: The Transformation of Work and Community in Lowell, Massachusetts, 1826–1860* (New York, 1979): 184–5.
42 This was true even of the Ballard daughters and of Parthena and Sally; see Feb. 15, 1790, June 23, 1786.
43 MMB: July 31, 1801.
44 Charles William Janson, "Stranger in America," in Gordon S. Wood, ed., *The Rising Glory of America, 1760–1820* (New York, 1971): 123. Although some seventeenth-century householders also complained about the impertinence of helpers, the independence of servants may have grown in the eighteenth century. Certainly, there is evidence for a larger breakdown in family government apparent in such things as rising premarital pregnancy rates.
45 Ruth Belknap to Sally Belknap, Aug. 28, 1786, MS, New Hampshire Historical Society, Concord.
46 MMB: July 20, 1802.

8

"BAUBLES OF BRITAIN": THE AMERICAN AND CONSUMER REVOLUTIONS OF THE EIGHTEENTH CENTURY

T. H. Breen

Like many other essays in this volume, the springboard for Tim Breen's argument is the diversity of early America. Early in the eighteenth century, he points out, colonies and regions had little in common with one another. But they came together. One way that they did involves an activity that touched all – getting and spending. Ordinary consumers began purchasing ever more British products. Exciting new commodities such as tea, sugar, chocolate, and tobacco whet appetites, while better and cheaper textiles, pottery, and glass improved the domestic environment. The self-sufficient frontier farmer is a myth.

But Breen is not content to document the mundane actualities of everyday life; rather, he explores the meaning of things. Essentially private acts like buying tea, shirts, or buckles could be transformed under certain conditions into public, even national concerns. Breen sees two developments. First, a consumer revolution integrated the colonies within an interdependent empire. Second, the constitutional crisis that enveloped the British Empire in the aftermath of the Seven Years' War transformed individual consumer acts into broader political statements. The first British Empire was built in large part on consumer goods and its dismemberment owed much to a discourse and rituals centered on those same consumer goods. Breen connects "pots and pans" history to political history.

Such challenging arguments invite responses. Although society united in the purchase of some goods – tea, for example – did not gentlemen buy other goods – fine furniture, for example – in order to differentiate themselves from other social ranks? Consumption, in other words, might produce both integration and differentiation. How far downward did the consumer revolution extend? Did it reach the poor in the eighteenth century? What was the impact of the new consumer amenities on household life? Surely women's lives were affected most of all? Was the discourse about goods necessary for the ideological abstractions of the American revolutionaries to acquire concrete meaning? Were they in fact abstractions?

* * *

Something extraordinary occurred in 1774. Thousands of ordinary American people responded as they had never done before to an urban political crisis. Events in Boston mobilized a nation, uniting for the first time artisans and farmers, yeomen and gentlemen, and within only a few months colonists who had earlier expressed neutrality or indifference about the confrontation with Great Britain suddenly found themselves supporting bold actions that led almost inevitably to independence.

At mid-century almost no one would have predicted such an occurrence. Some two million people had scattered themselves over an immense territory. They seemed to have little in common. In fact contemporary observers concluded that should the colonists ever achieve political independence, they would immediately turn on each other. "In short," declared one English traveler in 1759, "such is the difference of character, of manners, of religion, of interest, of the different colonies, that I think ... were they left to themselves, there would soon be a civil war from one end of the continent to the other."[1] John Adams agreed.[a] Reflecting in 1818 on the coming of revolution, he marveled that the Americans had ever managed to unite. Their own separate histories seemed to have conspired against the formation of a new nation. The colonies, Adams explained, had evolved different constitutions of government. They had also experienced:

> so great a variety of religions, they were composed of so many different nations, their customs, manners, and habits had so little resemblance, and their intercourse had been so rare, and their knowledge of each other so imperfect, that to unite them in ... the same system of action, was certainly a very difficult enterprise.

Very difficult indeed! And yet in 1776 these colonists surprised the world by successfully forming a new nation. In Adams's words,

"Thirteen clocks were made to strike together."[2] Somehow, Americans had found a means to communicate effectively with each other, to develop a shared sense of political purpose, to transcend what at mid-century had appeared insurmountable cultural and geographic divisions. The mobilization of strangers in a revolutionary cause eroded the stubborn localism of an earlier period. In other words, it was a process that heightened awareness of a larger social identity. In Benedict Anderson's wonderful phrase, these men and women "imagined" a community, a national consciousness which while not yet the full-blown nationalism of the nineteenth century was nevertheless essential to the achievement of political independence.[3]

Efforts to explain this political mobilization have foundered on an attempt to establish the primacy of ideology over material interest.[4] This is not a debate in which the truth lies somewhere between two extremes. Neither the intellectual nor the economic historian can tell us how Americans of different classes and backgrounds and living in very different physical environments achieved political solidarity, at least sufficient solidarity to make good their claim to independence. Economic explanations – those that analyze an individual's political loyalties in terms of poverty or profits, absence of business opportunities, or decline of soil fertility – are not only reductionist in character but also narrowly focused upon the experiences of specific, often numerically small, groups in colonial society. Though we learn, for example, why certain urban workers in Boston or Philadelphia might have been unhappy with parliamentary taxation, we never discover how such people managed to reach out to – indeed even to communicate with – northern farmers and southern planters. In other words, the more we know about the pocket-book concerns of any particular eighteenth-century American community, the more difficult it becomes to understand a spreading national consciousness which accompanied political mobilization.

Intellectual historians encounter a different, though equally thorny set of problems. They transform the American Revolution into a mental event. From this perspective, it does not matter much whether the ideas that the colonists espoused are classic liberal concepts of rights and property, radical country notions[b] of power and virtue, or evangelical Calvinist beliefs about sin and covenants. Whatever the dominant ideology may have been, we find that a bundle of political abstractions has persuaded colonists living in scattered regions of America of the righteousness of their cause, driving them during the 1760s and 1770s to take ever more radical positions until eventually they were forced by the logic of their original assumptions to break with Great Britain. Unfortunately, intellectual historians provide no clear link between the everyday world of the men and women who actually became patriots and the ideas that they articulated. We are thus hard-pressed to comprehend how in 1774 wealthy Chesapeake planters and poor Boston artisans – to cite two obvious examples – could possibly have come to share a political mentality. We do not know how these ideas were transmitted through colonial society, from class to class, from community to community.

These interpretive issues – those that currently separate the materialists from the idealists – may be resolved by casting the historical debate in different terms. Eighteenth-century Americans, I shall argue, communicated perceptions of status and politics to other people through items of everyday material culture, through a symbolic universe of commonplace "things" which modern scholars usually take for granted but which for their original possessors were objects of great significance.[5] By focusing attention on the meanings of things, on the semiotics of daily life, we gain fresh insight into the formation of a national consciousness as well as the coming of the American Revolution.[6]

The imported British manufactures that flooded American society during the eighteenth century acquired cultural significance largely within local communities. Their meanings were bound up with a customary world of face-to-face relations. Within these localities Americans began to define social status in relation to commodities. This was, of course, an expression of a much larger, long-term transformation of the Atlantic world. And though this process differentiated men and women in new ways, it also provided them with a common framework of experience, a shared language of consumption.

But in America something unusual occurred during the 1760s and 1770s. Parliament managed to politicize these consumer goods, and when it did so, manufactured items suddenly took on a radical, new symbolic function. In this particular colonial setting the very commodities that were everywhere beginning to transform social relations provided a language for revolution. People living in scattered parts of America began to communicate their political grievances *through* common imports. A shared framework of consumer experience not only allowed them to reach out to distant strangers, to perceive, however dimly, the existence of an "imagined community," but also to situate a universal political discourse about rights and liberties, virtue and power, within a familiar material culture. In this context the boycott became a powerful social metaphor of resistance, joining Carolinians and New Englanders, small farmers and powerful merchants, men and women in common cause.

This interpretive scheme gives priority neither to ideas nor experience. Some Americans undoubtedly boycotted British imports because of political principle. By denying themselves these goods they expressed a deep ideological commitment. Other colonists, however, gave up consumer items because their neighbors compelled them to do so. They were not necessarily motivated by high principle, at least not initially. But the very experience of participating in these boycotts, of taking part in increasingly elaborate rituals of nonconsumption, had an unintended effect. It served inevitably to heighten popular awareness of the larger constitutional issues at stake. In this sense, the boycott for many Americans was an act of ideological discovery. These particular colonists may not have destroyed tea because they were republicans, but surely they learned something fundamental about republican ideas by their participation in such events. Questions about the use of tea in one's household forced ordinary men and women to choose sides, to consider exactly where one stood. And over time pledges of support for nonimportation publicly linked patriotic individuals to other, like-minded individuals. Decisions about the consumer goods tied local communities to other communities, to regional movements and, after 1774, to a national association. Neither the consumer revolution nor the boycott movement can in itself explain an occurrence so complex as the American Revolution. That argument would amount to a new form of reductionism. The aim here is more limited: to explore the relation between the growth of national consciousness and the American rejection of the "baubles of Britain."

I

The eighteenth century witnessed the birth of an Anglo-American "consumer society." Though the Industrial Revolution was still far in the future, the pace of the British economy picked up dramatically

231

after 1690. Small manufacturing concerns scattered throughout England began turning out huge quantities of consumer goods – cloth, ceramics, glassware, paper, cutlery – items that transformed the character of everyday life. Merchants could hardly keep up with expanding demand. The domestic market hummed with activity. People went shopping, gawking at the wares displayed in the "bow-windows" that appeared for the first time along urban streets. Advertisements in the provincial English journals fueled consumer desire, and to those middling sorts who wanted to participate in the market but who did not possess sufficient cash, tradesmen offered generous credit.[7]

Americans were quickly swept up in this consumer economy. These were not the self-sufficient yeomen of Jeffersonian mythology. Eighteenth-century colonists demanded the latest British manufactures. Few would have disagreed with the members of the Maryland general assembly who once announced, "We want the British Manufactures."[8] In order to pay for what they imported, the Americans harvested ever-larger crops of tobacco, rice, and indigo. Northern farmers supplied the West Indian plantations with foodstuffs. Economic historians have traditionally concentrated on this flow of American exports or, more precisely, on the production of staple commodities in response to European market conditions. The problem with this perspective is that it depreciates the role of consumer demand in shaping the colonial economy. At a time when the American population was growing at an extraordinary rate, per capita consumption of British imports was actually rising. In other words, more colonists purchased more manufactured goods every year. Since this was a young population – half of the colonists were under the age of sixteen – one must assume that adults were responsible for this exploding demand. Their consumption raised per capita rates for the entire society. After mid-century the American market for imported goods took off, rising 120 percent between 1750 and 1773. Throughout the colonies the crude, somewhat impoverished material culture of the seventeenth century – a pioneer world of homespun cloth and wooden dishes – was swept away by a flood of store-bought sundries.[9]

These ubiquitous items transformed the texture of everyday life in provincial America. Even in the most inaccessible regions people came increasingly to rely on imports. One English traveler discovered to her surprise that in rural North Carolina women seldom bothered to produce soap. It was not a question of the availability of raw materials. Good ashes could be had at no expense. But these rural women were consumers, and they preferred to purchase Irish soap "at the store at a monstrous price."[10] In more cosmopolitan environments, the imports were even more conspicuous. Eighteenth-century Americans situated other men and women within a rich context of British manufacturers. John Adams betrayed this habit of mind when he visited the home of a successful Boston merchant:

> Went over [to] the House to view the Furniture, which alone cost a thousand Pounds sterling. A seat it is for a noble Man, a Prince. The Turkey Carpets, the painted Hangings, the Marble Table, the rich Beds with crimson Damask Curtains and Counterpins, the beautiful Chimney Clock, the Spacious Garden, are the most magnificent of any Thing I have ever seen.[11]

Like other Americans, Adams had obviously developed a taste for British imports.

How does one make sense out of this vast consumer society? There is much that we do not know about eighteenth-century colonial merchandizing. Still, even at this preliminary stage of investigation, it is possible to discern certain general characteristics that distinguished the colonial marketplace at mid-century: an exceptionally rapid expansion of consumer *choice*, an increasing *standardization* of consumer behavior, and a pervasive *Anglicization* of the American market.

Of these three, the proliferation of choice is the most difficult to interpret. We simply do not know what it meant to the colonial consumer to find himself or herself suddenly confronted by an unprecedented level of variety in the marketplace. Perhaps it was a liberating experience? Perhaps the very act of making choices between competing goods of different color, texture, and quality heightened the individual's sense of personal independence? After all, the colonial buyer was actively participating in the consumer economy, demanding what he or she wanted rather than merely taking what was offered.

Whatever the psychological impact of this change may have been, there is no question that Americans at mid-century confronted a range of choice that would have amazed earlier generations. A survey of New York City newspapers revealed, for example, that during the 1720s merchants seldom mentioned more

233

than fifteen different imported items per month in their advertisements. The descriptions were generic: cloth, paper, ceramics. But by the 1770s it was not unusual during some busy months for New York journals specifically to list over 9,000 different manufactured goods. And as the number of items expanded, the descriptive categories became more elaborate. In the 1740s New York merchants simply advertised "paper." By the 1760s they listed seventeen varieties distinguished by color, function, and quality.

If, as many scholars currently argue, human beings constitute external reality through language, then the proliferation of manufactures during the eighteenth century may have radically altered how Americans made sense out of everyday activities. The consumer market provided them with an impressive new vocabulary, thousands of words that allowed them not only to describe a changing material culture but also to interpret their place within it. Adams demonstrated this point when in his diary he recorded his reactions to the possessions of the wealthy Boston merchant. This language of goods was shared by all who participated in the market. It was not the product of a particular region or class, and thus furnished colonists with a means of transmitting experience across social and geographic boundaries. As we have seen, a visitor could engage the women of North Carolina in a discourse about imported soap. It was a conversation that the women of Virginia and Massachusetts would also have understood.

An example of this kind of cultural exchange occurred in a Maryland tavern in 1744. A traveling physician from Annapolis witnessed a quarrel between an innkeeper and an individual who by his external appearance seemed "a rough spun, forward, clownish blade." The proprietor apparently shared this impression, because she served this person who wore "a greasy jacket and breeches and a dirty worsted cap" a breakfast fit "for some ploughman or carman." The offended customer vehemently protested that he too was a gentleman and to prove his status, pulled a linen hat out of his pocket. He then informed the embarrassed assembly that "he was able to afford better than many who went finer: he had good linnen in his bags, a pair of silver buckles, silver clasps, and gold sleeve buttons, two Holland shirts, and some neat night caps; and that his little woman att home drank tea twice a day." What catches our attention is not the man's clumsy attempt to negotiate status through possessions – people have been doing that for centuries – but rather that he bragged of owning specific manufactured goods, the very articles that were just then beginning to transform American society. He assumed – correctly, in this case – that the well-appointed stranger he encountered in a country tavern understood the language of shirts, buckles, and tea.[12]

This expanding consumer world of the mid-eighteenth century led almost inevitably to a *standardization* of the marketplace. To be sure, as the previous anecdote suggests, Americans had begun to define status in relation to commodities. In this they were not especially unique. Throughout the Atlantic world choice created greater, more visible marks of distinction. Nevertheless by actually purchasing manufactured imports as opposed to making do with locally produced objects, by participating in an expanding credit network, and by finding oneself confronted with basically the same types of goods which were now on sale in other, distant communities, Americans developed a common element of personal experience.

One can only speculate, of course, why colonial shoppers purchased certain items. They may have been looking for status, beauty, convenience, or price. Whatever the justification may have been, the fact remains that people living in different parts of America were exposed to an almost identical range of imported goods. In part, this standardization of the marketplace resulted from the manufacturing process; after all, there were only so many dyes and glazes and finishes available during this period. The Staffordshire ceramics, for example, that sold in Charleston were of the same general shapes and colours as the Staffordshireware that sold in the shops of Philadelphia, New York, and Boston. Indeed an examination of newspaper advertisements in these colonial ports reveals no evidence of the development of regional consumer taste. British merchants sent to America what they could obtain from the manufacturers; the colonists bought whatever the merchants shipped. It is not surprising, therefore, to discover a Virginian in 1766 exclaiming, "Now nothing are so common as Turkey or Wilton Carpetts."[13] As we have already discovered, carpets of the same description had just made their appearance in the newspaper advertisements in New York and in the home of the Boston merchant described by John Adams.

The standardization of taste affected all colonial consumers. This is an important point. It is easy for modern historians to concentrate on the buying habits of the gentry.[14] Their beautiful homes – many of which are now preserved as museums – dominate

our understanding of the character of daily life in eighteenth-
century America. This interpretive bias is not a problem peculiar
to the colonial period. The consumer behavior of the wealthy has
always been more fully documented than that of more humble
buyers. But however much we are drawn to the material culture of
the colonial elite, we should realize that the spread of the consumer
market transformed the lives of ordinary men and women as
fundamentally as it did those of their more affluent neighbors.
Though wealthy Americans purchased goods of superior quality,
poorer buyers demanded the same general range of imports. Rural
peddlers, urban hawkers, Scottish factors responded to this eager
clientele, providing farmers and artisans with easy credit, the ticket
to participation in this consumer society. These people became
reliant on imported manufactures, so much so in fact that Francis
Fauquier, lieutenant-governor of Virginia, could note in 1763,
"These imports daily encrease, the common planters usually dressing themselves in the manufactures of Great Brittain [sic]
altogether."[15]

Tea provides an instructive example of the standardization of
consumer taste. Early in the eighteenth century this hot drink
became the preferred beverage in gentry households. Polite ladies
– perhaps as a device to lure gentlemen away from tavern society
– organized elaborate household rituals around the tea service. In
fact the purchase of tea necessitated the acquisition of pots, bowls,
strainers, sugar-tongs, cups, and slop-dishes. One writer in a New
York newspaper suggested the need for a school of tea etiquette.
The young men of the city, finding themselves "utterly ignorant in
the Ceremony of the Tea-Table", were advised to employ a knowl-
edgable woman "to teach them the Laws, Rules, Customs, Phrases
and Names of the Tea Utensils".[16]

Though less well-to-do Americans did not possess the entire
range of social props, they demanded tea. As early as 1734 one New
Yorker reported:

I am credibly informed that tea and china ware cost the
province, yearly, near the sum of L10,000; and people that are
least able to go to the expence, must have their tea tho' their
families want bread. Nay, I am told, they often pawn their
rings and plate to gratifie themselves in that piece of extravagance.[17]

It did not take long for this particular luxury to become a necessity.

"Our people," wrote another New York gentleman in 1762, "both in town and country, are shamefully gone into the habit of tea-drinking."[18] And when Israel Acrelius visited the old Swedish settlements of Delaware at mid-century, he discovered people consuming tea "in the most remote cabins."[19] During the 1750s even the inmates of the public hospital of Philadelphia, the city poor-house, insisted on having bohea tea.[20] All these colonists drank their tea out of imported cups, not necessarily china ones, but rather ceramics that had originated in the English Midlands where they had been fired at very high temperature and thus made resistant to the heat of America's new favorite drink.

Ordinary Americans adopted tea for reasons other than social emulation. After all, it was a mild stimulant, and a hot cup of tea probably helped the laboring poor endure hard work and insubstantial housing. Nevertheless in some isolated country villages the desire to keep up with the latest consumer fads led to bizarre results, the kind of gross cultural misunderstanding that anthropologists encounter in places where products of an alien technology have been introduced into a seemingly less-developed society. In 1794 a historian living in East Hampton, New York, interviewed a seventy-eight-year-old woman. "Mrs. Miller," he discovered, "remembers well when they first began to drink tea on the east end of Long Island." She explained that none of the local farmers knew what to do with the dry leaves: "One family boiled it in a pot and ate it like samp-porridge. Another spread tea leaves on his bread and butter, and bragged of his having ate half a pound at a meal, to his neighbor, who was informing him how long a time a pound of tea lasted him." According to Mrs. Miller, the arrival of the first tea-kettle was a particularly memorable day in the community:

> It came ashore at Montauk in a ship, (the *Captain Bell*). The farmers came down there on business with their cattle, and could not find out how to use the tea-kettle, which was then brought up to old "Governor Hedges." Some said it was for one thing, and some said it was for another. At length one, the more knowing than his neighbors, affirmed it to be the ship's lamp, to which they all assented.

Mrs. Miller may have been pulling the historian's leg, but whatever the truth of her story, it reveals the symbolic importance of tea in this remote eighteenth-century village.[21]

Standardization of consumer goods created a paradoxical situation. As Americans purchased the same general range of British manufactures – in other words, as they had similar consumer experiences – they became increasingly Anglicized. Historians sometimes refer to this cultural process as "the colonization of taste." The Anglo-American consumer society of the eighteenth century drew the mainland colonists closer to the culture of the mother country. In part, this was a result of the Navigation Acts[c] which channeled American commerce through Great Britain, a legislative constraint that made it difficult as well as expensive for Americans to purchase goods from the Continent. There is no reason to believe, however, that parliament passed these acts in a conscious attempt to "colonize American taste." That just happened. And during the eighteenth century this process is easy to trace. For most people, articles imported from the mother country carried positive associations. They introduced color and excitement into the lives of the colonists. Their quality was superior to that of locally made goods, silverware and furniture being two notable exceptions. It is not surprising that the demand for British manufactures escalated so quickly after mid-century. The market itself created new converts. Advertisements, merchants' displays, news of other people's acquisitions stoked consumer desire and thereby accelerated the spread of Anglicization. Booksellers – just to note one example – discovered that colonial readers preferred an English imprint to an American edition of the same title. "Their estimate of things English was so high," reports one historian, "that a false London imprint could seem an effective way to sell a local publication."[22]

Anglicized provincials insisted on receiving the "latest" English goods. They were remarkably attuned to even subtle changes in metropolitan fashion. "And you may believe me," a young Virginia planter named George Washington lectured a British merchant in 1760, "when I tell you that instead of getting things good and fashionable in their several kinds[,] we often have Articles sent Us that could have been usd [sic] by our Forefathers in the days of yore".[23] Washington may have envied his neighbors in Maryland. According to one visitor to Annapolis:

> The quick importation of fashions from the mother country
> is really astonishing. I am almost inclined to believe that a
> new fashion is adopted earlier by the polished and affluent

American than by many opulent persons in the great metropolis [London].... In short, very little difference is, in reality,
observable in the manners of the wealthy colonist and the
wealthy Briton.[24]

No doubt this man exaggerated, but as he well understood, after
mid-century American consumers took their cues from the mother
country.

Before the 1760s most Americans would not have been conscious of the profound impact of consumption upon their society.
They were like foot-soldiers who witness great battles only from a
narrow, personal perspective and thus cannot appreciate the larger
implications of thousands of separate engagements. Of course, the
colonists were aware of the proliferation of choice, but for most of
them the acquisition of British imports was a private act, one
primarily associated with one's own social status within a community or household. Manufactured goods shaped family routines;
they influenced relationships within a particular neighborhood. In
symbolic terms these articles possessed local meanings. Certainly
before the Stamp Act crisis[d] – a few extreme evangelicals like James
Davenport to the contrary notwithstanding – the Americans developed no sustained public discourse about goods.[25]

Nevertheless the totality of these private consumer experiences
deeply affected the character of eighteenth-century provincial society, for in a relatively short period following 1740 this flood of
British manufactures created an indispensable foundation for the
later political mobilization of the American people. Though these
highly Anglicized men and women were not fully aware of this
shared experiential framework, it would soon provide them with
a means to communicate across social and spatial boundaries. Only
after political events beyond their control forced them to form
larger human collectivities – as was the case after 1765 – did they
discover that a shared language of goods was already in place.

II

The importation of British goods on such a vast scale created social
tensions that the colonists were slow to appreciate. The very act of
purchasing these articles – making free choices from among competing possibilities – heightened the Americans' already well-
developed sense of their own personal independence. The acquisition

of manufactures also liberated them from a drab, impoverished, even insanitary folk culture of an earlier period. But consumption inevitably involved dependency. The colonists came increasingly to rely upon British merchants not only for what they now perceived as the necessities of daily life but also for a continued supply of credit. So long as the Anglo-American economy remained relatively prosperous and stable, it was possible to maintain the fiction of personal independence in a market system that in fact spawned dependence. But those days were numbered. An increasingly volatile international economy coupled with parliament's apparent determination to tax the colonists sparked an unprecedented debate about the role of commerce within the empire. Comfortable relations and familiar meanings were no longer secure. That was the burden of John Dickinson's[e] troubled remark in 1765, "under all these restraints and some others that have been imposed on us, we have not *till lately* been unhappy. Our spirits were not depressed".[26]

As Dickinson's observation suggests, the colonists' experiences as consumers no longer yielded the satisfaction that they had at an earlier time. The rising level of personal debt made the Americans' growing dependence upon British merchants increasingly manifest, and in this context of growing consumer "disappointment," the meaning of imported goods began to shift.[27] A semiotic order was changing. Articles that had been bound up with local cultures, with individual decisions within households, were gradually thrust into public discourse, and during the constitutional crisis with Great Britain these "baubles" were gradually and powerfully incorporated into a general moral critique of colonial society that traced its origins in part to radical country pamphleteers such as John Trenchard and Thomas Gordon[f] and in part to the evangelical preachers of the Great Awakening.[28] In other words, a constitutional crisis transformed private consumer acts into public political statements. Britain's rulers inadvertently activated a vast circuit of private experience and in the process created in the American colonies what they least desired, the first stirrings of national consciousness.

To understand the process of symbolic redefinition one must remember that the merchants of the mother country bore as much responsibility as did the members of parliament for the growing unhappiness of the American consumers. To be sure, during the Stamp Act crisis British merchants petitioned the House of Commons in support of the colonists. But at the same time these business-men pushed upon the American market more goods and credit than it could possibly absorb. Indeed, their aggressive, though shortsighted drive to maximize returns not only substantially in-creased colonial indebtedness but also alienated American wholesalers who had traditionally served as middlemen between the large British houses and the American shopkeepers.[29]

Parliament exacerbated these structural tensions within the American market. Though its efforts to raise new revenues after 1764 did not cripple the colonists' ability to purchase imported goods, parliament did remind the Americans of their dependence. If the colonists continued to purchase items such as glass, paper, and paint from British merchants – which seemed quite likely since they could not produce these articles themselves – then the Ameri-cans would inevitably have to pay unconstitutional taxes.

Considering the growing ambivalence of the colonists towards consumer goods – these items were immensely desirable, but also raised unsettling questions about economic dependency – it is not surprising that the Stamp Act crisis sparked a boycott of British manufacturers.[30] During the anxious months of 1764 and 1765 urban Americans endorsed nonimportation as the most likely means to bring about the Stamp Act's repeal and alleviate the burden of personal debt. As "Philo Publicus" explained to the readers of the *Boston Gazette*, "We have taken wide Steps to Ruin, and as we have grown more Luxurious every Year, so we run deeper and deeper in Debt to our Mother Country." After observ-ing how extravagantly the people of Boston decorated their parlors, how they piled their sideboards high with silver plate, how they collected costly china, this writer concluded, "I wonder not that my Country is so poor, I wonder not when I hear of frequent Bank-ruptcies."[31]

The boycott seemed an almost reflexive reaction to consti-tutional crisis. Of course, in 1765 angry Americans had little other choice. After all, there was no colonial Bastille for them to storm; George III and his hated ministers lived in safety on the other side of the Atlantic. But however circumscribed the range of responses may have been, the boycott served the colonists well. Participation in these protests provided Americans with opportunities to vent outrage against the policies of a distant government – much as Americans and others who boycott South African goods do today – and though it was not clear whether anyone in the mother country actually listened, the very act of publicly denying themselves these familiar imports began to mobilize colonists of different regions and backgrounds in common cause.

The success of this first boycott should not be exaggerated. Most activities were restricted to urban centers, and though nonimportation momentarily upset the flow of Anglo-American trade, it did not bring the British economy to its knees. Nevertheless, however limited its economic impact may have been, this initial confrontation reveals a mental process at work which in time would acquire extraordinary significance. As early as 1765 many colonists had begun to realize that patterns of consumption provided them with an effective language of political protest. In that sense, Americans discovered political ideology through a discussion of the meaning of goods, through observances of nonconsumption that forced ordinary men and women to declare where exactly they stood on the great constitutional issues of the day. British manufacturers thus took on a new symbolic function, and the boycott became a social metaphor of political resistance. If the mainland colonies had not already been transformed into a consumer society, the Stamp Act protesters would have found it extremely difficult to communicate effectively with each other at this moment of political crisis. The purchase of British manufactures was the one experience that most of them shared, and by raising the possibility that they could do without these goods patriotic Americans strained the bonds of Anglicization.

Revolution did not occur in 1765. The bonds of empire withstood the challenge, and as soon as parliament repealed the Stamp Act the Americans returned to the import shops. The confrontation with the mother country had eroded but not destroyed the traditional meaning of consumer goods. Newspaper advertisements carried the familiar words "just imported from England," a clear indication that many colonists still took their cultural cues from Great Britain. Until that connection could be severed, independence was out of the question. This does not mean that Americans deserted the political principles that they had mouthed during the Stamp Act protest; most certainly they were not hypocrites. The boycott had provided colonists with a behavioral link between a political ideology and local experience, and when it was abandoned ideas about liberty and representation, slavery and virtue were temporarily dissociated from the affairs of daily life.

The Townshend Act of 1767 returned consumer goods to the

center of American political discourse. This ill-conceived statute levied a duty upon imported glass, paper, tea, lead, and paint.[32] Patriotic leaders throughout the colonies advocated a campaign of nonconsumption, and though this boycott would ultimately disappoint some of its more fervent organizers, it revealed the powerful capacity of goods in this society not only to recruit people into a political movement but also to push them – often when they were unaware of what was happening – to take ever more radical positions. As in the Stamp Act crisis, imported British manufactures provided a framework in which many colonists learned about rights and liberties.

During the period of protest against the Townshend Act, roughly between 1767 and 1770, colonists began to speak of consumer goods in a highly charged moral language. Of course, these Americans were not the first people to condemn the pernicious effects of luxury and self-indulgence. That concern had vexed moralists for centuries. Nevertheless, during the Stamp Act crisis a dominant theme of the political discourse had been debt. The purchase of British manufactures undermined the personal independence of the American consumers and thus made them fit targets for tyrannical conspirators. But after 1767 the thrust of patriotic rhetoric shifted from *private* debt to *public* virtue. By acquiring needless British imports the colonial consumer threatened the liberties of other men and women. "Every Man who will take Pains to cultivate the Cost of Homespun," advised a writer in the *Boston Gazette*, "may easily convince himself that his private Interest, as well as [that of] the Publick, will be promoted by it."[33] In other words, how one spent one's own money became a matter deserving public scrutiny.

The artifacts of a consumer culture took on new symbolic meaning within a fluid political discourse, and before long it was nearly impossible for Americans to speak of imported goods without making reference to constitutional rights. The politicization of consumption was clearly evident in the December 22, 1767 instructions of the Boston town meeting to its representatives in the general assembly. We, your constituents, they announced, are worried about "the distressed Circumstances of this Town, by means of the amazing growth of Luxury, and the Embarrassments of our Trade; & having also the strongest apprehensions that our invaluable Rights & Liberties as Men and British Subjects, are greatly affected by a late Act of the British Parliament"; they urged

243

their representatives "to encourage a spirit of Industry and Frugality among the People."[34] Colonists living in different parts of America called for a boycott not just of those few imports specifically taxed by the Townshend Act but, rather, a long list of British manufactures, everything from clocks to carriages, hats to house furniture, even mustard.[35] The lists contained scores of items, a virtual inventory of the major articles of the mid-century consumer culture. The colonists seemed determined to undo patterns of consumption that had taken root in the 1740s, to return perhaps to a simpler period of self-sufficiency, which in fact had never existed, but which in this political crisis seemed the best strategy for preserving liberty. In this social context it made sense for colonial writers to declare: "Save your money and you can save your country."[36]

The Townshend boycotts – ineffective though they may have been in forcing parliament to back down – helped radical colonists to distinguish friends from enemies. Strangers communicated ideology through the denial of consumer goods. Rhetoric was not enough. One had to reveal where one stood. The nonconsumption movement forced individuals to alter the character of their daily lives, and as they did so, they formed collectivities of like-minded colonists, acts which inevitably reinforced their own commitment to radical politics. The leaders of Windham, a small village in southeastern Connecticut, scheduled a town meeting in response to correspondence they had received from Boston. This letter from the outside urged the people of Windham to join in a boycott; in other words, to think of politics in terms that extended far beyond the boundaries of the community. This invitation caused the villagers to take note of their "surprising fondness ... for the use and consumption of foreign and British manufactures." After a full discussion of the issues, they publicly pledged "to each other that we will discourage and discountenance to the utmost of our power the excessive use of all foreign teas, china ware, spices and black pepper, all British and foreign superfluities and manufactures."

By mobilizing people ordinarily excluded from colonial politics, the nonconsumption movement of this period greatly expanded the base of revolutionary activities. The Townshend boycott politicized even the most mundane items of the household economy and thereby politicized American women. Decisions about consumption could not be separated from decisions about politics. Within this electric atmosphere mothers and wives and daughters monitored the ideological commitment of the family. Throughout the colonies women altered styles of dress, wove homespun cloth and stopped drinking tea. At one wedding in Connecticut, country-women appeared in garments of their own making and insisted upon having "Labrador tea," a concoction brewed from indigenous herbs. Other women in New England participated in spinning and weaving competitions, community rituals of great symbolic complexity. The actual homespun was invested with political significance. But so too were the women themselves. Their efforts at the wheel, like those of Mahatma Gandhi[g] in another era, became local representations of a general ideology that connected the people of these communities – at least in their political imaginations – to unseen men and women in other American communities.[37]

The boycott of consumer goods also drew young people into the political debate. The students of Harvard, Yale, and the College of Rhode Island, for example, appeared at commencement during the late 1760s wearing homespun suits.[38] Though such displays irritated royal officials – that was the fun of it – they also transmitted political meanings through nonconsumption to other young people. This was an important element in the process of developing a national consciousness. In a society in which the average age was about sixteen, the young could not be taken for granted. A large percentage of the American population in 1776 had not even been born at the time of the Stamp Act crisis, and if college students had not been recruited into the boycott movement, they might not later as adults have appeared at Bunker Hill.

The circle of participation widened to include even the poorer members of colonial society, the kinds of people who were as dependent upon the consumer society as were their gentry neighbors. They collected rags required for the manufacture of "patriotic" paper. Goods – or in this case the denial of goods – were mobilizing an entire populace. Peter Oliver,[h] the Boston loyalist who later wrote an acerbic history of the Revolution, noted that during the protest against the Townshend duties, the city's radicals circulated:

A Subscription Paper ... Enumerating a great Variety of Articles not to be imported from *England*, which they supposed would muster the Manufacturers in *England* into a national Mob to support their Interests. Among the various prohibited Articles, were *Silks, Velvets, Clocks, Watches, Coaches & Chariots;* & it was highly diverting, to see the names & marks, to the Subscription, of Porters & Washing Women.[39]

Oliver found the incident amusing, an example of how a few troublemakers had duped the poorer sorts. But the porters and washerwomen of Boston knew what they were doing.[40] Affixing one's signature or mark to a document of this sort was a personal risk that they were willing to accept. Like the village women and the graduating students, these people had been mobilized through goods; it is difficult to see how independence could have been achieved without them.

The protest against the Townshend duties generated group activities that might best be termed "rituals of nonconsumption." These were focused moments in the life of a community during which continuing social relations were often, quite suddenly politicized. The spark for these events was usually a letter sent by some external body urging the villagers to support the boycott. In some towns large numbers of men and women took oaths before their neighbors swearing not to purchase certain items until parliament repealed the obnoxious taxes. These ceremonies possessed a curious religious character, much like the covenant renewals in the early Congregational churches of New England. In other communities specially selected committee-men carried subscription papers from house to house.[41]

Perhaps the most effective political ritual associated with nonconsumption, at least in New England, was the funeral. More than any other event connected with the life cycle, the funeral in eighteenth-century America had become an occasion of conspicuous consumption. Wealthy families distributed commemorative rings. Gloves were given out, and custom mandated that all attendants wear mourning dress made of the best imported cloth that they could afford. Indeed opulent funerals were in themselves an indication of the spread of the consumer society. "Such was the fashion," one colonist explained, that bereaved families imagined that if they disappointed their friends and neighbors, "they should have made themselves obnoxious to the censures of an ill-natured and malicious world, who would have construed their frugality into niggardliness."[42]

During the protest against the Townshend duties, such extravagant displays suddenly seemed inappropriate. A shift in the

symbolic meaning of British imports called forth a change in funeral etiquette. And since these were highly visible events, they
inevitably confronted those persons who had not thought deeply
about imperial politics with an ideological message. The freeholders and inhabitants of Boston agreed "not to use any Gloves
but what are manufactured here, nor any new Garments upon such
Occasion but what shall be absolutely necessary."[43] Everywhere
one saw signs of retrenchment at funerals, a trend that one anonymous writer declared "affected every true patriot with particular
satisfaction."[44]

The repeal of the Townshend Acts in 1770 retarded the growth
of national consciousness in the American colonies. Parliament's
apparent retreat on the issue of taxation revealed the symbolic
function that consumer goods had played in the constitutional
discourse. As political tensions within the empire eased, these
articles no longer carried such clear ideological meanings. Repeal,
in fact, unloosed a frenzy of consumption. Though the tax on tea
remained, the colonists could not be deterred from buying British
manufactures. Between 1770 and 1772 they set records for the
importation of foreign goods. Radical leaders such as Samuel
Adams warned the Americans that the threat to their political
liberties had not been removed. He begged them to continue their
resistance, to maintain the boycott. But few listened. Commerce
returned to the old channels, and as it did so, goods again became
associated with the Anglicization of American society. It is no
wonder that Adams grumbled in a letter to his friend Arthur Lee
that the colonial newspapers were once again filled with advertisements for "the Baubles of Britain."[45]

In 1773 parliament stumbled upon an element of mass political
mobilization that had been missing during the Townshend protest.
By passing the Tea Act, it united the colonists as they had never
been before. The reason for this new solidarity was not so much
that the Americans shared a common political ideology, but rather
that the statute affected an item of popular consumption found in
almost every colonial household. It was perhaps *the* major article
in the development of an eighteenth-century consumer society, a
beverage which, as we have seen, appeared on the tables of the
wealthiest merchants and the poorest laborers. For Americans,
therefore, it was not difficult to transmit perceptions of liberty and
rights through a discourse on tea. By transforming this ubiquitous
element of daily life into a symbol of political oppression, parliament

inadvertently boosted the growth of national consciousness. "Considering the article of tea as the detestable instrument which laid the foundation of the present sufferings of our distressed friends in the town of Boston," the members of the Virginia house of burgesses declared in August 1774, "we view it with horror, and therefore resolve that we will not, from this day, either import tea of any kind whatever, nor will we use or suffer, even such of it as is now at hand, to be used in any of our families."[46] And in the northern colonies, people now spoke of tea-drinkers not simply as enemies of our country – a term which in the 1760s had referred to one's colony or region – but as enemies "to the liberties of America."[47]

The public discourse over tea raised issues about the political effects of consumption that had been absent or muted during the previous decade. The language of goods became more shrill, hyperbolic. During the Stamp Act crisis, colonists associated consumption chiefly with personal debt. After parliament passed the Townshend duties, they talked more frequently in a moral vocabulary. By denying themselves the "baubles" of the mother country, they might thereby preserve their virtue. But in 1774 they spoke of tea as a badge of slavery, as a political instrument designed by distant tyrants to seize their property. "A WOMAN" argued in the *Massachusetts Spy* that:

> in the present case the use of tea is considered not as a *private* but as a *public* evil ... we are not to consider it merely as the herb tea, or what has an ill-tendency as to health, but as it is made a handle to introduce a variety of public grievances and oppressions amongst us.

Tea, A WOMAN concluded, is a sign of "enslaving our country."[48]

Throughout America the ceremonial destruction of tea strengthened the bonds of political solidarity. Once again, we must look to local communities for the embryonic stirrings of national consciousness. It was in these settings that a common commodity was transformed into the overarching symbol of political corruption. By purging the community of tea leaves – an import that could be found in almost every American home – the colonists reinforced their own commitment to certain political principles. But they did more. The destruction of the tea transmitted an unmistakable ideological message to distant communities: we stand together. The Boston Tea Party[i] is an event familiar to anyone who has heard of

the Revolution.[49] In many villages, however, the inhabitants publicly burned their tea. Everyone was expected to contribute some
leaves, perhaps a canister of tea hidden away in a pantry, a few
ounces, tea purchased long before parliament passed the hated
legislation, all of it to be destroyed in flames that purged the town
of ideological sin.

The seizure and destruction of tea became an effective instrument of political indoctrination, forcing the ignorant or indifferent
people of these communities publicly to commit themselves to the
cause of liberty while at the same time reinforcing the patriots'
commitment to a radical ideology. The individuals involved were
often ordinary men and women. Had they not become associated
with tea, they might have remained anonymous colonists, going
about their business and keeping their political opinions to themselves. But they were not so lucky. Early in 1774 Ebenezer
Withington, a "laborer" living in Dorchester, allegedly found some
tea on a road that ran along the ocean. Soon thereafter he was called
before a meeting of "Freeholders and other Inhabitants" where
Withington confessed in writing before his neighbors that:

> I found said Tea on Saturday, on going round the Marshes;
> brought off the same thinking no Harm; returning I met some
> Gentlemen belonging to the Castle [the British fort in Boston
> Harbour], who asked me if I had been picking up the Ruins?
> I asked them if there was any Harm; they said no except from
> my Neighbors. Accordingly, I brought Home the same, part
> of which I Disposed of, and the Remainder took from me
> since.

The townspeople decided that Withington had not realized the
political significance of his act. The people who had purchased tea
from him were warned to bring it to the village authorities immediately for destruction or risk having their names published as
enemies of the country.[50] The Dorchester committee – and committees in other towns as well – performed the same political function
that local militia units would serve during the Revolution. They
provided ideological instruction, and by so doing made it difficult
even for the poorest persons either to remain neutral or retain old
loyalties.[51]

During the summer of 1774 patriot spokesmen throughout
America called for some form of boycott. Boston's leaders, for
example, urged the people of Massachusetts to sign a Solemn

League and Covenant pledging to break off "all commercial connection with a country whose political Councils tend only to
enslave them".[52] Loyalists castigated this "infernal Scheme." In this
atmosphere almost any manufactured article could spark a dis-
pute. The League in fact threatened to bring the political battles of
the street into the home, "raising a most unnatural Enmity between
Parents & Children & Husbands & Wives."[53] People living in other
parts of America now looked to the Continental Congress for
guidance. As George Mason had recognized in 1770, a successful
boycott required the united and coordinated efforts of all the
colonists. When the congressional delegates convened in September 1774, they passed legislation almost immediately, creating the
Association, a vast network of local committees charged with
enforcing nonimportation. This was a truly radical act. In an attempt to halt further commerce with Great Britain, Congress
authorized every county, city and town in America to establish a
revolutionary government.[54] As Henry Laurens[j] explained in September 1774:

> From the best intelligence that I have received, my con-
> clusions are, that So. Carolina, No. Carolina, Virginia, Maryland,
> Pensylvania [sic], New Jersey, New York, Connecticut, Rhode
> Island, Massachusets [sic], New Hampshire, one chain of
> Colonies extending upwards of 1,200 Miles & containing
> about three Millions of White Inhabitants of whom upwards
> of 500,000 [are] Men capable of bearing Arms, will unite in an
> agreement to Import no goods from Great Britain, the West
> India Islands, or Africa until those Acts of Parliament which
> Strike at our Liberties are Repealed.[55]

The colonists responded enthusiastically to the call. The committees monitored consumption, identifying local patriots by the
garments they wore and by the beverages they drank, and demanding public confessions from those who erred. In Virginia counties
everyone was expected to sign the Association, a promise before
one's neighbors – almost a statement of one's new birth as a
consumer – not to purchase the despised manufactures of the
mother country. According to James Madison, these signings were
"the method used among us to distinguish friends from foes and
to oblige the Common people to a more strict observance of it [the
Association]."[56] As in earlier boycotts, people sorted themselves
out politically through goods. A committee in Prince George's

County announced, "That to be clothed in manufactures fabricated in the Colonies ought to be considered as a badge and distinction of respect and true patriotism."[57] The local associations also educated ordinary men and women about the relation between consumer goods and constitutional rights, in other words, about the relation between experience and ideology. A committee in Anne Arundel County, Maryland, helped Thomas Charles Williams understand that by importing tea he had "endangered the rights and liberties of America." Proceedings against Williams were dropped, after he proclaimed that he was "sincerely sorry for his offense."[58] Silas Newcomb of Cumberland, New Jersey, was more stubborn. The members of the local association failed to convince the man of his error in drinking "East-India Tea in his family," and they were finally compelled "to break off all dealings with him, and in this manner publish the truth of the case, that he may be distinguished from the friends of American liberty."[59]

III

The colonists who responded to Boston's call in 1774 were consciously repudiating the empire of goods. Within barely a generation the meaning of the items of everyday consumption had changed substantially. At mid-century imported articles – the cloth, the ceramics, the buttons – had served as vehicles of Anglicization, and as they flooded into the homes of yeomen and gentry alike, they linked ordinary men and women with the distant, exciting culture of the metropolis. By participating in the marketplace, by making choices among competing manufactures, the colonists became in some important sense English people who happened to live in the provinces. By taxing these goods, however, parliament set in motion a process of symbolic redefinition, slow and painful at first, punctuated by lulls that encouraged the false hope that the empire of goods could survive, but ultimately straining Anglicization to breaking-point. Americans who had never dealt with one another, who lived thousands of miles apart, found that they could communicate their political grievances through goods or, more precisely, through the denial of goods that had held the empire together. Private consumer experiences were transformed into public rituals. Indeed many colonists learned about rights and liberties through these common consumer items, articles which in themselves were politically neutral, but which in the explosive atmosphere of the 1760s and 1770s became the medium through which ideological abstractions acquired concrete meaning.

When the colonists finally and reluctantly decided that they could do without the "baubles of Britain," they destroyed a vital cultural bond with the mother country. "The country," explained James Lovell to his friend Joseph Trumbull in December 1774, "... seems determined to let England know that in the present struggle, commerce has lost all the temptations of a bait to catch the American farmer."[60] Lovell may have exaggerated, but he helps us to understand why in 1774 the countryside supported the cities. Consumer goods had made it possible for the colonists to imagine a nation; the Association made it easier for Americans to imagine independence.

EDITOR'S NOTES

a   John Adams (1735–1826), New England lawyer, prominent patriot, and later president of the United States.

b   Radical country thought stressed the dangers inherent in a powerful government, warning that political power was always to be feared, and arguing that the price of liberty was eternal vigilance.

c   The Navigation Acts (1651–73) asserted English control of its colonial trade by creating a closed system within which only citizens of the empire had the right to trade.

d   The Stamp Act of March 1765 placed taxes on legal documents, customs papers, newspapers, almanacs, college diplomas, playing cards, and dice. It was repealed in March 1766.

e   John Dickinson (1732–1808), Pennsylvania lawyer, pamphleteer during the Revolutionary crisis, and prominent nationalist.

f   John Trenchard and Thomas Gordon, opposition thinkers in Britain, collaborated on *The Independent Whig* (1720) and *Cato's Letters* (1720–3), which were extremely influential in the colonies.

g   In the early twentieth century Mahatma Gandhi promoted *swadeshi* (home) industries and the boycott of foreign goods as a key theme of Indian nationalism.

h   Peter Oliver (1713–91), chief justice of Massachusetts, went into exile after the Revolution.

i   The Boston Tea Party occurred on December 16, 1773.

j   Henry Laurens (1724–92), South Carolina merchant-planter, and notable patriot.

NOTES

World Copyright: The Past and Present Society, 175 Banbury Road, Oxford, England. This article is reprinted with the permission of the society and the author, from *Past and Present: A Journal of Historical Studies*, no. 119 (1988): 73-104.

1 Andrew Burnaby, *Travels through North America* (New York, 1904): 152-3.
2 *The Works of John Adams*, ed. C. F. Adams, 10 vols. (Boston, 1850-6), X:283; John Adams to Hezekiah Niles, February 13, 1818.
3 Benedict Anderson, *Imagined Communities: Reflections on the Origin and Spread of Nationalism* (London, 1983); Linda Colley, "Whose Nation? Class and National Consciousness in Britain, 1750-1830," *Past and Present*, 113 (November 1986): 97-117; Geoff Eley, "Nationalism and Social History," *Social History*, vi (1981): 83-107; Richard L. Merritt, *Symbols of American Community, 1735-1775* (New Haven, 1966).
4 I discuss this historiographic debate in *Tobacco Culture: The Mentality of the Great Tidewater Planters on the Eve of Revolution* (Princeton, 1985): chap. 1. See also Gordon S. Wood, "Rhetoric and Reality in the American Revolution," *William and Mary Quarterly*, 3rd ser., xxiii (1966): 3-32.
5 See Mihaly Czikszentmihalyi and Eugene Rochberg-Halton, *The Meaning of Things: Domestic Symbols and the Self* (Cambridge, 1981).
6 See Lynn A. Hunt, *Politics, Culture and Class in the French Revolution* (Berkeley, Calif., 1984); Anthony Giddens, *The Constitution of Society: Outline of the Theory of Structuration* (Berkeley, Calif., 1984); Marshall Sahlins, *Islands of History* (Chicago, 1985).
7 The literature on the development of an Anglo-American consumer society during the eighteenth century is quite large. Works that were particularly helpful for this investigation include Charles Wilson, *England's Apprenticeship, 1603-1763* (Cambridge, 1965); Ralph Davis, *A Commercial Revolution in English Overseas Trade in the Seventeenth and Eighteenth Centuries* (London, 1967); Roy Porter, *English Society in the Eighteenth Century* (Harmondsworth, 1982); Harold Perkin, *The Origins of Modern English Society* (London, 1969); Neil McKendrick, John Brewer, and J. H. Plumb, *The Birth of a Consumer Society: The Commercialization of Eighteenth-Century England* (Bloomington, Ind., 1982); Eric Jones, "The Fashion Manipulators: Consumer Tastes and British Industries, 1660-1800," in Louis P. Cain and Paul J. Uselding, eds., *Business Enterprise and Economic Change: Essays in Honor of Harold F. Williamson* (Kent, Ohio, 1973): 198-226; Lorna Weatherill, "A Possession of One's Own: Women and Consumer Behaviour in England, 1660-1740," *Journal of British Studies*, xxv (1986): 131-56; Joanna Innes, "Review Article: Jonathan Clark, Social History and England's 'Ancien Regime'," *Past and Present*, 115 (May 1987): 165-200.
8 *Archives of Maryland, lix: Proceedings and Acts of the General Assembly of Maryland, 1764-1765*, ed. J. Hall Pleasants (Baltimore, 1942): 210.
9 I have reviewed the literature of consumer behavior in eighteenth-century America in "An Empire of Goods: The Anglicization of Colonial America, 1690-1776", *Journal of British Studies*, xxv (1986): 467-99. See also John J. McCusker and Russell R. Menard, *The Economy of British America, 1607-1789* (Chapel Hill, N.C., 1985): chap. 13; Carole

Shammas "How Self-Sufficient Was Early America?", *Journal of Interdisciplinary History*, xiii (1982): 247–72; Gloria Main, "The Standard of Living in Colonial Massachusetts," *Journal of Economic History*, xliii (1983): 101–8; Lorena S. Walsh, "Urban Amenities and Rural Sufficiency: Living Standards and Consumer Behavior in the Colonial Chesapeake, 1643–1777," *Journal of Economic History*, xliii (1983): 109–17; Marc Egnal and Joseph A. Ernst, "An Economic Interpretation of the American Revolution," *William and Mary Quarterley*, 3rd ser., xxix (1972): 3–32. An interpretation of the character of the eighteenth-century American economy that differs substantially from the one advanced here can be found in James A. Henretta, "Families and Farms: *Mentalité* in Pre-Industrial America," *William and Mary Quarterly*, 3rd ser., xxxv (1978): 3–32.

10 [Janet Schaw], *Journal of a Lady of Quality ... 1774 to 1776*, ed. Evangeline W. Andrews and Charles M. Andrews (New Haven, 1921): 204.

11 *Diary and Autobiography of John Adams*, ed. L. H. Butterfield, 4 vols. (New York, 1964), I:294.

12 Alexander Hamilton, *Gentleman's Progress: Itinerarium of Dr. Alexander Hamilton*, ed. Carl Bridenbaugh (Chapel Hill, N.C., 1948): 13–14.

13 John Hemphill, "John Wayles Rates his Neighbors," *Virginia Magazine of History and Biography*, lxvi (1958): 305.

14 See Richard L. Bushman, "American High Style and Vernacular Cultures," in Jack P. Greene and J. Pole (eds.), *Colonial British America: Essays in the New History of the Early Modern Era* (Baltimore, 1984): 345–83.

15 Public Record Office, London, C.O. 5/1330, Francis Fauquier, "Answers to the Queries Sent to Me by the Right Honourable the Lords Commissioners for Trade and Plantation Affairs," January 30, 1763. See also Breen,"Empire of Goods": 485–96.

16 Cited in Esther Singleton, *Social New York under the Georges, 1714–1776* (New York, 1902): 380–1.

17 ibid.: 375.

18 William Smith, *The History of the Late Province of New-York ... 1762* (New York Hist. Soc. Collections, iv, pt. 2, 1829): 281.

19 Cited in Rodis Roth, "Tea Drinking in Eighteenth-Century America: Its Etiquette and Equipage," in *Contributions from the Museum of History and Technology*, paper 14 (U.S. National Museum, ccxxv, Washington, D.C., 1961): 66.

20 Billy G. Smith, "The Material Lives of Laboring Philadelphians, 1750 to 1800," *William and Mary Quarterly*, 3rd ser., xxxviii (1981): 168.

21 Henry P. Hedges, *A History of the Town of East-Hampton* (Sag-Harbor, N.Y., 1897): 142.

22 Stephen Botein, "The Anglo-American Book Trade before 1776: Personnel and Strategies", in William L. Joyce *et al.*, eds., *Printing and Society in Early America* (Worcester, Mass., 1983): 79.

23 *The Writings of George Washington*, ed. John C. Fitzpatrick, 39 vols. (Washington, D.C., 1931), II:350, George Washington to Robert Cary and Co., September 28, 1760.

24 William Eddis, *Letters from America*, ed. Aubrey C. Land (Cambridge,

Mass., 1969): 57–8.

25 D. D. Hall, "Religion and Society: Problems and Reconsiderations," in Greene and Pole, eds., *Colonial British America*: 337–8. The most famous evangelical of the period, George Whitefield, embraced the latest merchandizing techniques, literally selling the revival to the American people. The crowds flocked to hear Whitefield, while his critics grumbled about the commercialization of religion. One anonymous writer in Massachusetts noted that there is "a very wholesome law of the province to discourage Pedlars in Trade" and it seems high time "to enact something for the discouragement of Pedlars in Divinity also": *Boston Weekly News-Letter*, April 22, 1742.

26 John Dickinson, "The Late Regulations Respecting the British Colonies" (1765), in *The Writings of John Dickinson*, ed. Paul Leicester Ford, 2 vols. (Philadelphia, 1895), I: 217 (emphasis added).

27 The psychological implications of economic "disappointment" are imaginatively discussed in Albert O. Hirschman, *Shifting Involvements: Private Interest and Public Action* (Princeton, 1982). See also Tibor Scitovsky, *The Joyless Economy: An Inquiry into Human Satisfaction and Consumer Dissatisfaction* (New York, 1976).

28 Bernard Bailyn, *The Ideological Origins of the American Revolution* (Cambridge, Mass., 1967); Gordon Wood, *The Creation of the American Republic, 1776–1787* (Chapel Hill, N.C., 1969); Edmund S. Morgan, "The Puritan Ethic and the American Revolution," *William and Mary Quarterly*, 3rd ser., xxiv (1967): 3–43.

29 William T. Baxter, *The House of Hancock: Business in Boston, 1724–1775* (Cambridge, Mass., 1945): 239–42; Egnal and Ernst, "Economic Interpretation of the American Revolution"; Breen, *Tobacco Culture*: chap. 3–5.

30 See Edmund S. Morgan and Helen M. Morgan, *The Stamp Act Crisis: Prologue to Revolution* (Chapel Hill, N.C., 1953).

31 *Boston Gazette*, October 1, 1764. Also Arthur M. Schlesinger, *The Colonial Merchants and the American Revolution, 1763–1776* (Columbia University, Studies in History, Economics and Public Law, lxxviii, 182, New York, 1918): 63–5; Charles M. Andrews, "Boston Merchants and the Non-Importation Movement," *Transactions of the Colonial Society of Massachusetts*, xix (1916–17): 182–91. For a discussion of the cultural meaning of debt in this period, see Breen, *Tobacco Culture*.

32 Merritt Jensen, *The Founding of a Nation: A History of the American Revolution, 1763–1776* (New York, 1968): 237–344; Andrews, "Boston Merchants": 191–252.

33 *Boston Gazette*, January 11, 1768.

34 *A Report of the Record Commissioners of the City of Boston Containing the Boston Town Records, 1758 to 1769* (Boston, 1886): 227–8.

35 ibid.: 221. Also "Virginia Nonimportation Resolutions, 1769," in *The Papers of Thomas Jefferson*, ed. Julian P. Boyd, 22 vols. (Princeton, 1953), I: 28–9.

36 Cited in Andrews, "Boston Merchants": 92.

37 Andrews, "Boston Merchants": 193–4. Also Linda K. Kerber, *Women of the Republic: Intellect and Ideology in Revolutionary America* (Chapel Hill,

N.C., 1980): 38–41.
38 Andrews, "Boston Merchants": 195–7.
39 ibid.: 197; Peter Oliver, *Origin and Progress of the American Revolution: A Tory View*, ed. Douglass Adair and John A. Schutz (Stanford, 1961): 61.
40 See Alfred F. Young, "George Robert Twelves Hewes, 1742–1840: A Boston Shoemaker and the Memory of the American Revolution," *William and Mary Quarterly*, 3rd ser., xxxviii (1981): 561–623.
41 Andrews,"Boston Merchants": 209–14; Schlesinger, *Colonial Merchants*: chap. 3.
42 *Massachusetts Spy*, January 6, 1774. Also Robert A. Gross, *The Minutemen and their World* (New York, 1976): 33.
43 *Report of the Record Commissioners*: 224. Also Andrews, "Boston Merchants": 196; Morgan and Morgan, *Stamp Act Crisis*: 247–8.
44 *Massachusetts Spy*: January 6, 1774.
45 *The Writings of Samuel Adams*, ed. Harry Alonzo Cushing, 4 vols. (New York, 1904–8), II: 267.
46 "Virginia Non-Importation Agreement", August 1, 1774, in *Documents of American History*: 80.
47 "New York Sons of Liberty Resolutions on Tea", November 24, 1773; ibid.: 70.
48 *Massachusetts Spy*: January 6, 1774; also ibid.: January 13, 20, August 25, 1774.
49 See Benjamin Woods Labaree, *The Boston Tea Party* (New York, 1964).
50 *Massachusetts Spy*: January 13, 1774.
51 On the responsibility of the colonial militias to indoctrinate citizens, see John W. Shy, *A People Numerous and Armed: Reflections on the Military Struggles for American Independence* (New York, 1976): 193–224.
52 *American Archives*, comp. Force, 4th ser., i: 397–8; Jensen, *Founding of a Nation*: 468–75; Schlesinger, *Colonial Merchants*: 319–26; Gross, *Minutemen*: 47, 50–1.
53 Oliver, *Origin and Progress of the American Revolution*: 104.
54 Jensen, *Founding of a Nation*: 506–7.
55 *The Papers of Henry Laurens*, ed. George C. Rogers, Jr., 10 vols. (Columbia, S.C., 1981) IX: 552, Henry Laurens to Peter Petrie, September 7, 1774.
56 *Papers of James Madison*, ed. W. T. Hutchinson and William M. E. Rachal, 3 vols. (Chicago, 1962), I: 135, James Madison to William Bradford, January 20, 1775.
57 *American Archives*, comp. Force, 4th ser., i: 494.
58 ibid.: 1061.
59 ibid., ii: 34.
60 Cited in Jensen, *Founding of a Nation*: 561.

Part IV

CONCLUSION

In this concluding article, John Murrin engages themes central to all the previous essayists. His view of regional diversity and continental uniformities addresses the concerns of Bailyn and Greene; the prominence he attaches to the role of Indians and blacks dovetails with the work of Merrell and Berlin; and the importance he ascribes to religion, family, and the growing integration of empire connects with the studies of Butler, Isaac, Ulrich, and Breen. Murrin's assessments will not be the last word, but his essay indicates the promise of syntheses that encompass a multiplicity of approaches to colonial America.

9

BENEFICIARIES OF CATASTROPHE: THE ENGLISH COLONISTS IN AMERICA

John M. Murrin

John Murrin's essay provides an apt summary of many of the themes of this reader and an engaging overview in its own right. He begins by juxtaposing two views of colonial America: triumph or tragedy, heroic epic or nightmare? Murrin uses the findings of historical demographers to demonstrate that colonization's human toll was mind-numbing. The world's largest holocaust occurred in the Americas. Murrin recognizes that the interplay of cultural groups was extensive and often cooperative. Nevertheless, his summary of early Indian–white contact inspires the provocative conclusion that "Most American colonies were founded by terrorists." And he emphasizes that the same cheap land which provided unprecedented opportunities for Europeans also led many Africans into bondage. Liberation and enslavement were flip sides of the same coin. From these perspectives, Murrin's view of colonial America appears to be resoundingly negative. Early America was a catastrophe.

But focusing on the settler communities allows a more positive view. Free colonists did, after all, achieve a higher level of material wellbeing than any of their contemporaries. But Murrin is most impressed by the staggering diversity of colonial experiences. Again, he turns to historical demography to document the extraordinary variations in life expectancy, rate of natural increase, and family structure from one region to the next. He concludes that the colonies formed a "broad spectrum" of settlements, suggesting that proximity tended to mute differences, and distance enlarge them.

Murrin sees convergence, but it is brought about, he argues, only by the colonies' increasing integration within the British empire. For Murrin, the American Revolution was not the logical culmination of a growing sense of separateness among the American settlers. Rather, it was an ironic outcome of the absorption of the colonies by the empire.

* * *

Most Americans regard our colonial era as a heroic period. Bold men and women, often fired by a sense of divine mission or by a quest for a fuller and juster life than Europe could offer, braved the severities of an Atlantic crossing, attacked the "howling wilderness," erected their tiny settlements, established large and thriving families, and somehow still found time to create the free institutions that remain even today the basis for our democratic society. Eighteenth-century Europeans saw things differently. The generation that witnessed the American Revolution also debated the moral significance of the discovery of the Americas and the establishment of European trade and settlement in both the East and West Indies. Abbé Guillaume Thomas François Raynal in France and Dr. William Robertson[a] in Scotland found little to praise and much to condemn. "I dare to state it," agreed Joseph Mandrillon, a minor philosophe, "the discovery of America was an evil. Never can the advantages it brought about (no matter how one considers or depicts them) compensate for the harm it has caused." To educated and thoughtful Europeans, the opening of the Americas seemed one of the greatest moral monstrosities of all time.

The philosophes estimated that the conquest and settlement of the Americas cost the lives of some 20 million people, most of them Amerindians. They admitted that the process led to swift improvements in navigational techniques, shipbuilding, mapmaking, and related skills and that it certainly quickened the pace of European commerce. But, they insisted, most of these positive assets were used only to exchange vices between the hemispheres. Europeans carried cruelty, greed, slaves and enslavement, disease and death to the Americas. They brought back syphilis, gold and silver to fuel inflation and an interminable cycle of destructive wars, and such products as tobacco and sugar to undermine the health of people who never even got close to the New World. Early America was a catastrophe – a horror story, not an epic.

America's revolutionary leaders – such as Benjamin Franklin and Thomas Jefferson, who both served the new republic as ministers to the court of Louis XVI – resented these arguments and the related claim that the environment of the New World was so enfeebling that, over time, it caused all forms of life to degenerate. American plants and animals had less variety and vitality than those of Europe, Asia, or Africa, insisted most careful observers, who were particularly struck by the paucity of large mammals in the Western Hemisphere. Humans who moved to the Americas would surely inflict the same degeneracy upon their descendants, the philosophes warned. Jefferson once met this criticism by persuading a friend to ship a moose to France as a typical example of an American deer. But European sentiment was already beginning to shift by then. Many philosophes readily conceded that the American Revolution might herald a daring new departure for all mankind. Its message of liberty and equality, constitutionalism married to popular sovereignty, reverberated throughout much of Europe. Indeed, the success of the revolution ended the debate over whether America was a hideous mistake, or at least banished that perception to what is now the Third World. Even historians usually regard this controversy as more amusing than instructive.

Until recently, American colonial history recounted the activities of Europeans in America: the institutions they established, the liberties they fought to secure, the ideas they propounded about God, man, and society. But as in other fields of American history, since the 1960s scholars have turned to large problems of social history. Who were the settlers? Where did they come from? What sorts of communities did they struggle to create? Who was here when they arrived? Where did the colonists get their slaves? What happened when these very different cultures came together?

Research in elementary numbers during the 1970s and 1980s ought to revive the Enlightenment[b] controversy about early America. Reasonable estimates now exist for the flow of people across the Atlantic, including the volume of the African slave trade from the fifteenth through the nineteenth century. Some of the most imaginative scholarship of the past generation has gone into reconstructing the approximate size of the pre-Columbian Indian population in several major portions of the Americas, a necessary prelude to measuring the impact of European intrusion. Together these materials tell a story a good deal more dismal than even the philosophes had quite imagined.

The figure of 20 million dead falls far short of the true total, which was at least double and perhaps triple that number. Of course, many Europeans on both the eastern and western shores of the Atlantic benefited immensely from the settlement process. Most actors on all sides of the transatlantic drama made rational choices in their own best interests, including even the slaves, once they understood what few options they still retained. But using the elementary utilitarian criterion of the greatest good for the greatest number as a crude but revealing way of assessing the overall process, nobody can now make a compelling case that the settlement of the Americas was a net benefit to mankind until some time in the nineteenth century. In aggregate terms, losers far outnumbered winners until then. Unlike the philosophes, today's historians see what happened in early America not as a moralistic melodrama but as a tragedy of such huge proportions that one's imagination cannot easily encompass it all. The truest villains were microbes, whose predations acquired an inevitable momentum that quickly made human motivation all but irrelevant for the deadliest part of the process.

Before 1820 about 11 million people crossed the Atlantic from Europe and Africa to the Caribbean, North America, and South America. The overwhelming majority, about 8 million, came against their will – in chains. African slaves constituted almost three-fourths of the entire migration. Only in the period between 1820 and 1840 would the number of free passengers catch up with and then decisively surpass the volume of the slave trade throughout the Atlantic world. For more than three centuries, in other words, the slave trade was no unfortunate excess on the periphery of free migration. It was the norm.

The situation was less extreme in the English colonies, at least on the mainland, than elsewhere. About 380,000 people left the British Isles for England's North American and Caribbean colonies before 1700. A huge majority came from England and Wales, not Scotland or Ireland. They were joined by 10,000 or more other Europeans, mostly from the Netherlands and France. During the seventeenth century almost 350,000 slaves, or about 47 percent of the people crossing the Atlantic to the English colonies, left Africa to provide coerced labor for these new societies. Three-fourths of the entire human wave went to the West Indies, which attracted over 220,000 settlers (roughly 56 percent of the Europeans) and nearly 320,000 slaves (about 91 percent of the Africans). The Chesapeake colonies drew nearly 120,000 settlers (32 percent) and at least 25,000 slaves (7 percent). The Middle Atlantic region claimed a net of some 20,000 colonists (just over 5 percent) and a few thousand slaves. After outmigrants are subtracted, probably fewer than 20,000 Europeans and an insignificant trickle of Africans went to New England.

Patterns changed during the eighteenth century. The African slave trade hit its all-time peak as over 6.1 million people were dragged aboard ships headed for the Americas – nearly 45 percent of them traveling in British or American vessels. Losses in transit probably approached or exceeded 20 percent until at least mid-century but improved somewhat after that. Slaves were not the only unwilling migrants. Between 1718 and 1775 Great Britain shipped 50,000 convicts to North America, most of them to Maryland or Virginia.

Recent estimates indicate that between 150,000 and 230,000 Europeans entered the mainland colonies from 1700 to 1760, fairly close to the probable minimum of 180,000 slaves imported during the same period. Most of the voluntary immigrants came from new sources in the eighteenth century. Between 1700 and 1760 nearly 60,000 Germans and more than 30,000 Irish settlers and servants sailed for the Delaware Valley alone. Thousands of others – Irish, Scottish, English, and German – landed in New York, the Chesapeake, and the lower South. London registration records indicate that the British capital continued to send perhaps 800 indentured servants to the colonies per year from 1718 to 1759. No doubt the capital and the home counties provided other migrants as well. Northern England probably contributed a sizable (as yet untabulated) stream.

After the fall of New France in 1760, immigration exploded: 55,000 Irish, 40,000 Scots, 30,000 English, 12,000 Germans, and 84,500 slaves swarmed into North America. Totaling more than 220,000 people, the newcomers equaled nearly a seventh of the total population of just under 1.6 million people in the mainland colonies in 1760. Their story – where they came from and how they got to America – has been marvelously told in Bernard Bailyn's Pulitzer Prize-winning study, *Voyagers to the West* (1986). The typical colonist from southern England was an unmarried male in his teens or early twenties who often possessed artisanal skills and brought with him a set of optimistic expectations. He was most likely to settle in Virginia or Maryland, and he probably left home because of the pull of the New World, not out of exasperation with England. The characteristic *émigré* from north Britain (Ulster, Scotland, and northern England) sailed to America as part of an intact family. The head of the household was typically in his thirties, was frequently a farmer, and carried bitter memories of the social environment he was leaving – heavy taxes, rack-renting[c] landlords, unemployment or underemployment. He usually led his family to Pennsylvania, New York, or North Carolina.

Statistically, the British colonial world as a whole approximated the dismal norm set by other Atlantic empires in the eighteenth century. Over 1.5 million slaves left Africa for British colonies in the West Indies and North America, outnumbering by three to one the half-million free migrants who sailed for the same provinces. In the islands, however, slave imports overwhelmed free immigrants by about ten to one. On the mainland, slaves probably outnumbered other newcomers in most decades between 1700 and 1760, but for the continent and the century as a whole, free migrants exceeded slaves by a margin of roughly four to three over the entire period, with most of the edge for voluntary migrants coming after 1760.

Settlers and slaves carried with them microbes that were far more deadly than muskets and cannon to Indian peoples with virtually no immunities to smallpox, measles, and even simple bronchial infections. The result was the greatest known demographic catastrophe in the history of the world, a population loss that usually reached or exceeded 90 percent in any given region within a century of contact with the invaders. In warm coastal areas such as the West Indies and much of Brazil, it approached complete extinction in a much shorter time. By Russell Thornton's careful estimates, the pre-Columbian population of the Americas exceeded 70 million, or about one-seventh of the 500 million people then inhabiting the globe; high estimates for the Americas run to double this number. Mexico probably had more than 20 million when Hernan Cortés arrived in 1519, Peru from 8 to 12 million, the Caribbean at least 10 million (some estimates run much higher), the continent north of the Rio Grande close to 8 million (with about 5.7 million in what is now the lower forty-eight states), Brazil over 3 million, and the rest of South America several million more. By comparison, Europe east of the Urals probably had about 55 million people in 1500 – living, to be sure, in a much smaller geographical area. The Indian population of 1492 thus outnumbered all European immigrants to 1820 by a ratio of perhaps twenty-five to one and all the Africans who arrived by maybe nine to one.

Disease demolished these numerical advantages. The Carib Indians had virtually disappeared from the Greater Antilles by 1550. Mexico's 20 million had plummeted to 730,000 by 1620, and Peru's 10 million to 600,000. The Americas were never a "virgin land"; in Francis Jennings's melancholy but telling phrase, they became a "widowed land." By the mid-eighteenth century Europeans outnumbered Africans except in Brazil, the West Indies, and South

Carolina, but nearly everywhere south of Pennsylvania (except in Mexico and a few other localities that did not rely heavily on African slavery) blacks outnumbered Indians within regions of European settlement.

Interaction among the three cultures was extensive. The plants and animals of the Western Hemisphere seemed so strange to Europeans that without knowledgeable occupants to tell them what was edible and how it could be prepared, the intruders would have found far greater difficulty in surviving. The first explorers or settlers to arrive in a region, for instance, nearly always had to barter for food. Indian trails showed them the easiest ways to get from one place to another and where to portage streams and rivers. Indian canoes and snowshoes displayed an ingenuity and utility that Europeans quickly borrowed. Settlers also learned from their slaves. Africans, for example, may well have taught South Carolina planters how to cultivate rice. From their masters, in turn, Africans acquired knowledge of the prevailing European language and, more slowly, Christian convictions.

For their part, Indians greatly valued firearms whenever they could get them. Those who acquired them early, such as the Iroquois, won huge advantages over neighboring tribes. Indian women quickly discovered the benefits of European pots, but imported textiles took longer to find Indian markets. Not so alcohol. It exacted a fierce toll from a people who had no cultural experience with its intoxicating powers.

Yet Indian society had many built-in immunities to European influences. Although most Indian tribes in North America were agricultural, they also spent part of the year hunting. Their crops gave them a strong attachment to the land but not the European sense of exclusive ownership of individual plots. The need to move every year also prevented Indians from developing large permanent dwellings and necessarily restricted their desire and capacity to consume European goods. Because women erected and controlled the home environment (wigwam, tepee, or longhouse in North America), they had no wish to own any more products than they were willing to lug from one place to another several times a year. Women also did the routine agricultural labor in Indian societies, a practice that seemed degrading to male European observers. The consequences of their attitude were significant: however well intentioned, European efforts to "civilize" the Indians by converting warriors into farmers seldom succeeded, for at the deepest cultural level these demands amounted to nothing less than an attempt to turn men into women. When Indians did copy the agricultural practices of the settlers, slavery often provided a necessary intermediating mechanism. Nineteenth-century Cherokee warriors, for instance, were willing to become planters who forced other men to work for them in the fields.

War provided a grisly but frequent point of cultural contact, and perhaps no activity did more to intensify mutual misunderstanding. European geopolitical norms had little resonance among Indians, who were far more likely to fight for captives than for territory or trade. Aztecs waged continuous war to provide thousands of sacrifices for their gods every year. Most North American Indians practiced analogous rites but on a much smaller scale, and they were far more likely to keep their prisoners. Indeed, Indians often fought in order to replace losses by death, a phenomenon called "the mourning war." Epidemics, which utterly demoralized some tribes, accelerated warfare among others, such as the Iroquois in the northern or the Catawba in the deep southern region of what is now the United States. As the death toll from imported disease climbed at appalling rates, these tribes struggled to make up for their losses.

In the process Indian societies proved far more openly assimilationist than European colonies were. The Iroquois, for example, seem to have begun by absorbing such similar neighbors as the Hurons and other tribes who spoke Iroquoian dialects. When that supply ran thin, the Iroquois turned to Algonquian tribes. As early as the 1650s or 1660s, most of the people who claimed to be members of the Five Nations of the Iroquois Confederation had not been born Iroquois. They were adoptees. Only in this way could the confederacy preserve its numbers and its strength. Even this strategy was failing by the 1690s, when virtually all potential enemies had equal access to muskets and gunpowder, and the price of war became heavier than its benefits. In 1701 the Five Nations chose a policy of neutrality toward both the English and the French, and thereafter they usually confined their wars with other Indians to fighting distant southerly tribes.

During the eighteenth century some Indian communities adopted significant numbers of Europeans and granted them and their descendants full equality with other members of the tribe. Women usually decided which captives to adopt and which to execute, often after deliberate torture. Most of those tortured and killed were adult men; most of those adopted were women and children, whether Europeans or other Indians. European women who spent a year or more in captivity quite often made a voluntary choice to remain. This decision baffled and dismayed the European men they left behind, including in many cases a husband and children. Adult male settlers found it inexplicable that "civilized" women, some of whom were even church members in full communion, could actually prefer a "savage" life and would not object to toiling in the fields. In fact, Indian women enjoyed greater respect within their tribes than European housewives received from their own communities, and Indian women worked fewer hours and participated more openly in making important decisions, including questions of war and peace. Adoptees shared fully in these benefits; some adopted males even became chiefs.

On the other hand, Indian fondness for torture shocked and enraged most settlers. Warriors took pride in their ability to withstand the most excruciating torment without complaint. The ideal brave chanted defiant war songs or hurled verbal abuse at his tormentors until the end. Europeans, who did not share these values, screamed horribly, wept, and begged for mercy until they finally died. But their people nearly always won the war. From an Indian perspective, the weak were indeed inheriting the earth.

Europeans were accustomed to fighting for trade and territory; unlike Indians, they showed almost no inclination to capture opponents, adopt them, and assimilate them fully into their culture. Their Indian captives became slaves instead and seldom lived long. Exceptions to this pattern did occur, though rarely as a result of war. On Martha's Vineyard and Nantucket, for instance, most Indians did convert to Christianity in the seventeenth century, and in the eighteenth – until disease radically diminished their numbers – many of them went to sea as skilled harpoonists on whaling vessels.

Such examples of peaceful cooperation and borrowing did little to mitigate the ferocity of war when it occurred. Because the settlers regarded themselves as "civilized" and all Indians as "savages," they saw little point in observing their lingering rules of chivalry in these conflicts. Often encumbered in the early years by armor and heavy weapons, they could not keep up with Indian warriors in the wilderness and were not very skillful at tracking opponents through dense forest. But they could find the Indians' villages, burn them, and destroy their crops. In early Virginia, New England, and

New Netherland, the intruders – not the Indians – introduced the tactic of the deliberate and systematic massacre of a whole community, which usually meant the women, children, and elderly who had been left behind when the warriors took to the forest. The intruders went even further. Often women and children became their targets of choice, as in the Mystic River campaign of 1637 during the Pequot War, when Puritan soldiers ignored a fort manned by warriors to incinerate another a few miles away, which was packed with the tribe's noncombatants. The motive for this kind of warfare was not at all mysterious. It was not genocide in any systematic sense; settlers relied too heavily on Indians to try to get rid of all of them. The real purpose was terror. Outnumbered in a hostile land, Europeans used deliberate terror against one tribe to send a grisly warning to all others nearby. This practice struck the Indians as at least as horrible and senseless as torture seemed to the Europeans, but it could be grimly effective. Most American colonies were founded by terrorists.

Americans like to see their history as a chronicle of progress. Indeed it is. Considering how it began, it could only improve. The internal development of the settler communities is a story of growth and innovation. Ordinary free families in the English colonies achieved a level of economic autonomy and wellbeing difficult to match anywhere else at that time. Starvation, for example, was never a problem after the very early years, but it continued to threaten most other communities around the world. The main reason for the contrast was, of course, the availability of land in North America, which made subsistence relatively simple once the newcomers understood what crops to grow. It also tended to make younger sons the equals of the eldest, because in most families they could all expect to inherit land.

Before 1700, however, the human cost was immense for most colonists, and it got much worse for Africans in the eighteenth century, the period in which the Atlantic slave trade peaked. Cheap land meant scarce labor – the same principle that liberated Europeans enslaved Africans – and the coercion of outsiders became the most obvious answer to the shortage. The quest for material improvement motivated the vast majority of settlers and servants who crossed the ocean, and they had few scruples about depriving outsiders of their liberty in order to achieve their own goals. That is, they did in America what they would not have dared try in Europe; they enslaved other people. Even Puritans and Quakers, driven by powerful religious commitments, found prosperity quite easy to bear. To the extent that they resisted slavery, they acted less from principle than from a dislike of "strangers" who might cause them moral difficulties.

Historians have worked with patience and imagination to reconstruct the community life of English North America. Paying close attention to settler motivation, demography, family structure, community organization, local economy, and social values, they have uncovered not just a single "American" colonial experience but an amazing variety of patterns. Current scholarship is now beginning to link this diversity to specific regional subcultures within the British Isles and their expansion and even intensification in North America.

Here too the numbers are striking, particularly the contrast between those who came and those who survived. Within the English colonies before 1700, the huge majority of settlers that chose the West Indies over the mainland had become a distinct minority by century's end. The 220,000 Europeans and 320,000 slaves who had sailed for the islands left a total of fewer than 150,000 survivors by 1700, and the preponderance of slaves over free colonists, which already exceeded three to one, grew more overwhelming with each passing year. The 120,000 Europeans and at least 25,000 slaves who had gone to the southern mainland colonies before 1700 had just over 100,000 survivors at that date. By contrast, only 40,000 people had gone to the Middle Atlantic and New England colonies in the seventeenth century, but the survivors and their descendants numbered almost 150,000 by 1700, just over 5,000 of whom were slaves. Founded by some 10 percent of the free migration stream and only 5 or 6 percent of the total number of free and enslaved passengers, by 1700 the northern colonies accounted for considerably more than half of all the European settlers in English North America and the West Indies. This sudden and quite unexpected expansion of the area of free-labor settlement was the greatest anomaly yet in two centuries of European overseas expansion. The Middle Atlantic colonies in particular, which had gotten off to a slower start than New England, were by 1700 poised to become the fastest-growing region on the continent and probably in the world over the next century and a half.

One paradox is striking. Almost certainly, intense religious motivation was underrepresented among those leaving the British

Isles. The Puritans, Quakers, and other religious exiles were a tiny percentage of the transatlantic migration, but their coreligionists who remained at home were numerous enough to generate a revolution and execute a king between 1640 and 1660. Protestant dissent acquired its power in American life not because of its prominence among the migrants in general but because of the amazing ability of this small number of people to survive and multiply.

These enormous differences in rates of population growth stemmed from patterns of migration, family structure, and general health. Among the colonists, sex ratios tended to get more unbalanced the farther south one went. Men outnumbered women by only about three to two among the first settlers of New England, most of whom arrived as parts of organized families. In New Netherland the ratio was two to one, and it was probably somewhat lower in Pennsylvania. Early Maryland and Virginia attracted perhaps six men for every woman, a ratio that fell slowly. Because most Chesapeake women arrived as indentured servants, they were not legally free to marry and bear children until they had completed their terms. Most were in their mid-twenties before they could start to raise legitimate families. Not surprisingly, both the bastardy rate and the percentage of pregnant brides were quite high, cumulatively affecting something like half of all immigrant servant women. In the early West Indies, women were even scarcer, sometimes outnumbered by ten or twenty to one. To move from that situation to all-male buccaneering communities, as in Tortuga and parts of Jamaica in the 1650s and 1660s and in the Bahamas later on, did not require a radical transition.

Life expectancy and rates of natural increase also declined from north to south. The New England population became self-sustaining during the first decade after the founding of Boston in 1630. Immigration virtually ceased after 1641, and for the rest of the colonial period the region exported more people than it imported. Yet its population grew at an explosive rate from 20,000 founders to nearly 100,000 descendants in fewer than seventy years. New Netherland entered a similar cycle of rapid natural increase in the 1650s. Early New Jersey townships and Pennsylvania's first farming communities were almost certainly demographically self-sustaining from the decade of their founding, between the 1660s and 1680s.

By contrast, the Chesapeake colonies took most of the century to achieve natural growth. Although settled longer than any other part of North America, Virginia remained a colony dominated by immigrants until the decade after 1700, when native-born men (those born after 1680) finally took charge. Immigrants had already survived childhood diseases in England, but their life expectancy as young adults in the Chesapeake was much lower than that of Englishmen of the same age who stayed behind or those who went to more northerly colonies. Men could expect to live only to about age forty-five in Maryland and Virginia, and women died even sooner, especially if they were exposed to malaria while pregnant. This situation improved slowly as, for example, settlers planted orchards and replaced local drinking water with cider, and as a native-born population with improved immunities gradually replaced the immigrants. In the West Indies, life expectancy may have been as much as five years shorter. From the Chesapeake through the islands, even the men in power were often quite youthful.

These differences powerfully affected family size and structure. Although New England women married only slightly younger than their English counterparts, they averaged one or two more pregnancies per marriage, fewer died in childbirth, and they lost fewer of their children to disease. Thus eighteen of Andover's twenty-nine founding families had at least four sons who survived to age twenty-one, and fourteen of these twenty-nine families had at least four daughters who lived that long. The average age at death for the heads of these households was 71.8 years, and a third of them lived past eighty.

As these settlements matured, power gravitated naturally to their founders, who, as respectable grandfathers, continued to run most towns until the 1670s and even the 1680s. They often retained economic control over adult sons by withholding land titles until their own deaths, by which time their oldest children could be middle-aged or even elderly. They retained religious control, at least in the Massachusetts and New Haven colonies, by tying voting rights to church membership and by insisting on a publicly verified conversion experience before granting that membership. Most ministers and magistrates (the Puritan gentry who administered justice) favored a degree of compromise on this question. What later came to be called the Halfway Covenant, a measure approved by a New England synod in 1662, encouraged second-generation settlers to have their children baptized even though neither the father nor mother had yet experienced conversion. But

271

lay saints – the grandparents who still numerically dominated most churches – resisted the implementation of this policy. They believed in infant baptism, but only for the children of proven saints. Thus very few people took advantage of the device until the founding generation began to die and lose control in the decade after King Philip's War (1675–6).

In brief, New England families tended to be patriarchal, authoritarian, and severely disciplined at the same time that New England villages were a fairly egalitarian community of aging farmers. Few of them were inclined to tolerate any significant degree of religious nonconformity. Those who could not accept local standards often made their way to Rhode Island, where they explored the difficulties of trying to find some basis for unity other than sheer dissent. It took time.

In the Delaware Valley, Quaker families shared many of the demographic characteristics of New England Puritans, but the family ethos was very different. Far less troubled by the doctrine of original sin, Quakers tried to protect the "innocence" of their numerous youngsters and give them a warm and nurturing environment. This goal included the acquisition of enough property to give each son a basis for genuine independence at a fairly youthful age and each daughter an early dowry. Quakers amassed more land and built larger and more comfortable houses than either their Anglican neighbors or the New Englanders. Those who failed to achieve these goals had difficulty marrying their children to other Quakers and themselves lost status within the Society of Friends.

The colonies created largely by Quakers – the provinces of West New Jersey and Pennsylvania – were far less authoritarian and patriarchal than those in New England. Quakers did not suppress religious dissent except occasionally within their own midst. As pacifists, they objected to any formal military institutions, and the Pennsylvania government created none until the 1750s. But the governor, who had to deal on a regular basis with a war-making British government, was seldom a Quaker. He did not easily win deference or respect from the members of the Society of Friends who continued to dominate the assembly, and who insisted on winning for it a body of privileges that greatly exceeded those claimed even by the British House of Commons, but then seldom converted these powers into actual legislation. Quaker assemblymen were far less interested in making laws than in preventing others from using the powers of government against their constituents. Even the court system existed overwhelmingly for the use of non-Quakers, and taxes remained low to nonexistent. Pennsylvania acquired its reputation as the world's best poor man's country while almost abolishing everything that the eighteenth century understood by government – the ability to wage war, pass laws, settle disputes, punish crimes, and collect taxes.

Family structure in the Chesapeake colonies differed greatly from either of these patterns. Unbalanced sex ratios before 1700 and short life expectancy even into the eighteenth century meant that almost no settlers lived to see their grandchildren. Among indentured servants arriving during the seventeenth century, many men never married at all, and others had to wait until their late twenties or thirties. Servant women also married late, but as the native-born population came of age and grew in size, its women married very young, usually in their middle to late teens. A typical seventeenth-century marriage endured only seven or eight years before one of the partners died, often leaving the surviving spouse in charge of the property and thus in a strong position to remarry. Death might also dissolve the second marriage before the oldest child by the first one had reached adulthood. Although the experience was not typical, a child could grow up in one household but by age twenty-one not even be related by blood to the husband and wife then running the family. Under these conditions, Chesapeake families tended to spread their loyalties among broader kinship networks. Uncles, aunts, cousins, and in-laws could make a real difference to an orphan's prospects. Even the local tradition of lavish hospitality to visitors may have derived some of its intensity from these imperatives.

Although the organizers of both Virginia and Maryland believed in a hierarchical and deferential social and political order, demographic realities retarded its development. True dynasties of great planters began to take shape only as the seventeenth century faded into the eighteenth. The slave population became demographically self-sustaining about a generation later than the European and thereafter multiplied almost as rapidly, a phenomenon that made the American South unique among Europe's overseas empires. Only as this process neared maturity could a planter be reasonably certain of passing on property, prestige, and authority to a lineal son. Not even then was he likely to retain significant power over the lives of his adult children. Until the age of the American Revolution, he was not likely to live that long.

Yet the men who governed seventeenth-century Virginia achieved considerable success in holding the colony to at least an elementary Anglican loyalty. Maryland, by contrast, officially favored toleration under the Roman Catholic dynasty of the Calvert family, until Anglicans finally gained control in the 1690s and established their church. In the West Indies the Church of England also became an established institution, but contemporary commentators thought that its moral hold on the planters was rather weak. Mostly because sugar was a more lucrative crop than tobacco, while the supply of land was much more limited than on the mainland, extremes of wealth emerged early in the Caribbean. Slavery was already becoming well entrenched by the 1650s, and by the end of the century the richest planters were beginning to flee back to England to live affluently as absentees off their island incomes.

Regional differences extended to ethnicity as well. New England may have been more English than England, a country that had sizable Scottish, Irish, Welsh, French Huguenot, and Dutch Reformed minorities. The Middle Atlantic region was more diverse than England. It threw together most of the people of northwestern Europe, who learned, particularly in New York, that every available formula for active government was likely to antagonize one group or another. Pennsylvania's prescription of minimal government for everyone worked better to preserve ethnic peace until war with frontier Indians threatened to tear the province apart between 1754 and 1764. The Chesapeake settlers, while predominantly English in both tidewater and piedmont, contained sizable ethnic minorities from continental Europe and, in the backcountry, large Scottish and Irish contingents. But after 1700 their most significant minority was African. The southern colonies mixed not just European peoples but newcomers from different continents. Slaves came to constitute about 40 percent of Virginia's population in the late colonial era. In coastal South Carolina, Africans had become a majority of two to one by the 1720s, but not even South Carolina approached the huge African preponderances of the sugar islands.

The economies of these regions also varied from north to south. In somewhat different ways, New England and the Middle Atlantic colonies largely replicated the economies of northern Europe in their urban–rural mixture, their considerable variety of local crafts, and their reliance on either fish or cereal crops as a major export.

Within the Atlantic colonial world these free-labor societies were unique, but they could not have sustained themselves without extensive trade with the more typical staple colonies to the south. New Englanders learned as early as the 1640s that they needed the islands to sustain their own economy, a process that would eventually draw Rhode Islanders into the slave trade in a major way. Tobacco, rice, and sugar – all grown by forms of unfree labor – shaped Chesapeake, South Carolina, and Caribbean society in profound, almost deterministic ways.

In effect, then, the colonists sorted themselves into a broad spectrum of settlements with striking and measurable differences between one region and its neighbors. All retained major portions of their English heritage and discarded others, but what one region kept, another often scorned. David Hackett Fischer traces this early American regionalism to its origins in British regional differences. East Anglia and other counties on the east coast of England gave New England their linguistic peculiarities, vernacular architecture, religious intensity, and other folkways as diverse as child-naming patterns and local cuisine. Tobacco and slaves aside, the distinctive features of Chesapeake society derived in a similar way from the disproportionate recruitment of planter gentry from England's southern counties. The Delaware Valley, by contrast, drew its folkways from the midland and northern counties and contiguous portions of Wales that gave shape to the Quaker movement. Beginning about 1718 the American backcountry from New York south took most of its social character from the people of north Britain: the fifteen Ulster, Scottish, and north English counties that faced each other around the Irish Sea and shared both numerous cultural affinities and deep-seated hostilities. These people were used to border wars, and they brought their expectations to the American frontier, where they killed Indians – including peaceful Christianized tribes – with a zeal that shocked other settlers, particularly the Quakers.

These contrasts affected not only demographic and economic patterns and an extensive list of major folkways but also religion and government. England contained both an established church and eloquent advocates for broad toleration, mostly among the dissenting population. By the end of the seventeenth century, toleration for Protestants had finally become official policy, and England emerged as one of the most pluralistic societies in Christendom. All these tendencies crossed the ocean, but they clustered differently in particular colonies. Until the middle of the eighteenth century most colonies were more uniform and, certainly in formal policy and often in practice as well, more repressive than the mother country. By 1710 the Church of England had become officially established from Maryland south through the islands, but Virginia was far less willing than England to tolerate dissent. In New England, by contrast, dissent became establishment, and the Anglican Church had to fight hard and occasionally share an awkward alliance with Quakers and Baptists to win any kind of public recognition. But in Rhode Island, Pennsylvania, and for most purposes the entire mid-Atlantic region, the triumph of toleration meant death for an officially established church. Only in the aftermath of the Great Awakening of the 1730s and 1740s did pluralism and toleration take firm hold throughout the entire continent.

Provincial governments also varied along the spectrum. Corporate forms predominated in New England, where virtually all officials were elected, and charters – whether officially granted by the Crown or unofficially adopted by the settlers – provided genuine antecedents for the written constitutions of the eighteenth century. As of about 1670 the rest of the mainland except Virginia had been organized under proprietary forms, devices whereby the Crown bestowed nearly the totality of its regal powers upon one or more "lords proprietors," who organized the settlement and, less easily, tried to secure the cooperation of whatever settlers they could attract. Because the Caribbean was the most viciously contested center of imperial rivalries, the West Indies in the 1660s and 1670s emerged as the proving ground for royal government, a form in which the Crown appointed the governor and the council (a body that both advised the governor and served as the upper house of the legislature); they in turn appointed the judiciary; and the settlers elected an assembly to join with the council and governor in making laws. Crown efforts to control these societies led by the end of the century to standardized sets of commissions and instructions and to the routine review of provincial legislation and the less frequent hearing of judicial appeals, both by the Privy Council. These routine procedures, especially as organized under the Board of Trade after 1696, largely defined what royal government was, and they could be exported to or imposed upon other settlements as well. But as late as 1678, Virginia remained the only royal colony on the mainland of North America.

The American continents had taken one exceptionally homogeneous people, the Indians (whose genetic similarities were far greater than those of the people of western Europe or even the British Isles) and transformed them over thousands of years into hundreds of distinct linguistic groups and tribal societies. As the emerging spectrum of settlement revealed, the New World was quite capable of doing the same thing to European intruders, whose own ethnic identities were but a few centuries old. The process of settlement could, in other words, create new ethnicities, not just distinct regions. By 1700 it had already magnified a select number of regional differences found within Great Britain. The passage of time seemed likely to drive these young societies further apart, not closer together. To take a single example, the institution of slavery, although it existed everywhere in at least a rudimentary form, tended to magnify regional contrasts, not reduce them. The main counterpoise to increasing diversity came not from any commonly shared "American" experience but from the expanding impact of empire. Only through closer and continuous contact with metropolitan England – London culture and the central government – would the colonies become more like each other.

During the last half of the seventeenth century, England discovered her colonies. Unlike the Spanish Empire, which subordinated trade to religious and political uniformity, the English government reversed these priorities. Parliament's interest in these tiny settlements derived overwhelmingly from its determination to control their trade, which, from the Restoration of 1660 to the American Revolution, was indeed the most dynamic sector of London's rapidly expanding commerce and thus a major factor in propelling London past Paris as Europe's largest city. Through a series of Navigation Acts, Parliament confined all trade with the colonies to English shipping (a major benefit to colonial shipbuilders as well), compelled major staple crops to go to Britain before leaving the empire for other markets, and tried to make Britain the source of most manufactures consumed in the colonies and the entrepôt for other European or Asian exports shipped to America. Despite ferocious resistance at first, these policies had achieved an extremely high level of compliance by the early eighteenth century. Later attempts to restrict colonial manufacturing and regulate the molasses trade were much less successful.

Crown efforts to assert political control over the colonies arose mostly out of frustration at early attempts to enforce these mercantilistic policies. Virginia had been a royal colony since 1624, but it drew almost no attention from the home government until Nathaniel Bacon's Rebellion of 1676–7 severely threatened the king's very considerable revenues from the tobacco trade. In subsequent years the Privy Council imposed on Virginia the same kind of close oversight that had emerged in the West Indies since 1660. New England attracted London's interest not because of its religious peculiarities – which seemed to sophisticated Londoners both anachronistic and rather embarrassing – but because it controlled more shipping than any other part of North America. Yankee skippers could undermine the Navigation Acts. To destroy that possibility, England revoked the charter of Massachusetts Bay in 1684, merged all the New England colonies into one enlarged Dominion of New England in 1686, added New York and East and West Jersey to this union in 1688, and tried to govern the whole in an authoritarian manner without an elective assembly. The model for this experiment came from the autocratic proprietary colony of New York under James, Duke of York and brother of King Charles II. When the duke became King James II in 1685, he saw a way of salvaging these faltering efforts by imposing them on a broader constituency.

He got a revolution instead. After William of Orange landed at Torbay in November 1688 and drove James from England, Boston and New York copied this example and overturned James's representatives, Sir Edmund Andros and Sir Francis Nicholson respectively, in the spring of 1689. Maryland Protestants used the same occasion to overthrow the proprietary government of the Catholic Lord Baltimore. Thereafter, government by elective assembly was no longer in doubt. Massachusetts had to accept a new charter that imposed a royal governor on the province. Although the two leaders of the New York rebellion, Jacob Leisler and Jacob Milborne, were both hanged in 1691, the upheavals of 1689 permanently discredited autocracy in America. By the 1720s the Crown's only other option for effective control, the West Indian model of royal government, had become the norm on the continent as well. Only proprietary Pennsylvania and Maryland (the latter restored to the Calverts in 1716 when the fifth Lord Baltimore converted to Protestantism) and corporate Connecticut and Rhode Island held out from this pattern. Except for Pennsylvania, even they went formally bicameral, and all of them reorganized their court systems along stricter common-law lines. Throughout North America, government was acquiring structural similarities that it had never had in the seventeenth century.

This absorption into empire dramatically altered political culture in North America. The struggles surrounding the Glorious Revolution[d] persuaded most Englishmen that they lived on an oasis of freedom in a global desert of tyranny. Eighteenth-century political ideology emerged as an effort to explain this anomaly and give it a solid historical foundation. In Britain and the colonies everyone in public life affirmed the "Revolution principles" of 1688, which always meant some variant of the triad of liberty, property, and no popery. The English gloried in their "mixed and balanced constitution," which prevented any monarch from corrupting a virtuous Parliament. This theme had both "court" (statist) and "country" (antistatist) celebrants and interpreters, and both crossed the ocean to America. Virginia and South Carolina became the purest embodiments of country ideology. They idealized the patriotic role of the truly independent planter-citizen and allowed virtually no holders of profitable public offices to sit in their assemblies. In New Hampshire, Massachusetts, and New York, by contrast, royal success usually depended – as in Great Britain – on the loyal support of a corps of these "placemen" in the lower house. The governor gained strength from defense needs, which were much greater than in the Chesapeake colonies. In this environment, country ideology became the creed only of a minority opposition through the 1750s, but its appeal would expand dramatically after 1763, when the entire imperial establishment came to seem a direct threat to provincial liberties instead of a bulwark for defending them.

Other forces also drew the separate parts of the empire closer together in the eighteenth century. Trade with Britain grew enormously. It did not quite keep pace with per capita population growth in the colonies from the 1690s to 1740, but thereafter it expanded even more explosively. Port cities became a dynamic part of the Atlantic cultural world in a way that had simply not been possible in the seventeenth century when New York City, for instance, regularly received only about half a dozen ships from Europe each year. By the mid-eighteenth century, with these arrivals almost daily occurrences, the colonists tended to divide into two distinct blocs: "cosmopolitans," who nurtured strong contacts with the rest of the world, and "localists," who were relatively isolated from such experiences and often suspicious of what outsiders wished to impose upon them.

Almost by definition, colonial newspapers reflected cosmopolitan values. They rarely reported local events in any systematic way. Instead, they informed their communities of what was happening elsewhere, particularly in Europe. The *Boston Newsletter*, established by an enterprising postmaster named John Campbell in 1704, became America's first successful paper. By the 1720s all the major northern ports had at least one, and by the 1750s three or four newspapers. South Carolina and Virginia each acquired one in the 1730s, and Maryland a decade later.

By the end of the 1760s every colony north of Delaware had also established its own college, but from Delaware south only William and Mary in Virginia provided higher education for the settlers. This difference was symptomatic. On the whole, northern colonies *replicated* the institutional potential of Europe. With New England setting the pace, they trained their own ministers, lawyers, physicians, and master craftsmen. Plantation societies *imported* them instead, even though white per capita wealth was considerably higher from Maryland south. Northern provinces were already becoming modernizing societies capable of internalizing the institutional momentum of the mother country. Southern provinces remained colonies, specialized producers of non-European crops and importers of specialists who could provide necessary services. But all mainland colonies grew at a prodigious rate. In 1700 they had only 250,000 settlers and slaves. That figure topped a million in the 1740s and 2 million in the late 1760s.

Among large events, both northern and southern colonies shared in the Great Awakening and the final cycle of wars that expelled France from North America. Some historians like to interpret the Awakening – a powerful concentration of evangelical revivals that swept through Britain and the colonies mostly between the mid-1730s and early 1740s – as a direct prelude to the American Revolution, but even though awakened settlers overwhelmingly supported independence in the 1770s, the relationship was never that simple or direct. "Old Lights," or opponents of the revivals, would provide both the loyalists and nearly all of the most conspicuous patriots. At no point in its unfolding did the Awakening seem to pit Britain against America. It divided both.

By 1763 Britain had emerged victorious from its mid-century cycle of wars with France, a struggle that pulled together most of the trends toward imperial integration that had been emerging since the 1670s. The last of these wars, what Lawrence Henry

Gipson called the Great War for the Empire (1754–63), marked the fourth-greatest mobilization and the third-highest rate of fatality of any American military struggle from then to the present. (Only World War II, the Civil War, and the Revolutionary War mustered a higher percentage of the population; only the Civil War and the American Revolution killed a larger proportion of participants.) Despite widespread friction in the first three years, no other event could rival that war in the intensity of cooperation it generated between imperial and provincial governments. Both New Light and Old Light preachers saw nothing less than the millennium issuing from the titanic struggle. The result was more prosaic but still as unique as the effort. Great Britain expelled the government of France from North America and, in the Peace of Paris of 1763, asserted control over the entire continent east of the Mississippi except New Orleans, which France temporarily transferred to Spain along with the rest of Louisiana west of the great river.

The war left several ironic legacies. To North Americans who had participated, it seemed a powerful vindication of the voluntaristic institutions upon which they had relied for their success. To London authorities, it seemed to demonstrate the inability of North Americans to meet their own defense needs even under an appalling emergency. The British answer would be major imperial reforms designed to create a more authoritarian empire, capable of answering its vast obligations whether or not the settlers chose to cooperate.

Neither side noticed another heritage. During the struggle the Indians throughout the northeastern woodlands had shown a novel and intense distaste for shedding one another's blood. The Iroquois ideal of a league of peace among the tribes of the confederacy seemed to be spreading throughout the region, fired by universalist religious justifications for resisting any further encroachments from the settlers. The Delawares and Shawnees in the upper Ohio Valley provided most of this religious drive for Indian unity, which had a striking impact as early as Pontiac's war of resistance in 1763–4.[e]

As events would show, it was too little, too late. But for the next half-century, this movement inflicted one disaster after another upon the settlers and subjected first the empire and then the United States to a rate of defense spending that would have enormous political consequences. Considering the limited resources upon which Indian resistance could draw, it was at least as impressive as the effort toward unity undertaken by the thirteen colonies themselves after 1763. It also suggests a final paradox. Without Indian resistance to seal British commitment to imperial reform, there might have been no American Revolution at all.

EDITOR'S NOTES

a Raynal was a philosophe, much interested in the New World, and Robertson was a historian, much admired in America.
b The Enlightenment was an eighteenth-century movement of European and American intellectuals that emphasized liberalism, progress, and rationality.
c Rack-rent was excessive or extortionate rent.
d The Glorious Revolution (1688) refers to the bloodless *coup d'état* in which William III and Mary succeeded to the English throne in place of James II. It represented a victory for Protestantism, parliamentary power, and limitations on royal prerogatives.
e Pontiac, an Ottawa chief, organized a pan-Indian movement that attacked most of the British outposts in the Great Lakes region.

NOTE

Reprinted from *The New American History*, edited by Eric Foner (Philadelphia, 1990). Copyright 1990 Temple University Press. Used by permission of the author and publisher.

SUGGESTIONS FOR FURTHER READING

GENERAL STUDIES

Bailyn, Bernard, *The Peopling of British North America: An Introduction* (New York, 1986).

Bailyn, Bernard, *Voyagers to the West: A Passage in the Peopling of America on the Eve of the Revolution* (New York, 1986).

Bailyn, Bernard, and Morgan, Philip D. (eds.), *Strangers within the Realm: Cultural Margins of the First British Empire* (Chapel Hill, N.C., 1991).

Butler, Jon, *Awash in a Sea of Faith: Christianizing the American People* (Cambridge, Mass., 1990).

Fischer, David Hackett, *Albion's Seed: Four British Folkways in America* (New York, 1989).

Greene, Jack P., *Pursuits of Happiness: The Social Development of Early Modern British Colonies and the Formation of American Cultures* (Chapel Hill, N.C., 1988).

Greene, Jack P. and Pole, J. R. (eds.), *Colonial British America: Essays in the New History of the Early Modern Era* (Baltimore, 1984).

Katz, Stanley N., Murrin, John M., and Greenberg, Douglas (eds.), *Colonial America: Essays in Politics and Social Development*, 4th ed. (New York, 1992).

McCusker, John J. and Menard, Russell R., *The Economy of British America, 1607–1789* (Chapel Hill, N.C., 1985).

Meinig, D. W., *Atlantic America, 1492–1800* (New Haven, Conn., 1986).

Steele, Ian K., *The English Atlantic, 1675–1740: An Exploration of Communication and Community* (New York, 1986).

LOCAL STUDIES

Anderson, Fred, *A People's Army: Massachusetts Soldiers and Society in the Seven Years' War* (Chapel Hill, N.C., 1984).

Isaac, Rhys, *The Transformation of Virginia, 1740–1790* (Chapel Hill, N.C., 1982).

Merrell, James H., *The Indians' New World: Catawbas and their Neighbors from European Contact through the Era of Removal* (Chapel Hill, N.C., 1989).

Morgan, Edmund S., *American Slavery, American Freedom: The Ordeal of Colonial Virginia* (New York, 1975).

Ulrich, Laurel Thatcher, *A Midwife's Tale: The Life of Martha Ballard, Based on Her Diary, 1785–1812* (New York, 1990).

Wood, Peter H., *Black Majority: Negroes in Colonial South Carolina from 1670 through the Stono Rebellion* (New York, 1974).